# UNENDING DESIGN

# UNENDING DESIGN

*The Forms of Postmodern Poetry*

Joseph M. Conte

*Cornell University Press*

Ithaca and London

First published 1991 by Cornell University Press.


International Standard Book Number 0-8014-2469-0 (cloth)
International Standard Book Number 0-8014-9914-3 (paper)
Library of Congress Catalog Card Number 90-55732
Printed in the United States of America
*Librarians: Library of Congress cataloging information*
*appears on the last page of the book.*

Pages x–xii, "Acknowledgment of Copyright Material,"
constitute a continuation of this copyright page.


⊗ The paper in this book meets the minimum requirements
of the American National Standard for Information Sciences–
Permanence of Paper for Printed Library Materials, ANSI Z39.48-1984.

*For my parents*

# Contents

Acknowledgments      ix

1   Introduction      1
     Defining a Postmodern Poetics      5
     Seriality and Proceduralism: A Typology of Postmodern
       Poetry      13

SERIAL FORM

2   The Infinite Serial Form      47
     The Unbound and the Uneven: Robert Duncan's *Passages*      47
     Against the Calendar: Paul Blackburn's *Journals*      69
     One Thing Finding Its Place with Another: Robert Creeley's
       *Pieces*      87

3   The Finite Serial Form      105
     The Dark House: Jack Spicer's Book of *Language*      105
     The Subway's Iron Circuit: George Oppen's *Discrete Series*      121
     Sounding and Resounding Anew: Louis Zukofsky and Lorine
       Niedecker      141

PROCEDURAL FORM

4   A Predetermined Form      167
     Renovated Form: The Sestinas of John Ashbery and Louis
       Zukofsky      167
     Canonic Form in Weldon Kees, Robert Creeley, and Louis
       Zukofsky      192

5  A Generative Device                                          214
      Constant and Variant: Semantic Recurrence in Harry
         Mathews, William Bronk, and Robert Creeley            214
      Arbitrary Constraints and Aleatory Operations: Harry
         Mathews and John Cage                                 238

6  A Polemical Conclusion: The Language Poetries and the
   New Formalism                                               267

   Notes                                                       283

   Index                                                       309

# Acknowledgments

Certainly of all the pages numbered in this book, this one gives me the most pleasure since it is the acknowledgment of many gifts received. I am especially grateful to Diane Middlebrook, Gilbert Sorrentino, and Albert Gelpi, who read this book in its original form; their enthusiasm, generous criticism, and artful direction were invaluable. Simone Di Piero and Marjorie Perloff offered shrewd assessments at critical junctures in the early formulation of the book; Michael Davidson and James E. B. Breslin provided insightful and indispensable critiques of the final version. I also thank my colleagues and friends at the State University of New York at Buffalo who have offered timely advice on individual sections: Victor Doyno meticulously read drafts of the revised manuscript; Carl Dennis and Neil Schmitz contributed significantly to my understanding of contemporary poetics; Robert Bertholf's exhaustive knowledge of Robert Duncan's life and poetry improved my treatment of his work; and Robert Creeley offered important advice and encouragement regarding "the company." My gratitude must also go to those close friends and fellow students who offered not only readings but life support as well, especially Robin Appleby, Robert Basil, Elisabeth Frost, and Marc Tognotti. I am thankful for the gracious assistance of the staff of the Stanford University Library (especially William McPheron) and the Poetry Collection of the Lockwood Library of the State University of New York at Buffalo. A version of the essay on Paul Blackburn appeared in *Sagetrieb*; my thanks to the editors of that journal. The Julian Park Publication Fund at the State University of New York at Buffalo awarded a grant to cover permissions fees for *Unending Design*. The Whiting Foundation provided me with a fellowship in 1987–88 which allowed me to make significant, undistracted progress toward the completion of the manuscript. Lastly, I offer the greatest thanks to my parents, without whose support and encouragement I could not have undertaken this work.

J. M. C.

## Acknowledgment of Copyright Material

# UNENDING DESIGN

# Introduction

In this work I wish to establish a systematic typology of postmodern poetic forms. The success of such a typology requires that it be inventive enough to account for the unanticipated shapes of recent poems and that it be disciplined enough not to force them into a mold of the critic's own making. My intention has been not to restrict but to articulate the surprising diversity of formal approaches in postmodern poetry. Too often discussions of recent American poetry have taken place without particular attention to formal types, their origins, and the relationships of affinity or antagonism which poetic forms (no less than their practitioners) enjoy. One encounters attempts at classification which conflate types—as when any poem of less than a page is designated a "lyric," and of more than ten pages a "long poem." Or one encounters the comparison of examples exhibiting distinct or conflicting formal properties. I have taken some trouble to enunciate and define the formal types presented here, and I hope that they will at least be (as Charles Olson said of his "Projective Verse") of some essential use. In selecting the various poems described either at length or in passing, I have endeavored, like a good hôtelier, to see to it that each example is perfectly comfortable with its typological accommodations. My first concern has always been to respect the formal integrity of the poem rather than to bolster some ambitious schema of my own, one of the risks inherent in working out any sort of typology. I do not intend to offer a static, Aristotelian classification of the familiar species—no sooner has one got the bug in the bottle than someone else suggests that the bottle's not right or that the bug be moved. I would prefer to take as a model for my activities those of Darwin, who in his voyage aboard H.M.S. *Beagle* discovered several new species and thought to see them in movement through time as well as from one archipelago to another. I favor the exploratory over the inventory. My intention then is not so much to arrange familiar works as in the formulation of my typology to reveal the innovative in twentieth-century poetic form.

This century (which now seems to be accelerating to its close) has unquestionably experienced a cult of the new. Whether the product is laundry soap or literature, we have become accustomed to the rapidity with which things change. Accordingly, the turnover rate among literary movements and manifestos since 1913 has been alarmingly high. It seems that almost as soon as a thing is done, it must be undone or done over. Despite such apparent turmoil, we need to distinguish in kind among the various "new" movements in poetics which have emerged in the last fifty years. In the 1940s a New Criticism touted an academic *style* or method, featuring allusion, ambiguity, and irony, which quickly became orthodox. In keeping with a reactionary cultural agenda, the New Critics were determined to maintain the hegemony of traditional attitudes toward poetic form and metrics, actively "disallowing" much of what was innovative. I consider their widely accepted designation as formalists to be valid only in the most limited sense, because their discussion of poetic form is arguably the least revolutionary and most mechanical aspect of their program. The concern of such "formalist" critics rarely extends beyond the static codification of already acknowledged poetic forms. In their estimation the evolution of a new poetic form promises only decline, and not the successful adaptation of poetry to changing conditions. In turn, I do not adhere to the designation of their subsequent rivals (many of whom I discuss in this book) as anti-formalists. Rather, these postmodern poets are nontraditionalists who have concerned themselves fundamentally with a reexamination of poetic forms and their appropriateness to contemporary life and thought.

Among those poets who were inclined to challenge certain aspects of the New Criticism, Robert Lowell, Anne Sexton, and John Berryman introduced the possibility of a new *content*, or subject matter, which some maligned as "confessionalism" but others hailed as a liberation from the tyranny of poetic decorum. This group extends the boundaries of poetry by admitting the personal through intimacies of the body and extremities of the mind. But we must also consider as related those poets, such as Adrienne Rich, Robert Bly, and Denise Levertov, whose work becomes aggressively politicized, or public, during the Vietnam War era. The unnerving songs of the madhouse and the graphic songs of antiwar protest expand our conception of a subject matter suitable to expression in verse.

As important as they are to the history of American poetry after 1945, these movements are, I maintain, revolutions of style or content. Of greater interest to me is the emergence among postmodern poets of a new perception of poetic *form*. As evidence, I wish to identify and explore the attributes of the two poetic forms I consider to be peculiar to and in many ways typical of postmodernism: serial and procedural form. The series is determined by the discontinuous and often aleatory manner in which one thing follows another. In an age of instant telecommunications and the motley of metropolitan life, the series accommodates the rapidly shifting contexts and the overwhelming diversity of messages that we now experience as part of our daily routine. Serial form offers itself as a distinct alternative to the organic sequence—a product of romanticism—whose development reflects the more leisurely pace and unitary quality of the nineteenth-century British house and garden or mountain-lakes resort. As a complement to the series, procedural form consists of predetermined and arbitrary constraints that are relied upon to generate the context and direction of the poem during composition. No longer able to suppose that a grand order is either discernable or desirable in the world, the poet discretely enacts a personal order that, if not cosmic, is no less real. Procedural form presents itself as an alternative to the well-made, metaphorical lyric whose practitioners, from Shakespeare and Donne to Baudelaire and Eliot, were the subject of much New Critical explication.

Serial and procedural forms are strictly postmodern innovations that can easily be distinguished—as I will elaborate—from their romantic and modernist predecessors. Although I discuss prototypes that are incipient in the 1930s (when high modernist poets are joined by a new generation), I also attend to examples published in the last year or two by poets who have titled their work a "series" or adamantly declared its "predetermined" structure. Casting about in the often contentious waters of contemporary poetry, I have caught several "live ones" still flapping vigorously as they hit the air.

In searching for examples of these two poetic forms, I found that their authors were frequently unacknowledged by the canon. This relative obscurity I took to be a good omen because, as William Carlos Williams or Arnold Schönberg attest, that which is truly new at first must seem discordant and so gains recognition slowly.[1] To be sure, certain poets whose work I examine, such as John Ashbery and Robert Creeley, have been much discussed of late. But many others have been undeservedly ignored: the Objectivist poets as a class, including Louis Zukofsky, Lorine Niedecker, and George Oppen, are grossly under-valued; Paul Blackburn remains a virtually unknown member of the Black Mountain movement; Jack Spicer has only recently come to be recognized as a catalyst of the San Francisco Renaissance; Weldon Kees is an important precursor of the New York School; and William Bronk has yet to emerge from the mists of the Hudson Valley. It is no surprise to me that in the pursuit of the new in poetic forms I have come upon several excellent poets who are largely unknown outside of their small pool of devoted admirers.

Each poet under discussion in this work has assumed the role of a formal innovator, partly as a response to the legacy of modernism, and partly out of the need to formulate a distinctly postmodern poetry. Among the now-canonized modernists, Ezra Pound argues against the priority of style in the poem, for which reason he abandons the elabo-rate Pre-Raphaelite rhetoric that he favored in his early verse. William Carlos Williams speaks repeatedly against the priority of content in the poem, thus abjuring all types of narrative or philosophical verse. Both demand a new perception of form itself. In *Gaudier-Brzeska* (1916), Pound extols the "vorticist artists," whom he had in fact cre-ated: "These new men have made me see form, have made me more conscious of the appearance of the sky where it juts down between houses, of the bright pattern of sunlight which the bath water throws up on the ceiling, of the great "V's" of light that dart through the chinks over the curtain rings, all these are new chords, new keys of design."[2] Pound's newfound perception does not regard the beauty of the object or the light itself (as might have been expected of an imagist) but the "pattern" or "design" that it makes. Williams is even more explicit in his introduction to *The Wedge* (1944): "There is no poetry of distinction without formal invention, for it is in the intimate form that works of art achieve their exact meaning, in which they most resemble the machine."[3] Williams emphasizes not only the exactitude with which any literary Edison must submit his invention for patent approval, but also the primacy of such innovation to the quality of the poetry. Elsewhere he speaks of "the necessity for a new form *before* a *new* poetry of any sort can be written."[4] The validity of such a state-ment has not lapsed with the close of the modernist era—nor did Williams intend it to be a dictum appropriate only to the passing concerns of his moment in literary history. In fact, Williams's convic-tion remains axiomatic among the postmodern poets discussed in this work: formal invention is a prerequisite for any new poetry.

There are those "formalists" who believe in the unchanging pertinence and applicability of traditional forms, convinced that there are few contemporary experiences that cannot be appropriated within the confines of a sonnet. But each succeeding period in Anglo-American literature, secure in its sense of "difference" with regard to critical issues and the immediate complexities of the human condition, has brought forth in its poetry certain identifiable forms that are distinct in their structure and to some degree representative of the concerns of the period at large. The briefest catalog of familiar types would include the neoclassical couplet, the greater romantic lyric, and the modernist fragment. The postmodern poets to whom this book is devoted are fully aware that their period also requires the defining of a new formal identity. Seriality and proceduralism have provided those new definitions. By exploring the complementary alternatives of the aleatory and the predetermined in their works, postmodern poets have given a verifiable identity to the shape of poetry in the latter half of the twentieth century. The serial and the procedural form are not the only new forms to emerge during this period—there are concrete poems, minimalist poems, and talk poems—but they are virtually unanticipated by existing formal types and essentially unique in what they tell us of contemporary thought and culture. The poets of our time have in fact exercised that new perception of form which is essential to any poetry of distinction.

## Defining a Postmodern Poetics

Much of the meaning we impart to words in conversation is a matter of emphasis. The inflection of the voice often does more to convey our intentions satisfactorily than the words do themselves. So useful distinctions about a postmodern poetics depend on how we hear the poet or critic accenting that crucial period term. For some the term is pronounced "post-Modern," with the emphasis on the Modern. In this case the company admitted and the topics of conversation are necessarily more historical, concerned with whatever it is that comes after modernism. As such the term becomes synonymous with "contemporary." It has not been mispronounced; it gives, however, a somewhat different meaning. Advocates of a "post-Modern" literature deny that a rupture has occurred between contemporary and modernist poetics.[5] Instead the poets of today maintain a continuity with their predecessors, and (however many qualifications may apply) they extend and modify modernist poetics. Nothing here fully rebuts the charges of belatedness and influence, or the image of pale epigones toiling after the monumental work of their masters. Nor can this pronunciation of the "post-Modern" evade the rather bland inclusiveness of what is at base a temporal distinction: a generation of poets which has matured post-1945.

The alternative pronunciation carries the somewhat more fluid arch of "Postmodern." This "Postmodern" is largely taken as synonymous with the hydra-headed avant-garde; it thus ignores historical boundaries in the search for radical innovation. The avant-garde typically courts rupture, a dramatic and absolute break in linear-temporal continuity. The "Postmodern" (for those who pronounce it in this gliding fashion) is not to be regarded as the period after modernism, but as something entirely beyond it, laying claim to a new human consciousness. Among the harbingers of the new cosmology is Charles Olson, who argues:

> This is the morning, after the dispersion, and the work of the morning is methodology: how to use oneself, and on what. I am an archaeologist of morning. And the writing acts which I find bear upon the present job are (I) from Homer back, not forward; and (II) from Melville on, particularly himself, Dostoevsky, Rimbaud, and Lawrence. These are the modern men who projected what we are and what we are in, who broke the spell. They put the men forward into the post-modern, the post-humanist, the post-historic, the going live present, the "Beautiful Thing."[6]

The "live present" of which Olson considered himself to be the prophet was 1950. By his own estimation he had passed beyond the modern order of things. Olson's "post-historic" argument, linking Homer, Melville, and himself, is indicative of a "Postmodern" that ignores traditional historical boundaries in the definition of its peculiar psyche. In its pursuit of a new order, the "Postmodern" has placed a heavy accent on experimentalism. An inevitable argument regarding the relevance of experimental forms ensues. For some critics such works of the "Postmodern" articulate actual and immediate cultural criteria; they describe more accurately than traditional forms the convolutions of our current condition. For others the apparently haughty pursuit of the radically new guarantees a marginal audience composed largely of the practitioners themselves, a few aficionados, and the academics who deconstruct these elaborate games.[7]

Olson's vatic, stirring announcement of the "Postmodern" present can, however, be contrasted to the apocalyptic anxieties of the prophet-historian Arnold J. Toynbee, whose rather more negative assessment was also voiced in the early 1950s. For Toynbee, the "post-Modern

Age" (which he sees as beginning in the mid-1870s) is characterized by irrationality, anarchy, indeterminacy, and the general breakdown of modern Western civilization.[8] The conflict between these two early assessments of the "Postmodern" has become typical of the debate centered on the period term, a debate in which postmodernism is problematized well beyond the dimension of aesthetics to include political, philosophical, economic, and historical disputes. Hal Foster deftly summarizes the problem—which is rather too extensive to be treated in full here—when he says, "In cultural politics today, a basic opposition exists between a postmodernism which seeks to decon-struct modernism and resist the status quo and a postmodernism which repudiates the former to celebrate the latter: a postmodernism of resistance and a postmodernism of reaction."[9] On behalf of a resis-tant postmodernism, poststructuralist, feminist, and psychoanalytic critics celebrate the death of the subject, the revaluation of the su-preme fictions of modernism, and a rising pluralism and heterogeneity. The reactionary position, often taken up by cultural neoconservatives (perhaps following the lead of Toynbee), laments the dissolution of a distinct high culture and the hierarchical social structures that sup-port it.

The case for a "post-Modern" contemporary literature can be sup-ported by the facts of literary history. Contemporary poets provide the most significant evidence in the homage they pay to their illustrious predecessors. The following poem by Paul Blackburn is a worthy ex-ample of such homage, partly for its clear devotion to its subject, William Carlos Williams, and partly because its immediacy enacts the poetics it celebrates:

> Phone Call to Rutherford
>
> "It would be—
>                 a mercy if
> you did not come see me . . .
>
> "I have dif-fi / culty
>                 speak-ing, I
> cannot count on it, I
> am afraid it would be too em-
>                 ba
>                 rass-ing
> for me ."
>
>                 —Bill, can you still
>                 answer letters?

"No . my hands
are tongue-tied . You have . . . made

a record in my heart.
                    Goodbye."
                                        Oct 1962[10]

The difficulty with presenting such a record is that it can only be partial. Blackburn (who acted on Pound's advice to provide a contemporary translation of the troubadours) did not extend such devotion to T. S. Eliot or his poetics. Although Blackburn is "post-Modern," his poetics discriminates among the moderns, rejecting the symbolist mode of Eliot and the meditative mode of Wallace Stevens for an immediate contact and a precise articulation of the real. That is, modernism itself is not monolithic, and the "post-Modern" poet does not feel obliged by each of its authorities. Records of physical contact, pilgrimages by younger poets to the residences of their graying masters, are similarly partial or ambiguous. Witness Elizabeth Bishop's ambivalent record of her visits to Pound in St. Elizabeths Hospital:

These are the years and the walls and the door
that shut on a boy that pats the floor
to feel if the world is there and flat.
This is a Jew in a newspaper hat
that dances joyfully down the ward
into the parting seas of board
past the staring sailor
that shakes his watch
that tells the time
of the poet, the man
that lies in the house of Bedlam.[11]

In "Visits to St. Elizabeths" (1950), Bishop refers to Pound in the cumulative stanzas of this parodic nursery rhyme as tragic, talkative, honored, old, brave, cranky, cruel, busy, tedious, and wretched; all of these attributes were undoubtedly true, but none quite explain her attendance in the sanitarium. These homages and visits are part of "literary history," but they are in no way definitive of a poetics. Bishop's style owes little to Pound, and as if to illustrate the difficulties of temporal period distinctions, Blackburn dies of cancer in 1971, more than a year before the aged Pound.

The temporal criteria of a "post-Modern" poetry leave us with a disturbing sense of simultaneity in which the major late works of the modernists and the important early works of the postmodernists coexist. Thus one finds Robert Creeley's landmark *For Love: Poems 1950–1960* (1962) alongside Williams's remarkable *Pictures from Brueghel: Collected Poems 1950–1962* (1962); Zukofsky's first half of *"A" 1–12* (1959) alongside the last complete volume of Pound's *Cantos, Thrones de los Cantares* (1959); John Ashbery's *Some Trees*, tapped by W. H. Auden for the Yale Younger Poets series in 1956, alongside Stevens's *Collected Poems*, published on his seventy-fifth birthday in 1954. It may be that the long-lived and highly productive modernists have precluded discussion of a distinct postmodernist poetics until a respectful interim following their departure has transpired.

If we cannot trust literary history to provide us with an accurate gauge of a postmodern poetics, what criteria can we then turn to? First there is language. The modernists still held aloft the sacred and symbolic chalice of the Word, as *Logos*. At the same time they promoted the palpability of the word over its referential function—prompting Williams to exclaim, "My dear Miss Word let me hold your W."[12] But for the postmodernist, language has fallen entirely into the secular realm; it is a more plastic medium that he or she can reshape without lingering impressions and employ for multifarious purposes. Next there is the world. The modernist laments the lost promise of a cultural *risorgimento*; the postmodernist experiences the world with dread, as more than slightly out of control and possibly beyond reparation. Atomic irrationalities, gross economic imbalances, and an ecological crisis brought about by several of our most cherished activities contribute to the general *angst*. Finally one can mark the divergence of postmodern from modern poetics by conducting an inductive examination of formal criteria. The formal relations between the two periods can be more precisely determined than their historical relations. The postmodern formal response to changes in language and the world is just as pronounced, inventive, and various as that of modernism; accordingly, it is this postmodern formal response that concerns me most in the discussions that follow.

A growing number of critical theorists—using the sense of "Postmodern" described earlier—associate the movement with an avantgarde that has always been present in the arts. In an effort to disentangle the postmodern from its immediate historical predecessor, these critics assert the presence of a postmodern impulse in such works of the past as Stein's *The Making of Americans*, Rimbaud's *Illuminations*, Sterne's *Tristram Shandy*, Rabelais's *Gargantua et Pantagruel*, and Apuleius's *The Golden Ass*. And in an assault on the future, the radical avant-garde has occupied the coffeehouses, lofts, and performance spaces in order to challenge the already acknowledged and lucratively rewarded works of postmodernism.[13] In his argument against an historical definition of postmodernism, William V. Spanos rather closely tailors the term to a radically disruptive avant-garde fringe: "The word [postmodernism] is misleading in suggesting that the literature I call postmodern is restricted to a moment within and emanating belatedly from a developing historical narrative which has some kind of original source (*archè*) and ultimate end (*télos*). It thus obscures one crucial aspect of my sense of what the postmodern impulse is: that there has been a 'postmodern' urge to art throughout the literary history of the West." He identifies postmodern literature as a marginalized, parodic impulse of the folk imagination which seeks "to mock and de-stroy the utterly completed, linear yet circumscribed, monoglotic, distanced, hierarchical, and timeless world" of official genres and the sociopolitical authorities that legitimate them.[14] Matei Calinescu offers something of a corrective to Spanos's ambitious proposal:

> Typically, the avant-garde, as the experimental cutting edge of modernity, has historically given itself a double task: to destroy and to invent. But negation certainly is the most significant moment in the twofold logic of radical innovation: it is the old, the institutionalized past, the Library and the Museum, that must be effectively rejected, demystified, torn down; the new—unanticipated, radiant, abrupt—will follow by itself.
>
> In postmodernism, it has been observed, it is precisely this purely destructive aspect of the old avant-garde that comes under question. What could justify so much ruthless devastation? Is this the price to be paid for access to the new? But the new, a relative value, not an absolute one, cannot be worth such a steep, exorbitant price. Abandoning the strictures of the avant-garde and opting for a logic of renovation rather than radical innovation, postmodernism has entered into a lively reconstructive dialogue with the old and the past.[15]

Both Spanos and Calinescu describe a postmodernism that is not bound by temporal relations. But Calinescu pulls back from the brink, refusing to identify postmodernism with a marginal, destructive avant-garde: innovation has been tempered by renovation, destruction by appropriation. The predominant postmodern impulse has been not to destroy, or rupture, but to mutate and fuse as a process of "making it new." Certainly the hierarchical, timeless works of modernist poets have been challenged by the anarchical, occasional works of postmodern poets. But the two poetics of modernism and postmodernism can be set in apposition without requiring that the latter wholly reject, disrupt, or destroy the various activities and products of the former.

In practice the postmodern tempers its penchant for innovation and its avant-gardist tendency to absolute rupture by relying on mutation (gradual change as an articulation of difference), fusion (the synthesis of diverse attributes to produce a distinctly new quality), and renovation (reviving the castoffs and misfits of formerly threadbare poetics). Fragments of bar talk in *The Waste Land* mutate—cancerously, and no less gravely—in Charles Bukowski and David Antin. Eliot maintains his distance in "A Game of Chess" from Cockney corruption, but the participation of Bukowski and the talk-performance of Antin bleed to the very edge of the page.[16] High culture fuses with low in Ashbery's difficult *and* silly "Daffy Duck in Hollywood." Unlike Pound, who disdains the "pianola" in "Hugh Selwyn Mauberley," Ashbery successfully absorbs popular culture without catering to it. Recent fiction and poetry have revived the dark textures of the baroque and the elaborate artifice of the rococo. Williams insisted on an entirely "new form" for the American poetry of 1947 or thereabouts, but Harry Mathews plunders the history of formal invention for lipograms and haiku, palindromes and combinatoric plots. Postmodern poetics is neither a belated "happening" of modern poetics, nor does it demand a destructive and adversarial confrontation with its immediate predecessor. Postmodern poetry maintains its very high level of interest because of its subtle blend of innovation and renovation, mutation and fusion.

Postmodern poets have sought a distinct formal identity in their work through two complementary methods. Poets such as Creeley, Oppen, and Spicer have discerned a serial order that is "protean" and provisional. It incorporates random occurrences without succumbing to formlessness. Poets such as Ashbery, Mathews, and Cage have entertained a procedural order that is "proteinic" and predetermined. It employs arbitrary constraints to generate the content of the poem instead of merely containing it, as in traditional fixed forms. These complementary methods transcend the now familiar dichotomy between "closed" and "open" forms. The poet who experiments with a procedural order concedes, indeed welcomes, results that are beyond his immediate determination. The poet who incorporates the aleatory likewise welcomes each shape as it occurs, and not as she determines it. Neither makes pronouncements on the world; each articulates a form. In a "protean" order the poet as Menelaus struggles to capture the incessantly changing, fluid, and contiguous phenomena as they occur. In a "proteinic" order the poet initiates an encoded structure or network that builds on itself, replicates with variation, and produces the text.[17] In his survey of the major works of postmodern music, visual arts, and fiction, Christopher Butler discerns "a contrast between those which are dominated by a theory of their own rule-dominated means of creation, and those whose method is antithetical to this, being irrationalist, indeterminate, or aleatory."[18] Certainly postmodern poets deserve equal billing with the composers of serial music, the abstract expressionists, and the new novelists. Similarly inventive principles of form have been applied in verse. Postmodern poets have by no means viewed form suspiciously, nor have they been particularly devoted to "antiformal" methods of composition. These poets have in fact a decidedly imaginative and innovative approach to formal methods, easily challenging in its diversity the formal innovation of the great modernists. Serial and procedural orders, an aleatory or a rule-dominated method of composition, constitute a distinctive formal identity in postmodern poetics.

In a statement for the *New American Review* in 1969, Robert Creeley argues that period labels are irrelevant, consigning them appropriately to the domain of critical discourse: "Terms such as 'modern' and 'post-modern' are habits of art history. One tends to use all that he can get hold of, and I don't know that one 'time' is thus distinct from another, in the actual practice. *Here* is where one seems to be."[19] Period distinctions are of far more importance to the historian than to the practicing artist; or, as Malcolm Bradbury has noted, " 'Postmodernism' has in some ways become a critic's term without ever quite being an artistic movement."[20] As a poet Creeley need neither deny the continuing relevance of the modernist writers, nor pledge absolute fealty to their principles. He can, however, enumerate the literary principles that inform his practice. He first reminds us that "the previous conception of a Newtonian universe—with its containment" has yielded to new measures and new formal orders. Thus he claims, "Most interesting to me is the insistent presence of what has been called the *chance factor* in the activity of all the arts of the past several years. . . . [O]ne sees that a discipline, so to speak, is being gained to discover a *formal* possibility in a highly variable context of activity."[21] Reluctant to proclaim an altogether separate era, Creeley nevertheless enunciates aspects of a distinctly postmodern poetics. In proclaiming the advent of aleatory methods of composition, he does not seek the utter dissolution of form but the discovery of a new formal possibility that is variable, relative, or provisional. Much the same can be said for those artists who explore rule-dominated or procedural forms as a creative means, not as a device for containment requiring mechanical assembly. These aleatory and rule-dominated methods provide the basis in postmodern poetics for a formal identity that is innovative, distinct from that of its predecessors, and representative of our present concerns.

## Seriality and Proceduralism: A Typology of Postmodern Poetry

By far the most divisive and contentious debate in the field of poetics since about 1960 has been that regarding the relative merits of an "open" and a "closed" form. Each has its readily recognizable shape on the page. One should not attribute to "sour grapes" (the ironic and self-deprecating title of Williams's fifth collection of poems) or discount as "poet lore" the fact that the editors of various small magazines firmly attached to one camp have for some time returned at a glance the stray submission from a poet firmly attached to the opposing camp. The shape of the poem on the page is the first apparent criterion: one first sees Stanley Kunitz and Richard Wilbur as regular stanza lengths, flush left, often with the initial word capitalized; one first sees Charles Olson in ragged left and right, indented parentheticals, and the occasional line printed on the diagonal. For the veteran of the "poetry wars" of the middle decades of this century, many estimations flicker through synapses before the poem has even been read. Thus poetic form is truly an advance guard, the initial point of contact )
between opposing forces.

By 1950 the skirmish lines in American poetry were already drawn )
between the academy and bohemia. Academic poets have relied rather
more on tradition than individual talent for their authority; they have consequently been prescriptive in their few essays on poetics; and as editors they have guarded their prestigious, funded magazines with Cerberean ferocity. Bohemian poets have more often relied on a cult of the hero (the commanding presence of one who has persevered in hostile environs) for support; as a result of their disenfranchisement, they have felt pressed to defend their poetics in many polemical essays; and they have predominantly depended on the literary equivalent of guerrilla tactics in their publishing efforts. Robert Creeley remarks in retrospect, "Given the time, and the enclosing orthodoxy with respect to either poetry or prose, there seems little wonder in the fact that my early essays have an embattled manner. I was quite

certain that we faced an indefatigable army of resistance, a sense I've never really been able to persuade otherwise."[22] Joel Oppenheimer likewise testifies to his lasting conviction that the poets and critics associated with the academy are "the enemy."[23] In the clash between bohemia and the academy, poetic form is the emphatic declaration of one's allegiance, the sudden flashing of one's colors.

It would be fair to concede the decades of the forties and fifties to academic poetry and its closed forms. The sociopolitical complacency and conservatism of the period, culminating in Eisenhower's eight-year administration, finds its match in a poetics overawed by tradition and ruled by its sense of decorum. The containment of the traditional forms was invoked not merely as a shape on a typescript page but as a political gesture of conformity and as a psychological testament to the triumph of self-restraint—particularly among those poets struggling for their sanity. Likewise one acknowledges in the decades of the sixties and seventies the increased prominence of a Beat, bohemian, open-form poetics which was readily adopted as the mouthpiece—the genre—of the free speech, free love, antiauthoritarian, and anti–Vietnam War movements. Fulfilling the prophecies and invocations of Whitman, poetry rises from its place as an elitist genre at the fireside or in the classroom to become a populist genre of campus protest and coffeehouse readings.[24] The repeated clashes between academia and bohemia over the viability of open forms or the applicability of closed forms to the contemporary ethos give evidence that these were not peripheral spats over technique; such formal concerns constituted an active engagement with the sociopolitical goals and values of their adherents. In fact, the dichotomy implied by the formal terms "open" and "closed" was frequently restated as the "raw" and the "cooked," in the mythological terms introduced by Claude Lévi-Strauss in 1964. The "raw" evokes Whitman's barbaric yawp and Ginsberg's plaintive howl, Dionysian impulse and romantic spontaneity, progressive politics and projective verse. The "cooked" evokes the civilized yawn and what Olson calls the "verse which print bred,"[25] Apollonian form and Ivory Tower ruminations, conservative politics and instructional handbooks on versification. In the siege and sway of the fifties and sixties the issue of poetic form required a declaration of one's stance toward reality and one's position in society.

By the late eighties much of the vehemence that fired the debate between academia and bohemia had abated, in part because many of the once ostracized poets had found positions as university instructors, and in part because bohemian poetics had found eloquent defenders within the academic community. Despite this apparent truce, a handful of poets and critics have claimed to foresee the imminent return to prominence of the metrical verse forms that characterized the academic poetry of the forties and fifties. One such critic, Robert Richman, argues, "After two decades of obscure, linguistically flat poetry, there has been a decisive shift" to rhymed and metered verse.[26] Such an argument—whatever its empirical evidence—implies a "pendulum effect" in which the aesthetic sensibility, once it has swung to one terminus, must as easily swing back over the same course to its opposite terminus. But the arguments over open and closed forms will not simply repeat themselves in reverse; it seems foolish to regress to an understanding of poetic form as it stood for John Crowe Ransom in 1940. Rather I would propose that the postmodern poet has arrived at a new position of synthesis with regard to poetic form, having grown beyond the frequently exaggerated antithesis of the open and the closed. The poet's understanding of open and closed forms has not remained static during this period; the defining characteristics of both forms have been modified, and each has adapted to the new contingencies of postmodernity. This disturbing sense of the inadequacy with which we have been "typing" contemporary poetry—in the terms of an argument over forty years old, if we take Olson's "Projective Verse" (1950) as a first salvo—leads me to propose the existence of serial and procedural forms that are not antithetical to one another but complementary responses to postmodernity.

The open form of the poetic series is defined by its limitless set of relations; it takes its shape from the diverse ways in which items come together, undetermined by (in Umberto Eco's terms) an "external *necessity*" that would prescribe its organization,[27] or by the "internal" necessity that is the claim of organic form. The series is distinct from the neoromantic sequence because its discontinuity and radical incompleteness are at odds with the latter's basis in an organic theory of continuity and development. The series as an open form—with its aleatory and indeterminate qualities—thus supersedes in its postmodernity an organic sequence that still hopes to discover an immanent form and a unity in creation. Poets have been redefining the characteristics of an open form since Coleridge first proposed a "form as proceeding" as an alternative to a "form as superimposed." Motivated by the presence of such an alternative, contemporary poets have also begun to reconceive the function of closed or fixed forms. A procedural form is "closed" by virtue of its entirely predetermined structure, but the function of that structure is radically different from that of traditional closed forms. A traditional form is imposed on an already *known* content in an effort to contain and shape it as an object of art; it is a product of a hierarchical cosmos in which all things can be known and situated accordingly. The procedural form is a generative structure that constrains the poet to encounter and examine that which he or she does not immediately fathom, the uncertainties and incomprehensibilities of an expanding universe in which there can be no singular impositions.

The sonnet and the organic sequence have a rich history of magnificent examples to recommend them, but it is precisely because these forms have their origins in another time that we must look to the contemporary response. Serial and procedural forms have their beginnings in the postmodern era because they reflect an understanding—a formal perception—of conditions that the poet of the fourteenth century in Italy or the late eighteenth century in England could not have had. The humanism that Petrarch was so influential in spreading has given way to a post-humanism in which man is no longer the measure of all things; the reasoning mind is cast into shadows by celebrated irrationalities, and the individual ego finds itself to be at the periphery rather than the focus of modes of order. The organicism in which Coleridge sought the unity of natural processes and the creative mind yields to a technological person divorced from an environment that he gamely attempts to "manage" or "condition." A poet cannot hope to practice in a poetic form that is irrelevant to the immediate concerns of her contemporary reality. The work must perforce be ineffectual.

The concept of a poetic form must respond to the conditions of the modern world and to an understanding of how that world functions. Not all "new" verse forms are equal to the task of confronting reality. Poets may correctly observe that theirs is a printed medium requiring the extended concentration of the reader; and they may also observe that the audiovisual media that now dominate our culture offer an almost instant gratification that barely requires the attention of its audience at all. Thus some poets have devoted their energies to producing concrete or "visual poetry" that could easily be flashed on a video monitor; or they have composed "sound poetry" that can be chanted like a mantra, recorded, spliced, or broadcast over loudspeakers in some public forum.[28] But in my opinion such poetic forms seem too much to bear the stamp of their reality. They are formal effects that seem not so much devised by the poet as thrust upon him by the exigencies of his condition. They reflect a world that has grown too impatient to tolerate the "defamiliarization," the increase in the "difficulty and length of perception" that Victor Shklovsky argued poetic language ought to pursue.[29] Such forms do not confront or interpret contemporary reality; they submit to it. A literary form has always been best understood in terms of its function, what it hopes to accomplish. It is a *device* whose attributes can be enumerated and codified—not unlike a socket wrench—but it best defines itself by its use. Thus the most effectual forms are those that most actively engage and clearly interpret phenomena, those that foresee implications rather than reflect them in an unmediated way, those that present the world as it has become—even if we are ourselves not fully aware of the changes.

Serial and procedural forms provide alternative and complementary responses to postmodernity. Both are acutely aware of what has generally been perceived as the lapse of governing orders in our existence. The divine order as a single voice of authority has withdrawn to be replaced by a cacophony of channeled voices, or by no voice at all; the New Age offers us either the comic confusion of a hundred cajoling, admonitory sources, or a sublime but empty "space music" of planetary motion and interstellar dust. The pantheistic solace that many of our great nineteenth-century writers found in the vast and supposedly indomitable American continent and its wildlife has been negated by the acknowledgment that humanity is at once the ecology's greatest enemy and its only recourse for survival. Natural order, like Melville's fated leviathan, finds itself all too dependent on our graces. The postmodern artist has little confidence in suprahuman orders, and she will readily concede that whatever order may be apparent in the world is largely a projection of the human mind. Our sense of the universe as ineffable is stronger now than a century ago because we are that much more inclined to disbelieve the fictions of its coherence. Consequently, postmodern artists consider human orders to be arbitrary and occasional, and they are rather skeptical regarding any claims that such orders are endorsed by anything beyond our own immediate political, ethical, or utilitarian convenience. Among the poets of my own discussion, the active responses to this condition can be sorted into two distinct but complementary types: either they make (in Robert Creeley's words) "a quick graph" of the acknowledged disorder as it occurs; or they enlist an admittedly arbitrary and personal order as mediation between the mind and its environs. One creates a somewhat desultory topological map of the "ground" of existence; the other produces a grid transparently superimposed on—and as easily lifted from—existence. The one describes the process of seriality; the other declares the product of proceduralism.

The reciprocal relationship of seriality and proceduralism, aleatory procedures and arbitrary constraints, is founded on attitudes toward chaos and order which are newly effective in the postmodern era.

Chaos no longer evokes the terrifying disruption that a modernist such as Wyndham Lewis meant to convey by the title of his magazine *BLAST*. The concept returns to its pre-Socratic value as the *absence* of a determining order. Science must now investigate the indeterminate as well as the determinate in order to describe our condition; its field of inquiry thus expands immensely. Conversely, all orders that make a claim for hierarchy or orthodoxy are seriously challenged. In his essay "The Poetics of the Open Work," Umberto Eco recognizes this development when he states, "In every century, the way that artistic forms are structured reflects the way in which science or contemporary culture views reality." In a display of his own rather remarkable breadth of inquiry, he contrasts this relationship in the medieval and postmodern eras:

> The closed, single conception in a work by a medieval artist reflected the conception of the cosmos as a hierarchy of fixed, preordained orders. The work as a pedagogical vehicle, as a monocentric and necessary apparatus (incorporating a rigid internal pattern of meter and rhymes) simply reflects the syllogistic system, a logic of necessity, a deductive consciousness by means of which reality could be made manifest step by step without unforeseen interruptions, moving forward in a single direction, proceeding from first principles of science which were seen as one and the same with the first principles of reality.[30]

Following the dissolution of such hierarchical orders, contemporary science has proposed the notion of "field" which, as Eco observes, "implies a revised vision of the classic relationship posited between cause and effect as a rigid, one-directional system."[31] Eco cites the composer Henri Pousseur as his example of the influence of such scientific concepts on the artistic community, but students of American poetry will recall that Charles Olson declares in "Projective Verse" that "any poet who departs from closed form . . . ventures into FIELD COMPOSITION—puts himself in the open."[32]

Eco also observes the philosophical and scientific currency of the notion of "possibility," the "discarding of a static, syllogistic view of order, and a corresponding devolution of intellectual authority to personal decision, choice, and social context." He concludes that our understanding of contemporary reality is marked by "a general breakdown in the concept of causation":

> Multi-value logics are now gaining currency, and these are quite capable of incorporating *indeterminacy* as a valid stepping-stone in the cognitive process. In this general intellectual atmosphere, the poetics of the open

work is peculiarly relevant: it posits the work of art stripped of necessary and foreseeable conclusions, works in which the [musical] performer's freedom functions as part of the *discontinuity* which contemporary physics recognizes, not as an element of disorientation, but as an essential stage in all scientific verification procedures and also as the verifiable pattern of events in the subatomic world.[33]

Eco's thesis is provocative and compelling: that the abandonment by science of a unidirectional system of causation for a multidirectional field of possibilities encourages a corresponding shift in the arts from closed to open forms. His argument is particularly useful to a definition of seriality in poetry. No longer bound by the fixed, preordained orders of closure, the series articulates both the indeterminacy and the discontinuity that the scientist discovers in the subatomic world and that we are compelled to consider in our own interaction with reality. The concept of serial form could not be convincing without the "granular" physics of subatomic particles and molecular combination and recombination. Postmodern poets recognize such qualities not as elements of disorientation or as a disruptive chaos, but as an essential aspect of their own investigation of contemporary existence.

I would like to suggest one small emendation to Eco's lucid analysis of the relationship between contemporary science and artistic form: that the contemporary artist's concept of a closed form has not remained the same as it was for the artist in a medieval library. Ihab Hassan has also suggested this overly neat progression in which "literary forms seem to develop from closed to open to antiforms."[34] Such an argument is sustained by the paradigm of a classical model, its "modern" reinterpretation, and finally its parody. But the closed forms of postmodern poetry are not anachronistic slaves to a hierarchical order; nor are they satisfied to parody that concept of order. The poets in this discussion who have adopted procedural forms are very much aware of the resignation of hierarchical orders, but they have as a consequence felt justified in asserting their own, very arbitrary systems of organization; in this sense they agree with Eco's assessment of the "devolution of intellectual authority to personal decision." Form is not dictated by tradition, but assembled as a set of choices that can be disassembled or reconstituted according to the poet's assessment of their effectiveness. Form is not "endowed" by some suprahuman or historical authority, but "fabricated" with an emphasis on displaying the poet's artifice. The alternative to a practice that engages the flux and indeterminacy of contemporary existence is one that acknowledges the arbitrariness of all assertions of a fixed order. The aleatory procedures of serial form and the arbitrary constraints of procedural form thus represent the complementary alternatives to the hierarchical order discredited by modern physics, made untenable in contemporary reality, and abandoned by postmodern poetics.


### Serial Form

The series is the one form of the "long poem" which truly has its origin in the postmodern era. In the interest of providing some historical parameters, it is worth noting that the serial form can claim as its prototype William Carlos Williams's *Spring and All* (1923). The book consists of twenty-seven numbered, untitled poems interspersed with prose arguments whose concern is the defense of the author's poetics. This book is a manifestation of Williams's demand in one argument that poetry be "new form dealt with as a reality in itself."[35] The poems of this series have been so frequently excerpted, with the addition of individual titles, that I would venture to say that very few readers recognize "The Red Wheelbarrow" (XXII) or "To Elsie" (XVIII) as parts of a larger, more complex work.[36] The series distinguishes itself from the neoromantic sequence principally because it forgoes the linear, thematic development of that form. Thus excerpts taken from Keats's "The Eve of St. Agnes," Tennyson's *In Memoriam*, or Stevens's "The Auroras of Autumn" would be wholly unsatisfactory, and in the case of Tennyson, the anthologies seldom agree as to what should be left in or out. But it was Williams himself who first excerpted, and titled, the separate but related poems of *Spring and All* in the preparation of his *Collected Poems, 1921–1931* (1934). In effect, the fame of his "lyric" poems comes at the expense of a more general knowledge of his daring formal innovation during this decade. Although I will not discuss Williams's book at length, it can be considered the prototype for those poems whose form is both discontinuous and capable of recombination.[37] Serial poems of course continue to be written, and I discuss such current examples as Michael Palmer's "Series" in *The Circular Gates* and the title poem of Leslie Scalapino's *that they were at the beach* (which she designates an "aeolotropic series") in my concluding essay.[38] From its prototype to the present, the series asserts itself as a uniquely postmodern form.

The series can be described in semiotic terms as a poetic form in which the syntagmatic relation of the sign is predominant. Roland Barthes describes a "syntagmatic imagination," which no longer sees the sign in terms of its "depth" (or symbolic) relation, but in terms of "its antecedent or consequent links, the bridges it extends to other signs."[39] An authoritative voice in the *Princeton Encyclopedia of Poetry and Poetics* claims in an entry on literary signification that "the more interesting and important semantic problems of poetry have to do with its employment of, and shifting relations to, depth symbols."[40] But Barthes argues for the aesthetic complexity with which signs combine. Such literary forms as the series are the product of "a 'stemmatous' imagination of the chain or network." They function as "an arrangement of mobile, substitutive parts, whose combination produces meaning, or more generally a new object."[41] The serial form is thus based on the complex and multifarious means by which, as Robert Creeley points out, one thing finds its place with another. A linear or temporal sequence is only the most logical, or the most readily comprehensible, means by which combinations are brought about; but signs or events are rarely so simple in their convergence.

The serial form in poetry is one of "those works," as Barthes puts it, "whose fabrication, by arrangement of discontinuous and mobile elements, constitutes the spectacle itself."[42] The discontinuity of its elements—or their resistance to a determinate order—distinguishes the series from the thematic continuity, narrative progression, or meditative insistence that often characterize the sequence. At the same time, the series does not aspire to the encompassment of the epic; nor does it allow for the reduction of its materials to the isolated perfection of the single lyric. The series demands neither summation nor exclusion. It is instead a combinative form whose arrangements admit a variegated set of materials.

Each element of the series is a module that asserts its position in combination with other elements; its place is not assigned by any external schema. Among sequences, on the other hand, perhaps the most recognizable types are those with a "mechanic" or imposed organization. In a temporal sequence, for example, one fully expects after the presentation of poems titled "Spring," "Summer," and "Autumn," that the final section will declare the arrival of winter. Each part follows from that immediately preceding it, as surely as middle age follows from youth and old age from middle age. Any reshuffling of such an order would cause consternation among the readers. As Barbara Herrnstein Smith points out, "These sequences are generated by an *extraliterary* principle of succession."[43] Narrative progression of character or event, as in Keats's "Eve of St. Agnes," would not be sustained by the serial form. The rejection of an external or predetermined order by the series is a contributing factor in its status as an open form.

The distinction between the sequence and the series can also be expressed as follows. A sequence is a hypotactic structure (meaning, "arranged one under another") whose elements are subordinate to or dependent on other elements for their meaning. For example: the local newspaper prints a synopsis of this week's soap operas; the episodes are thus sequential (not discontinuous) because each episode contains information that the viewer must know in order to comprehend those that follow. The series, however, is a paratactic structure (meaning, "arranged side by side") whose elements, although related by the fact of their contiguity, are nevertheless autonomous.[44] For example: a line of parked cars assembles itself on the street each evening shortly after six P.M. The cars are related by their bumper-to-bumper contiguity and by their general participation in this phenomenon. Yet the make and model of the cars differ and their order along the curb frequently changes; occasionally, one arrives or departs at an odd hour. Their relationship is serial, or paratactic, subject to a multiplicity of combinations. As Herrnstein Smith points out, "The dislocation or omission of any element will tend to make the sequence as a whole incomprehensible, or will radically change its effect. In paratactic structure, however (where the principle of generation does not cause any one element to 'follow' from another), the thematic units can be omitted, added, or exchanged without destroying the coherence or effect of the poem's thematic structure."[45] In postmodern poetry, the complexity with which such units of meaning can be brought together, and the phenomena they describe, attain a level of artistic maturity comparable to particle physics.

The series is an open form in large part because it does not require the "mechanic" imposition of an external organization. It is not, however, an "organic" form. In *The Modern Poetic Sequence*, M. L. Rosenthal and Sally Gall define a neoromantic sequence, "a grouping of mainly lyric poems and passages . . . which tend to interact as an organic whole."[46] The discontinuous elements of the series, however, are rather more atomistic or molecular than plantlike in their behavior. It would be impossible to dispense with continuity among the parts of an organic structure—there cannot be a leaf detached or a bud clipped from its root. "The organic form," as Coleridge claims, "shapes as it develops itself from within."[47] We can observe the thematic development of Tennyson's *In Memoriam*, the character development of Pound's "Hugh Selwyn Mauberley" or Berryman's "Homage to Mistress Bradstreet," and the thematic continuity of such meditative sequences as Crane's "Voyages" or Stevens's "Auroras of Autumn." But the discontinuity of elements in the series, as Creeley's volume *Pieces* demonstrates, disrupts any internal development or progression of its materials. The sections of a series are not hierarchical. There is no initiation, climax, or terminus precisely because there can be no development. In the sequence, the reader must, so to speak, enter through the front door and exit through the rear; but in a series such as Robert Duncan's *Passages*, the reader is encouraged to select any of these "passages" as an entrance. The reader does not require the information of any one section in order to comprehend the others.

Narrative discourse endeavors to create the illusion of movement that is both linear and continuous. When we praise such writing for the progression of its terms toward some conclusion, we use such phrases as "seamless logic" or "smooth transition." The movement of the serial poem, however, is curvilinear and disjunctive. It generates a centrifugal force, which is always directed away from a central axis. Although we expect from prosaic writing that its materials will march along the designated path, a series such as Paul Blackburn's *Journals* displays an arc whose momentum will carry it, with the odd leap, beyond a single focus and on to other foci. If on the other hand we consider the lyric mode in poetry, we find a propensity for various types of comparison, especially metaphor. The impulse of the lyric is to equate disparate materials, to draw them toward a central axis that expresses some unity of the whole. But if the discourse of the lyric is in a metaphoric mode, the discourse of the series is in a metonymic mode. The series expresses its structure as a set of tangencies. Each contiguous part (or metonym) on the poetic line, aware of its antecedent and consequent links, implies a contextual whole. But the intersection of these contexts will be small, and frequently they will meet only at discrete points. Such is the implication of the title of George Oppen's *Discrete Series*.

I have been at some pains to distinguish between serial form and sequential form precisely because of their apparent similarities, which have caused a number of critics to use the terms interchangeably and thus confusingly. Furthermore, it needs to be stated explicitly that the series is not simply an extension or revision of a Coleridgean metaphor for the creative process; it necessarily engages a comprehension of the world which is considerably more current than that of the German idealist philosophers. Roland Barthes's proposal of a "syntagmatic imagination" may strike some readers as unnecessarily technical, or they may be inclined to limit it to the perception of semiologists alone. But Umberto Eco, in his essay "Series and Structure," augments Barthes's proposal with his own defense of a "serial thought." Based on "the philosophy that underlies post-Webern musical aesthetics," serial thought is not simply a different methodological stance but a different vision of the world.[48] Eco quotes the composer Pierre Boulez for an initial exposition of the "distinctive features" of serial thought:

> Serial thought has become a polyvalent thought process. . . . As such, it is in complete contrast to classical thought, according to which form is a preexisting entity and at the same time a general morphology. Here (within serial thought) there are no preconstituted scales—that is, no general structures within which a particular thought could inscribe itself. A composer's thought, operating in accordance with a particular methodology, creates the objects it needs and the form necessary for their organization each time it has occasion to express itself. Classical tonal thought is based on a world defined by gravitation and attraction; serial thought, on a world that is perpetually expanding.[49]

Eco comments that "this hypothesis of an oriented production of open possibilities, of an incitement to experience choice, of a constant questioning of any established grammar, is the basis of any theory of the 'open work,' in music as well as in every other artistic genre. The theory of the open work is none other than a poetics of serial thought."[50] If seriality were nothing more than a methodology, its practice would not extend beyond modern music. But confirmation of a "serial thought" exists in the other arts. Thus Robert Creeley, as we noted earlier, similarly discerns the collapse of a Newtonian universe, a classical world based on gravitation, containment, and centripetal force. Serial thought announces the presence of an expanding universe in which centrifugal force predominates. It is a world in which, as Yeats predicted, "the center cannot hold."[51] But whereas Yeats, who expresses the former consciousness, sees "mere anarchy . . . loosed upon the world," the postmodern theorist proposes an open structure that welcomes possibility, choice, and chance. Serial thought is the expression of a world concept that lies, luxurious in its possibilities, between the systemic and the anarchic.

Boulez's statement makes the important contrast between the classical concept of form as a preexisting entity and the serial concept of form as an occasional entity. In classical thought, the form is systemic, hierarchical, and preconstituted. But serial thought, as Boulez argues, "creates the objects it needs and the form necessary for their organization each time it has occasion to express itself." The serial form constitutes itself on the instant from a set of mobile and discontinuous objects; and it may reconstitute itself at the next instant from a varied set of objects. Each new combination produces a new meaning, reorients itself as a new aesthetic object. The classical form aspires to the permanent and the crystalline; the serial form is occasional and recombinative.

The polyvalence of serial thought concerns itself neither with grand summation nor with the reduction of multiple alternatives to a single "truth." Instead, as Eco describes it,

> a series, qua constellation, is a field of possibilities that generates multiple choices. It is possible to conceive of large syntagmatic chains (such as Stockhausen's musical "group"; the "material" ensemble of action painting; the linguistic unit extracted from a different context and inserted, as a new unit of articulation, within a discourse where what matters are the meanings that emerge out of the conjunction and not the primary meanings of the syntagmatic unit in its natural context; and so on)—chains that offer themselves as ulterior instances of articulation in relation to their initial articulations.[52]

Serial thought recognizes that each conjunction of objects has a meaning; that the objects are capable of rearrangement; and that that subsequent arrangement also has a meaning which is in no way "secondary" to its initial articulation. Nor does the initial articulation determine the pattern or arrangement of those that follow. This recombinatory quality does not negate form; it acknowledges its pliability in an expanding, relative universe.

The serial form accommodates the contemporary experience of reality in which the perceiving mind is not solely directed to a few prominent features but continually presented with its full texture. Seriality does not chart the peaks of experience only, but the full pattern in all its divertissements and divagations. In the following passage from Harry Mathews's epistolary novel *The Sinking of the Odradek Stadium*, a conversation among Italian semioticians is recorded by the Southeast Asian woman who is one of the novel's two correspondents. Her broken English, replete with typographical errors, struggles to reconstitute a conversation whose jargon she does not comprehend but which she finds charming for its reference to the city of Miami (the residence of the librarian to whom she writes). Her experience should not seem entirely "foreign" to us.

    1: "When I say, *slab,* I maen, *slab.*"
    2: "But whut do you dou with the *signifiant*? A road sign say, Miami 82 mile. What re-ality do this indicate? Miami? The distans be-tween the sing and the sity? The location of the sign? The semi-ottic (?) re-ality, the mmediate realita, posit a structsure . . ."
    3: "I like Miami—of coarse it *is* infect-ed with Amerihans."

4: "Why strutcher it though? The elemens of the consep 'sign' thath you naem, and othrs giust as importort, are grasp by our outerd con-sciouscnesce in a kine of frifloatin jazz continume, so when I see the in for-mation containt, the so call content, I all so *feel* the grainy-ness of the would or flaky-ness of the pent, which ar part of the so-call form, in factt I can feel too the in-formation at any rat it's only one hork of many bob-ing in the opent see of simultanity . . ."[53]

The first comment—an allusion to Wittgenstein's *Philosophical Investigations*—attests to the arbitrariness with which words, as sig-nifiers, adhere to the objects they signify. The postmodern mind recog-nizes that there is no intimate bond between its articulation in lan-guage and its experience of the world as object. The second comment confronts the difficulty of determining the precise referent of even so simple a signifier as a road sign: Miami 82. Is it possible to limit its meaning by agreement to "the distance between the sign and the city"? In fact, we must contend with the unreliability of all systems of signification to indicate precisely the same reality in each instance and for all observers. The fourth comment rather concisely sums up the postmodern perception of reality. The individual consciousness perceives each sign in "a kind of free-floating jazz continuum." Reality is itself "grainy" or "flaky," and it is a fond illusion that one can sift and extract from it the profound nugget of symbolic meaning. The serial thought of postmodernism recognizes that each sign is "one cork of many bobbing in the open sea of simultaneity," and that to attempt to isolate an element of causality or a linear sequence is to violate the nature of that reality. The open, polyvalent, and protean structure of serial form is most in accord with this understanding of the nature of reality.

## The Postmodern Long Form

The "long poem" has been the measure and the lifework of many significant modernist and postmodernist poets. The serial form is a distinct type of the long poem, and it is remarkable for being the one long form whose characteristics are unique to a postmodern poetics. All other types of the long poem as practiced by contemporary poets are adaptations or renovations of forms whose theoretical and struc-tural underpinnings were set in previous periods. Since I have offered some means of distinguishing seriality from other types of poetic order, I think it important to identify the characteristics and the origins of these rival types of the long poem. Too many critics speak indiscriminately of the "epic," the "sequence," and the "series" as if they were all versions of the same poetic structure. One encounters critics who use the terms interchangeably (even within a single paragraph) and critics who casually compare examples of one type to examples of another. As a case in point, M. L. Rosenthal and Sally M. Gall treat in a single essay such structurally diverse poems as Hart Crane's "Voyages," *The Bridge*, and Charles Olson's *The Maximus Poems* as examples of the "modern poetic sequence."[54] The three poems are linked by the thematic relationship of American neo-regionalism, but this concern obscures the distinctions in their formal types: the first is a true sequence of lyrics closely united by its thematic concerns; the second is more accurately described (by Crane) as a "jazz symphony" than as an epic; the third, a book of some 635 oversized pages, makes a legitimate claim as a modern, transcultural epic. In each case the poems are better served if we acknowledge their structural diversity rather than obscuring it under the single rubric of the "sequence" or subordinating their distinct formal characteristics to thematic comparisons.

Among the prominent types of the long poem in the latter half of this century are those in which the reemergence of the Coleridgean theory of organic form has been most pronounced. These poems adhere to a central tenet of what Roland Barthes calls the "symbolic consciousness," namely that the form of the poem "is constantly exceeded by the power and the movement of its content."[55] This concept can be clearly traced to the writings of Coleridge. In his *Lectures on Shakespeare*, Coleridge distinguishes between the properties of a mechanic and an organic form: "The form is mechanic when on any given material we impress a predetermined form, not necessarily arising out of the properties of the material, as when to a mass of wet clay we give whatever shape we wish it to retain when hardened. The organic form, on the other hand, is innate; it shapes as it develops itself from within, and the fullness of its development is one and the same with the perfection of its outward form. Such is the life, such the form."[56]

There are two dichotomies at work in this description, one temporal and the other spatial. In the mechanic model, form precedes content; it is predetermined and applied to the "material." The force of the form as it shapes and molds the rather inert clay exceeds that of the content. In the organic model, Coleridge claims that the "fullness" of the content's development and the "perfection" of an outward form are simultaneous. But it is the very stuff of the poem-plant which is continually developing and shaping itself; the perfection that is the outward form is not the prior cause but the secondary effect of the "innate properties," the power and movement of the content. When a disciple of organicism such as Dylan Thomas refers to "the force that through the green fuse drives the flower," he does not praise the outward form of his "crooked rose" as the neoclassical poet praises his lady, but stands "dumb," in awe of its inner life force.[57]

The second dichotomy, between "inner" and "outer" forces, firmly indicates that organic form adheres to Barthes's description of the predominance of content in the symbolic imagination. Barthes argues that "the symbolic consciousness implies an imagination of depth; it experiences the world as the relation of a superficial form and a many-sided, massive, powerful *Abgrund*, and the image is reinforced by a very intense dynamics: the relation of form and content is ceaselessly renewed by time (history), the superstructure overwhelmed by the infrastructure, without our ever being able to grasp the structure itself."[58] M. H. Abrams provides the relevant discussion of a superficial form and a powerful content in Coleridgean terms: "An artefact needs to be made, but a plant makes itself. According to one of Coleridge's favorite modes of stating this difference, in life 'the unity . . . is produced *ab intra*,' but in mechanism, '*ab extra*.' "[59] We need only compare Barthes's claim that in the symbolic mode, "form resembles the content, as if it were actually *produced* by it."[60] In organicism, it is the content that produces the poem's unity from within; form then and therefore becomes its superficial resemblance.

Coleridge, however, offers an alternative to the terms "organic" and "mechanic" which I find more useful. If we abandon the analogy to plant and machine for a more abstract, yet functional description of the two forms, we can adopt for the one *form as proceeding* and for the other *shape as superinduced*.[61] Although this second set of terms loses the evocative power of metaphor, it approaches the subject on a somewhat larger scale. Using related terms, Donald Wesling, in *The New Poetries: Poetic Form since Coleridge and Wordsworth*, makes a useful distinction between system and structure: "*System* is here taken to mean the conditioning set, the assumptions that direct poetic creation (now, after 1795); *structure* is the term referring to interrelations between constituent units. . . . *System*, as applied here to concepts of language, nature and art, innovation, and genre theory, is the broader term; it describes, by and large, the attitudes that determine the more precise aspects of structure, namely organization, the device, and the buildup of segment and line."[62] Even though Wesling himself prefers the term "form as proceeding" to "organic form," he neglects to identify it as the broader of the two that Coleridge employs. In the discussion of an open form poetics, I would claim that "form as proceeding" is a description of the *system;* similarly, in a closed form poetics, "form as superimposed" describes certain assumptions regarding the functions of language and art.

But as surely as there are many closed forms, so there are many types of open form. In "Some Notes on Organic Form," Denise Levertov broaches an argument with Robert Duncan:

> Thinking about how organic poetry differs from free verse, I wrote that "most free verse is failed organic poetry, that is, organic poetry from which the attention of the writer had been switched off too soon, before the intrinsic form of the experience had been revealed." But Robert Duncan pointed out to me that there is a "free verse" of which this is not true, because it is written not with any desire to seek a form, indeed perhaps with the longing to *avoid* form (if that were possible) and to express inchoate emotion as purely as possible.[63]

Whatever the merits of Duncan's formless "free verse," the suggestion that Levertov objects to is that there could be an accomplished open form that is not organic. But the series is just such a form. Again, I would claim that the term "organic" describes the *structure* of a particular kind of open form. Although serial form could be described as a type of "form as proceeding," its organization, the buildup of segment and line, is as significantly different from the organic sequence as Duncan's *Passages* is from the *Lyrical Ballads*. As a poetry of process, both serial and organic forms are "exploratory,"[64] but in organization the one displays a discontinuity of parts whereas the other prizes their assimilation.

If the Coleridgean theory of organicism is the still-fertile trunk of an old apple tree, it has managed even after a hundred years to produce in postmodern poetry two rather green and vigorous shoots. The first thrived in rural North Carolina, c. 1950, in the poetics of Charles Olson's Black Mountain College. Since library shelves hold more than one dissertation and several books on the school's poetics, I will not attempt a comprehensive discussion but rather select a few apt phrases and slogans as evidence for the place of Black Mountain in my typology. The essential document is Olson's "Projective Verse." His discussion of a projective or exploratory verse takes place largely at the level of *system*, so that much of his commentary pertains to all open forms. He does in fact distinguish "the *principle*, the law which presides conspicuously over such composition, and, when obeyed, is the reason why a projective poem can come into being. It is this: FORM IS NEVER MORE THAN AN EXTENSION OF CONTENT."[65] Although Olson does not avail himself of the term "organic," his maxim is heavily in debt to Coleridgean poetics because it asserts in all cases the primacy of content over form. Form is an "extension" of content, as the outer wall of an amoeba is an extension of its cytoplasm; or, to repeat Barthes's formulation, "form resembles the content, as if it were actually produced by it." Olson next describes what Wesling would define as *structure*: "the *process* of the thing, how the principle can be made so to shape the energies that the form is accomplished. . . . ONE PERCEPTION MUST IMMEDIATELY AND DIRECTLY LEAD TO A FURTHER PERCEPTION."[66] Although Olson attempts to describe the "shape" or structure of an open form—its organization—in this latter maxim, it seems to me that this *process* describes all open forms, whether organic or serial, unified or fragmented. I would say that Olson's maxim of *principle*, though he presumes it to be the "broader" term, is actually limited to the organic mode, whereas his statement of *process*—"form as proceeding"—actually encompasses the greater number of formal types.

In "An Admonition," Denise Levertov argues that "form exists only *in* the content and language." She then revises Olson's phrasing to read, "Form is never more than the *revelation* of content."[67] As I see it, this phrasing only reinforces the essential primacy of content in Coleridgean poetics. For Levertov, it is the numinous essence of content which is revealed. In serial composition, it is the "arrangement" (as Barthes puts it) which "constitutes the spectacle itself." Each new form is a revelation. In defense of her argument, Levertov cites Coleridge, but also Frank Lloyd Wright ("Form follows function") and Emerson ("Ask the fact for the form"). In each case, function, fact, experience, and content precede and appear to produce form.

Since Coleridge, poets have variously described the organic form as "innate," "inherent," or "intrinsic" in the materials at hand. Duncan asserts that "the poet desires to penetrate the seeming of style and subject matter to that most real where there is no form that is not content, no content that is not form."[68] The romantic poet argues that content does not "produce" form but that the form has always been present in the material, the experience, the content. But what Duncan describes as the "most real" is actually an ideal union of form and content which the New Critics were equally prepared to claim as the pursuit of any able poet. In practice, however, we can make the following distinction: the organicist adheres more closely to the claim that "there is no form that is not content"; and the formalist is far more comfortable with the claim that "there is no content that is not form." So the Russian Formalist critic Boris Eichenbaum, reacting to the symbolist movement, claimed, "Poetic form . . . is not contrasted with anything outside itself—with a 'content' which has been laboriously set inside this 'form'—but is understood as the genuine content of poetic speech."[69]

The second type of the long poem which derives its poetics ultimately from Coleridgean organicism is the Stevensian meditative sequence.[70] In an essay dedicated to the revival of the "Romantic spirit" and to the "pleasures and thrills in Coleridge and Poe," Robert Duncan claims that he is "conscious of the debt to Wallace Stevens—that there is a route back to the Romantics in Stevens."[71] Both Harold Bloom and Helen Vendler have established with extensive examination of the genealogy that Stevens is a direct descendant of Coleridge and Keats, and so their findings need not be repeated here. But I am concerned to establish that the Stevensian theory of form is both derived from Coleridge and related to the organic form of Black Mountain. Because the Stevens "school" apparently has not felt required to state its poetics in manifestos as the members of the Black Mountain school have, I will attempt to represent their views in a brief selection of poems.

A fine place to start for virtually any topic in Stevens is the poem "Notes toward a Supreme Fiction." In what some have described as the climax of this three-part sequence,[72] Stevens rebukes the Canon Aspirin, his figure for the neoclassical poet of rational thought and predetermined form:

> He imposes orders as he thinks of them,
> As the fox and snake do. It is a brave affair.
> Next he builds capitols and in their corridors,
>
> Whiter than wax, sonorous, fame as it is,
> He establishes statues of reasonable men,
> Who surpassed the most literate owl, the most erudite
>
> Of elephants. But to impose is not
> To discover. To discover an order as of
> A season, to discover summer and know it,
>
> To discover winter and know it well, to find,
> Not to impose, not to have reasoned at all,
> Out of nothing to have come on major weather. . . .[73]

The two approaches to the question of order—in the world, in language—which Stevens presents are ultimately derived from Cole-

ridge. We see in Canon Aspirin's imposition a mechanic form, one that
in Coleridge's phrase "impresses" or molds our conception of order
upon material. Though he begins in some affinity with the natural
world—the fox and snake—as a "reasonable" man, he asserts or *imposes* personal orders "as he thinks of them." Soon he "builds" (constructs, rather than grows) centers of government, mythologizing the
tokens of his own organization. Even the natural world assumes the
shape of his thoughts—he anthropomorphizes the "literate owl" and
"erudite elephant." But, Stevens says, when we *discover* the innate
order of a season, when we can know winter without recourse to
weather maps, without the shaping of Snow Men, without the jingle
bells of preconception and association, only then are we able "to find
the real." The language of Robert Duncan's own call to natural order is
so similar that it merits juxtaposition: "The order man may contrive
or impose upon the things about him or upon his own language is
trivial beside the divine order or natural order he may discover in
them."[74] The barometer provides only a trivial and inaccurate forecast
when what one seeks is "major weather." Both Duncan and Stevens
seek to substitute for an organized religion a faith in some immanent
natural order. The assertion of a natural order beyond our own personal constructs reappears in "The Man with the Blue Guitar" as "a
tune beyond us, yet ourselves,"[75] an order in which we participate but
which is not ours to construct.

Stevens might be said to introduce this opposition of general and
personal order in "The Idea of Order at Key West." In "the maker's rage
to order words of the sea," he pits the temperamental poet as a fabrica-
tor of personal order against the rhythmic yet monotonous sound of
the sea which, from Sophocles to Hart Crane, connotes the annihilation of ego.[76] But in the somewhat more didactic "Of Modern Poetry"
Stevens introduces a new, meditative mode of organic form. He calls it
"the poem of the mind in the act of finding / What will suffice. It has
not always had / To find: the scene was set; it repeated what / Was in
the script."[77] Again we see the opposition between romantic "finding"
or discovery of an innate form and the neoclassical imposition of
order—the passive acceptance of a predetermined form. The slight
shift of emphasis in the latter poem commands our attention: not
whether a perceptible general order exists, but whether the poet can
graph the presence of that order in the mind itself. So Stevens sets out
to write "the poem of the act of the mind."[78] As in Coleridge's exchange of the metaphoric "organic" description for the functional
"form as proceeding," Stevens adopts the meditative terminology, to
find in the mind itself an order, a thought rhythm that is not personal

or idiosyncratic but basic and general; the difference is as great as that between the current in the toaster or the frequency of an AM radio and the cosmic hum recorded by a radio astronomer's instruments.

Coleridge anticipates this version of open form in "On Poesy and Art" when he presents in several guises the idea that art is "the union and reconciliation of that which is nature with that which is exclusively human," or the object and the mind, the external and the internal.[79] Or as Stevens says in "Notes," "Two things of opposite nature seem to depend / On one another . . . the imagined / On the real."[80] Stevens's most successful renditions of the "poem of the act of the mind" occur in his later long poems. In "The Auroras of Autumn," he considers the prospect of "form gulping after formlessness" and repeatedly bids "farewell to an idea."[81] In "An Ordinary Evening in New Haven," he posits, "Suppose these houses are composed of ourselves . . . Impalpable habitations that seem to move / In the movement of the colors of the mind . . . object / Of the perpetual meditation . . . So much ourselves, we cannot tell apart / The idea and the bearer-being of the idea."[82] Suppose, that is, the reconciliation of mind and nature, accomplished in the abstract, not by the idiosyncratic. Suppose, to begin with, Coleridge's definition of the primary imagination "as a repetition in the finite mind of the eternal act of creation in the infinite I AM."[83]

Although I do not have the space for an exhaustive analysis, I would like to present two postmodern examples of "the poem of the act of the mind." A. R. Ammons's book-length poem *Sphere: The Form of a Motion* (1974), effectively demonstrates the "route back to the Romantics" through Stevens. Ammons's punctuation—no full stops, only colons—designates the poem's structure as an ongoing process and indicates an evolution or development of subject matter until, in a final exclamation of wonder, man born of mud learns to fly: "we're clear: we're ourselves: we're sailing."[84] The first of 155 strophes displays Ammons's organicism:

> The sexual basis of all things rare is really apparent
> and fools crop up where angels are mere disguises:
> a penetrating eye (insight), a penetrating tongue (ah),
>
> a penetrating penis and withal a penetrating mind,
> integration's consummation: a com- or intermingling of parts,
> heterocosm joyous, opposite motions away and toward
>
> along a common line, the in-depth knowledge (a dilly),
> the concentration and projection (firmly energized) and
> the ecstasy, the pay off, the play out, the expended

nexus nodding, the flurry, cell spray, finish, the
haploid hungering after the diploid condition: the reconciler
of opposites, commencement, proliferation, ontogeny:[85]

The scientific diction garnered from a master's degree in biology and
Ammons's ever-present epistemological queries (what can we know,
how can we know it) accompany a prolonged pun on the modern
orgasm and a Coleridgean organicism. Throughout the poem, in fact,
we encounter a postmodern slippage of diction—a melange of frank-
ness and ribaldry, the metaphoric and the scientific, a "dilly" and a
"diploid." But most prominent in this passage is the concept of the
"reconciler / of opposites," the integration in terms both sexual and
intellectual of the mind and nature which Coleridge first proclaimed
for the imagination. *Sphere* is in part an extended discourse on the
"synthetic" properties of the imagination: in the fourth strophe, Coleridge's "multeity in unity" appears as "an isosceles triangle" at whose
base we find "diversity" and individuality and at whose peak we find
"unity," "symbol," and "abstraction."[86]

Although the debt to Coleridge's synthetic imagination is extensive
and an organic form the celebrated structure, the poem offers evidence
of the Stevensian "act of the mind" in the second strophe:

often those who are not good for much else turn to thought
and it's just great, part of the grand possibility, that
thought is there to turn to: camouflagy thought flushed

out of the bush, seen vaguely as potential form, and
pursued, pursued and perceived, declared: the savored
form, the known possession, knowledge carnal knowledge:[87]

What is pursued is the potential form of thought, and Ammons is
fairly sure that such a form, not idiosyncratic but of a natural order, is
there to be "perceived, declared." So the mind and the body, "knowledge" and "carnal knowledge," become one (to use a favorite Stevensian phrase). The search for pattern in nature and its image in thought
is proposed in the ninth strophe, accompanied by the transcendence
that such a pattern must provide: "though the surface is crisp with
pattern still we know / that there are generalized underlyings . . . but if
we // pass through the discrete downward to the general, may we / not
also pass upward, to the high syntheses of overlyings / and radi-
ances. . . ."[88] Even in these few passages, the essential structure of
Ammons's *Sphere* is disclosed: Coleridgean in its organicism and in
the exercise of a synthetic imagination, and Stevensian in its search
for the general pattern of thought.

A second example of "the poem of the act of the mind" is the long title poem of John Ashbery's collection *A Wave* (1984). Here the choice of the indefinite article should not be overlooked, for this is not the tsunami of significant events or as they say, of "catastrophic propor-tions," but one wave among many—ripples of thought. Again the opposition of form imposed and form as proceeding surfaces early in the poem:

> One idea is enough to organize a life and project it
> Into unusual but viable forms, but many ideas merely
> Lead one thither into a morass of their own good intentions.
> Think how many the average person has during the course of a day, or night,
> So that they become a luminous backdrop to ever-repeated
> Gestures, having no life of their own, but only echoing
> The suspicions of their possessor. . . .[89]

If one has a single, predetermined idea, it can be imposed to give form to a life or a poem—thus the sestina, the canzone, and the pantoum are "unusual but viable forms." But how does one cope with "a morass of good intentions," what Stevens encountered as "form gulping after formlessness," or Duncan as the longing "to express inchoate emotion as purely as possible"? The form of such a poem presents "the act of the mind" itself, but will it record only the *process* of thought or will it discover an *organic* pattern? I pose these questions because Ashbery sustains the indefinite quality introduced by the title; his skepticism of natural order and of language itself lingers, a trait perhaps more typical of postmodernism than the affirmations of Levertov, Duncan, or Ammons. Unlike Ammons—who declares a "potential form" of thought—Ashbery entertains the concept only as one more in the morass of ideas. Perhaps he tips his hand in the long title poem of a previous volume, "Self-Portrait in a Convex Mirror." Speaking of the forms in Parmigianino's portrait, he realizes their beauty "only at a point where they lapse / Like a wave breaking on a rock, giving up / Its shape in a gesture which expresses that shape."[90] It is impossible to fix these forms; their beauty is only apparent in their proceeding.

Though a practitioner of the "poem of the act of the mind," Ashbery seems rather more cautious about its organic quality or the prospects for the revelation of a suprahuman order. The analogy of the wave, like Coleridge's plant, is drawn from nature. But can the monotonous and transitory pattern be perceived? In "A Wave," these gestures may only be "echoing / The suspicions of their possessor." The indecision as to where the pattern lies or whether it even exists continues:

                                             Then the advantage of
Sinking in oneself, crashing through the skylight of one's own
Received opinions redirects the maze, setting up significant
Erections of its own at chosen corners, like gibbets,
And through this the mesmerizing plan of the landscape becomes,
At last, apparent. It is no more a landscape than a golf course is,
Though sensibly a few natural bonuses have been left in. . . .[91]

Are these patterns idiosyncratic, "one's own / Received opinions," the mind's own "significant / Erections"? Or can one claim to have discovered the "landscape" of the mind? With typical indecision, this landscape appears to be no more than a "golf course" with its manicured greens, manufactured sand traps, and water hazards. Ashbery never quite shuts the door, however, qualifying his qualifications; a few natural elements are observable—the compromise of a hillock or meadow. One can imagine Robert Trent Jones claiming that the best golf courses respect the lay of the land, but it remains that we tread up and down them in the pursuit of a game. It may well be that Ashbery's idolatry of indeterminacy constitutes for him the essential "act of the mind." In the central metaphor of the poem, language is "an ocean . . . that comes to be part of us" and "the mind / Is the beach on which the rocks pop up, just a neutral / Support for them in their indignity." We know that the slope of the beach creates the form of the wave. And this offers hope of "reality. Explained. And for seconds / We live in the same body, are a sibling again." Though we are offered no great synthesis of the mind and nature, we have—if only for the moment—its prospect.

The epic is the classic type and model for the long form in poetry. Its history, and the many examples both ancient and modern, can be adequately treated only at length; any attempt to define the epic form would require—has produced—a book in itself.[92] But in the limited space available it is necessary for me to distinguish the modern epic from other, postmodern versions of the long form, especially the series. The open, non-narrative models for the modern epic share some of the aesthetic concerns of the serial form. And yet a very clear structural difference between the epic and the series exists. The primary characteristic of the modern epic is its comprehensiveness. I do not mean—in a narrow sense of the word—a "comprehensive" treatment of a particular subject, since no epic limits itself to a single thematic concern, nor seeks the rather suspect satisfaction of having "exhausted" a given subject. (That job has fallen to the textbook.) But the concept of comprehensiveness, in the sense of a complete world view, a breadth of intellectual range, or mental capaciousness, stands foremost among the achievements of epic poetry, ancient or modern. The long poem (even when it does not assume the epic form) has pursued this quality. Lucretius's *De Rerum Natura*, on everything from atomism to Zeno, or Ovid's *Metamorphoses*, with its definitive re-creation of the Greek mythology, offer themselves as models, though neither presents an extended narrative with an heroic figure. Both works do, however, illustrate the requirement of comprehensiveness in later epic poems. Golding's translation of Ovid is a primary source for Pound's re-inspiring of classical mythology. The cosmogony in Book I of the *Metamorphoses* and Lucretius's treatment of science and philosophy can be said to anticipate James Merrill's *The Changing Light at Sandover* (1983) or Frederick Turner's *The New World* (1985), though Ovid seems to my taste a good deal more sensible and less extravagant. Central to the epic then (whether narrative or otherwise) is its capaciousness: its length is only justified by its breadth. Thus the form demands a complete portrait of the culture (not an excerpt), or a whole system of belief (not a single idea). The serial form by comparison is desultory, radically incomplete, and aleatory rather than systematic. As stated earlier, the epic goal is encompassment, summation; in contrast, the serial process is accumulation.

The modernist epic can be distinguished from postmodern long forms by its characteristic desire for "totality." Pound's *Cantos* demand—even if they do not achieve—a coherent synthesis. They posit an authoritarian hierarchy, so that Pound's claim for the sponsorship of Mussolini ("'Ma questo,' / said the Boss, 'è divertente'" [Canto XLI]), should not be surprising given Vergil's endorsement of the Augustan reign at the conclusion of Book VI of the *Aeneid*, or Ovid's reverential treatment of the deification of Caesar in the final book of the *Metamorphoses*. The modernist epic is characteristically concerned with "centering," bringing diverse materials into a synthesis. In postmodern long forms, a "dispersal" or separation is more characteristic, as is the case in serial form. The modernist epic feels compelled to assert complete control over its materials; the postmodern series enjoys its own abandonment to the materials of its presentation. In this sense, the series is more appropriate to an increasingly heterodox culture. Totality for the modernist is an attempt to realize a grand design upon the world; the postmodern series accedes to the condition of flux, revels in the provisional state of things. The epic, assertive in principle, gives way to the serial articulation of particulars. The series forsakes mythic permanence in the recognition of cultural transience.

*The Maximus Poems* of Charles Olson (composed between 1950 and the poet's death in 1970) can be considered both a late modern epic and a postmodern long poem. Displaying the recognizable features of both periods, it is an important transitional work. Olson's praise for, and objections to, the method of Pound's *Cantos* (as "ego-system") and of Williams's *Paterson* (as "emotional system") establish these two modernist works as "halves" of a job *The Maximus Poems* would encompass and complete.[93] Consequently, in its relation to its modernist precursors, the book retains (even as it revises) certain modernist assumptions about the long form. Its reliance on the superhuman persona of "Maximus," through whom the poet assumes a didactic authority, is a late modern, totalizing device. And, as Robert von Hallberg points out, in its use of the city of Gloucester (like *Paterson*) as focal point, "the local is a major structural device" of *The Maximus Poems*.[94] Olson's use of persona and locale attempts to provide the comprehensiveness, the coherence, and the closure to which both the *Cantos* and *Paterson* aspired.

If in this aspect *The Maximus Poems* is late modernist, its division into letters—rather than cantos or books—is a postmodern structural device. Von Hallberg argues: "Williams' lead [in the locale of Paterson] is an Ariadne thread through the wayward serial structure Olson took from the *Cantos*. Yet Olson's serial structure is far from Pound's, partly because letters just aren't cantos. Cantos lay claim to comparison with the *Divine Comedy*, especially in terms of overall structure; letters are less presumptuous."[95] While von Hallberg does not arrive at a stable definition of "serial structure" here, he makes an important distinction: cantos demand an absolute structure, whereas the discrete, distinct address of each letter is more closely related to seriality. One letter need not predicate the next, though a descent into hell requires an ascent into paradise. The postmodern essence of Olson's use of letters is reinforced by an actual letter to Cid Corman in 1952 in which, at one point declaring himself a "post-modern," he feels the need to distinguish between technique and form. Olson cites Pierre Boulez's definition of serial structure in music and concludes that "form must be carefully extricated" from technique, "just as carefully as Boulez is after form in serial *structure*."[96] Although persona and locale conspire to make *The Maximus Poems* a late modern epic, Olson's use of letters confirms that he sought a new form for the postmodern long poem in a serial structure.

### Procedural Form

Robert Duncan assesses the conventional wisdom regarding poetic form at mid-century—and the social milieu that sustained it—with as much wit as accuracy:

We are just emerging from a period that was long dominated by the idea of a poem as a discipline and a form into which the poet put ideas and feelings, confining them in a literary propriety, giving them the bounds of sound and sense, rime and reason, and the values of a literary—a social— sensibility. Poetry was to be brought to heel, obedient to the criteria of rational discourse, of social realities, of taste. For the New Criticism of the 1930's and 1940's, it was most important that the poet not put on airs. The dominant school of that time thought of form not as a mystery but as a manner of containing ideas and feelings; of content not as the meaning of form but as a commodity packaged in form. It was the grand age of Container Design; and critics became consumer researchers, wary of pretentious claims and seeking solid values. Ideas were thought of as products on the market.[97]

Duncan's partisan appraisal of New Critical formalism is deliberately couched in capitalist terms. He perceives a relationship between the approach to poetic form (aesthetics), a conservative social agenda (politics), and the advancement of consumerism (economics as methodology). Thus the "ideas or feelings" expressed in the poem are its primary commodity or value; such ideas should advance—or at least submit to—the community standards of rational and decorous behavior. The form assumes a secondary relationship as packaging, an attractive window dressing used to enhance sales. The market is the university and its affiliated publications. And the critic as market researcher advances the prospects of suitable goods and values to the detriment of nonconformist materials.[98] As a poet who often spurned commercial publication and promotion (he declared a fifteen-year hiatus after *Bending the Bow* in 1968), and who preferred his solitary work as an adept typist of manuscripts, Duncan means his analogy of New Critical formalism to merchandising as dire condemnation.

Duncan analyzes the methodology of New Critical formalism with similar acuity. The "idea"—or paraphrasable content—of the poem is thought to precede the making of the poem. The idea cannot be deemed appropriate unless the poet has "something to say," which presupposes a functional message—capable of indefinite resale in the classroom—of suitable relevance and discretion. This idea is then set within the container of the form in an effort to shape or "package" the product in accordance with "literary propriety." Traditional verse forms are designed to restrain or confine the idea in a seemly shape; they discourage the flamboyant or inchoate. For Duncan and so many like-minded poets at mid-century, such restraint was insufferable. Thus alienated by the literary industry and at odds with the social structure that endorsed it, the "New American" poets rejected poetic "closure" virtually in unison. They created a poetry of "unconscious, multiphasic accommodations" which welcomed irrational thought processes and polyvalent structures.[99] As the vanguard of an increasingly heterodox society, they rejected the overweening proclamations of the New Critics and the literary "product" they had marketed.

And yet a number of postmodern poets have introduced innovations in both the methodology and the intent of closed forms. The new method of proceduralism likewise rejects the concept of a form superimposed on preexistent content; instead, it proposes a system of arbitrary constraints which functions as a generative device. In this new conception of "formal verse," the poet decides on a set of restrictions or chooses an elaborate form prior to composition. Formal choices thus precede content, and the arbitrary constraints are relied on to generate, not contain, the material of the poem. The poet who proceeds according to a priori formal choices willfully commits himself to an arbitrary order, the results of which he may not have anticipated. Such rule-dominated composition relieves the poet of the burden of the self, since the "personality" of the artist is no longer called on to direct the creative process. At the same time, the necessarily idiosyncratic order set in place by the poet's formal choice rejects any ulterior, societal determination of an appropriate message or the form that should accommodate it. Arbitrary constraints, as Ashbery says, "have a paradoxically liberating effect," from both the inhibitions of the psyche and the restraints of societal mores.[100]

A procedural form sustains its own momentum by virtue of its formal rigor. Poets such as John Ashbery and Harry Mathews have sought out the more arcane and intricate predetermined forms precisely for the stricture they impart. But only certain predetermined forms have the generative capacities of a procedural form. The more traditional formalist has indeed claimed that the imposition of a rhyme scheme acts as a kind of "divining rod" with which one seeks the unexpected—but revealing—word. In such forms, however, the moderate constraint of rhyme or stanzaic structure compels the poet to modify his or her word selection, presumably in a fruitful manner; the same is true for modifications to the rational progress of the poet's thought or argument. But there is no assumption that the logical paraphrase or intended meaning of the poem is ever more than modified—however scintillating the results—by the imposition of such predetermined forms. On the other hand, the procedural form assumes as its first rule and intention that the formal choices that precede composition actually generate that process of composition. The formal intent is not to prepackage ideas or feelings for subsequent disposition; rather, the procedural form is radically exploratory.

Such forms are not auxiliary to content, but primary to the creative process.

The ability of procedural forms to sustain their own momentum derives from their relationship to the "paradigmatic consciousness." According to Roland Barthes, "the paradigmatic consciousness . . . is a formal imagination; it *sees* the signifier linked, as if in profile, to several virtual signifiers which it is at once close to and distinct from; it no longer sees the sign in its depth, it sees it in its perspective; thus the dynamics attached to this vision is that of a summons; the sign is chosen from a finite organized reservoir, and this summons is the sovereign act of signification."[101] The symbolic consciousness sees the sign in its "depth" and thus has a tendency to neglect form as a superficial concern in a work. But the paradigmatic consciousness sees the sign in its "profile" and thus pays particular attention to the formal relations of signs and to the regular constraints of a work; it is, after all, attention to the *system*. The comparison of signs "in profile" occurs in works that exhibit a high degree of recurrence. Barthes cites as examples Mondrian's squares, which "must have both certain affinities by their shape as squares, and certain dissimilarities by their proportion and color," and "the American automobiles (in Butor's *Mobile*)," which "must be constantly regarded in the same way, yet they must differ each time by both their make and color."[102] These are works "whose esthetic implies the interplay of certain commutations (Robbe-Grillet's novels, for example)."[103] In fiction or the visual arts, such commutations can occur on a decidedly grand scale, or as a relation among multiple works.[104] In poetry, the commutation of a single word may instigate the paradigmatic relation. For the poet in particular, "the formal (or paradigmatic) imagination implies an acute attention to the *variation* of several recurrent elements."[105] By its repeated evaluation of the affinity and dissimilarity of its elements, the procedural form generates a centripetal force that provides the momentum for its composition.

Earlier I relied on the ubiquity of the automobile in American life—surely no one item has more thoroughly transformed the national consciousness since the 1920s than the car—in order to describe a mundane instance of the series. I would now like to turn from the street to the showroom to illustrate the function of the paradigm in a procedural form. As a onetime owner of a 1968 Volkswagen Beetle, I was taken by a VW advertisement that provided a handsome photograph of each yearly model from the inception of the design (in the 1940s I think) until the (then) present model, touting a "Super" Beetle. Why was this advertisement so engrossing? The unsuspecting consumer has been caught up in a rather simple example of the paradigm. The ad elicits acute attention to the variation of several recurrent elements in this car's rather peculiar design. One studies the affinities and dissimilarities of successive models. Almost beside the point is VW's claim that the "Super" Beetle is of better manufacture than its predecessors—though its demise might indicate otherwise. Rather, this ingenious promotion so involves the prospective customer in the minute comparison of one model to the next that he entirely omits to consider how this odd little car compares to something outside its class, like the huge Cadillacs or Buicks that once dominated the American road. The centripetal force of the paradigm is adapted to the hard sell; by encouraging comparisons within a single make, the sales representative shuts out any thought of the competition. To say that a predetermined form generates its own momentum is to say that one is caught, forced to move in the direction that the form dictates.

Serial works are characterized by the discontinuity of their elements and the centrifugal force identified with an "open" aesthetic. Procedural works, on the other hand, are typified by the recurrence of elements and a centripetal force that promises a self-sustaining momentum. While virtually any pattern implies some sort of recurrence, the poetry I discuss in detail is notable for two very pronounced modes of recurrence, lexical and semantic. In forms such as the sestina, pantoum, or round, lexical recurrence prevails: the commutation of several words or phrases from one place in the poem to another is the principal structural motive. Each reappearance of a word or phrase summons a reevaluation of the sign and of the form itself. Traditional types of wordplay such as rhyme, metaphor, and symbol involve or imply the comparison of two distinct terms; we recall the separation of metaphor into its two constituent parts, a "tenor" and a "vehicle." But the verbal art of the paradigm turns on a comparison of the variations of a single term in each instance. The recurrence of a word or phrase immediately recalls its previous appearance and underscores any shift in meaning or context. The structure of the sestina is thus based on lexical recurrence and semantic variation. Its rigorously predetermined form generates a shifting and indeterminate meaning. Postmodern poets such as John Ashbery have renovated the sestina in order to fully exploit the generative capabilities—the compounding dynamics—of its lexical recurrence. The repetitions of its end-words propel the mind of the poet from one stanza to the next.

I also examine poems in which semantic recurrence prevails and demands a lexical variation. The texts by Harry Mathews and William Bronk make repeated reference to what they are about—as is typical of the paradigm—even as they employ a variety of terms with which to convey their "message." The significance of each stanza remains largely the same, though the words and phrases chosen to express that meaning change. Whereas the serial form relies mainly on contiguity, the procedural form exhibits a fondness for substitution.

Finally, there are procedural forms whose constraints have been formulated without literary precedent. They defy simple categorization because they are not merely occasional variants of familiar stanzaic patterns, but wholly inventive structures assembled by the poet. These forms employ a variety of extraliterary organizational methods: musical forms, mathematical formulae, combinatorics, and the *I Ching*, among others. For instance, Harry Mathews's *Trial Impressions* and John Cage's *Themes & Variations* are two book-length poems organized according to a structure of constant and variant. In this sense, they resemble other predetermined forms whose attention is given to the recurrence of one element or another. But the emphasis in these poems falls more heavily on elaborate constraints. Mathews draws on several restrictions devised by the Oulipo group in Paris to enliven his twenty-nine variations on an "ayre" by John Dowland. Similarly, Cage's volume engages in an intriguing interplay of arbitrary and "motivated" constraints. He composes "mesostics" on the names of fifteen composers and writers of personal importance to him, further complicated by the use of time constraints, Japanese renga (an interlocking stanzaic form), and chance operations. Such constraints compel the poet to say what he would not normally say. He avoids a recitation of conventional subjects in a comfortably familiar tone, urged by the form itself to explore new ideas and to compose in a new idiom.

Postmodern proceduralism can be distinguished from traditional formal verse by its attitude toward artifice. Although the New Critics praised "craft" in a poem, such technique was not to be flaunted but always to be given the appearance of natural ease. No matter how complicated the verse form, its arrival should seem a matter of gentlemanly grace. Procedural forms are by comparison more militant in their proclamation of artifice. All literary devices should be marked, or in the Russian Formalist phrase, "laid bare." When Mathews employs a constraint, its directives are boldly advertised. Cage even supplies a lengthy introduction to the formal parameters of his own work. No longer feigning the naiveté of the inspired romantic, these poems are obviously made, deliberately assembled.

Accordingly, the voice in these poems is programmatic—not false or misleading, but rather a recognized element in the poem as assemblage. The traditional lyric speaker who is firmly established and thought to preside over the business of the poems is evicted by a variety of recycled rhetoric, multiple voices to which no priority has been assigned. Without the endorsement of a dominant persona, the language of the poem can be said to speak for itself.

# SERIAL FORM

# The Infinite Serial Form

## The Unbound and the Uneven:
## Robert Duncan's *Passages*

What is an epigraph if not an invitation to enter the text, an offering that extols the qualities of things to come? The epigraph of Robert Duncan's *Passages* is certainly an invitation to a reading, but it is also an announcement of the poem's principle of form. The two "passages" selected from the Emperor Julian's *Hymn to the Mother of the Gods*, according to Duncan, "stand as inscriptions to the entry which Passages 1 is upon a series having no beginning and no end as its condition of form."[1] The second passage of the epigraph is a door opening on a long corridor:

> For the even is bounded, but the uneven is without bounds and there is no way through or out of it. (BB 9)

*Passages* is obedient to both the unbound and the uneven. The first informs us that the poem is an infinite series, without beginning or end; it speaks to the openness of the whole. The second, "uneven," speaks to the relation of the parts of the series, their method and movement. Together these two concepts in the pantheon of aesthetics comprise the formal principle of *Passages,* and it is important to consider them at some length.

"Without bounds," or so it is translated; Duncan takes his first principle of the poem's form ultimately from the pre-Socratic philosophers. For Anaximander the concept of *apeiron* involves the absence of both external boundaries which would bind or contain the whole, and internal boundaries which would group or compartmentalize in some rigid fashion. The first state of matter is infinite and explains its own movement—a condition to which the serial form of *Passages* aspires. For Heraclitus all things are in a constant state of flux. The river flows, and that which appears to be solid is changing. This same observation arises in Duncan's discussion of Whitmanic form: the New Critics "thought of form not as mystery but as a manner of containing ideas and feelings. . . . But Whitman's ideas flow as his work flows." His verse is a "pouring forth of thought, not a progression" (FC 179–80). Whitman is "most Heraclitean" insofar as he believes "in a Universe in the process of Its Self-realization" (FC 181). So *Passages* as an infinite series aspires to constant motion and the self-description of form.

The immediate corollary to a Heraclitean form without bounds is the assertion of an ongoing process without either the initial "given" of a procedural form or a teleological progression toward some end-point or climax. Duncan accepts the "incorporation of struggle as form, this Heraclitean or Lucretian or Darwinian universe as a creation creating itself. . . . Form had its principle of survival not in its derivation from an eternal paradigm but from its variability and plasticity in functioning in the changing totality" (M 49). Duncan's invocation of "the Creation as universal Process" calls to mind Charles Olson's romance with Alfred North Whitehead's *Process and Reality* (1929) and his exhortation in the essay "Projective Verse" (1950) to "USE USE USE the process."[2] Although Duncan was recruited to the faculty of Olson's Black Mountain College, he and Olson frequently challenged one another on intellectual and aesthetic grounds.[3] Duncan records his appearance at Olson's deathbed and finds there one last disagreement in their poetics: "He told me that he had completed *Maximus* which shocked me. Although I had already seen that *Maximus* was a poem which wasn't open. I mean, in my sense of open. Because Olson had never observed that open would mean that you wouldn't begin or end. He always remained a good Roman Catholic who does begin and end" (EF 56). Duncan endorses Olson's theory of projective verse while lamenting that the composition of Olson's *Maximus* does not fully realize the essence of an ongoing process. Duncan claims that *Passages* is constantly "moving between an initiation and a terminus I cannot name" (BB v); his creation of an infinite serial form seeks to transcend the simple dichotomy of open versus closed form.[4] In Olson's conception, even open forms are finite—they should begin and end.[5] But for Duncan the full extension of a poetics of process is the infinite form capable of encompassing portions that are open as well as closed and having neither an initial given nor an endpoint.

Duncan is dismayed by what he considers the last-minute and unnecessary efforts of Pound and Olson to bring their poems to "completion" or to some greater degree of "coherence." While a modernist epic such as *The Waste Land* is composed of fragments shored against the ruins of a once viable whole,[6] Duncan's *Passages* is an articulation of parts which is intentionally incomplete; it is neither the mending of a modern culture fractured by mortar fire nor the romantic failure of the poet to realize his aspirations. In an infinite series, the unbound is an assertion of the incomplete as its condition of form.

Umberto Eco in "The Poetics of the Open Work" describes a number of "works in movement" which "characteristically consist of unplanned or physically incomplete structural units."[7] These works "display an intrinsic mobility, a kaleidoscopic capacity to suggest themselves in constantly renewed aspects to the consumer." Eco cites as examples Henri Pousseur's *Scambi* (Exchanges), which the composer describes as a "field of possibilities,"[8] Alexander Calder's mobiles, and as the obligatory representative of literary production, Mallarmé's *Livre*. Declining to entertain the "metaphysical premises" of this last work, Eco prefers to concentrate on "the dynamic structure of this artistic object which deliberately set out to validate a specific poetic principle: 'Un livre ni commence ni ne finit; tout au plus fait-il semblant'" [A book neither begins nor ends; at most it pretends to]. Mallarmé's book, for which—appropriately enough—only provisional notes and proposals exist, was conceived as a "mobile apparatus" with even greater flexibility than *Coup de dés*, "where grammar, syntax, and typesetting introduced a plurality of elements, polymorphous in their indeterminate relation to each other." Citing Pousseur, Eco claims that such "works in movement" place the reader or performer "at the focal point of a network of limitless interrelations, among which he chooses to set up his own form without being influenced by an external *necessity* which definitively prescribes the organization of the work."[9] Mallarmé's *Livre* and Duncan's *Passages* (whose title connotes movement) share the properties of a work without bounds: having no beginning and no end; a limitless interrelation of parts; the absence of an externally imposed schema; mobility; and an intentionally incomplete condition of form.

In its publication history alone *Passages* provides several indications of its unbound condition. The poems are scattered through three volumes: 1–30 in *Bending the Bow* (1968), ten more in *Ground Work: Before the War* (1984), and the final twelve in *Ground Work II: In the*

Dark (1987); additionally, "Passages 22–27" have appeared separately as *Of the War* and "Passages 31–35" as *Tribunals*.[10] Always interspersed with other concurrent poems or excerpted into chapbooks, the *Passages* poems have never appeared sequentially in a single book. Duncan clearly intended that these poems remain, in a very literal sense, unbound. Given his declared war against the constraints of commercial publishing,[11] his decision to allow the poems to remain uncollected indicates the intentionally incomplete status of the series; for the reader, a sequential encounter with the entire series is discouraged. In addition, Duncan ceases to number the individual poems, beginning in *Ground Work*; in one such unnumbered section, he states that "the series does not signify / beyond the incident of a numeration" (GW 135). As one critic, Ian Reid, has said, they are "emancipated from ordinal placing."[12] Freed from any semblance of a right order in which to be read, the poems attain what Eco describes as an intrinsic mobility.

Duncan does not consider the unbound condition of *Passages* to be either the absence of form or an invitation to *kaos*; he frequently endorses the concept of *kosmos*, the universe as an ordered whole.[13] To understand his position, we must redraw the lines of an ancient philosophical skirmish. Among the pre-Socratic philosophers, Pythagoras exalts the idea of limit. Pythagoras is a moral dualist who believes that the "good" is that which is limited, in addition to unity, light, and the masculine; the "bad" is that which is unlimited, in addition to plurality, darkness, and the feminine. For Pythagoreans, the imposition of limit (*peras*) on the unlimited (*apeiron*) creates the inherent order of the universe (*kosmos*). Heraclitus rejects the Pythagorean ideal of a peaceful and harmonious world as an ideal of death; that which is permanent or stabile is stagnant. He argues instead that everything is born of conflict; form is not the harmony but the struggle of opposites. Duncan participates in this skirmish when he claims that he finds himself "emotionally incapable of entertaining the notion of a non-integral universe." Like Pythagoras, he claims, "I have a closed form at this point" (EF 62). So he refuses to make concessions to *kaos*: he exclaims against a disruptive or deconstructive tendency manifest in Allen Ginsberg's *Howl* or the "cut-ups" of William Burroughs and the aleatory aspects of John Cage's compositions; he asks, "Are we really going to dissolve all the boundaries?" (EF 66). And yet Duncan remains a committed Heraclitean. In the same interview he states: "In the early *Passages* there is a proposition that the universe has only the boundaries we imagine. Every step in science is the imagination of a new boundary and every boundary gives us a new figure of the universe. . . . This would suggest exactly what an open field or an open mind is. And it may actually be an intuition about the nature of the universe" (EF 61). Duncan's boundary is provisional and expansive, allowing the ongoing process to express its inherent order. He makes no concession to the random or chaotic, and yet he will not accept the imposition of limit as a moral necessity for the universe. He is committed to "a cosmos in which the poet and the poem are one in a moving process" (FC 81).

If the figures of Heraclitus and Charles Olson are prominent in Duncan's aesthetics, between them must stand Coleridge. It is impossible not to hear in the central conviction of Duncan's poetics an echo of *Biographia Literaria*: "The order man may contrive or impose upon the things about him or upon his own language is trivial beside the divine order or natural order he may discover in them" (FC 82–83).[14] This statement is of course a repetition in the postmodern mind of the romantic opposition of an order mechanically imposed and an inherent order discovered. Neither science nor poetics, however, has stood still since Coleridge wrote his literary autobiography; it is important to examine in what way Duncan's figure of the universe has compensated for their motion. As representative of Coleridge's view, M. H. Abrams provides the following encapsulation:

> Organic growth is an open-ended process, nurturing a sense of the promise of the incomplete, and the glory of the imperfect. Also, as a plant assimilates the most diverse materials of earth and air, so the synthetic power of imagination "reveals itself," in Coleridge's famous phrase, "in the balance or reconciliation of *opposite* or *discordant* qualities." And only in a "mechanical" unity are the parts sharply defined and fixed; in organic unity, what we find is a complex interrelation of living, indeterminate, and endlessly changing components.[15]

We must remember that Coleridge formulated his famous distinction on two separate occasions and that the two sets of terms are not exactly interchangeable; it seems to me that "form as superimposed" and "form as proceeding" are larger categories than "mechanic" and "organic" form—not every open form will exhibit an organic growth. There is ample evidence of the unbound in this passage—the poem as an "open-ended process" with a "promise of the incomplete." While *Passages* is certainly a manifestation of the unbound (i.e., an example of "form as proceeding"), it does not adhere to the analogy of "organic growth." Unlike the plant, *Passages* does not attempt to "synthesize" or "reconcile" opposite or discordant qualities. Duncan claims that he wishes to maintain "the juncture in the music that appears discordant" (BB ix–x).[16] He cites an aphorism of Heraclitus, "They do not apprehend how being at variance it agrees with itself" (BB iv), which seems to challenge Coleridge's synthetic imagination. Although *Passages* is indeed open-ended and incomplete, it seeks rather to *maintain* the disequilibrium of opposites than to *balance* them. This desire is an expression of the Heraclitean "form as struggle," the essential uneven condition of the poem.

In a letter to Charles Olson (6 February 1960) reprinted in *Maps 6*, Duncan recounts a passage in Whitehead's *Process and Reality* which "speaks of our particular kosmos as atomic" (M 62). He recognizes in this statement a "repeat in history," since it was Democritus among the pre-Socratic philosophers who first offered an atomic theory of the universe; his views were revived by Lucretius in *De Rerum Natura* but remained unchanged in essentials until the advent of modern physics in the nineteenth century. Duncan then observes that the order of his poems must participate in such an atomic universe and so arises from "a kosmos as order or harmony, that includes a void, and *cannot possibly be a wholeness*, but is a mathematical incomplete (our own versions of harmony, our own scales, are always incomplete and what had been dis-cord is being added)" (M 62; the emphasis is Duncan's). Once again we note the expression of a poetic form which is unbound; atomism posits the existence of a void in which the particles are constantly moving, and so demands the incomplete as a condition of form. But the atomic kosmos also welcomes the uneven; it demands the inclusion, not the resolution of discord. Only in the Pythagorean concept of musical harmony as mathematical limit and just proportion can one exclude certain tones as discordant. So Duncan cites Heraclitus in defense of atonal music and a concept of poetic order: "Couples are wholes and not wholes, what agrees disagrees, the concordant is discordant" (M 63). The Heraclitean paradox is not meant to be resolved but sustained; his concept of "struggle as form" depends on disequilibrium, the uneven. This is the second principle of the form of *Passages*.

The atomism of the ancient Greeks reemerges in modern particle physics, and Heraclitus finds his reincarnation in the German biophysicist Erwin Schrödinger. In his essay "Towards an Open Universe," Duncan exclaims, "What gnosis of the ancients transcends in mystery the notion Schrödinger brings us of an aperiodic structure in *What is Life?*" (FC 78). Schrödinger, as cited by Duncan, claims that in an organic molecule "every atom, and every group of atoms, plays an individual role, not entirely equivalent to that of others." All living matter, Schrödinger declares, "evades the decay to equilibrium." Duncan seizes on this passage because it reaffirms the Heraclitean emphasis on discord in the nature of things: a world of concord and equilibrium is stagnant; all things are born of discord and disequilibrium. So the atoms of an organic molecule resist the equivalence of structure or function which would bring them to the stasis of equilibrium; each atom plays its individual role and yet, in its struggle to fulfill its semiautonomous function, it maintains the form of the molecule. Duncan finds an image of the uneven in the biophysicist's description of "an intricately articulated structure, a form that maintains a disequilibrium" (FC 78). He subsumes the dichotomy of closed and open form into the larger categories of *periodic* and *aperiodic* structure, suggested by his reading of both Heraclitus and Schrödinger. So "rhyming lines and repeating meters . . . evoke our powerful longing to fall back into periodic structure, into the inertia of uncomplicated matter" (FC 77). The formal repetitions of the sonnet or sestina are like the lattice structure of an inorganic crystal.[17] But the uneven condition of *Passages* is aperiodic. Each poem is complete in itself, an event enacted; but in the context of the series, each is but a part of the ongoing process, and thus incomplete. A Heraclitean condition is reaffirmed by the experiments of a contemporary scientist: the disequilibrium of the parts maintains the vital form of the whole.

For Duncan, Schrödinger's notion of an organic molecule as an aperiodic structure implies that "life is by its nature orderly and that the poem might follow the primary processes of thought and feeling, the immediate impulse of psychic life" (FC 78). In the Pythagorean universe, order is achieved solely by the imposition of limit. But Schrödinger confirms a Heraclitean world in which an order inherent in the life processes themselves can be realized. Heraclitus declares that the universality of change is an ongoing process[18] that nevertheless expresses the "measure" (*metron*) inhering in change, the stability that persists through it and ensures that change does not produce a random or chaotic plurality.[19] The river flows, but it does not wildly overrun its banks.

Duncan finds an appropriate model for the form of *Passages* in an organic molecule, which, in Schrödinger's phrase, "goes on 'doing something,' moving, exchanging material with its environment" (FC 78). Duncan extends the theory of organicism to his *Passages*, but a new physics has taken over from the old physiology. Coleridge's elected analogue, the plant, cannot anticipate the structure of Duncan's infinite series. The analogy of a plant suggests a continuous, linear development—organic growth: from the seed the roots and stem sprout; the flower bud cannot appear before the leaves which photosynthesize, and so on. Schrödinger's "field" of view is not agricultural but atomic: in organic molecules, the semiautonomous atoms are in constant motion, changing places as easily as they exchange functions. Duncan's analogy, following Olson, is drawn from particle physics; he insists on "a form as a field of things in action instead of the development of a path" (BH 4). His serial form not only disputes the necessity of *telos*, completion, but it also challenges the validity of direct consequence—any situation in which *A* must follow *B*.[20] Although the organic growth of a plant may, according to M. H. Abrams, account for a structure that is ongoing and incomplete (the unbound), it cannot account for the absence of a linear development (the uneven). Duncan's atomic *kosmos*, however, consists of particles that are both *discontinuous* and *ahierarchical*. Unlike the leaves of a plant, molecules move freely in the void that separates them from other molecules. Unlike the flower, which serves as the culmination of an organic cycle, no one molecule in the flux can claim a predominant position. So Duncan endorses (M 59) Olson's claim in Letter 6 of the *Maximus Poems* that "there are no hierarchies."[21] No one poem in the series explains, orients, or proves climactic for the others. Coleridge's plant reconciles the discordant qualities of earth and air (a metaphor for the synthesis of the romantic imagination), but Schrödinger's organic molecules maintain a disequilibrium. Or as Heraclitus put it, "Fire lives the death of air, and air of fire; water lives the death of earth, earth that of water."[22]

In the introduction to *Bending the Bow*, Duncan compactly expresses the compositional method of *Passages* under the heading "Articulations":

> The artist, after Dante's poetics, works with all parts of the poem as *polysemous*, taking each thing of the composition as generative of meaning, a response to and a contribution to the building of form. The old doctrine of correspondences is enlarged and furthered in a new process of responses, parts belonging to the architecture not only by the fittings— the concords and contrasts in chronological sequence, as in a jigsaw puzzle—by what comes one after another as we read, but by the resonances in the time of the whole in the reader's mind, each part as it is conceived as a member of every other part, having, as in a mobile, an interchange of roles, by the creation of forms within forms as we remember. (BB ix)

The form described here embraces plurality; inasmuch as Duncan considers himself to be "multiphasic" (EF 66), so every part of the poem is *polysemous* in its contribution to the building of form. This claim is "derivative" (as Duncan wryly labels himself) in one respect, and innovative in another. It recalls Pound's imagist credo, "To use absolutely no word that does not contribute to the presentation,"[23] and Williams's claim that in a poem "there can be no part, as in any other machine, that is redundant."[24] But Duncan goes beyond modernist economy to declare that each part of the poem is a *sign* with several functions. The "correspondences" or "concords" of a periodic form, the sweet harmonies of meter, rhyme, and simile, are enlarged to include the discord, the multiple significations of an aperiodic form.

Duncan admits somewhat casually in an interview, "I myself have taken a whole bunch of things from Barthes" (EF 63), so it is not surprising to find a reformulation of his polysemic compositional method in his essay "Kopóltuš: Notes on Roland Barthes, *Elements of Semiology*": "The concept of significant form in aesthetics is the feeling of parts belonging to a whole as a *sign*. We see in every part signs of the formlessness of the whole; the formlessness of the work then is a significant form. How else did we know it?" (FC 106). The "old doctrine" of two-term correspondences enforced a periodic form as if by law, largely by its insistence on a patent and comprehensive *unity* (patent meaning "available to inspection," as opposed to the Heraclitean opinion cited by Duncan that "the invisible attunement is better than the visible" [M 63]). The polysemous parts of *Passages* produce an aperiodic form, each part able to signify and interrelate a plurality of concerns. The old doctrine cannot accept the formlessness of the whole (i.e., the lack of a patent unity), while in Duncan's "new process," if *every* part signifies that formlessness then the whole is itself a single sign, a significant form.

Duncan describes two different "responses" in "Articulations." The first involves the fitting of parts "one after another as we read." A semiologist would identify this response as the syntagmatic relation; it occurs on the *combinatory* axis of language, establishing chains, networks, "jigsaws" of meaning. This relation is of particular importance to serial form because the syntagm—the "lateral" drive of language to move, move on—is primarily responsible for the ongoing process of the form; it is the linguistic response to a world in flux. At the same time, each part resonates "in the time of the whole in the reader's mind." Acknowledging the reduced role of such correspondences as meter, rhyme, and metaphor in an aperiodic structure, Duncan stresses the importance of the metonymic function: each part or section of the series implies a whole that is its context as well as a whole that is the full extent of the series—the whole itself as a *sign*. As a second response, then, Duncan claims that each part is "conceived as a member of every other part" (BB ix), or as he says elsewhere, "my concept of form is the co-inherence of all parts and . . . every single particle of that poem is different from or the same as every other part" (BH 24). A semiologist would describe this response as the paradigmatic relation, apprehending the resemblance of whole classes of dissimilar but related signs. In an aperiodic serial form, the interrelation of all parts, the ability to *substitute*, is important if one is to posit an ahierarchical structure.

At the close of this section of "Articulations," Duncan offers another analogue for the structure of *Passages*: the mobile is also an aperiodic form that maintains a disequilibrium. Like the atoms of an organic molecule constantly exchanging material with its environment, the parts of a mobile have "an interchange of roles." Such criteria as sequence or developmental path, hierarchy, or organic unity at the botanical level yield to an intrinsic mobility, discontinuity, and the interchange of parts as formal characteristics. Roland Barthes, in a comment appropriate to the form of *Passages*, claims that it is the syntagmatic imagination (the driving force behind all serial compositions) which nourishes "all those works whose fabrication, by arrangement of discontinuous and mobile elements, constitutes the spectacle itself." Duncan abandons the notion of a static, fixed form for what Barthes describes as "an arrangement of mobile, substitutive parts, whose combination produces meaning, or more generally a new object."[25] Thus Duncan can suggest that *Passages*, by virtue of its mobility, is capable of "the creation of forms within forms as we remember," each combination producing a new object.

Similarly, we find in Umberto Eco's description of a "work in movement" that Calder's mobiles are "elementary structures which possess the quality of moving in the air and assuming different spatial dispositions. They continuously create their own space and dimensions to fill it with."[26] Duncan, Barthes, and Eco seek to define a "plural form" whose mobility grants the status of the "many in one." The fascination with this possibility lies in the number of forms one can create for which all parts are indispensable. If we closely examine the mobile, we find that the finest of wires connect all the parts; so Duncan claims, regarding *Passages*, that "in the true form of the poem all its parts co-operate, co-exist" (M 53). While the whole turns in a state of disequilibrium, all parts are intrinsically necessary to the maintenance of the form; if a wire were to snap and one of the parts fall off, the object would collapse.

An important conjunction exists between Roland Barthes's proposal in *S/Z* of a "plural text" and Robert Duncan's composition of *Passages*.[27] Barthes proposes that texts can be regarded as either "readerly" (*lisible*) or "writerly" (*scriptible*).[28] The readerly text is a "classic" text, one that offers itself as a finished product to be consumed by a canonically informed reader. The classic text is always a "beautiful artifact," adhering to Duncan's criteria of periodic form—fixed and tightly bound by its conventions; there is only one way through or out of it. The writerly text, however, is one that encourages the reader to become a "producer of the text" and by an active role in its composition, to gain "access to the magic of the signifier, the pleasure of writing." A writerly text offers its producer "the plurality of entrances, the opening of networks, the infinity of languages."[29] While Barthes's argument is couched in the language of an "ideal case," we can find very similar descriptions of a plural form both in Eco's comments on the "work in movement" and in Duncan's comments on *Passages*. First, Eco:

> The *possibilities* which the work's openness makes available always work within a given *field of relations*. As in the Einsteinian universe, in the "work in movement" we may well deny that there is a single prescribed point of view. But this does not mean complete chaos in its internal relations. What it does imply is an organizing rule which governs these relations. . . . The *work in movement* is the possibility of numerous different personal interventions, but it is not an amorphous invitation to indiscriminate participation.[30]

In accordance with Duncan's Heraclitean belief, the plural text, like the atomic cosmos, is not an invitation to chaos, even if the author or the earth is displaced from its center. Although as Eco claims, the work "always remains the world intended by the author," an "open" work is "characterized by the invitation to *make the work* together with the author."[31] On behalf of *Passages*, Duncan confirms the "plurality of entrances" suggested by Barthes: "For those who at last see the cloth there is no first strand or second strand; the design does not begin in a certain place but where the admirer's eye chooses to begin in seeing" (M 53). This collaboration of author and reader in the plural text echoes a declaration by Walt Whitman, as cited by Duncan: "The reader will always have his or her part to do, just as much as I have mine" (FC 202).

The writerly text is a structuralist's conception of an open, aperiodic form—a text with a plurality of entrances and no way through or out of it. If, as Barthes proposes, the text is "moderately plural," it succeeds in being (as Duncan claims for *Passages*) "polysemous." But

Duncan's criteria for the structure of *Passages* very nearly match Barthes's description of an *ideal* plural text:

> In this ideal text, the networks are many and interact, without any one of them being able to surpass the rest; this text is a galaxy of signifiers, not a structure of signifieds; it has no beginning; it is reversible; we gain access to it by several entrances, none of which can be authoritatively declared to be the main one; the codes it mobilizes extend *as far as the eye can reach*, they are indeterminable (meaning here is never subject to a principle of determination, unless by throwing dice); the systems of meaning can take over this absolutely plural text, but their number is never closed, based as it is on the infinity of language.[32]

Barthes's description of the writerly text provides a thorough elucidation of the formal theory of *Passages* as an infinite series. To sum up their conjunction: all parts of the series are interrelated or interact; no hierarchy among parts exists; each part is a signifier of the whole; because the text neither begins nor ends, one can enter it at any point; and the meaning of the text is indeterminate, neither limited nor centered, since its language is coextensive with the cosmos.

To extract a linear reading from *Passages* would be to pull a single thread out of a tapestry's weave; tugging at one strand, we ruin the design of the fabric. To search for a "first strand" and unravel it to some endpoint would be to invalidate the principle of the form which Duncan proposes: "As we comprehend the form, all its parts are present in one fabric" (M 53). We can begin in this plural text wherever "the admirer's eye chooses to begin in seeing" the design. Duncan's metaphor of the text as fabric, which describes both his compositional method and the role of the reader, nevertheless draws me to an "early" entrance to the poem, "Passages 2," "At the Loom." In his introduction to *Scales of the Marvelous*, Robert Bertholf claims that Duncan, as a self-declared "derivative" poet, "projects both the romantic tradition of the theology of poetry and the Poundian disciplines of the intense search for poetic forms."[33] Before becoming enmeshed in the poem's weave, we note that the "first" poems of *Passages* set forth these two traditions: "Passages 1," "Tribal Memories," with its invocation to Mnemosyne[34] and meditation on an orphic cosmogony (a pre-Socratic concept of a primal "World Egg"[35]), represents the entrance of the romantic poet-priest; "Passages 2" begins with an allusion to Pound at Rapallo, the poet as maker of forms. Because this admirer's eye is drawn not to Duncan's theology but to his formal inventiveness, I turn to the latter entrance for what it tells of the poem's making rather than its incantation.

The first stanza of "At the Loom" describes Ezra Pound weaving his poem of gists and fragments, feeding the stray cats of Rapallo[36] his table scraps:

A cat's purr
in the hwirr thkk     *"thgk, thkk"*
of Kirke's loom on Pound's Cantos
*"I heard a song of that kind . . ."*

(BB 11)

As an infinite series, *Passages* is at once derivative of the Poundian epic and corrective: it is woven at the loom of many materials and so offers no single narrative "line" to tug at; and yet (the emphasis should be positive here) it is less "ambitious" than Pound's compulsive desire for bounds, his initial limit of one hundred cantos and his final efforts to make it "cohere" (see BB iv). After this tribute to "the greater craftsman," Duncan employs the loom as an analogy for the compositional method of *Passages* and for the structure of language itself:

my mind a shuttle among
          set strings of the music
lets a weft of dream grow in the day time,
          an increment of associations,
     luminous soft threads,
the thrown glamour, crossing and recrossing,
          the twisted sinews underlying the work.

Back of the images, the few cords that bind
     meaning in the word-flow,
               the rivering web
          rises among wits and senses
gathering the wool into its full cloth.

(BB 11)

The horizontal strands of the woof are analogous to what Saussure terms *parole* (individual utterances). The mind of the poet is a shuttle carrying the woof, crossing and recrossing; each utterance, or line, in the poem occurs on the horizontal axis of syntagm. This syntagmatic mode of language, "what comes one after another as we read" (BB ix), is predominant in a Poundian poetics of "an increment of associations." Duncan translates this function of language into Heraclitean terms as "the word-flow, / the rivering web." Extensive and centrifugal in force, the syntagm drives the serial poem onward.

The vertical "set strings" of the warp are analogous to what Saussure terms *langue* (the abstract system of language). The system, or para-

digmatic mode of language, is characterized by similarity and substitution rather than combination; so Duncan describes the warp as
"the few cords" (with a pun on "chords") "that bind the meaning" into
the poem. The paradigmatic mode is the intensive, centripetal force of
language which, although it does not determine the form of the series,
enables Duncan to claim that each part of *Passages* is "conceived as a
member of every other part." With a shuttle and set strings, Duncan
demonstrates in images an essentially Saussurian concept of how
language composes itself. But one might add that Duncan's citation
from the *O. E. D.* of the etymologies of warp and shuttle (BB 12)
indicates a diachronic approach to the language unlike Saussure's.
Duncan accepts etymology—like Darwinian evolution—as evidence
of constancy within change (the shuttle was *skutill*, an arrow or bolt;
even as the lexical entry and the object referred to change, the concept
of "that which moves horizontally" remains the same). Etymology
offers Duncan some proof that an inherent linguistic structure indicates an order inherent in the cosmos as well. On this point, Duncan's
orphic connection of language system and world order is more amena-
ble to Heidegger (who shares his interest in Heraclitus) than to Saussure.

"Passages 9," "The Architecture," is woven onto and through a
selection from Gustave Stickley's *Craftsman Homes* (1909), a treatise
on home design, the source supplied by Duncan's own notes to *Bending the Bow*. The passage both begins and ends with Stickley, and the
architect's advice provides the warp, the set strings on which the poet's
mind as shuttle plays. Duncan's own craft is on display in this tight
weave, an "embroidery" (BB 27), since the syntax of the quoted passage
is several times held in suspense—on significant phrases—to be resumed after the poet's commentary without the drop of a stitch.
House and garden, the poet's domesticity, is the setting of "The Architecture," reinforced by the analogue of weaving as compositional
method, Kirke at her loom.

But *Craftsman Homes* is chosen for more than its applicability to
the setting of the poem. The house itself becomes yet another analogue for the structure of *Passages*, and the specific virtues of the
model described by Stickley have a bearing on the poem's composition. "The Architecture" begins with Stickley's claim that a room
"must have recesses." By no means do we want to enter the front door,
the main entrance, and possess an unobstructed sightline down a
corridor, through the living room to the kitchen, and out the back
door. In short, we do not want a house or a poem whose structure and
endpoint are apparent at a glance; the sonnet from this vantage appears
boxlike and boring. Duncan's serial poem and Stickley's ideal home

abandon the regular measurements of a fixed form or a six-by-eight-foot rectangular room and encourage instead the discovery of form in the process of making our way through. From this gradual discovery, Stickley claims, a "feeling of mystery [. . .] arises when you cannot see the whole room from any one place . . when there is always something around the corner" (BB 26).

A similar feeling of mystery arises in *Passages* because we cannot "see" the whole series (incomplete now and always) from any one poem; each is a corridor like that of a house that is easily entered but from which there appears to be no way out.[37] The poet's own home at Stinson Beach with its "window-shelter" and "recesst" set of bookcases (BB 26) and its "garden's recesses" (BB 27) seems proudly to conform to Stickley's recommendation. But if a touch of mystery is a desirable attribute, we do not wish to be altogether lost in the structure: the architect stresses that such links as "French doors opening out upon a porch" or a staircase between the "social" part of the house and the "upper regions" of the private individual should be prominent features. Duncan is likewise very attentive to the "fittings" and contextual links of his materials, however diverse in source.

Curled up in the satisfying warmth of his domesticity, the poet offers his account of "a little night music" on the phonograph and an array of titles glimmering from the bookcases: Hesiod, Heraclitus, the Egyptian Gnostics, a Hermetic tract and theosophical essays. Duncan intends these "secret books" to impart something of the universal mystery that the poem ought to suggest; they function in his series like the many recesses of Stickley's ideal house. But these titles also function as links or, as he says, "keys." The poet's reading list connects several of the issues we have been discussing, and a passage from the introduction clicks into place:

> Hermes, god of poets and thieves, lock-picker then, invented the bow and lyre to confound Apollo, god of poetry. *"They do not apprehend how being at variance it agrees with itself,"* Heraclitus observes: *"there is a connexion working in both directions."*
>
> The part in its fitting does not lock but unlocks; what was closed is opend [sic]. Once, in the scale of Mozart, a tone on the piano keyboard could be dissonant; then, in Schönberg's scale, the configuration uses all the keys, only the tone row is set. . . . The poet of the event senses [that] the play of its moralities belongs to the configuration he cannot see but feels in terms of fittings that fix and fittings that release the design out of itself. (BB iv)

Hermes the lock-picker confounds the Apollonian order that binds poetry with a tight formal control; his skeleton key fits the door of every house and unbinds every poet's work. The fittings of a poem can be concordant and fix the design in the poem, or as Heraclitus reminds us, they can be discordant and release the poem's design. Likewise, Mozart's harmonies in "Eine kleine Nachtmusik" (referred to in line 10 of "The Architecture") are based on a tonal scale which excludes certain keys as dissonant; his fittings are Apollonian and so permit only the concordant.[38] But Schönberg's twelve-tone serial compositions include all the keys; there can be no dissonance in his open scale because all "conflicts are transformd in their being taken as contrasts" (BB iv). Like the warp of the loom, the tone row is set; but this fact enables the composer or poet to run infinite combinations across its strings. Schönberg's serial music provides a model for Duncan's open series, and it is not surprising to see that one of Schönberg's students makes a cameo appearance in "Passages 17": "John Cage's open scales" (BB 62). The syntagmatic fittings of serial composition are meant to be all-inclusive, or as Duncan says in one interview, "immensely conservative of everything" (BH 5). There are no discordances that cannot be subsumed in an infinite form—by Schönberg's row, Barthes's syntagm, or Kirke's loom.

A home with many recesses, corridors, and adjacent rooms provides Duncan with an analogue for serial composition, but the concept also occurs in Jack Spicer's description of serial form in his "Vancouver Lectures." The use of this analogue has its common origin in a Berkeley boardinghouse in the early spring of 1947, in which Duncan, Spicer, and several other poets gathered on ten successive nights for a séance of sorts and the composition of what was to be Duncan's *Medieval Scenes*. In his preface to a revised edition of the poem issued in 1978, Duncan claims: "For Spicer *Medieval Scenes* was the initial spectacle of the dictated poem and of the serial poem—by which he meant nothing as recondite as serial composition in music might lead one to believe, but the episodic appearance of a movie serial."[39] The slightly arch tone in Duncan's comment is an indication of the competitiveness that these two "poet-kings" of the budding San Francisco Renaissance had begun to feel toward one another, and Duncan suggests that Spicer has taken a distinctly lowbrow approach to the series. Although Duncan's study with the medieval historian Ernst Kantorowicz at the University of California at Berkeley later in 1947 provides some measure of his interest, the poem suffers from the *table parlant* rhetoric and rampant unicorn imagery for which W. C. Williams frequently scolded Duncan but in which he persisted (EF 60).

Nevertheless, the distinction Duncan makes in his preface of 1978 (ten years after the inception of *Passages*) is important. In the old movie serials or in today's soap opera, an irresolution of dramatic action can be expected in the last scene of each episode; this suspension of the plot, also known as a cliff-hanger, is only effective because of the development of various themes—treachery, adultery, the reunion of long-lost siblings. The soaps are constructed in this episodic or sequential fashion to insure the networks daily viewers; a missed episode requires a trip to the local supermarket for a soap digest. In Duncan's more recondite approach to serial composition, however, each passage is autonomous rather than episodic. In a letter dated 15 June 1957, Duncan discusses "Crosses of Harmony and Disharmony" (OF 44) with Robin Blaser: "In form I wanted to let go as far as I could bring myself of any thematic development . . . and to stress a serial composition. We got the complete Webern. In which have been revelling—and what an impeccable ear he has for possible inner structures in a passage of a poem being set."[40] Duncan abandons the linear development of the thematic sequence—a rather obvious and low-brow method of retaining an audience's attention—in favor of the more recondite serial form, which is in this case represented by the music of Webern, yet another student of Schönberg. Reminiscent of the Heraclitean claim that "the invisible attunement is better than the visible," serial composition allows for the exploration of the possible inner structures of a passage. Joined by Spicer, Robin Blaser, and Michael McClure, Duncan began to examine serial composition as a possible alternative to composition by field in San Francisco in the late 1950s.

Duncan's recognition that the autonomy of the individual sections of a serial composition distinguishes it from an episodic sequence prompts his claim that "there's nothing open about an individual 'Passage.' . . . All of them have closure."[41] The closure of the individual poems is chiefly an assertion of molecular independence, not an insistence on thematic resolution. No section is reliant on or consequent to any other, and thus a linear-sequential reading of *Passages* is not permissible; each poem is independent of its predecessor, and so cannot be episodic. Nevertheless, Duncan strives to articulate in his own series what he hears in the music of Webern as the "possible inner structures" of the passage. Although autonomous, each section continues to be conceived as a member of every other section, contextually interrelated.

"Passages 10," "These Past Years," readily demonstrates that it retains its own autonomy and yet is interrelated with other sections of the series. If "The Architecture" is a hymn to the household gods, "These Past Years" is a celebration of the poet's most important relationship:

Willingly I'll say there's been a sweet marriage
         all the time          a ring
    (if wishing could make it so)   a meeting
         in mind      round      the moon
    means rain.

(BB 29)

The composition of these five lines is not syntactic but paratactic (the placing of related clauses side by side), which demonstrates at the sentence level something of the molecular autonomy attributed to the individual sections of the series. We can separate the two clauses that intermingle and float freely in the text ("all the time a meeting in mind" and "a ring round the moon means rain"), but Duncan's compositional method is intended to emphasize the interrelatedness of his impressions. The parenthetical phrase, "if wishing could make it so," performs this task nicely; it at once recalls "wishing on the moon" and reinforces the hint of uncertainty or longing in his earlier use of the future subjunctive, "Willingly I'll say." The paratactic construction of these lines is a function of the ahierarchical quality of the sections themselves;[42] the poet strives for "overlapping structures, so that words are freed, having bounds out of bound" (BB ix). The interrelations among the elements of this poem occur as "correspondences" along a single plane of discourse: a ring and the moon correspond as circles; a meeting (as the lines that trace a circle meet) corresponds to marriage (the union of two halves of a circle); and the ring as both "round" and "around" the moon corresponds to the concentric circles of a marriage in "sweet" harmony. Precisely because each part of this poem is floating free of syntactic bonds it can recognize itself "as a member of every other part, having, as in a mobile, an interchange of roles" (BB ix).

As further evidence of the "inner structure" of the series, the elements of this poem also correspond to those in other parts of *Passages*. The moon does not become a fixed symbol with limited relations but as a sign enters a limitless network of associations. "Passages 5," "The Moon," a homage to Oberon and Titania, also presents the concentric circles of a marriage:

so pleasing              a light
     round,          haloed,          partially
disclosed,          a ring,
     night's wedding signet   •

(BB 17)

"Passages 6," "The Collage," unites the erotic with the poetic:

> the moon taking over tides of the mind,
>
> pulling back
> > whatever cover love had
>
> until the reefs upon which we lie are exposed,
>
> > the green water going out over
>
> > > the rock ledges,
>
> body upon body
>
> > turning keys as the tide turns
>
> > > > > (BB 21)

The moon moves bodies of water, it moves the bodies of the lovers in their nocturnal embraces, and it moves "the body of the poem, aroused" (BB 19). The ocean at Stinson Beach, the companion of the poet, and the poet's self-reflexive act of composition are not bound to the moon as symbol but unbound in a series of interrelationships compassing several poems of *Passages*.[43]

"These Past Years" achieves its own form of closure with a reprise of the initial line:

> > > Willingly I'll say there's been a sweet
>
> > marriage
>
> > > and I would fill your arms
>
> > as if with flowers      with my forever
>
> > > being there  •
>
> > > > "French doors
>
> > opening out upon a porch which
> > links the house with the garden."
>
> > > > > (BB 30)

As in the rondeau, the recurrence of the first line with a certain gain in emotional emphasis (in this case, an added measure of confidence in the relationship) indicates the closure that Duncan claims for the individual sections of the series. The poet also recalls from "Passages 9" the garden of Stickley's *Craftsman Homes*, now in the somewhat different context of a love-gift, as the source of "sweet flowers." Especially in evidence in "These Past Years" is Duncan's lyric gift, and the motive for closure is very much that of the traditional love lyric. Even so, we have observed that in the entire series "each part is a thing in itself; the junctures not binding but freeing the elements of configuration so that they participate in more than one figure" (BB ix). The moon and the garden participate in multiple poems and figures, their contexts and significance constantly shifting.

In "Passages 18," "The Torso," Duncan revives the erotic genre of the *blason*. As Michael Riffaterre notes, the "grammar" or basic rule of this genre is that "every part of the feminine form must be celebrated. One required motif, and the most frequent, is praise for the lady's snowy breasts."[44] But Duncan as a homosexual insists on his own variation of the tradition; although "The Torso" follows every other rule of the genre, the essential twist is that the body is that of a male. When the poet arrives at that familiar resting place in the genre's progress, the breast, he offers in place of such traditional metaphors of nourishment as "little green apples" or "milk-white lawns" a description of the man's more massive pectorals, the nipples of which are useless except for their erotic possibilities:

> At the rise of the pectoral muscles
>
> *the nipples*, for the breasts are like sleeping fountains
>     of feeling in man, waiting above the beat of his heart,
>     shielding the rise and fall of his breath, to be
>     awakend
>
> (BB 63)

Poetic closure can be achieved through the completion of a fixed stanzaic form, or in the case of the *blason*'s descending survey of the beloved's attributes, through the fulfillment of the set rules of the genre. Certainly the poem stands on its own as a celebration of Eros. But "Passages 18" extends beyond the bounds of the traditional genre and in so doing asserts its position in the serial poem. After the somewhat more dramatic climax of this *blason*, an "other" speaks as in a dream to the poet:

> wherever you are
>     my hand in your hand    seeking    the locks, the keys
> I am there.   Gathering me, you gather
>
>     your Self •
>
> For my Other is not a woman but a man
>
> *the King upon whose bosom let me lie.*
>
> (BB 64–65)

We hear in the echo of Whitman's *Song of Myself* the click of the key that unlocks, unbinds "Passages 18." The homoerotic subversion of the genre liberates the poet in the expression of his sexuality, opening that which was previously closed to him.

"Passages 15," "Spelling," begins with a testament to the open, incomplete structure of the series:

> He did not come to the end of the corridor.
>
> He could not see to the end of the corridor.
>
> What came beyond he did not know.
>
> (BB 48)

The headnote to the poem promises a lecture in etymology as poetic genre, "an earnest mimesis of a classroom exposition."[45] The topic under scrutiny is the linguistic similarity/opposition of *chi* and *kappa*: "Christos, Chronos, chord are spelld with *chi*, **X**   not / **K**   (*kappa*)." The interchangeability of these two letters which gradually occurs in the spelling of words from classical Greek to Renaissance and contemporary English confirms for Duncan the kind of paradigmatic interrelatedness possible in an infinite series—a corridor, like language itself, without end. The essential "chord" or harmony under study is that between the etymology of words (language) and the evolution of living forms (nature). Changes in spelling—"*thunder was þunor / tapestry, tapisry*" (BB 49)—are interpreted as a kind of Darwinian natural process. Duncan claims that "as an evolution of elements comes into our picture of living and dying forms, so, the drama of poetic form in our special language-world must change to include new propositions" (M 50). "Spelling" is a self-reflexive "Xrestomathy" or notation of remarkable "passages" from the *O. E. D.*, Liddell and Scott, Shakespeare, and Dr. Johnson. Despite the pedagogic threat in his headnote, Duncan brings this poem to an elegant and poetic closure:

> And Jespersen recites:
>
>> *She was a maid • the maiden kween.*
>> *It is made of silk • a silken dress.*
>> *The man is old • in olden days.*
>> *The gold is hid • the hidden gold.*
>> *The room is nice • all nicen warm.*
>
> and quotes from Conan Doyle's *The Great Shadow*:
>
>> "I wish your eyes would always flash like that, for
>>  it looks so nice and manly."
>
>> It looks so nicen manly.
>>
>> (BB 50)

The grammarian's recitation on noun-adjective conversions is applied to the rather "straight" language of Conan Doyle. Duncan's pronunciation is a more coy and suggestive "It looks so nicen manly." This closing reference to the changes wrought on language by (mis)pronunciation reopens the motif of Eros, specifically homoerotic, throughout the series. Each figure in an interrelated series of poems holds multiple significance; the excerpt from Conan Doyle is made to function as both the close of the lecture and the opening line of a proposition.

"Passages 21," "The Multiversity," is a Vietnam war–era poem set in the midst of a Free Speech Movement demonstration at U.C. Berkeley. Duncan protests against the "heads of usury, heads of war" (BB 70), against all forms of hierarchy whether economic, military, political, or poetic. He disparages the unnatural order of an imposed will which would "over-rule / the Law man's inner nature seeks" (BB 72), and extols the "communion" resulting from "the freedom of / individual volition" (BB 73). In an earlier essay, Duncan discovers this natural law in the specialization of cells whose autonomy is defined by their ability to adjust to their surrounding condition, and in the anarchist Bartolomeo Vanzetti's "proposition of a voluntary State, a social order utterly arising from just that social action that each autonomous cell-member volunteers" (M 48). The theory of social action which Duncan adopts intersects with his theory of poetic form in *Passages*. The point of contact seems to be Ezra Pound, invoked by the reference to *usura*. Duncan continues Pound's battle with the unnatural monster Usury, and yet he contests the "absolute authority" (BB 70) that Pound thought necessary to make the *Cantos* cohere, and that drew him to "Mussolini's Bossism and the simplistic rigor of the structure of total control that Fascism proposes in its authoritarian model for all social behavior" (M 49).[46] The ahierarchical serial form of *Passages*, whose autonomous "cell-members" are not assigned to but "voluntarily" assert their position in the structure as a whole, represents a postmodern break from the comprehensive superstructure that the modernist epic attempts to establish. Duncan employs Pound's method of an "increment of association" (as we noted in "At the Loom"), but he avoids his "authoritarian superego" for which "order meant the order of totalitarian idealogues and neo-Platonic hierarchies" (FC 190). The peculiarly postmodern aspect of the serial form is the ahierarchical mobility of sections, not only the refusal to enforce closure, the "lock" of coherence, but the willingness to "unlock" individual sections from a developmental sequence and from the conventions of a genre.

Robert Duncan's *Passages* is an infinite serial form whose rejection of limit is derived from both the Heraclitean concept of flux and the

Coleridgean theory of form as an ongoing process. But Duncan is always alert to the "new propositions" of form presented in the sciences or the other arts: in Schrödinger's theory of a molecular disequilibrium, he finds the confirmation of a form as struggle (on which point both Heraclitus and Darwin offer supporting evidence); in the tone row of Schönberg's serial music, he finds the inclusion of dissonant keys and of discord itself; and in the mobile, a visual representation of a centrifugal force and the interchange of roles among elements. These propositions combine to set the parameters of Duncan's postmodern series: ahierarchical, autonomous sections which are nevertheless interrelated in the constant movement of an aperiodic structure. One commentator on *Passages*, Michael André Bernstein, has warned that "the critical terms with which we might account for success or failure in a poetics in which there is no *telos* to identify, and in which we cannot measure the individual poem's trajectory in terms of an already known project are still vexingly imprecise."[47] Roland Barthes's semiological description of a "writerly," plural text provides us with at least some of the critical tools we require. But only if we cease to think of *Passages* as a linear form will we arrive at an appropriate measure of its success; having ceded *telos*, we should abandon the concept of trajectory as well. We need to acknowledge a condition of form which is both deliberately incomplete and in a state of disequilibrium, unbound and uneven.

## Against the Calendar:
## Paul Blackburn's *Journals*

The biographical note prepared for the recent collection of Paul Blackburn's poetry is a chronological presentation of the major events of his life: born on November 24, 1926, in St. Albans, Vermont, he attended New York University and received his B.A. from the University of Wisconsin in 1950; he was awarded a Fulbright in 1954 and a Guggenheim in 1967; he published poetry and translations. Closure is provided in the respectful, declarative style of the genre: he died of cancer on September 13, 1971, in Cortland, New York. The biographical note fixes dates and places, as it were, in stone. But those of us who read Blackburn's serial poems "The Selection of Heaven" or *The Journals*, attendant to the dates and places he provides, will be disappointed in our expectation of dramatic events or closure. In an autobiographical note, written for what was to become the posthumous publication of *Early Selected Y Mas*, Blackburn says of himself: "He is Mediterranean by adoption and lusts after French food, Greek wines, Spanish coñac, and Italian women. His tastes are broad and indelicate: he would gladly settle for Italian food, French wines, Spanish coñac and Greek women."[48] Instead of the dramatic event, a continental dinner for two is proposed; rather than closure, he offers the beginning of a permutation of eight elements (Spanish coñac, probably because it was cheap, appears to be a constant). The endless process of selection, not the progress of events on a calendar, defines the serial form of these poems; and when that selection is, as he says with characteristic modesty, "broad and indelicate," the serial poem is all the more likely to defy closure.

In section 15 of "The Selection of Heaven," there is a rectangle, like a grave marker, in which Blackburn inscribes the deaths of his paternal grandparents: "Hannah died Mar 23, 1963 / John Henry, April 17."[49] The mode of this lyric is elegiac, and the mood more consistently somber than usual in Blackburn's work. And yet, the event of death or meditation on the theme of death does not consume the form of the poem. Rather, the serial form of the poem enables its author to evade the almost foreordained resignation to death and its finality which is characteristic, for example, of Tennyson's sequence *In Memoriam*. The serial form of the poem subsumes the closing of two lives, and more.

The poem begins:

> 1.  GOD,      that it did happen,
>     that loose now, that
>     early configuration
>             of birds, the texture set in
>             words,  1945,
>     a Staten Island beach in early October
>     here in more than flesh and brick,
>     9th Street, March 1963.
>
> (CP 246)

A correspondence of two places and two dates is established. The events are unnamed, but the point of contact is the "configuration of birds." In his Author's Note to *The Cities*, Blackburn claims, "Finally, it is a construct, out of my own isolations, eyes, ears, nose, and breath, my recognitions of those constructs not my own that I can live in."[50] The "it" here is both the volume of poems and any city in which the poet has lived. "It" is not a sequence of events or meditations on a theme, but the observations (sensual) or recognitions (intellectual) of "constructs"—figures, forms. Acts of love and the event of death have their place in "The Selection of Heaven"; they are perhaps the all-informing contexts of the poem. But their places are "set," just as "the texture" of this early configuration of birds is "set in words." Blackburn's note to *The Cities* claims that there are no events, no correspondences of years and seasons, which are not part of the construct of the poem. There is no content that, by process of selection and configuration, is not form.

The second section notes a correspondence among the materials with which the poet-translator works:

> 2.  ROYAL EBONY
>     is the name of a carbon paper  .  Is
>     also title of a poem by Nicolás Guillén.
>
> The smoke rises in a thread, a
> curled stream from between
> his thumb and forefinger
> as he snuffs it out.
>                         We live.
>                         Pity?  It
>                         is the waste of their lives.
>                                                       (CP 247)

Remarkably, neither narrative progression nor metaphoric comparison binds these lines; rather, they meet tangentially, as Guillén's title and the carbon paper that the translator uses meet in a name, a color. Every element in these lines, each sign, occurs in some permutation further along in this serial poem. The poem is a network, a construct in which signs (for example, Ebony) exist in a contiguous relationship with other signs (Guillén's title) and a paradigmatic relationship with dissimilar but related signs elsewhere in the text. For instance, the sixth section, ÁSHARA, begins and ends with the phrase "in Arabic it is the number 10 / Color is black" (CP 250). A black crow, a black cat, and "the black cypress spires" are joined to the number 10 by contiguous association. Whenever the number 10 is invoked, as in sections 10 and 14, things black reappear. In this paradigm, Guillén's title and the carbon paper are related to crow and cypress. Contextually—as every metonymic part has its semantic whole—black is the obvious color of elegy.

There is no metonym in section 2 which does not have its correlative at some other point in the poem. Although section 2 narrates no event, contains no metaphor, it initiates a complex network of motifs. Section 10, for example, presents a similar conjunction among the materials the translator requires to get the job done:

> 10.   IT EXISTS.        There↓
>        is the very spot to place the ashtray
>        so that              my hand
>        may reach it without looking while I read
>        And that is where I place it,
>                      exactly │
>                              │
>                              │
>           THERE  ↓
>
>        The   3
>        brandies I have had after lunch are
>                      exactly
>                          enuf
>        to create the vulnerability the
>        translator needs to bring him
>        open to the text, that other life
>        than his own
>                      /
>                          or how to share
>        another man's glory, exaltation,
>        love, penury, lust,   700
>        years agone, the gap gone,
>        No, not bridged, baby,
>        YOU ARE THERE!

                                                          (CP 254)

Translation, which seemed incidental in section 2, becomes the focus of the later section. The THERE's of the ashtray and of the translator's transmigration of soul are an ironic conjunction. The exact placement of the ashtray, THERE, the packs of cigarettes methodically extinguished, metonymically represent the repeated and methodical revisions by which the THERE of the troubadour's exaltation is achieved. Although the three brandies facilitate the process, it is the ironic conjunction of ashtray and exaltation—a metonymy, not a metaphor—which gives this section its structure.

The gesture of extinguishing the cigarette, first described in section 2, is repeated with slight variations at the close of section 10, as well as in sections 14 and 16. It is a free motif which punctuates the poem as the poet-translator puts out one cigarette after another:

> Smoke
> rises in a thread from between his
> thumb and middlefinger as
> he snuffs it out   .   continues   .

(CP 255)

Such repetition is free from a rhetorical continuity that, as Barthes says, "will agree to repeat only if it can transform." This repeated gesture is not bound to any development of plot, character, or event, nor does it require any prior information to be understood. Rather, the free motif is indicative of what Barthes calls "fugal" continuity, in which "identifiable fragments ceaselessly appear."[51] Such a motif, then, is characteristic of the "unbound" structure of the infinite serial poem. Each section of this serial poem is as disjunct and autonomous as the free motif. Because of this disjunction, the *significance* of the gesture changes with each *context* in which it occurs: the relationship is, once again, contiguity. In section 10, the cigarettes that the translator chain-smokes and methodically snuffs without looking are indicative of the laboriousness of his ceaseless revisions.[52] In contrast, the motif no longer signifies laboriousness when it recurs in section 16. The poet is smoking during the graveside services of his grandfather. The smoke rises and the ashes fall, leading metonymically to the phrase from the Catholic service, "ASHES TO ASHES" (CP 262). The snuffing of the cigarette, like the color black, signifies death. Habitual, ubiquitous, mundane—and like the taste, hot and bitter.

"Pity is hate," the poet conjectures in section 2—only to retract the statement. In section 16, the poet concedes that John Henry's children could at least pity, if not love, a severe man who at last slipped into senility:

> John Henry survived Hannah twenty-five days,
> would wander about that section of the rest home
> peering into the empty room.
>    "I can't seem to find my wife."
> They'd tell him his wife had died
> and he'd remember that for five minutes.

(CP 258)

Bitterness remains, though Blackburn says of Hannah: "Everybody loved her" (CP 253). "The Selection of Heaven" is in the elegiac mode, but the ongoing process of the poem's serial form defies the finality of death.

A similar formal tension occurs in an elegy for the novelist Robert

Reardon, "Sixteen Sloppy Haiku" (CP 396). As the title suggests, it is a
series of short poems which, nevertheless, defy closure. Referring to
Reardon, the last section declares:

> He had a tendency to finish
> what he did
> cleanly,
> minus something
> Find it.
>
> (CP 400)

What is that something? The poet cannot deny the death of his friend,
but he can offer an absolute defiance of closure in the poem that he
fashions. The "final" line damns us to search for something we cannot
hope to find.

"Elegy" to Propertius and Ovid meant a "lover's complaint." See
how terms get away: a lover's complaint in Lower Manhattan sounds a
good deal harsher. Federico García Lorca is a more recent model whose
elegies display an obsession with the presentiments of death. In a
stanza from "Song of the Small Dead Girl," translated here by Blackburn, Lorca laments:

> I found myself with the girl.
> Mortal meadow of earth.
> A small dead girl.[53]

But Blackburn's approach to the elegiac mode is a more exquisite
blend of love (often enough, the procreative urge) and death, the lover's
complaint and the graveside lament. This blend of Eros and Thanatos
is most pronounced in *The Journals*—a blend of such fruits as these:

> Because I have left the door open
> there is always a matter of insects
> the wind in these high valleys blows
> in . I
> have to take a butterfly out in my hands before he
> batters himself to death against the
> glass pane
> between the livingroom & the kitchen .
>
> Then a wasp discovers the fruit bowl in the corner.
> He checks out the oranges and the mayonnaise-jar
> and settles on the bruised portion of a pear . O, yes!

> Lemons
> peaches
> a melon
>            but returns to
>                        the bruised pear, its
>                        speckled skin, he
>     hovers and sucks, he checks my outgoing mail,
>     my empty pastis glass, the story now translated,
>     even the lines of this notebook where he walks
>
>         for a bit, but returns,
>
>                 makes love to the pear .
>
> (CP 539–40)

Blackburn presents this scene directly to the senses without comment. His craft is so clean—there are but three or four adjectives employed—that I feel compelled to supply an adjective or two: so *gentle* with the butterfly, which seeks to batter out its life; so *mellifluent*, as he follows the sucking wasp. One adjective that he does allow, however, is at the core of things: the wasp sucks at, "makes love to," the "bruised" portion of the pear, the one spot of decay. Blackburn, like the wasp, draws love out of death. In the only metaphor permitted, the procreative force draws life from death. At Julio Cortázar's house, in the hills of Saignon-par-Apt, August 1968, Blackburn presents a late pastoral elegy.

The wasp, "checking out" the fruit and other objects on the table with an apparently random intent, seems to me like Blackburn himself in action. Hovering over and touching upon the aspects of the *vita quotidiana*[54] (to quote his one Italian critic, Annalisa Goldoni)—the outgoing mail, the drink, and the work just completed—Blackburn throws us a feint: what we take to be aleatory, there by chance, is rigorously selected and meticulously "placed" on the table—and in an instant, the poet as wasp returns to it. The immediacy, the *presence* that the demonstrative pronoun in "this notebook" signifies, is of course a device, an effect of the poet's chosen words. This entire episode, finally, is chosen from so many working days as a translator throughout Europe: *The Journals* is not an immediate, chronological record of what happened from 1968 to 1971 at all. *The Journals* is a series of discontinuous poems which, like a still life of notebook, glass, and bowl of fruit, are placed or arranged according to the artist's sense of order, not the calendar's.

But elegy, yes—the moments of crisis are here too, though never excerpted, never allowed to become melodramatic events removed from the realm of the quotidian. The entry for December 13, 1968, begins casually, with "A saturday-seeming sunlight in the front room." Blackburn observes:

> The black cats sit on the dirty couch and observe me reading,
> drinking my coffee, first of the day . They are waiting for me
> to feed them.
>
> (CP 561)

There is a kind of ellipsis in time; we do not hear the telephone ring—Blackburn shifts all at once into the past tense, to dramatic effect:

> I came back from the telephone and got into bed in the cold room.
> The covers were still warm. She was raised on her left elbow,
> looking at me . It wasn't fear, nor acceptance, nor anticipation.
> The cusp of necessity. I stroked her hair a few times and told her:
>
> "Your father is dead." Her hair is long & black & fine, her head
> rounded underneath it, under my stroking hand. It breaks, falls
> against my chest, my shoulder suddenly wet with tears . Sobs come
> openly from the throat, not choked back, neither opened to scream .
> I hold her hard against me, continue stroking. I wish she cd/
> scream . I wish I cd/ .
>                    R O A R
>
> The cats sit together on the bathmat near the door & observe me
> sitting on the pot . First of the day . They
> are waiting for me to feed them. I clean their box.
> In the front room, one sits in the single spot of sun on the floor, the
> other climbs the wooden louver, swings up to the top as the blind
> swings with her weight, rides it to the centersash . sits there .
>
> (CP 562)

Certainly, the attention paid to the cats and their scatological curiosity is a rupture of the traditional decorum of elegy, its serious tone and eschatalogical meditation. But the repeated stanzas, in which the cats observe a daily routine that must go on, bind death to the process of life. The melodramatic event—and there is a strident expression of grief here—is bound to the quotidian. In *The Journals*, as in "The Selection of Heaven," it is not the advance and arrival of the event of death which define and control the form but the network of motifs in their recurrence.

Blackburn continues:

I hold her and she weeps for a long time. We are naked and alone in the world, lie there as one, and one and two, I hold her and we sleep . for an hour.

> "Stone already knows the form"

He quotes Michelangelo (via Pound), "Stone already knows the form / of the statue within it" (CP 564); the artist only discovers it. This profession of immanence is critical to the poetry of process. The poet must recognize the form of an event, "those constructs not my own that I can live in." Even so, the statue is not dis-covered without the craft, the artisanship, of the sculptor.

> Warm & desolate under the blankets in a cold room
>
> in another man's house / in Annandale, New York
>
> somewhere in time
>
> sleep.
>
> Wake.
> Telephone calls . when is the wake?
>
> (CP 562–63)

Hypnos and Thanatos, Sleep and Death, nearly identical twins on a Mycenaean vase, remind us, as the pun on "wake" does, how very much death is a process of our lives, an event that cannot be estranged, nor separated from the flux and the repetition of the *vita quotidiana*.

The final section of "The Selection of Heaven" was written in 1967, four years after the composition of the first sixteen sections. As with Robert Duncan's infinite series, *Passages*, it is entirely appropriate to the form of the poem for the poet to make additions at wide intervals, over the course of several volumes. Edith Jarolim, editor of the *Collected Poems*, claims that the last section is thematically bound to the preceding sixteen because it presents the "death of the poet's second marriage" (CP xxix). Of course, no such phrase occurs in section 17; Jarolim is reading the biographical note. What the section does present is a repetition of motifs from the earlier sections:

> The dead man sits at the table
> a dead cigarette in his mouth,

> drinks, the mind-gears turn
> repetitiously over the same materials,
> the same images return, murderously.
>
> (CP 263)

The structure of 17 and its connection to the earlier sections are found
not so much in the contexts of love and death—nor the death of love—
but in the relation of repeated metonymic details. An interesting
physiological connection, like the synapse of a nerve ending, is described by the apparently injured speaker:

> a right arm broken in two places, and
> everytime there's a twinge in the interosteol musculature, the
>
> pickup truck will return, with the
> sound of glass smashing, with
> hysterical vision of a wet rock
> and a pink flower in the identical spot a week later .
>
> (CP 265)

Each time the speaker feels the twinge in his arm, the pain triggers a
reiteration of details associated with his marital separation (merely
implied by the poem; *we* must supply the context). This association is
based on contiguity—the twinge is not *similar* to the sound of glass
smashing but *tangent* to it. The physical pain, while not a metaphor
for divorce, is related paradigmatically to an emotional pain, his murderous impulse. Finally, the poem contains in its last stanza one more
repetition of the free motif:

> O,   L O V E !
>                Smoke
> rises from between the first and middle fingers of his left hand
> which came to life,
> so passive it was before .
>
> (CP 266)

The free motif, the repetition of metonymic details, and in effect, the
primacy of the syntagmatic relation over context, event, or chronological narrative, assert the structure of the series "The Selection of
Heaven."

Edith Jarolim's arrangement of Blackburn's work in *The Collected
Poems* is by the chronological order of composition. But very often the
chronological order does not coincide with the numerical order given
to the series. "Rituals I–XVII," for example, written over a span of nine

years, has its "first" section appearing fourth in this volume; as a further complication, only eleven of the seventeen sections are extant—a series with lacunae. Clearly, Blackburn has something other than an autobiographical portrait in mind as the controlling structural device of these poems. The interesting effect is that the reader who begins on page one and proceeds to the back cover will read several of the serial poems out of numerical sequence. But since these poems are not *sequences*, the order in which they are read will make no difference. One does not need to have read "Rituals I" to understand II or IV which precede it; and if the poems were not numbered at all, one could not know that there were sections missing. As Robert Duncan says of *Passages*, there is no initiation and no terminus to the infinite series, and no bound sequence. Reading *The Collected Poems*, then, is empirical proof of the autonomy of the individual sections of the series.

The chronological ordering of poems (and this should be kept in mind in regard to *The Journals*) is finally more arbitrary than the assignment of Roman or Arabic numerals by the poet. What do the dates tell us about the form of the poem in *The Journals*? Or as Duncan says, "the series does not signify / beyond the incident of a numeration."[55] I would like to gauge the difference between the series and the sequence by reading Blackburn's four-part "Signals" in chronological order—that is, out of sequence. "Signals I: Tanger, August 1956" is in two parts: essentially a pair of street scenes, not very pretty, like deuces in a poker game. In the first, people scramble to pick up "the empty cones of the ice cream vendor / the gust had scattered" (CP 70). The revelation is in the lack of conflict where an American might expect to find one: "Even in Algeciras / that cesspool," the cones are a welcome windfall; the hot wind initiates a gentle scramble—not for ice-cream (how American!) but for the dry, empty cones. In part 2, we have a contextual disjunction:

> Tonite,
> after   10   minutes watching
> and listening to early roosters
> a dog joining in from the street
>                         a lonesome ass
> screaming from the market
> for company
> or food
>            one
>                    burst toward the Spanish coast
>                    It was orange.
>
>                                     (CP 71)

What bursts? A flare, fireworks, a shell? It was orange. Part 2 is a series of observations related contiguously; these sights and sounds are described without comment and without any effort to join the animal cries to the "burst." Only the lack of punctuation and the isolated "one" indicate a syntagmatic connection: we are to "read through," pivoting on an isolated word. It is difficult to tell how these two parts are "signals." What are their signifieds?

"Signals III," written and published in 1958, is the next to appear. Ironically, it is a poem of spring in a series with no motif of seasonal progression:

> Spring, being what it is this year,
>
> > and it has been cold up to now
> > and the heat later will be, my
> > god, how shall we stand it?
>
> > but after that storm Sunday, we
> > have acquired several slug-
> > > gish flies.   I
> > am very tender with them.

(CP 108)

This poem contains a rather nice, and deviously appropriate, example of anacoluthon—in classical rhetoric, "without sequence," or a "failure to follow." The poet's supposition as to what "the heat will be" is abandoned in favor of an exclamation of dismay: "my / god, how shall we stand it?" In a "failure" of rhetorical continuity, no finite verb completes the sentence for which "spring" is the subject. This abandonment of a syntactical structure is quite common in spoken discourse, and Blackburn is attuned to the rhythms of everyday speech. Anacoluthon suggests a sluggishness and/or befuddlement on the part of the speaker—so both the speaker and the flies are similarly surprised by the spring heat. But this rhetorical device, though it betrays the laziness of the speaker, displays the craft of the poet. Instead of a syntactic completion, we have two autonomous clauses set side by side, paratactically. Not only does the anacoluthon establish the mood of the speaker, it also establishes at the level of sentence structure the aperiodic, asequential structure of the serial poem. I especially enjoy the ambiguous meaning of the final line. By "tender," does the poet mean a lazy, soft swat? Here the poet is neither the savior of the butterfly at Saignon (in *The Journals*), nor is he "murdering flies" as in the final section of "The Selection of Heaven."

"Signals II" was composed five to six years after "Signals III." "Signals I & II" appeared in *The Cities*, published by Grove Press in 1967, but the three poems have never appeared in sequence. "Signals II" concerns the breakup of the poet's relationship with . . . whom? It would be better to say that the poem engages in a mimetic fashion the breakup of a relationship through the breakup of syntactic structure. We are so continually frustrated in our attempts to assign a poem to biographical events, or to compose a coherent biography from poetic statement, that we must finally admit that the referential function of language in poetry is subordinated to the relational (signs among themselves)—that is, to the very form of the poem:

> Aside,
> that you wd not come to me
> that neither of us can, nor want to
> share the other, nor can we help it,
> I wd not come to you, either, nor
> need I have
> The gin and tonic begun or never drunk, I
> shall sit here with my red wine and mull
> I shall mull my red wine and think
> I shall think
> red gin . mulltonic . sitwine
> red mullet, ginthink, miltown, drink
> the atonic mulled red, bink, bink,
> bink, bink, bink. . . .

(CP 306)

Ostensibly, the disconsolate lover has made the mistake of following gin with red wine, mixing or mulling them—in the homonym he fuses the act of drinking with that of repetitive consideration (the two senses of "mull" are etymologically related). As the poet becomes progressively more inebriated, syntactic combination virtually disappears, leaving words or word particles to recombine in a free-associative manner: a small red fish, an Orwellian "ginthink," the tranquilizer Miltown widely prescribed in the 1950s, and a tribute to atonal music. The speaker's last act before lapsing into unconsciousness is the ironically poetic "drink . . . bink" rhyme. The repetitive "bink," like the sound of a cardiac monitor recording the heartbeat of the unconscious patient, is the device in this series which is most clearly a "signal," not a "verbal icon."

Blackburn added a fourth part to "Signals" in 1967, consisting of the last third of the poem "Paris-Toulouse Train"—that poem being a part of *The Journals*. This intersection, or series-crossing, also occurs when

"Rituals XVII. It Takes an Hour," which the poet writes on the bank's "Hispano-Olivetti" while waiting for a check to be cashed, appears in *The Journals* (CP 522). Robert Duncan's serial poems also intersect: "Passages 20" is also "Structure of Rime XXVI"; "Passages 36" is also No. 8 in "A Seventeenth Century Suite."[56] This may sound like the notational nattering of a conductor fussing over the score instead of listening to the music, but these intersections are in fact a positive proof of the autonomy of individual sections in the series; their ahierarchical, achronological structure is capable of being read without prior narrative or thematic information.

The fourth part of "Signals" shows us the poet encountering, in the train's restroom, the sign *eau non potable*, which "has been carefully edited down to / 'no pot'" (CP 490). An interesting aspect of this poem is that we have a sign, with both an official and an abbreviated message in French (*pot* can be taken as a shortened version of *pot de chambre*), which is almost, but not quite, effaced by another sign with two more subversive messages in English: in 1967, "no pot" might either refer to the unavailability of marijuana on French trains, or it might command that we not use the sink for a toilet. Thus, we have at least four signs in all, not one of which confidently achieves signification—four "messages" that refuse to mean in any stable or fixed way. Who has done the editing? How can we assign a determinate meaning to "no pot"? Remarkably, Blackburn fashions a "poetic sign" from an act of vandalism; although he appears to be merely reporting, he arrives at a polysemic quality in this poem without resorting to a play on words.

"Signals" is, I think, one of the more interesting of Blackburn's short serial poems because the contexts of the four poems are so diverse and unrelated thematically. From line to line, Blackburn's materials fiercely resist a confident "this is one to take home" paraphrase. The train's conductor forbids him to play his tape recorder:

> There are
> sonsofbitches
> everywhere .
> Bonjour, monsieur Blackburn!
> Welcome back to Toulouse!
> and rain, I swear .

Clearly the invective and the curse on the weather are the speaker's; but whose voice greets him in such an amiable, though formal, tone? Who gives the signal, and how do we read it?

The poetics of *The Journals* is elegantly stated in "ROADS":

> Thus qualified, I
> want to write a poem abt/ roads
> that they are there, that
> one travels them & is not obtuse
> nor obliged to take anymore in, onto the mind, than
> the body in time and space taketh unto itself, the
> mind in its holy vacuum
> breaking out of   past the fact
> to other   FACTS?
>
> (CP 485)

Blackburn's "elected analogue" for the form of *The Journals* is the open road: form as proceeding. Literally, he is almost always "on / the road" in these poems, on the subway, on French or Spanish trains, in his VW camper—why not *The Travelogues* as a title for the record of wanderlust? Neither Coleridge's analogue for poetic form, the rooted plant, nor Duncan's analogue for *Passages*, the mobile, accommodate the motive of *The Journals*. These poems are centrifugal, always "breaking out of past the fact / to other FACTS" in an encompassing arc. No portentous metaphors or imposing schema force the poem to turn back on itself; instead, the force of the syntagm driving past one fact and on to the next results in a metonymic journey. We hear the echo in Blackburn of Olson's statement in "Projective Verse": "ONE PERCEPTION MUST IMMEDIATELY AND DIRECTLY LEAD TO A FURTHER PERCEPTION."[57] The poetry of process is opposed to the notion of progress, and in Blackburn, as in Duncan, we hear a denial of *telos*, closure, or climax—any sense of an ending. Each arrival signals a new departure:

> so there's this road
> & one stays on it forever until one
> (it) stops (roads
> go on forever, so do parentheses) or
> gets some WHERE else in his body or his head,
> finds there's another place to be, comes
> or goes
> quietly to one side, & there
> lives
> or dies
> accident
> -ly .
>
> (CP 486)

*The Journals*, like these roads, could go on forever. But we are not on the interstate, trying to make time from one big city to the next.

Although *The Journals* proceeds without closure, it is not as linear or continuous as the long white line. Blackburn's poem is more like the "blue" highways, the county roads that wind twenty miles east even though the sign reads north; they are often as broken and discontinuous as the dashes of white on a back road. It doesn't matter if we've been here before, if we got on in Cortland, New York, or Saignon-par-Apt; and we don't have to know where we've been to get where we're going—there isn't any predetermined route.

*The Journals*, as a serial form, is centrifugal and infinite; but if the poem were linear and continuous it would have to contain nearly everything that took place in the last four years of Blackburn's life. We like to see Blackburn in the present tense, getting it down *right then*, until "the black cat comes over and stages a sit-in directly on the notebook / in which one is trying to write a poem" (CP 559). The illusion—and this is *craft*—is that the poem he is writing is *this* one. This "interruption" by the cat in need of attention is inserted between descriptions of an analogue that disturbs the idea of a continuous natural process in poetry:

> . . . I'm dreaming of an absolutely natural hair, a single
> intricately curled, long, brown hair in a tiny plastic container
> you can see thru like a fuse, loose at both ends, beautifully
> involuted and fine. This is an absolutely indispensable item in
> a list of objects which must be collected, this wild hair in its
> artificial little glass tomb, carefully random, carefully
> natural. An absolute fake essential to the collection, essential
> for a correct life.
>
> (CP 559)

Blackburn addresses in his metaphor an essential conflict between the ideas of "organic form" (*right then* and inspired) and the precise selection that the poet must make (*poiein*, to make). Even in an open form, in the poetry of process, the artifice of the poet (represented here by the "artificial little glass tomb") must be imposed on the natural, organic hair. One result of this process of selection is that, instead of a continual development of a single context (often the form of auto/biography or traditional narrative poetry), we have a series of contextual disjunctions. For example, the poet's "dream" of the encapsulated hair is followed by a careful description of "The Ft. Moultrie flag on a recent 6¢ stamp"; the cat stages its sit-in in the next stanza. Are these things "a list of objects which must be collected," an inventory of the desk-top? It is tempting to say that the process is aleatory, that something like the random collision of organic molecules has occurred.

Blackburn's poem, however, is "carefully random": the poet intervenes to select only the "absolutely indispensable item."

The complexity of the infinite series comes not from the layering of metaphor (similarity and comparisons) but from the multiplicity of disjunct contexts. We have three metonymic, "indispensable" items arranged contiguously on the page: the hair in its capsule, the flag on its stamp, and the cat on the poet's notebook. Yet how do the contexts of these three items meet? Is there a complete disjunction or a point of tangency? We cannot even say that the items themselves meet contiguously on the desk, since the encapsulated hair has been "dreamt." Perhaps we must say that these items are "placed" together, if not on the desk, then in the poem alone. The infinite series proceeds metonymically, from item to item, and not by metaphoric comparisons. Blackburn concludes:

> And it doesn't stop. None of it
>
> stops, ever, it needs that wild hair in its
>
> plastic container, the essential image . So .

While this serial poem is a process without closure, it nevertheless requires the craft, the careful selection of the poet—anything and everything won't do.

Blackburn heads one Journal entry for August 1969 "THEY ARE NOT THE SAME" (CP 588). A rebuke to those who think that all gulls (his favorite bird) look alike, this phrase is also the rebuke of the metonymic poet to the poets of metaphor. In his prologue to *Kora in Hell: Improvisations*, William Carlos Williams incites the revolt against "the coining of similes": "Much more keen is that power which discovers in things those inimitable particles of dissimilarity to all other things which are the peculiar perfections of the thing in question."[58] Blackburn exhibits this ability for the most precise observation:

> The gull stands on the piling hits my eye between
> the locker shacks on the pier painted a dull identical
> tan, consecutively numbered, they are not the same, not
> by content or location of door, nor by width of board, nor
> how the corner joints are laid & nailed or finished.
>
> (CP 589)

The metonymic poet shuns the synthetic metaphor and the simile, which Williams claims depends on a "nearly vegetable coincidence";

what then is the virtue of this peculiar vision? Blackburn answers that one sees

> . . . another sameness always changing, never quite
> identical . the same timelessness . it is not the same
> gull
>
>                                                      (CP 589)

The poet needs to see not generically or randomly, but carefully; he needs to see through the Heraclitean flux to the "peculiar perfection" of a thing, or in Blackburn's words, the "essential image." The payoff for precise observation is in the vision of the timelessness that the essential gist of an object offers. The poet of "Plaza Real with Palm-trees" (CP 50) can return to Barcelona ten years later and find, in "Plaza Real with Palm Trees: Second Take" (CP 493), that the apparently random movements of people and birds about the plaza can be made timeless through careful observation. The poet of process could write "Plaza Real" every day, a different poem. "Once again," he rejoices, "I am *looking* at it" (CP 496).

In the last entry of *The Journals*, Blackburn exclaims:

> What a gas, maybe
> Louie Armstrong & I
> die, back to back,
> cheek to cheek, maybe the same year.    "O,
> I CAN'T GIVE YOU
> ANYTHING BUT LOVE,
> Bay-aybee"
>                                  1926, Okeh a label then
>                                      black with gold print, was
> one of my folks' favorite tunes, that year
> that I was born . It is all still true
> & Louie's gone down &
> I, o momma, goin down that same road.
> Damn fast .
>
>                                                      (CP 676–77)

The physiological progression of Paul Blackburn's cancer is subverted by the very form of his poem. His infinite series not only denies closure but also rejects a linear and continuous development—any sense of a progression. These fourteen lines, written in the year of his death, refer to an event from the year of his birth, thus creating a neat circumscription of a life. But *The Journals* cannot be read as autobiography; rather than attempt to fit each poem into the context of a life, we must recognize that these poems are a series of indispensable items whose structure can only be understood by their syntagmatic and paradigmatic relations. Discontinuity obstructs the process of the poem, and the resulting disjunction of contexts makes it impossible to say that, biographically, "it is all still true." Such is the evidence that even in "form as proceeding," the form of the poem is a made thing. The physiological and the poetic truth of Blackburn's final declaration are not the same: "Bigod, I must have been full of shit."

## One Thing Finding Its Place with Another: Robert Creeley's *Pieces*

Robert Creeley observes that in his later writing he has arrived at the "admission of serial order as a complex and diversely organized phenomenon."[59] The almost neoclassical "hit singles" of the early *For Love* ("give it form certainly, / the name and titles" [CP 115]) give way to a "common audit of days" (EF 186):

> One day after another—
> perfect.
> They all fit.
>
> (CP 564)

As John Cage says, "no matter what, one thing follows another."[60]

Creeley's "serialogy," the way one thing follows another, informs the structure of his later poetry, *Pieces* (1969), *In London* (1972), *Thirty Things* (1974), and the prose of *Mabel: A Story* (1976). Those critics enamored of the referential poetics of the sequence, in an effort to chart romantic quests or record the poet's strained marital relations, exhaust themselves with a poetry they must eventually find too spare or loose. Instead, we find in the relational poetics of the series much more than a simple linear relation. These books are, as Creeley claims, complex and diversely organized phenomena, opposing the continuum of experience and the poet's disjunctive perception, the aleatory and the systematic, and the contiguous relation of components and the autonomy of individual sections.

In his interview with Creeley, Ekbert Faas asks, "Is there any modern music which you feel moves in the directions you follow in your poetry?" Creeley responds that the music of John Cage offers such a parallel. Cage attended Black Mountain College from 1948 to 1952 and had been a student of Arnold Schönberg,[61] the inventor of the twelve-tone serial form. In a circuitous fashion, Creeley explains their affinities:

> I've been fascinated by re-qualifications of senses of "serial order." I was reading a text called *The Psychology of Communication*, by George A. Miller. For example, the human situation has difficulty regaining the context if there is something interpolated, like: "That man, whom you saw yesterday, is my father." "That man is my father" is the basic statement—"whom you saw yesterday," is the element that's being inserted. This is also applicable to computer structure. If you keep putting in statements into the basic statement, after about three or four such insertions, the hearer or witness gets very, very confused. The human attention apparently is not recursive and tends to be always where it is, so the more that is interpolated in that fashion the more difficult it is for the human to regain locus. (EF 176–77)

Creeley's interpolation of Miller to describe his structural affinities with Cage makes perfect sense, allowing him to relate his verbal experience, poetry and conversation, to the more abstract concept of serial order in musical form. One might compare Miller's "nonrecursive human attention" to Roland Barthes's postulation of a "syntagmatic imagination." The poetry of *Pieces* is very much the product of what Barthes calls "a 'stemmatous' imagination of the chain or the network."[62] The syntagmatic imagination is that which readily claims, "*Here* is where one seems to be" (CTP 186). It does not double back on itself in an effort to recollect or recoup the "gone" moment. This is a poetry of what *is* happening, not of the transcendental *there*, or of an initial, and now lost, *locus*.

Since I am obliged to be recursive, I would like to recall to our attention Paul Blackburn's "Signals III" in which conversational interpolations drive the speaker further and further from the initial syntactical structure, "Spring, being what it is this year . . . ," until it is finally lost. The sluggish conversational style of the speaker is a rhetorical effect that the poet implements, and the "nonrecursive human attention" it presents is called, in the jargon of the classical rhetorician, *anacoluthon*.[63] The metaphoric style, which always refers back to one thing or another, is largely absent from the poetry of Blackburn or Creeley. Creeley's *In London* offers a lyric in the style of an anacoluthic Catullus:

Do you think that if
I said, *I love you*, or anyone
said it, or you did. Do you
think that if you had all
such decisions to make and could
make them. Do you think that
if you did. That you really
would have to think it all into
reality, that world, each time, new.

(CP 475)

For the nonrecursive mind of this poet, it is contiguity and not comparison that forwards the process of poetry.

Despite his interpolation of Miller's text, Creeley does return to his initial point on Cage and brings his statement on serial order to a rondo-like closure: "Poetry obviously is a way to regain a situation in the recursive, that is, to remind us where we are constantly by structure. Now I am fascinated by what happens when we aren't so reminded, when we break and move into different patterns to locate the experience of being somewhere, and that's what I find extraordinary with Cage: the attempt to requalify the experience of serial order, which to me is really crucial" (EF 177). Creeley sets up an opposition in his statement between a poetic structure that is recursive and a serial order that is not recursive. We recognize the recursive mode in traditional form, "poems *bien fait* to some dull mold" (CTP 187). Creeley explicates: "Say, you write a poem about 'a day at the beach' or a poem in a certain meter, or a poem having rhymes of this or that order. All of these elements could be variously used to locate the reader, to give him a reassurance that he knows where he is. If he can't understand what's happening in the third verse, then the very structure of the fourth relocates him and lets him continue" (EF 177).

The sonnet form continually "locates" the reader semantically by such structural devices as the recurrence or parallelism of sound (rhyme), similarities in rhythmic patternings (meter), and stanza form (three quatrains and the final couplet). Gerard Manley Hopkins, cited by Roman Jakobson, claims that this recurrence of rhyme and meter begets "a recurrence or parallelism answering to it in the words and thought and, speaking roughly and rather for the tendency than the invariable result, the more marked parallelism in structure whether of elaboration or of emphasis begets more marked parallelism in the words and sense."[64] Jakobson then summarizes, "Briefly, equivalence in sound, projected into the sequence as its constitutive principle, inevitably involves semantic equivalence." The formal properties of the sonnet, as both Jakobson and Creeley agree, are recursive; semantically, the attention of the reader is continually "located" by the parallelisms of sound and rhythm.

In his essay "Poetry of Grammar and Grammar of Poetry," Jakobson contends that "either [the poet] is striving for symmetry and sticks to these simple, repeatable, diaphanous patterns, based on the binary principle, or he may cope with them, when longing for an 'organic chaos.' "[65] The New Critical "formalists" seem to fall into the former category while the Black Mountain poets fall into the latter.

I doubt that Jakobson, however, in making his very useful observations, ever considered the possibility of a poetry such as Creeley's *Pieces* in which contiguity, not similarity, is the predominant function. Creeley has rejected the binary principle of equivalence in favor of the nonrecursive serial form. Kenneth Burke, in *The Philosophy of Literary Form*, seems better able to appreciate this possibility, as well as the problem of the dislocation of the reader—all, happily, in another musical analogy: "The symphonic form contained a 'way in,' 'way through,' and 'way out.' It sought to place a spell of danger upon us, and in the assertion of its *finale* to release us from this spell. But the tone poem sought *to lead us in and leave us there*."[66] The tone poem to which he refers has its development in Liszt and Debussy—in opposition to the classical symphonies of Beethoven. Our final exam in music theory would certainly contain an exercise in "drop the needle": assuming the student is aware of the basic formal elements of the symphony, the instructor should be able to drop the needle on a platter of Brahms and demand to know which movement is playing. As in the sonnet, the symphony continually relocates the listener, showing him the "way through"; likewise, the *finale* offers closure, a "way out." Not so in the tone poem, and especially not so in the serial music of Schönberg, whose programmatic "tone row" is essentially syntagmatic. Both the music of John Cage and the infinite serial poems of Robert Creeley resist leading the listener-reader at all: "We break and move into different patterns to locate the experience of being somewhere."

We have said that the sonnet form is essentially paradigmatic, that it is composed of phonic, semantic, and grammatical parallelisms or similarities. The serial poem is essentially syntagmatic, and it is the process of contiguity which Creeley identifies in his later poetry: "I am fascinated by how one thing can follow another, and how diverse that pattern can be" (EF 177). The syntagmatic imagination is fascinated, not by the symbolic or the similar, but by the chain of, as

Barthes puts it, "antecedent and consequent links, the bridges [a sign]
extends to other signs."[67] Creeley provides an interesting example:
"Bill Eastlake is a very pleasant friend and novelist and in one of his
books this Navaho lady is saying that she knows the TV story is over
when she sees the lady hand another the box of soap. That's the end of
the story. It's like: *and so they all went home* or something" (EF 177).
No similarity exists between the conclusion of a daytime drama and
the metonymic box of soap, and yet, by the contiguous relationship of
the two signs, however apparently diverse in context, the Navaho lady
attempts to locate her experience. The tension or complexity that
traditional form assigns to metaphor is here, in the serial order, taken
up by the diversity of patterns established among metonymic particulars and their contexts. Or as Charles Altieri has phrased it, "Multiplicity of relations can replace the attributions of depth that justify
scenic, metaphoric styles."[68]

I've interpolated discussion from several sources in the midst of
Creeley's conversation with Faas, not to dislocate the reader but to
demonstrate how fully formed with respect to music and linguistics
Creeley's conception of serial order is in 1978. But, as I have said,
Creeley has been considering the "diverse ways in which an active
*seriality* might be manifest" in his writing since about 1969 (see also
CTP 179, 187, 198). John Cage is a frequent compatriot in this endeavor, as Creeley notes again in an interview in 1973: "Serialogy—
one thing finding its place with another—becomes a far more complex
situation in writing as elsewhere. John Cage is a brilliant instance of
this new sense of how things come together, how they find place with
one another."[69] Creeley's serial poems are infinite; as Burke, Cage, and
Robert Duncan would claim, there is no way out of them. Nor are they
a predetermined form; on the contrary, the use of sudden breaks or
disjunctions, and the aleatory or *"chance factor"* (CTP 186) which is
also one of Cage's signature devices, are prominent compositional
methods that reinforce Creeley's frequent claims that he does not
know what the outcome will be when he sits down to write. Most
importantly, *Pieces* asserts the complexity of the syntagmatic imagination, with its diverse network of contiguously related particulars, at
a level of artistic value equal to the symbolic "depth" of New Critical
formalism. The metonymic poet argues for a tension in poetry previously thought by such as Allen Tate to reside only in the metaphoric.

A serial form, warns Cage, is not a "two-dimensional linear-fact."
Complete dominance by the contiguity relation would result in "a
series of *components*, not a *series* of components";[70] the result would

hold as much interest as a telephone book or the inventory of a grocery store. A conflict exists between the continuum of experience and the ability of the poet to record only fixed moments, or a series of such moments. Creeley addresses this problem directly in the 26 February 1969 entry of *A Day Book*: "Back and forth, in some endless interchange, apparently (but of no actual?) necessity. The consciousness *thinks* it has experience of this or that. Conceptualizes. Like Alpert's note of the ratio between conceptual units and the content admissible in perception, something like 1 to 20,000 per second. Itself a somewhat unwieldy 'idea'" (MS 55). In *Pieces*, the purely syntagmatic impulse to proceed is countered by the poet's disjunctive perception and the necessity of fixing particulars in complex interrelationships. Charles Altieri notes that "as early as the 1965 Berkeley poetry conference we find [Creeley] insisting that Williams' and Olson's ideas of measure entail fixing particulars in terms of 'relational qualifications.'. . . His recent work embodies these qualifications in poetic structures capable of capturing multiple forms of relationship and shifting degrees of relevance among particulars."[71] *Pieces* negotiates the interstice between a projective verse, the "process" of Charles Olson, and the "made" poem of particulars which Williams espouses in his introduction to *The Wedge*.

We recall Olson's uppercase dictum: "ONE PERCEPTION MUST IMMEDIATELY AND DIRECTLY LEAD TO A FURTHER PERCEPTION." Discourse in obedience to Olson's law would be forwarded by contiguity, "how one thing follows another," not by similarity. And with all this moving "INSTANTER, ON ANOTHER!" the poet's attention will be nonrecursive.[72] We notice that the "series of tensions" that are made to hold objects in a "field" are relational.[73] Cage, in fact, claims that "it would be perfectly acceptable for a series to enter into a field situation."[74] As Olson says, if "any ideas or preconceptions from outside the poem" were to hold the objects, the poem, governed by external motifs, would be the predominantly referential utterance of the "philosopher."[75] The contiguous, nonrecursive, and relational functions of the serial poem are an extension of Olson's projective verse.

At several points in his early collection of essays *A Quick Graph*, Creeley quotes from the introduction to Williams's *The Wedge* to make a statement of his own poetics: "When a man makes a poem, makes it, mind you, he takes words as he finds them interrelated about him and composes them—without distortion which would mar their exact significance—into an intense expression of his perceptions and ardors that they may constitute a revelation in the speech that he uses."[76] Creeley's small, tight stanzas, like knotted fists, have an almost physiological tension. He could no sooner deny the fact of his own body than deny the tension of the poem as a "made thing." As he says in "A Note on Poetry," "A poem will be a *thing* of parts, in such relation, that the tension created between them will effect an actual coherence of form" (QG 25). This effect is most pronounced in the early poetry, but in the serial poems it manifests itself as a counterbalance to the purely syntagmatic impulse to proceed; particulars become multivalent or act as destructive interferents, creating tension while thwarting referential narrative or metaphoric analogy.

In "Notes Apropos 'Free Verse,'" Creeley says, "Jakobson's use of 'contiguity' and 'parallelism' as two primary modes of linguistic coherence interests me. Too, I would like to see a more viable attention paid to syntactical environment, to what I can call crudely 'grammartology'" (CE 493). The metonymic poet, whose discourse is forwarded by contiguity, rejects aspects of similarity. In *Pieces*, Creeley claims, "I hate the metaphors" (CP 442), and deplores "the damn function of *simile*, always a displacement of what *is* happening" (CP 419). Williams shares his disgust for simile, preferring "those inimitable particles of dissimilarity to all other things which are the peculiar perfections of the thing in question."[77] Olson prefers to ride the syntagmatic pulse; Williams stresses a binding tension—but what fundamentally informs the structure of *Pieces* is the predominance of the contiguity relation over the similarity relation.

Creeley's poem "Having to—" will serve to illustrate in *Pieces* the syntagmatic current and the counterbalancing interference of complexly related particulars. Here are the first two sections:

> HAVING TO—
> what do I think
> to say now.
>
> Nothing but
> comes and goes
> in a moment.
>
> •
>
> Cup.
> Bowl.
> Saucer.
> Full.
>
> (CP 382)

The title line recalls Williams's "interview" in "The Desert Music":

You seem quite normal. Can you tell me?   Why
does one want to write a poem?

Because it's there to be written.

Oh.   A matter of inspiration then?

Of necessity.

Oh.   But what sets it off?

I am he whose brains
are scattered
aimlessly[78]

The necessity of the poem is nothing so metaphysical as inspiration.
Not *Meta ta physika*, beyond the body, but as Williams says earlier in
the same poem, "Only the poem / only the made poem, to get said
what must / be said."[79] In the second section of Creeley's poem, the
tabletop setting conforms to Williams's sense of the poem's intrinsic
necessity. One effect is that we infer the context, the table, from the
metonymic particulars actually presented. As the contexts of a series
of metonymic particulars become more diverse or disjunct, the interrelations of the words-as-signs become correspondingly more complex. "Full," as an adjective, describes the condition of the crockery; it
refers to all three items. A cup, a bowl, and a saucer—all full, seemingly, out of necessity. To ask, "With what are they full? Liquor, gall,
honey?" is to require the particulars to comment symbolically on the
poet's life. As Williams asserts in the introduction to *The Wedge*, "It
isn't what [the poet] says that counts as a work of art, it's what he
makes, with such intensity of perception that it lives with an intrinsic
movement of its own to verify its authenticity. . . . To me all sonnets
say the same thing of no importance. What does it matter what the
line 'says'?"[80] "Full" causes what threatens to be a dull inventory of
the cupboard to cease, orients the items in an upright position, and
most importantly, forces the reader to question the relations of the
items: why would the cup, the bowl, *and* the saucer be full? By its final
position in this tiny series, the adjective forces the reader into a *retrospective* consideration of the objects' "condition of being." The tabletop setting, then, is a fixed moment of rather intense perception which
counterbalances the projectivist impulse of the second stanza: what is
said "comes and goes / in a moment."

The poem "One thing" also illustrates the counterbalancing in
*Pieces* of the continuum of experience and the necessity of the fixed
moment or place; the poem corresponds nicely to the first sections of
"Having to—":

ONE THING
done, the
rest follows.

•

Not from not
but in in.

•

Here here
here. Here.

(CP 388)

While the first section declares the contiguity of "form as proceeding,"
the third sets like concrete into an obstinate, nonreferential block.
How does one claim, "*Here* is where one seems to be," without reference to a *there*? One says, "I'm in San Francisco, at Market and Grant,"
locating oneself on a referential grid according to the street signs. In
the poem, the *here* of each particular is located by its relation to other
word signs, not by its referential meaning. Street signs are fixed; in the
experience of a serial order, particulars "break and move into different
patterns to locate the experience of being somewhere."

Creeley has said, "I tend to posit intuitively a balance of *four*, a
foursquare circumstance, be it walls of a room or legs of a table, that
reassures me in the movement otherwise to be dealt with" (CE 494).
The four "heres" of "One thing" assert such a balance, providing the
reassurance or sense of control over the projectivist movement of
"One thing / done, the / rest follows." We can compare these stanzas
from "Numbers":

FOUR

This number for me
is comfort, a secure
fact of things. The

table stands on
all fours. The dog
walks comfortably,

and two by two
is not an army
but friends who love

one another. . . .

(CP 398)

The second half of "Having to—" somewhat more vividly presents this necessity of a relational balance, essentially the set of tensions among metonymic particulars, as it encounters the pull to go on, one after another:

> The way into the form,
> the way out of the room—
>
> The door, the hat,
> the chair, the fact.
>
> •
>
> Sitting, waves on the beach,
> or else clouds, in the sky,
>
> a road, going by,
> cars, a truck, animals, in crowds.
>
> (CP382)

The stable forms of a room or a chair counterbalance the movement, random and ongoing, of waves, clouds, and traffic on a road. In effect, the resolution between the fixed moment and the ongoing process is in the making, in Williams's sense, of the poem. The grammatical parallelism of the first couplet allows one to interchange "form" and "room" without the rhetorical annoyance of an explicit metaphor. This association of form and room indicates Creeley's concern for a system of containment "into" which the aleatory moves.

There are two additional series of four items in these sections to complement the tabletop setting of the second section. Just as the adjective "full" appears as the fourth item in the series to enliven relationally an otherwise dull inventory of crockery, so in these two groups, the final item provides the relational tension. The syntagmatic impulse, having named "the door, the hat / the chair," would continue with an immediately adjacent item: the welcome mat. But Creeley's "the fact," even as it settles the couplet into a foursquare balance, is contextually disjunct—not a member of a set of household objects. The foursquare balance, however, convinces us that it "belongs," and immediately we must consider: are facts objects, are hats facts, are words things? In "Oh, Love . . . ," Creeley claims that "the words one / tries // to say are / facts" (CP 508). Or as Williams says, "My dear Miss Word let me hold your W."[81] The purely syntagmatic impulse, which would lead to a kind of inventory, is checked by these fourth items (full, the fact, in crowds); subsequently, a much more complex set of interrelations occurs. If this spare, asymbolic poem is successful, it is because of the balance struck between the contiguous process and the tension among particulars which "effect[s] an actual coherence of form" (QG 25).

"I. A. Richards talks about progression in a poem," Terry R. Bacon suggests, interviewing Creeley, "where, simply because the poet uses language, the poem must follow some sort of syntactic sequence. . . . Some of your poems do not seem to exhibit this sort of progression."[82] One reason, Creeley responds, is a poetics of "conjecture," a favorite term of Olson's, in which semantic resolution is seen as boring and closure is resisted.[83] In a second approach to this lack of sequential progression, Creeley discusses the "disjunct couplet." "Two things" could be brought together in an apparently "rhetorical situation" (rhyme, rhythm, or some aspect of grammatical parallelism) which were nevertheless contextually disjunct. The concluding couplets of "Pieces of cake" function in this manner:

> PIECES OF CAKE crumbling
> in the hand trying to hold
> them together to give each
> of the seated guests a piece.
>
> •
>
> Willow, the house, an egg—
> what do they make?
>
> Hat, happy, a door—
> what more.

(CP 383)

In the first section, someone attempts to impose an external form on these "Pieces" with his hands; perhaps what is required for this dry cake is the internal adhesion or tension that "an egg" will provide. The first couplet has an off-rhyme, the second a perfect; we should be reminded by such a poetic structure of where we are. Phonic resolution should involve a semantic resolution. But the disjunct couplet deliberately obstructs sequential progression, refusing to relocate the reader as the sonnet or the heroic couplet would.[84] In the series "willow, the house, an egg," contextual disjunction denies semantic sequence—this despite, or in an exquisite tension with, the contiguous relations of the particulars. Creeley is not interested in what the series says, but in the diverse ways in which one thing finds its place with another. At the structural level of the entire poem, *Pieces*, contextual disjunction contributes significantly to the autonomy of sections despite the contiguous relation of components.

Gertrude Stein, in her essay "Poetry and Grammar," suggests a method of counting which can be compared to Creeley's "Numbers" series in *Pieces*:

> After all the natural way to count is not that one and one make two but to go on counting by one and one as china men do as anybody does as Spaniards do as my little aunts did. One and one and one and one and one. That is the natural way to go on counting.
> Now what has that to do with poetry. It has a lot to do with poetry.[85]

Stein distinguishes between summation and accumulation. Summation involves a final tally, a resolution, whereas the open-ended process of accumulation—in which one thing follows upon another—is syntagmatic. Stein's own accumulation of china men, Spaniards, and little aunts is itself a product of the syntagmatic imagination, contextually disjunct yet contiguous, expanding to the all-inclusive "anybody." The infinite serial poem, then, is a predominantly syntagmatic method of counting, not a summation.

Stein's syntagmatic impulse refuses to acknowledge the numerals beyond "one and one." Creeley's "Numbers," however, "commissioned" for Robert Indiana's number serigraphs, adopts the decimal system as a framing device. The poem is accumulative, and so predominantly syntagmatic, but its systematic aspects distinguish it (as a portion of the *Pieces* text) as a finite series. As Robert von Hallberg points out, "Creeley meditates on the psychological valences of an arbitrary construct, the decimal system. He is interested in the way feelings have accrued to a purely formal set of conventions; the feelings have nothing to do with the signification permitted by the system, only with its structure."[86] Since Creeley has begun with an arbitrary construct, his series is at least partially predetermined. As a system of containment, the decimals function as a limit for the syntagmatic impulse of accumulation. Aleatory associations must contend with a relational, not metaphoric, system:

THREE

They come now with
one in the middle—
either side thus
another. Do they

> know who each other
> is or simply walk
> with this pivot between them.
> Here forms have possibility.

(CP 397)

"Three" is the first "closed" shape, the triangle; it is a pivot, or fulcrum—a precarious balancing act.

> When either this
> or that becomes
> choice, this fact
>
> of things enters.
> What had been
> agreed now
>
> alters to
> two and one,
> all ways.

(CP 397–98)

"One" is identity; "two" is union or opposition; "three" is choice or dialectic. Each numeral accrues dissimilar as well as diverse associations within the limit of a formal system. The finite series is itself a precarious balancing act between multiplicity and containment.

Creeley's "Numbers" is a closed system of relations within the larger infinite series *Pieces*. He remarks in his interview with Ekbert Faas, "I certainly use closed forms with very decisive patterns. . . . It's like Duncan's sense of enclosing the closed in the open" (EF 194–95). Each numeral poem, while bound to the decisive patterns of the decimal system, retains its autonomy. The association "Is a door / four— but / who enters" (CP 399) does not depend on a sequential reading of the series. At the same time, poems throughout the larger infinite series *Pieces* continue to interrelate:

> One, two,
> is the rule—
>
> from there to three
> simple enough.
>
> Now four
> makes the door
>
> back again
> to one and one.

(CP 440)

Creeley's way into the form of his "quatrains" reflects the comfort he feels in the number four, and the "foursquare circumstance" discussed in *A Quick Graph*. "Numbers," a finite series whose individual sections retain a degree of autonomy, can still be related to the larger setting of the infinite *Pieces*. Duncan's *Passages*, then, is an appropriate parallel.

Creeley's use of the decimal system in "Numbers" is structurally analogous to some programmatic aspects of the tone row in serial music. The conventions of the tone row typically result in the avoidance of any sense of tonal center—the hierarchy or dominance of one section or key over another. Composers such as Schönberg or Cage also avoid symmetry and periodicity of the kinds encountered in the symphony—neither *finale* nor tonic resolution is to be found. "Numbers," as a finite series, obstructs thematic progression or semantic resolution in a similar fashion.

The advantage of pitch to the composer is that it does not bear the burden, as the word must, of a signified. Consequently, programmatic features of serial music are more pronounced than those of the serial poem. D. M. Randel summarizes the possible permutations of the tone row: "The particular series (or the *row* or *set*) of the twelve pitch classes on which a composition is based has four principal forms: the original or prime form, the inversion of the original form (produced by inverting the intervals separating the adjacent elements of the row), the retrograde of the original form, and the retrograde of the inversion. Each of these principal forms of the row can be transposed to begin on any of the twelve pitch classes, with the result that there is a total of forty-eight forms."[87] Although this might seem an impossible task for the poet to make "good verse" of, Creeley's *In London* contains a brief example of what might be called lexical permutation:

> Small dreams of home.
> Small of home dreams.
> Dreams of small home.
> Home small dreams of.
>
> (CP 460)

Creeley's interest in a "foursquare circumstance" seems to combine with what he has termed "a repetitive relocation of phrasing, where words are curiously returned to an almost objective state of presence so that *they* speak rather than someone speaking with them. It is something that Gertrude Stein had been concerned with" (CTP 88). The semantic weight of each of the four lines shifts slightly, so that by the final line of the "quatrain" their signifieds have become curiously detached, or as Creeley says, the words begin to mouth themselves.

The transpositions of the tone row, as Randel describes it, are generally relevant to the serial poem. We have said with reference to the work of all three infinite serialists, Duncan, Blackburn, and now Creeley, that the reader can begin at any section. Since the serial poem, unlike the sonnet sequence, makes no effort to relocate the reader, one is then free to initially locate oneself.

A frequent complaint of the dislocated audience at a concert by John Cage or of the critics of "Numbers" is that, despite evidence of the systematic, there is an apparent randomness in these works. Certainly, the serial order delights in the coexistence of the programmatic,

> The serial diminish-
> ment or progression of
> the products which
> helped me remember:
> *nine times two is one-eight*
>           *nine times nine is eight-one—*
> at each end,
>
> move forward, backward,
> then, and the same
> numbers will occur.
>
> (CP 404–5)

with the aleatory,

> She is eight
> years old, holds
> a kitten, and
> looks out at me.
>
>           •
>
> Where are you.
> One table.
> One chair.
>
> (CP 402–3)

One ambition of Creeley's *A Day Book* is to record the "continuous *it is*," the experience of the present (MS 25). He admits, however, that "the ratio between conceptual units and the contents admissible in perception" is "something like 1 to 20,000 per second" (MS 55). *A Day Book* is itself thirty pages of writing on thirty *discontinuous* days. "Numbers" also engages the dynamics of the continuous and the disjunct. William Sylvester notes that "the continuum of numbers forces us to a disjunctive perception."[88] Amid the flux of fractional and irrational numbers on the continuous number line, we perceive the whole, rational numbers: $1°2°3°4°5°6°7°8°9°0$ (the title of a long poem by Creeley with illustrations by Arthur Okamura). "Numbers" is not a linear, continuous sequence but a series of disjunct perceptions organized according to an arbitrary system.

Creeley comments in one interview, "This friend in Detroit, Ken McClosky, wants 500 original postcards, one or two lines, which is already a thousand lines. I like the idea that they'll be dispersed."[89] *Thirty Things* includes this sample:

> Post Cards
>
> Each thing,
> you didn't even taste it.
>
> •
>
> A red flag
> on a red pole.
>
> •
>
> Heaven must spell something.
>
> •
>
> If the telephone rings,
> don't say anything.
>
> •
>
> A beating around
> the bush. Green
> growth.
>
> •
>
> Dad's mother's
> death.
>
> •
>
> Up on the top the
> space goes further than
> the eye can see. We're
> up here, calling
> over the hill.
>
> (CP 557)

We have discussed three book-length infinite serial poems: Duncan's *Passages*, Blackburn's *The Journals*, and *Pieces* itself. "Post Cards," although short, is nevertheless an infinite series as well. As Cage would point out, this poem is "a fluent component open at both ends."[90] Creeley could have written 493 more postcards from Bolinas, California, to add to these seven. Our ability to read these postcards in a "retrograde" or "transposed" order with, if anything, an enhanced appreciation of their relations, is particularly evident in so short a poem. A serial order, as opposed to a sequential progression, is indicated by Creeley's desire to "disperse" the postcards separately; they must then be contextually disjunct.

*Thirty Things* is "a house book or a domestic book. . . . The random poems come simply like they were."[91] There is a relational constant in the domesticity of items in *Thirty Things* and in "Post Cards" in particular: mealtime, a flagpole, the telephone, a garden. At the same time there is a random, if not wild, shift in emotional register from one section to another: from the mild displeasure of "you didn't even taste it" to the serious concerns of a child's recognition of mortality in "Dad's mother's / death" or "Heaven must spell something." Again, the success of the series seems to depend on the ability of the poet to check the syntagmatic impulse to list, or take inventory, with the necessity of a relational complexity.

In *A Day Book*, Creeley discusses the opposition in a series of photographs between the fixed moment and continuous movement: "Like Bob, yesterday, involved with a photograph that tracks movement, in the essentially static context of the photo-image—so that you 'anchor' the image by having some of its detail, anything, or one, or more, stay in very particularized containment of focus, very sharp; and then let the hand, head, whatever, move—and with strobes, you get a one, two, three phasing manifest in the image" (MS 35–36). Creeley claims in his introduction to *Mabel: A Story* that he wanted an arbitrary system of containment, "a focus, or frame, with which to work, and *one, two, three* seemed an interesting periodicity or phasing" (MS 6). All three texts in the volume have an arbitrary limit of thirty single-spaced pages. In *Thirty Things* we observe: an arbitrary limit (each poem is isolated on one of thirty pages); a particularized focus on the domestic; and yet the ability to "track" random movements or events. The placement of an infinite series, "Post Cards," within the predetermined limit, or frame, of *Thirty Things* is an interesting result of this structural tension.

The serial order of Creeley's later poetry and prose is a distinctly postmodern form of predominantly syntagmatic writing, an extension of Charles Olson's late-modernist projective verse. Creeley feels compelled to counterbalance the syntagmatic impulse with the relational complexities of particulars. This necessity is partly the influence of Williams and partly the physiological tension in the hand of the poet: "I think I grow tensions / like flowers" (CP 194). Although not procedural forms, his arbitrary systems of containment in "Numbers," *Thirty Things*, and *Mabel: A Story* mark in his later work an interest in the finite series. Perhaps as a response to the open form of *Pieces* or *In London*, Creeley investigates structures that allow him the ability both to track random movement *and* to retain a particularized containment of focus. Or as John Cage says, in an uppercase dictum to replace Olson's: "PERMISSION GRANTED. BUT NOT TO DO WHATEVER YOU WANT."[92]

# The Finite Serial Form

## The Dark House: Jack Spicer's Book of *Language*

The cover of the White Rabbit Press edition of Jack Spicer's *Language* (1965) is a facsimile of the July–September 1952 issue of *Language*, the Journal of the Linguistic Society of America. In a thick crayonlike scrawl, the poet's name partially obscures the coauthors and title of one article: David W. Reed and John L. Spicer, "Correlation Methods of Comparing Idiolects in a Transition Area."[1] From linguist to poet, from John to Jack, Spicer undergoes what Noam Chomsky might term a "transformation." By "defacing" his one professional publication in linguistics, Spicer gives identity to himself as a poet. Yet this transformation does not totally eclipse his concern for the structure of language. The grammar of poetry and the poetry of grammar (to appropriate a phrase from Roman Jakobson) is very much the subject of Spicer's book. *Language* as a work replicates in the relationship of the poet to his book the relationship of a speaker to the closed system that is his language. It is a finite structure, or *langue* (here the terms are Saussurean), within which an infinite number of transformations, *parole*, are possible. On the closed cover of his book, Spicer's study of language as system contends with the individual utterance of the poet.

If there is a "transformation" in the poetics of Jack Spicer, it occurs in 1957. In a "letter of admonition" to Robin Blaser which assumes the declarative posture of a manifesto, Spicer dismisses the ten years of his work prior to 1957 as "one night stands filled (the best of them) with their own emotions, but pointing nowhere."[2] (Appropriately, the post-

humous collection of these poems edited by Donald Allen is titled
*One Night Stand and Other Poems*.) All subsequent work by Spicer
would be composed in the form of "books." Allen and Blaser are
invited to weep over the possible books buried in the early work. These
poems fail in part because they are expressions of the poet's "anger" or
"frustration," like purple welts that appear following trauma to the
ego. But they also fail, in Spicer's opinion, because they attempt to
stand as isolate, "unique" expressions. Curiously, the model for
Spicer's mature work had been given to him ten years before. In a
boardinghouse at 2029 Hearst Street in Berkeley, 1947, Spicer was
witness to the composition of Robert Duncan's *Medieval Scenes*, the
first instance of a "dictated," "serial" poem. Spicer admits in this same
letter to Blaser: "The trick naturally is what Duncan learned years ago
and tried to teach us—not to search for the perfect poem but to let your
way of writing of the moment go along its own paths, explore and
retreat but never fully realized (confined) within the boundaries of one
poem" (CB 61). Spicer's practice in a serial, book form marks a period
of intense creativity: twelve books in eight years. But it is as inevitable
as it is salutary that his practice in serial form differs from Duncan's in
at least one crucial aspect. Duncan not only rejects the boundaries of a
single poem, but all boundaries—formal, aesthetic, political, and
metaphysical. The resulting serial form of *Passages*, for instance, is
*infinite*. Spicer, however, posits the limiting presence of the book—the
presence, as I will show, of the ghost of Mallarmé. This limiting
presence, while not interfering with the serial form of the poems,
makes for a *finite* structure.

Spicer's only statements on the serial poem occur in the "Vancouver
Lectures," excerpted in *Caterpillar* and *The Poetics of the New American Poetry*, but nowhere in print in their entirety.[3] Under the guard of
his literary executor, Robin Blaser, or withdrawn by the reluctant
ghost of Spicer himself, the lectures are as difficult to apprehend as
Spicer's transparent spooks. But this much is clear: Spicer's serial
poems are finite forms. Intricately structured, his books nevertheless
"occur" without forewarning, as might an apparition:

> A serial poem, in the first place, has the book as its unit as the individual
> poem has the poem as its unit, the actual poem that you write at the
> actual time, the single poem. And there is a dictation of form as well as a
> dictation of the individual form of the individual poem. And you have to
> go into a serial poem not knowing what the hell you're doing. That's the
> first thing. You have to be tricked into it. . . . What I'm saying is you have a
> unit, one unit the poem, which is taken by dictation, and another unit,
> the book, which is a more structured thing. But it should be structured by
> dictation and not by the poet. (NAP 233)

Dictation is Spicer's private *ballo in maschera*: an unverifiable, seriocomic hoax, "a game like Yeats' spooks or Blake's sexless seraphim" (CB 51). But the displacement of agency from the poet-as-maker to a Yeatsian ghost is a spectral insurance policy against predetermined form. The poet enters the ballroom of the serial poem not knowing the steps to the waltz; he cannot preside over the ball because he is not wearing his crown of sonnets.

The book is the "more structured thing" and becomes for Spicer the unit of composition. He admonishes Robin Blaser: "There is really no single poem. . . . Poems should echo and reecho against each other. They should create resonances. They cannot live alone any more than we can" (CB 61). The resonance, or correspondence, of poems within the closed system of the Spicerian book can be distinguished from Duncan's open sprinkling of *Passages* across several volumes, in "a series that extends in an area larger than my work in them."[4] This resonance between one poem and another, Spicer says, is a product of a combinatory structure: "Things fit together. We knew that—it is the principle of magic. Two inconsequential things can combine together to become a consequence. This is true of poems too. A poem is never to be judged by itself alone. A poem is never by itself alone" (CB 61). The combinative function in the serial form produces from two or more inconsequential (i.e., not "perfect," not anthologizable) sections an unknown (not predetermined) consequence. Spicer indicates that this unknown is "magic"; Mallarmé considers it to be the "third aspect" that emerges from the exact relationship between two images. The system of correspondences occurs within the "closed book," which is a prominent symbol in Mallarmé's poetry ("Mes bouquins refermés sur le nom de Paphos" [My books, closed on the name of Paphos])[5] and the product of his symbolic method as well: "The inner structures of a book of verse must be inborn; in this way, chance will be totally eliminated and the poet will be absent. From each theme, itself predestined, a given harmony will be born somewhere in the parts of the total poem and take its proper place within the volume; because, for every sound, there is an echo."[6] For both Mallarmé and Spicer, the book is a closed structure within which one poem asserts its position in resonance with the others; its place cannot be assigned by any external thematic progression.

Duncan's analogue for the infinite serial form of *Passages* is the ever-shifting mobile; Spicer's analogue for the finite series is the haunted house. The house is a closed structure within which there are several contiguous rooms. The haunted house that one enters is the book, each room is an individual poem, and the furnishings that Spicer's spooks move about are the words of the poem. Spicer takes us on a metalinguistic tour of the finite series in his "Vancouver Lectures": "It's as if you go into a room, a dark room, the light is turned on for a minute, then it's turned off again, and then you go into a different room where a light is turned on and turned off" (NAP 233). The closed structure of the house situates each room through a system of correspondences: because the rooms are contiguous, the couch or divan knocking against the wall in one room will resonate in another. But the light from no one room is allowed to enter another. Each individual poem retains its contextual autonomy, never illuminated by the thematic or narrative fixtures of preceding sections. The passive voice haunts Spicer's description: the light is turned on and off, but not by the poet. Spicer suspects that "if you can get focused on the individual poem you have a better chance of dictation." The haunting of the house, in Spicer's parlance, assures that the structure of his finite series, however intricate, will not be predetermined, nor will the composition of one section be allowed to inform the next.[7]

The length of a section is a significant denominator in Spicer's consideration of the serial form: "When you're writing a long poem not composed of separate parts but a long poem say five or ten pages, well naturally you can't write a five or ten-page poem if you're a good poet within a humanly recognizable period of one sitting because the next morning you've had great ideas of what the poem means and it's you not the poem talking" (NAP 233). Partitioning, "the take from one room to another, from one frame to another," and the compositional time limit of one sitting, preclude in the Spicerian series the "great ideas" or developmental superstructure that govern the epic. The serial form is a postmodern halfway house for the addicts of the single lyric's perfectionism or the epic's totalitarian coherence.

Edgar Allan Poe, in "The Philosophy of Composition" (1846), makes a similar criticism of the long poem from a reader's viewpoint: "If any literary work is too long to read at one sitting, we must be content to dispense with the immensely important effect derivable from unity of impression—for, if two sittings be required, the affairs of the world interfere, and every thing like totality is at once destroyed."[8] After one sitting, the poet's own ideas about the composition of the poem, for Spicer, or the reader's experience of the world, for Poe, break the hermetic seal of the poem as closed system. Poe concludes: "What we term a long poem is, in fact, merely a succession of brief ones—that is to say, of brief poetical effects. It is needless to demonstrate that a poem is such, only inasmuch as it intensely excites, by elevating, the soul; and all intense excitements are, through a psychal necessity, brief." Poe argues his preference for the perfectly made short lyric against the inevitably prosaic "depressions" of the Miltonic epic. Spicer's serial form, with its autonomous and yet resonant sections, is a postmodern solution to the dilemma of the long poem; the light flicking on and off produces a series of brief poetical effects which exclude the poet's morning hangover of reconsideration.

Poe is America's first antiromantic. He rejects "ecstatic intuition" for a predetermined method of composition, "with the precision and rigid consequence of a mathematical problem." As W. C. Williams claims, "His whole insistence has been upon method, in opposition to a nameless rapture over nature."[9] Spicer's method, the dictation of the series to the poet-as-medium, prevents an a priori consideration of the poem's form; however, dictation also rejects by its displacement of the poetic ego the romantic process of composition by, in Poe's words, "a species of fine frenzy."[10]

Spicer's book *Language* is composed of seven closely related series. The first series, *Thing Language*, is an objectification of language, asserting the hermeticism of the poem as an object not dependent on either poet or audience for its presence. The first section obliterates the "listener" in a sea of static:

> This ocean, humiliating in its disguises
> Tougher than anything.
> No one listens to poetry. The ocean
> Does not mean to be listened to. A drop
> Or crash of water. It means
> Nothing.
> It
> Is bread and butter
> Pepper and salt. The death
> That young men hope for. Aimlessly
> It pounds the shore. White and aimless signals. No
> One listens to poetry.
>
> (CB 217)

The ocean corresponds with, though it is no metaphor for, the transmitter of those messages that are the poem. Yet for the listener, its messages are "white and aimless signals" that mean nothing. Perhaps if the ocean itself shouted practical warnings, SLIPPERY ROCKS, KEEP OFF or STAY BACK FROM EDGE OF CLIFF, we would heed its messages. No one listens to poetry, Spicer says, but poetry, like the ocean, persists. This is not the ego of the poet decrying his lack of a readership but the annihilation of the necessity of a reader. The ocean swallows all ego.

In the second section of *Thing Language*, Spicer goes to work on the poet, crossing the wires of two metaphors for the poet's role:

> The trouble with comparing a poet with a radio is that radios
>     don't develop scar-tissue. The tubes burn out, or with a
>     transistor, which most souls are, the battery or diagram
>     burns out replaceable or not replaceable, but not like that
>     punchdrunk fighter in the bar. The poet
> Takes too many messages. The right to the ear that floored him
>     in New Jersey. The right to say that he stood six rounds
>     with a champion.
> Then they sell beer or go on sporting commissions, or, if the
>     scar tissue is too heavy, demonstrate in a bar where the
>     invisible champions might not have hit him. Too many of
>     them.
> The poet is a radio. The poet is a liar. The poet is a
>     counterpunching radio.
> And those messages (God would not damn them) do not even
>     know they are champions.
>
> (CB 218)

The system of correspondences, poet–radio–punchdrunk fighter, generates a series of exquisitely senseless (i.e., lacking signifieds) and positively germane syntagmatic crosses: the poet takes too many messages.

Roland Barthes describes the effect of the double metaphor in Georges Bataille's novel *Histoire de l'oeil* (The Story of the Eye): "Everything changes once we disturb the correspondence of the two chains; if instead of pairing objects and actions according to laws of kinship (to break an egg, to poke out an eye), we dislocate the association by assigning each of its terms to different lines; in short, if we permit ourselves to break an eye and to poke out an egg; in relation to the two parallel metaphors (of eye and tear), the syntagm then becomes *crossed*, for the link it proposes will seek from the two series not complementary but distant terms."[11] Barthes proposes we call "*metonymy* this transfer of meaning from one chain to the other, at different levels of the *metaphor*."[12] The two chains establish relations of contiguity, not similarity: a term from the first, "counterpunching," attaches itself to a term from the second, "radio." If the cross-wired phrases are sense-short, it is because there is no deducible *signified*; the lines of the two *signifiers* are engaged in a closed circuit. But the effect is germane to Spicer's poetics, which is also Mallarmé's, of a book from which the poet will be absent. Spicer comments on his monophonic, and non-aural, system in the "Vancouver Lectures": "I don't think the messages are for the poet any more than a radio program is for the radio set. And I think that the radio set doesn't really worry about whether anyone is listening to it or not, and neither does the poet" (NAP 232). *Thing Language* is the message alone, the closed circuit of signifiers; there is no necessity either to appease the poet's ego in displays of barroom bravado or to please the listeners with lies or practical advice for right living—or ducking right crosses.

Roman Jakobson provides this schematization for the "constitutive factors" of any speech event, to which I have added parenthetically the functions he associates with each factor:

CONTEXT
(referential: informative)

(poetic/aesthetic:
for its own sake)
ADDRESSER————MESSAGE————ADDRESSEE
(emotive: toward the addresser)          (conative: toward the addressee)

CONTACT
(phatic: are all channels working?)

CODE
(metalingual: are we speaking the same language?)

Jakobson then summarizes his findings:

> The ADDRESSER sends a MESSAGE to the ADDRESSEE. To be operative the message requires a CONTEXT referred to ("referent" in another, somewhat ambiguous, nomenclature), seizable by the addressee, and either verbal or capable of being verbalized; a CODE fully, or at least partially, common to the addresser and the addressee (or in other words, to the encoder and decoder of the message); and, finally, a CONTACT, a physical channel and psychological connection between the addresser and the addressee, enabling both of them to enter and stay in communication.[13]

Although no verbal message fulfills only one function, "the verbal structure of a message depends primarily on the predominant function." For the poem, "the set (Einstelung) toward the MESSAGE as such, focus on the message for its own sake, is the POETIC function of language."[14] As Jonathan Culler reminds us: "By 'message' Jakobson does not, of course, mean 'propositional content' (that is stressed by the referential function of language) but simply the utterance itself as a linguistic form. In Mukarovsky's words, 'the function of poetic language consists in the maximum foregrounding of the utterance.' "[15] In the section of Spicer's *Thing Language* just discussed, the "foregrounding" of poetic language consists of the "ungrammatical" crossing of the two metaphors: the poet as radio, and the poet as punchdrunk fighter.

The predominant lyric mode, if such a thing exists, should conform to Jakobson's schematization of the speech event: the poet is the addresser; the reader is the addressee; the contact is a printed book; the "set" is toward the message itself. The analysis of Greek monody by W. R. Johnson, a classicist, is in accordance with Jakobson's rule. Johnson categorizes lyric modes according to pronomial structure. The predominant mode is "the I-You poem, in which the poet addresses or pretends to address his thoughts and feelings to another person—in William Wordsworth's phrase to Samuel Taylor Coleridge, 'as if to thee alone'; in this category the person addressed (whether actual or fictional) is a metaphor for readers of the poëm and becomes a symbolic mediator, a conductor between the poet and each of his readers and listeners. This pronomial patterning (*ego-tu, ego-vos*) I take to be the classic form for lyric solo, or, as the Greeks came to call it, monody."[16] Johnson considers the I-You, with its internalized reduplication of the speech event, to be the predominant mode of lyric from the ancients (Sappho and Catullus) to the romantics. Not unexpectedly, it is Mallarmé who is the first insurgent to disrupt the I-You lyric with an "impersonality that has increasingly become the characteristic mode of modern lyric," and for whom the poetic ego has become "irrelevant."[17]

In *Thing Language*, Spicer reinforces this Mallarméan insurgency. The addresser is no longer the poet or his persona but, for Spicer, the absent, unknown, outside spooks—the transmitters of the message in a white ocean of signals. The addressee is not Wordsworth's intimate "thee alone," but the nameless radioland listeners—who have apparently gone out for the day, leaving the unperturbed radio blaring in the room. The poet, as radio, shifts from the position of addresser to the contact, the "physical channel" between the absent addresser and addressee. The message, however, which the poet as "receiver" takes on the ear, remains pretty much what Jakobson claims it to be: not propositional content, warning, or entertainment, but the poem itself, *thing language*. Or as Louis Zukofsky says, "A poem as object . . . experienced as an object."[18] Spicer's phatic radio-in-a-room, by erasing addresser and addressee, and by relegating the poet to the channel of contact, very nearly does what Jakobson claims can't be: the "set" of

Spicer's *Language* is so predominantly tuned to the message that it appears to be the only fully operational function. Spicer's radio is an attempt to eliminate *parole*, individual utterance, and to broadcast only *la langue*, language as system, "the utterance itself as linguistic form."

When Spicer claims in the "Vancouver Lectures" that "language is a complex system that involves words," and that it is "a structure that hasn't yet been described," and most important, that "it's doubtful if any two people have the same language" (NAP 229–30), he speaks "as a professional linguist" aware of Saussure's distinction between *langue*, system, and *parole*, individual utterance. One could say that the final four series in *Language* (*Transformations, Morphemics, Phonemics*, and *Graphemics*) describe the abstract system of relations known as *la langue*. The linguistic headings of the four series demarcate that "more structured thing," the book. The four series squelch individual utterance, the persona or ego of the poet; each generates, however, its own particularized linguistic form.

*Transformations*: the process of converting a syntactic construction into a semantically equivalent construction according to the rules shown to generate the syntax of the language. (*The American Heritage Dictionary*)

In "Transformations I," Spicer converts an individual utterance, the accusation of the poets Robert Duncan and George Stanley that he deliberately exacerbates their rivalry, into a basic sentence structure.[19] The interpersonal rivalry is converted into a system of syntactical relations:

> They say "he need (present) enemy (plural)"
> I am not them. This is the first transformation.
> They say "we need (present) no enemy (singular)" No enemy in
>     the universe is theirs worth having. We is an intimate
>     pronoun which shifts its context almost as the I blinks at it.
>     Those
> Swans we saw in the garden coming out of the water we hated
>     them. "Out of place," you said in passing. Those swans and
>     I (a blink in context), all out of place we hated you.
> He need (present) enemy (plural) and now it is the swans and
>     me against you
> Everything out of place
> (And now another blink of moment) the last swan back in
>     place. We
> Hated them.
>
> (CB 232)

The major transformation of Spicer's career, from the earlier solo lyrics to the serial poems of *The Collected Books*, is prompted by "a need for a poetry that would be more than the expression of my hatreds and desires" (CB 51). "Transformations I" is, ironically, successful: the poet desires to wring the neck of the romantic swan, ego. He accomplishes this murderous little endeavor by the transformations, or "blinks" as he calls them, which make the rivalries of "I" and "you," "he" and "they," ridiculously indeterminate: "We is an intimate / pronoun which shifts its context almost as the I blinks at it"; or "now it is the swans and / me against you." In the basic syntactical constructions of *la langue*, shifts in pronomial relations are irrelevant; only in *parole*, individual utterance, does pronomial definition, the identification of addresser and addressee, become important. Spicer stifles the accusations of his rivals by squeezing the windpipe of the Wordsworthian "to thee alone." Who, in the final line, are "we," and who are "them"?

Spicer, as the host of a 1949 KPFA (Berkeley) radio program, the "Most Educational Folk-Song Program West of the Pecos," persuaded his friend Jim Herndon, after a sufficient quantity of red wine, "to make terrible changes in some revered 'authentic' version" of a folk song (CB 375). "Transformations II" performs such an operation on the grammar of the folk song:

> "In Scarlet Town where I was born
> There was a fair maid dwelling."
> We make up a different language for poetry
> And for the heart—ungrammatical.
>
> (CB 233)

The second line of this folk song, which promises to be a love lyric, is "ungrammatical" because of its syntactic inversion and the redundancy of "where" and "there." These are deviations from standard English (a language no one speaks), required by the poetic strictures of meter and rhyme; or, in a medieval sense, the grammar of passion, for another or for language itself, governs the lyric. A Chomskyan transformation to the more basic, yet semantically equivalent, syntactical construction (without the complex verb) would be: A fair maid dwelled in Scarlet Town where I was born.

Transformations are one method by which Spicer establishes correspondences: "what makes it possible for a poet to translate real objects, to bring them across language as easily as he can bring them across time" (CB 34). Scarlet Town becomes the Americanized Charlotte; Jack Spicer, host of KPFA's radio program, rewrites folk song history. As Jim Herndon claims, "Jack wanted association, *not* authenticity" (CB 375). "It is not that the name of the town changes," the poem concludes,

> But that the syntax changes. This is older than towns.
> Troy was a baby when Greek sentence structure emerged. This
>     was the real Trojan Horse.
> The order changes. The Trojans
> Having no idea of true or false syntax and having no recorded
>     language
> Never knew what hit them.

> (CB 233)

The Trojans meet their Nemesis, not in the shield of Achilles, but in the inexhaustible phalanx of Greek syntactical forms. Their culture is wiped out—and this is less fanciful than it seems—by an epic; they are struck by the *Iliad* much as Spicer's poet is floored by too many messages. The *Iliad* is the first recorded folk song in Western culture, a correspondence brought across time.

"Transformations III" works its magic on the nursery rhyme, concluding in a sort of self-portrait:

> This is the crab-god shiny and bright
>     who sunned by day and wrote by night
>     And lived in the house that Jack built.
> This is the end of it, very dear friend, this
>     is the end of us.

> (CB 233)

All three poems in the *Transformations* series clamp shut with the unmistakable rhetoric of poetic closure. The swans get it in I; the Trojans, like the Eskimo village wiped out by an earthquake ("a poem about the death of John F. Kennedy") in *Thing Language* (CB 221), get it in II; and last, the poet and his mockingly addressed "very dear friend" get it in III. In this series, the poet as addresser, friends and enemies as addressees, are struck out on three pitches. Transformational grammar, the correspondence of syntactical constructions, is a closed system of relations.

*Morphemics*: the study of linguistic units of relatively stable meaning that cannot be divided into smaller meaningful parts. (*The American Heritage Dictionary*)

The third poem of the *Morphemics* series begins with an example of this irreducible linguistic unit:

> Moon,
>           cantilever of sylabbles
> If it were spelled "mune" it would not cause madness.
> Un-
> Worldly. Put
> Your feet on the ground. Mon-
> Ey doesn't grow on trees. Great
> Knocker of the present shape of things. A tide goes past like
>      wind.
> No normal growth like a tree the moon stays there
> And its there is our where
> "Where are you going, pretty maid?"
> "I'm going milking, sir," she said.
> Our image shrinks to a morpheme, an -ing word. Death
> Is an image of sylables.
>
>                                                              (CB 235)

The irreducible morpheme corresponds, on a linguistic level, to "the thing itself." Spicer comments, in a letter from *After Lorca*, "I would like the moon in my poems to be a real moon, one which could be suddenly covered with a cloud that has nothing to do with the poem—a moon utterly independent of images. The imagination pictures the real. I would like to point to the real, disclose it, to make a poem that has no sound in it but the pointing of a finger" (CB 33–34). Folk wisdom has attached the image of a man's face to the moon with such adhesion, and so cloaked it in "madness," that the image has become semantically bonded to the morpheme: lunacy. Spicer's celestial satellite is "covered" and "disclosed" as the contexts of the poem shift: the maid a-milking is "a cloud that has nothing to do with the poem," having at best a correspondent whiteness. Images, metaphors, have so occluded the moon that even a romantic poet such as Wallace Stevens feels, in "The Man on the Dump," that he must salvage it:

> Everything is shed; and the moon comes up as the moon
> (All its images are in the dump) and you see
> As a man (not like an image of a man),
> You see the moon rise in the empty sky.[20]

The "man on the moon" and the surrounding "constellations" must be dissolved. No such images adhere, in Spicer's poem, to a moon brought to the verge of not-meaning: "mune." The twice misspelled "syllable" passes in front of the moon, perhaps to remind us that the morpheme is constantly threatened by "sylabbic" babbling which has no stable meaning. No image can be attached to a submorphemic syllable— hence "Death / Is an image of syllables"—and it is to this point that Spicer brings that favorite romantic object. His moon, as a real object, is utterly independent of images; his language, also a thing, always reminds us of itself *as language.*

> *Phonemics*: the study of the smallest units of speech that distinguish one utterance or word from another in a given language. (*The American Heritage Dictionary*)

The "m" of "mat" and the "b" of "bat" are phonemes; the "a" of "mat" and the "i" of "mit" are also phonemes. Thus:

$$\begin{array}{ccc} \text{mat} & — & \text{mit} \\ | & & | \\ \text{bat} & — & \text{X} \end{array}$$

where X is home plate, as every home has its welcome mat. So, a basic lesson in phonemics discovers Spicer's ruling passion: baseball, the game with a rule book larger than the Gutenberg Bible. The last section of *Phonemics* makes this correspondence explicit:

> The emotional disturbance echoes down the canyons of the
>     heart.
> Echoes there—sounds cut off—merely phonemes. A ground-
>     rules double. You recognize them by pattern. Try.
>
> (CB 238)

Spicer recognizes phonemic patterns in these echoes and so, as Mallarmé does, hears "the inner structure of a book of verse . . . because, for every sound, there is an echo." With the acuity of a big-league umpire, Spicer perceives those smallest distinctions with semantic, or poetic, effect: ball or strike, safe or out. Images and metaphors *connect* objects in a hazy similarity—the way diamonds become ovals if you file down the edges. "Mit" and "bat" *correspond* in a manner that exploits their phonemic difference; they share a "third aspect," at first unknown, the mat or plate that the poet comes up to—the system that is baseball, with its rule book, or language, with its grammar.

In the first poem of the series, a phonemic distinction establishes a correspondence, defeating the conventional employment of an image:

> No love deserves the death it has. An archipelago
> Rocks cropping out of ocean. Seabirds shit on it. Live out their
>     lives on it.
> What was once a mountain.
>
> (CB 236)

The first sentence, comfortable in its self-commiseration, is jolted by the archipelago, itself the product of some violent upheaval. Seabirds shit on an archipelago, but the referent of "it" in the second line could as easily be "love," which doesn't deserve the treatment it gets. The phonemic shift, love-live, is the catalyst, familiar to the lyric: "Vivamus, mea Lesbia, atque amemus" (Let us live, my Lesbia, and let us love), Catullus's sweetheart, in the end, a common prostitute. Could the shattered, shipwrecked image be "love on the rocks"? The once gaping-wide channel between "love" and "an archipelago" closes on us like the Symplegades; we find that, in fact, the two correspond. A mountain does not deserve the death it has. With a "logic" equalled only by the maritime poetry of Hart Crane, the seabirds, last on the scene, supply the "third aspect" of the love-live phonemic shift: death is shit.

The third and fourth poems answer the riddle: what do the Bell System, linguistics, and Spicer's *Language* have in common? AT&T gets the call first:

> On the tele-phone (distant sound) you sounded no distant than
>     if you were talking to me in San Francisco on the telephone
>     or in a bar or in a room. Long
> Distance calls. They break sound
> Into electrical impulses and put it back again. . . .
>
> (CB 237)

The poet, as *receiver*, must construct from the emotional impulses sent to him a language system, the poem, as the Bell System constructs from electrical impulses a long distance call:

> Your voice
>         consisted of sounds that I had
> To route to phonemes, then to bound and free morphemes, then
>     to syntactic structures. . . .

AT&T is:

> An electric system.
> "Gk. ἠλέκτρον, amber, also shining metal; allied to
> ἠλέκτωρ, gleaming."

But then, in the fourth poem, language is also systematic:

> Believe me. Linguistics is divided like Graves' mythology of
>     mythology, a triple goddess—morphology, phonology, and
>     syntax.
>
> (CB 237)

Spicer's *Language*, an enactment of the route from phonemes to mor-
phemes to syntactical structures, is itself an intricately structured,
closed system: from poem to series to book. Such a service is not free
of charge. Though these two poems transmit a message of erotic
longing, the poet as *amator* is absent—"This is no nightingale." These
are:

> Tough lips that cannot quite make the sounds of love
> The language
> Has so misshaped them.
>
> (CB 237)

*Graphemics*: the study of the letters of an alphabet, or the sum of letters
and letter combinations that represent a single phoneme. (*The American
Heritage Dictionary*)

Spicer's *Graphemics* is a semiological system: graphemes and traffic
lights are signifiers; graphemes, cars, and pedestrians crash together at
intersections to make words or to kill people; or, as Spicer said on his
deathbed, "My vocabulary did this to me" (CB 325). The conjunction
of semiology, poetry, and the traffic system occurs in the third poem of
the series:

> Let us tie the strings on this bit of reality.
> Graphemes. Once wax now plastic, showing the ends. Like a
>     red light.
> One feels or sees limits.
> They are warning graphemes but also meaning graphemes
>     because without the marked ends of the shoelace or the
>     traffic signal one would not know how to tie a shoe or cross
>     a street—which is like making a sentence.
> Crossing a street against the light or tying a shoe with a granny
>     knot is all right. Freedom, in fact, providing one sees or
>     feels the warning graphemes. Let them snarl at you then and you
>     snarl back at them. You'll be dead sooner
> But so will they. They
> Disappear when you die.
>
> (CB 240)

Graphemes are "strings" laced by an arbitrary convention to a real
shoe. We use them, claims Spicer in a letter from *After Lorca*, "to drag
the real into the poem. They are what we hold on with, nothing else.
They are as valuable in themselves as rope with nothing to be tied to"
(CB 25). Spicer opposes the orphic unity of word and being; he is,
rather, a hermetic poet, for whom graphemes and all components of a

language, because they are arbitrarily connected to things in the world, are "valuable in themselves" when made into a closed structure of relations.[21] The antiromantic poet joins the semiologist, whose domain, as Jonathan Culler says in explaining Saussure's thought, "is that of conventional signs, where there is no intrinsic or 'natural' reason why a particular *signifiant* and *signifié* should be linked. In the absence of intrinsic one-to-one connections, he cannot attempt to explain individual signs in piecemeal fashion but must account for them by revealing the internally coherent system from which they derive."[22] Because graphemes are arbitrarily, not intrinsically, significant, they "disappear" when we do. However, they form an internally coherent system of relations whose warnings or "limits" we are free to transgress, in crossing the street or making a sentence, at our peril—the extreme consequences being, of course, death and illegibility.

In the fifth poem of the series, the legibility of the traffic sign, the rules in the game of love, and the grammar of poetry collide:

> You turn red and green like a traffic light. And in between them
>     orange—a real courting color. Neither
> The pedestrian or the driver knows whether he is going to hit
>     the other. Orange
> Being a courting color
> Doesn't last long. The pedestrian
> And the driver go back to the red and green colors of their
>     existence. Unhit
> Or hit (it hardly matters.)
> When we walked through the Broadway tunnel I showed you
>     signs above green lights which said "ON A RED LIGHT
>     STOP YOUR CAR AND TURN OFF YOUR IGNITION."
>     On an orange light—
> But their was not an orange light
> In the whole tunnel.
>
> (CB 241)

Roland Barthes explains the semiological peculiarity of the traffic system: "The Highway Code must be immediately and unambiguously legible if it is to prevent accidents; therefore, it eliminates the oppositions which need the longest time to be understood, either because they are not reducible to proper paradigms (equipollent oppositions) or because they offer a choice of two signifieds for a single signifier (suppressible oppositions)."[23] The orange light is as close to an ambiguous signal as the traffic system gets; a "warning grapheme," it nevertheless "courts" accidents. On this two A.M. walk from Gino &

Carlo's Bar to a basement apartment in Polk Gulch, the poet's companion (an I-You lyric, this one) is in an unambiguous mood—"their" (grammatically jaywalking) are no courting lights in the tunnel of love tonight. Spicer recognizes that both linguistic and nonverbal signs, when language approaches its poetic function or when two people approach one another in courtship, are not unambiguously legible. As he notes in *Transformations*, the language of poetry is "ungrammatical" (CB 233); unlike the Highway Code, it is polysemic. The poetic function, Barthes says, is a "defiance of the usual distribution *syntagm/system*, and it is probably around this transgression that a great number of creative phenomena are situated."[24] Or, as the jaywalking Jack Spicer says of the warning graphemes, "Let them snarl at you then and you / snarl back at them."

W. R. Johnson discovers the crypt of the I-You lyric in the poetry of Mallarmé; Roland Barthes, as chief inspector, places Mallarmé alone at the scene of the "death of the author"; Gerald Bruns names *Un Coup de dés* as the first instance of a hermetic, closed book. Jack Spicer, as an American Mallarmé in a San Francisco Giants cap, plays a similar position in our league. The poet-as-radio achieves what Johnson regrets and Barthes celebrates: the absence of the poet from the book of verse. The serial poem *Language* is a significant example of the closed book, a hermetic system of relations. The poet Jack Spicer and the professional linguist John L. Spicer conduct a correspondence; the echoes of the inner structures of Mallarmé's book correspond with the internally coherent system of Saussure's semiotics. The house that Jack built is a haunted house, and it has been boarded up; but if we dare to enter it, the radio will play and the lights, from room to room, will go on and off.

## The Subway's Iron Circuit:
## George Oppen's *Discrete Series*

When The Objectivist Press was inaugurated at the Brooklyn apartment of George Oppen in 1933, a few blocks from the site where Walt Whitman first printed with his own hands a book called *Leaves of Grass*, it was agreed that the authors would pay for the publication of their own work, alternative financing being unavailable. The advantage to George Oppen, acting as editor and publisher of his *Discrete*

*Series* in 1934, was that this slender green book of thirty-seven pages was made as he wanted it: one poem, however short, to a page.

In an interview, George and Mary Oppen frequently answer for one another, finish sentences the other has begun, and occasionally speak the same words in unison; so it can be assumed that Mary registers George's discontent with the "poetical economy" with which New Directions reprinted his first book in *The Collected Poems of George Oppen*: "Well, Jay Laughlin just got a little bit too Scotch and wouldn't give a whole page to each poem and the way they've been reprinted makes some people think that if there are three little bits on a page, that's one poem, whereas that wasn't the way the *Discrete Series* was printed."[25] This edition, black and white as an old TV, emphasizes a commercial publisher's parsimony and not the true economy of words which William Carlos Williams marks in the title of his 1934 review. The serial form of the book is the unfortunate casualty of the confusion over which "lumps, chunks,"[26] as Oppen calls his verse, constitute poems and which do not. Like the steel cables that are at once the structural support and the aesthetic appeal of the Brooklyn and Golden Gate bridges (landmarks of two of Oppen's *residencie en la terra*), an essential structural tension of the serial poem occurs between the series as relational system and the autonomy of each poem: the whole must act as a taut mechanism, just as the parts must have their independent sway. Oppen chose not to number his poems consecutively, 1 through 31, as Robert Duncan has, until recently, numbered his *Passages*; so it is critical to the book as a discrete series that his decision be respected to isolate the poems, each on its own page, as Creeley has done in his *Thirty Things*.

In an interview with L. S. Dembo, Oppen stresses the structural tension between the series and the individual poem as he defines the title of his book:

> My book, of course, was called *Discrete Series*. That's a phrase in mathematics. A pure mathematical series would be one in which each term is derived from the preceding term by a rule. A discrete series is a series of terms each of which is empirically derived, each one of which is empirically true. And this is the reason for the fragmentary character of those poems. I was attempting to construct a meaning by empirical statements, by imagist statements.

> Q. Each imagist statement being essentially discrete from the statement that followed or preceded it?

> A. Yes, that meaning is also implicit in the word "discrete." The poems are a series, yet each is separate, and it's true that they are discrete in that

sense; but I had in mind specifically the meaning to the mathematician—
a series of empirically true terms.[27]

Oppen attempts to "construct a meaning" as one might build a bridge:
should he impose a too rigid "rule," his serial structure will snap in a
high wind. Each poem is neither derived from the preceding nor does it
generate the next—each must be, as he says, "empirically true." This
discretion is also contained in Jack Spicer's house-room analogy for
serial structure: each room has its functional place in the house as a
whole, yet the poet discretely douses the light from each room before
proceeding.

In a letter to Rachel Blau DuPlessis, Oppen makes a late addendum:

I thought too late—30 years too late—that the fly leaf should have carried
the inscription

14, 28, 32, 42

which is a discrete series: the names of the stations on the east side
subway.[28]

These four numbers are a mathematical example of a discrete series,
but they also function analogously: the stops on a subway line which
they indicate offer, as one rises out of the dark tunnel onto the cross-
streets of Lower Manhattan, a series of empirically derived observations. Hart Crane shares Oppen's experience of New York in the section of *The Bridge* (1930) which he calls "The Tunnel":

> The intent escalator lifts a serenade
> Stilly
> Of shoes, umbrellas, each eye attending its shoe, then
> Bolting outright somewhere above where streets
> Burst suddenly in rain. . . .[29]

For Crane as well as Oppen, the enormous metropolis offers itself to
the individual view only in discrete parts.

After the neo-Jamesian proem to the book, whose source in Henry
James's "The Story in It" has been perhaps too thoroughly
researched— down to the additional *e* that clings to Oppen's version of
Maude Blessingbourne's surname—the second poem of the series offers a more characteristic example of Oppen's mechanism, if one can
find the machine in the rubble of his syntax:

> White. From the
> Under arm of T

    The red globe.

    Up
    Down. Round
    Shiny fixed
    Alternatives

    From the quiet

    Stone floor . . .

                         (CP 3)

Charles Tomlinson, the British ally of the Objectivists, first suspected that the empirical object (which this poem does not, finally, represent) is the control handle of a circa 1929 elevator.[30] The scene could easily be the floor of the New York Stock Exchange, white ticker tape strewn about, strangely quiet after the stocks, their precipitous rise complete, had suddenly crashed: "Up / Down." My own ignorance of economics, by which all stocks appear enigmatic alternatives, seems to support this interpretation. But the more salient question is, do we need to know what the referential object of this verbless poem is, and if we entirely satisfy our curiosity upon learning what it is, is the poem then a good one? William Carlos Williams, in his review of *Discrete Series*, answers this question in the following extended argument. The importance of a poem

> cannot be in what the poem says, since in that case the fact that it is a poem would be a redundancy. The importance lies in what the poem *is*. Its existence as a poem is of first importance, a technical matter, as with all facts, compelling the recognition of a mechanical structure. A poem which does not arouse respect for the technical requirements of its own mechanics may have anything you please painted all over it or on it in the way of meaning but it will for all that be as empty as a man made of wax or straw.
>
> It is the acceptable fact of a poem as a mechanism that is the proof of its meaning and this is as technical a matter as in the case of any other machine. Without the poem being a workable mechanism in its own right, a mechanism which arises from, while at the same time constitutes the meaning of, the poem as a whole, it will remain ineffective. And what it says regarding the use or worth of that particular piece of "propaganda" which it is detailing will never be convincing. (MP 267–68)

The preceding statement has been brought to you by a counterrevolutionary modernist intent on eradicating the weed of romantic organicism. Oppen is not so interested in compelling our recognition of some machine in an urban landscape, whether elevator, ticker-tape machine, or as one critic rather perversely suggested, a shower stall, as compelling our recognition of the poem itself, the series itself, as mechanical structure. As critics, we would be a good deal too smug to think that, having exhumed Maude from the collected tales of Henry James or, like urban archaeologists tunneling under New York City, having unearthed the elevator car, half a century old at the bottom of its shaft, our job was done.

How, then, does the poem work? White and red are dialectical adjectives, the colors of the two globes, round, shiny, and fixed, which indicate alternatives of movement. As such, these adjectives are signifiers of an opposition. Lacking a verb, the poem relies heavily on prepositions to convey a sense of movement. The central pair, "Up / Down," reinforces the opposition of the color adjectives. The syntactical impulse of the poem depends almost entirely on prepositional phrases: "From the / Under arm of T," where "Under," disassociated by a space from the anatomical description "underarm," functions more as a reduplicated preposition. It may well be that the poet stands in an elevator, making an empirical observation of the white-up, red-down indicators of his own or other cars, noting the hush of a large, marbled lobby of an office building. But the prepositions that govern this poem are relational—like the lights, they are signs of an opposition. They are gears that, as they mesh, turn in opposite directions. We never *get* the referential, substantive noun—and if we agree with Williams that the poem is to *be* an object among the other objects of the empirical world, it cannot assume a secondary, representational relationship with the world.

How good is this poem? TO Publishers, begun in France by the Oppens and the forerunner of The Objectivist Press, included the poem in *An "Objectivists" Anthology* (1933) with the title "1930's." The title implies that the referent of the poem is the entire Depression era, a formidable task for a poem of such modest means. We can propose, as Louis Zukofsky did of Charles Reznikoff's contribution to the Objectivist number of *Poetry*, that the particulars of the poem function metonymically to suggest the larger contexts: "It is a salutary phase of Reznikoff's sincerity that the verbal qualities of his shorter poems do not form mere pretty bits (American poetry, circa 1913) but suggest . . . entire aspects of thought: economics, beliefs, literary analytics, etc."[31] But, as Robert Creeley has said of his own early work, the poem strains under the obligations of being an anthology-bound "hit single." The poem becomes good, in a sense, when Oppen sees fit to drop the unwieldy title and to include the poem in a discrete series, not an anthology; numbered 1, it is paired with the third poem in the series, numbered 2 and located on the facing page. The poem succeeds, not *solus*, but as a part of the whole series, its small gears meshing with larger; at the same time, it is discrete, requiring neither a substantive referent nor the rule or information of any preceding or following poem in the series.

The poetry of the Objectivists is predominantly metonymic; Oppen in particular is concerned with the relationship of part to whole. In one of his few essays, he rejects, with a nod to both Williams and Pound, the metaphors of nineteenth-century romanticism: "It is possible to find a metaphor for anything, an analogue; but the image is encountered, not found; it is an account of the poet's perception, of the act of perception; it is a test of sincerity, a test of conviction, the rare poetic quality of truthfulness."[32] The third poem of *Discrete Series*, and the partner of the poem just discussed, illustrates the metonymic concerns of the Objectivists:

> Thus
> Hides the
>
> Parts—the prudery
> Of Frigidaire, of
> Soda-jerking——
>
> Thus
>
> Above the
> Plane of lunch, of wives
> Removes itself
> (As soda-jerking from
> the private act
>
> Of
> Cracking eggs);
>
> big-Business

(CP 4)

Metaphors, of which there are none in this poem, are no better than refrigerator cases, glossy and white, which prudishly cover the nuts, bolts, and flywheels of the machine; the metonymic "parts" are what is real and functioning in the Objectivist poem, the rest is all appearance. To the general public, metaphors are synonymous with poetical writing; to the consumer of the quick lunch in a bourgeois capitalist society, the corned beef hash emerges with its poached egg already nesting in the center. The Objectivist poet is an Apex Tech repairman not afraid to get his hands dirty.

Unlike the previous poem, this one supplies its context, or whole; the abstract noun subject is detained until the final line—"big-Business." As Williams indicates in his review, unless the poem is first "a workable mechanism in its own right," it will never be a convincing piece of "propaganda." Oppen's gentle Marxism succeeds because of the poem's precise metonymic style, free of the bombast and sweeping gestures of condemnation which he found in much of the poetry of the Left.[33] No soda-jerk, (and here Oppen departs from Pound) he does not make his poetry a service industry for any political party or economic program; it is a "private act," like cracking eggs, which one can and should do for oneself.

Oppen has praised William Bronk's poems as "a permanent part of literature," saying that his is "a poetry of the use of his own senses, for the universe is not an abstraction . . . it cannot be derived by abstracting."[34] One of Bronk's poems provides expert commentary on the Objectivist's metonymic approach to poetry and the world:

Metonymy as an Approach to a Real World

Whether what we sense of this world
is the what of this world only, or the what
of which of several possible worlds
—which what?—something of what we sense
may be true, may be the world, what it is, what we sense.
For the rest, a truce is possible, the tolerance
of travelers, eating foreign foods, trying words
that twist the tongue, to feel that time and place,
not thinking that this is the real world.

Conceded, that all the clocks tell local time;
conceded, that "here" is anywhere we bound
and fill a space; conceded, we make a world:
is something caught there, contained there,
something real, something which we can sense?
Once in a city blocked and filled, I saw
the light lie in the deep chasm of a street,
palpable and blue, as though it had drifted in
from say, the sea, a purity of space.[35]

Bronk's promotion of the pronoun "what" to a substantive in line 2 and the lurching "which what?" of line 4—a precarious suspension of syntax—demonstrate a stylistic and epistemological affinity for what

Oppen refers to as "the little words that I like so much"—that one knows the world only through a series of particulars, met and connected. While Oppen's verbless snippets and Bronk's fully formed clusters might not, at first, indicate an alliance of poetics, both poets recognize, as T. S. Eliot could not, that the form of the whole world is not within the circumference of the poet's perception. Charles Altieri codifies this distinction: "Where objectivist poets seek an artifact presenting the modality of things seen or felt as immediate structure of relations, symbolist poets typically strive to see beyond the seeing by rendering in their work a process of medi[t]ating upon what the immediate relations in perception reflect."[36] Or as Bronk says more simply: we can make a world, but does what we make contain something of the real? Only the poem that employs metonymy as an approach to the real world can meet Oppen's "test of conviction, the rare poetic quality of truthfulness."

Bronk's travelers, eating foreign foods and adjusting to local time, could comfortably appear in the eleventh poem of Oppen's series:

> Party on Shipboard
>
> Wave in the round of the port-hole
> Springs, passing,—arm waved,
> Shrieks, unbalanced by the motion——
> Like the sea incapable of contact
> Save in incidents (the sea is not
>         water)
> Homogeneously automatic—a green capped
>         white is momentarily a half mile
>         out——
> The shallow surface of the sea, this,
> Numerously—the first drinks——
> The sea is a constant weight
> In its bed. They pass, however, the sea
> Freely tumultuous.
>
> (CP 8)

The effect of a "party on shipboard" is conveyed in the first three lines with an economy possible only through the contiguity, or tangency, of two perceptions: a single wave seen through the porthole (with its implied context, the sea); and, abruptly, a flailing arm (with its implied context, the remainder of the body of, the general group of, party-going passengers unbalanced by their "first drinks" and the white-capped waves). The wave and the "arm waved" are metonymies that, in a contiguous relationship, establish a complex scenario—revelry on the open sea.

The lines "Like the sea incapable of contact / Save in incidents" introduce an epistemological investigation which Oppen claims was not fully engaged until the series "Of Being Numerous" (1968). Contact, or empirical observation, is basic to the Objectivist program and to the method of *Discrete Series* itself. Williams, in the journal called *Contact*, claims as the essential quality in literature "contact with an immediate objective world of actual experience."[37] Although the poet can know parts of the real world in incidents (the splash of a wave against the porthole, or someone's drink against your arm), how can anyone, by direct contact, know the whole sea or the whole of humanity? Oppen collapses the terms of the simile, which in line 4 is syntactically detached, in his discussion of the poem with L. S. Dembo:

> You see the separate waves but somehow there is *the sea*, just as you see people and somehow there is, or could be found, *humanity*. . . . The waves are the individual person. Humanity can't be encountered as an incident or something that has just happened. But all one has is "this happened," "that happened"; and out of this we try to make a picture of what a man is, who these other people are, and even, what humanity is. . . . I left it as a contradiction, that I *know* there is such a thing as "the sea," the whole. But the poem doesn't manage to see it, and it records the poet's—my own—inability to see it. (MP 201–2)

As Bronk says, "conceded, we make a world"; so Oppen recognizes that out of discrete incidents we make a picture of what humanity is, hoping something real is contained there. A metonymic poetics is then the most tightly fitting wrench for this epistemological nut.

The epistemological "contradiction" that Oppen "left" in "Party on Shipboard" is closely related to the structural tension of a discrete series of poems. Oppen is "attempting to construct a meaning by empirical statements." Each poem is an autonomous, discrete observation, but the poet recognizes that each poem, as a *part*, must participate in the relational system of the *whole*, the series, if he is to construct a meaning. He also recognizes that if each statement remains discrete, empirically derived, he will not be able to see the whole from any one part; the individual poem will not depend on the information of the whole, what precedes or follows it, for its meaning. How can the poet "construct" a meaning from statements that are "empirically," separately, valid? The epistemological contradiction between the empirically encountered part and the implied but unverified whole finds its structural equivalent in the discrete series; if metonymy is the wrench, the series is the engine itself.

How can we know, from its "shallow surface," that "the sea is a constant weight / In its bed"? The adverb "Numerously," itself syntactically afloat, suggests that one approaches the whole through a multiplicity of separate incidents; it also directs us, for further inquiry, to the later series "Of Being Numerous," which begins:

> There are things
> We live among 'and to see them
> Is to know ourselves'.
>
> Occurrence, a part
> Of an infinite series. . . .
>
> (CP 147)

Oppen, aware that a discrete series is a structural reinforcement of the epistemological contradiction between the encountered part and the implied whole, considers whether, through the numerosity of occurrences in an infinite series, he may come to know himself as an object among other objects—that is, both himself as an individual and "ourselves," humanity. The process, though, is still metonymic; each occurrence is only a part of that infinite series which might include the whole of a person's life. In these forty consecutively numbered poems, Oppen contemplates the relationship of a discrete, or finite, series (which emphasizes the separate validity of the individual poems) to an infinite series (which emphasizes the continuous process and the multiplicity of poems which find their validity in that process). In this endeavor, he approaches the poetics of Robert Creeley, whose infinite series, *Pieces*, was published in 1969, one year after the collection *Of Being Numerous*.[38]

Metaphor has been the traditional mode of language for those poets, from Coleridge to Eliot, who aspire to a comprehensive view of the world; they are able, as Oppen claims, to find an analogue for anything. The circumference of their perception is coextensive with the world, and their esemplastic imagination, with which they scope the field of similarities, is located at the focus of this one great circle. The "vehicles" of each metaphor orbit the central "tenor," held by the centripetal force of the poet's imagination. This metaphoric mode of language is especially suited to the single, well-made lyric (figure 1).

Metonymy as a mode of language is, by contrast, most appropriate to the structure of the series. Contiguity, the method by which metonymies combine to make larger structures, rather neatly describes the tangent and yet autonomous relationship of the individual poems of the series. The poems are like gears which, as they mesh, are only in contact one tooth at a time. Each metonymy is a point on the periphery of some whole or context; the force upon it is centrifugal, and so

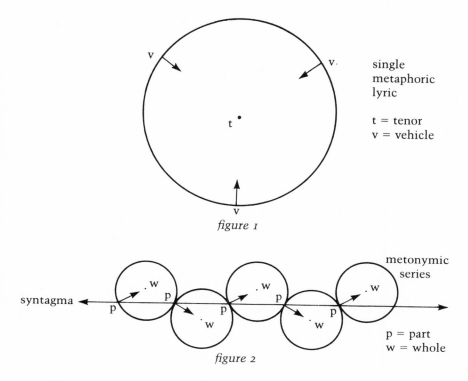

*figure 1*

single
metaphoric
lyric

t = tenor
v = vehicle

*figure 2*

metonymic
series

syntagma

p = part
w = whole

not directed toward a central poetic ego (figure 2). Williams provides the graphic illustration in his essay on Marianne Moore: "There is almost no overlaying at all. The effect is of every object sufficiently uncovered to be easily recognizable. This simplicity, with the light coming through from between the perfectly plain masses, is however extremely bewildering to one who has been accustomed to look upon the usual 'poem,' the commonplace opaque board covered with vain curlicues. They forget, those who would read Miss Moore aright, that white circular discs grouped edge to edge upon a dark table make black six-pointed stars (figure 3)."[39]

Or compare this image of "faces in a crowd" at the train depot, from the twenty-first poem of *Discrete Series* (closer, actually, to the semiotic apprehension of Creeley's "Numbers" than to Pound's painterly "Metro"):

> The shape is a moment.
> From a crowd a white powdered face,
> Eyes and mouth making three——

(CP 11)

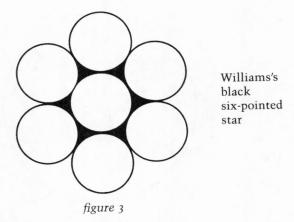

Williams's
black
six-pointed
star

*figure 3*

A number of similar things, like modular seating or penny rolls, will stack up, paradigmatically, for easy storage. "Numerous" metonymies will form chains, contiguously linked, their contexts like "circular discs grouped edge to edge," or to put it more sociably, like the bronze rings of the old Ballantine beer label. For this reason, the metonymic mode of language finds its structural correlative in the serial poem. Oppen approaches "the whole" through the numerosity of occurrence, not the comprehensiveness of the ego; his chosen form, with a postmodern humility, is the discrete series, not the epic (*The Waste Land* or *The Cantos*) or the sequence (*Four Quartets* or *Hugh Selwyn Mauberley*).

The nineteenth poem of *Discrete Series* illustrates the combinatory aspect of metonymic poetry:

> Bolt
> In the frame
> Of the building——
> A ship
> Grounds
> Her immense keel
> Chips
> A stone
> Under fifteen feet
> Of harbor
> Water——
> The fiber of this tree
> Is live wood
> Running into the
> Branches and leaves
> In the air.

(CP 10)

Three discrete metonyms, bolt, keel, and fiber, combine to give form to the poem. The three contexts, while diverse, are not distressingly scattered or in any way surreal; it would certainly be possible, though not required, to find a pier in Lower Manhattan from which one could observe a building, a ship, and a tree. Such a referential justification is not the true test of poetry. Rather, we ask, is the construction of the poem sufficiently adroit that, as with a machine or system, there is nothing redundant or superfluous? In answer to this question, Williams states in his review: "Oppen has moved to present a clear outline for an understanding of what a new construction would require. His poems seek an irreducible minimum in the means for the achievement of their objective, no loose bolts or beams sticking out unattached at one end or put there to hold up a rococo cupid or a concrete saint, nor either to be a frame for a portrait of mother or a deceased wife" (MP 269).

Certainly Oppen's disposition of his nouns on the line is as careful as a grand master's placement of his rook or queen; the three punctuation marks in the poem are like the best of a spot-welder's craft. The larger contexts, building, water, and air, close each of the three sections. At the same time, they interact with the opening noun of the next section: we move from one human construct, "building," to another, "a ship"; "water" keeps the nutrients running through "the fiber" of the tree. The metonyms themselves, though discrete, are also seen to be related: the bolt in the frame of the building is not decorative but structural; a sturdy keel is such a *sine qua non* that it is the traditional metonymy for a ship; and the fiber is that which gives form to all plant life. In short, these three metonyms are the indispensable items in their respective structures. Interestingly, none of them can actually be seen by the poet, like the parts of the Frigidaire. They are not decorative, "vain curlicues," but structural elements, both in the empirical object from which they are drawn as well as in the poem-as-construct in which they now occur.

A discrete series is a closed system; it is, to provide an analogue, "the subway's iron circuits" (CP 46). The poet and his metonymic mode of language are "the welder and the welder's arc," joining part to part, rail to rail. In a later series, "A Narrative," from *This in Which* (1965), Oppen acknowledges the necessity of a closed system when he says, "things explain each other, / not themselves" (CP 134). In agreement with this statement, Saussurean semioticians might don Oppen's "firm overalls," since they too recognize that the link between the signifier and the signified, between word and thing, is arbitrary and not intrinsic; as a result, the single sign cannot explain itself and things cannot name themselves—they can only be accounted for in terms of an internally coherent system. A discrete series, then, is a hermetic rather than an orphic poetry.

In his interview with L. S. Dembo, Oppen admits, "The little words that I like so much, like 'tree,' 'hill,' and so on, are I suppose just as much a taxonomy as the more elaborate words; they're categories, classes, concepts, things we invent for ourselves" (CW 175). His preference for the concrete, substantive nouns, like Zukofsky's obsession with the particles "a" and "the," results in poems that Hugh Kenner has called "systems of small words." Kenner elucidates Oppen's confession to Dembo:

> This is important; it avoids Hemingway's implication that the small words have a more intrinsic honesty. It is cognate to Mallarmé's famous realization that nothing is producible of which we can say that "flower" is the name. ("I say, 'a flower,' and musically, out of oblivion, there arises the one that has eluded all bouquets.") That the word, not anything the word is tied to, is the only substantiality to be discovered in a poem gave Mallarmé ecstatic shivers. . . . Oppen prefers to note that whatever words may be, men cannot survive without them.[40]

This knack of survival is indicated by the ninth poem of "A Narrative":

> The lights
> Shine, the fire
> Glows in the fallacy
> Of words. And one may cherish
> Invention and the invented terms
> We act on. But the park
> Or the river at night
> She said again
> Is horrible.
>
> (CP 138)

In a dark and meaningless world ("And Bronk said / Perhaps the world / is horror," as quoted in the eighth poem), even the word, an invented term arbitrarily linked to its signified, is warmth and comfort; we may act on words *because* we trust in the coherence of the system.

Kenner grants absolution to Oppen for his false faith in the little words: "We need not suppose that abstract nouns are empty whereas there is virtue in concrete ones. Rather, all nouns, all words, exist in a network of trust."[41] But Oppen is not so eager to do penance for his sin. In the Dembo interview, he says, "I, too, have a sense—I hesitate to say it because I have no way of defending it—of the greater reality of certain kinds of objects than others. It's a sentiment" (CW 180). Although he recognizes that the little words are just as much a "taxonomy," he cannot suppress a yearning for the elemental word and the colloquial object; the contradiction, as he has said, is "left" in the poem.

Again, as in "Party on Shipboard," the contradiction that Oppen leaves stranded—his sentiment that the little words are more closely attached to the real and his acknowledgment that language is a system whose signifiers are arbitrarily assigned—is closely related to the structural tension of a discrete series. On the one hand, each term of the series, each individual poem, is to be empirically derived. He claims that "it's been the feeling always that that which is absolutely single [separate, discrete] really does exist," and that it is "absolutely inexplicable" (CW 176). Oppen insists on empirical truth: "That they are there!" (CP 78). However, he can no more present in words the "absolutely single" than Mallarmé can present a flower from a real bouquet. He attempts, instead, to construct a meaning (i.e., the series itself) from these empirical statements. So the series, as an internally coherent system, allows these discrete observations, which cannot explain themselves, to explain each other. The structural tension, then, between a discrete observation and a closed system of relations is in part a manifestation of the contradiction in Oppen's thought regarding language itself—which he rather amiably, and productively, preserves.

Williams, like any economical building contractor, commends Oppen for the "irreducible minimum in the means" with which he constructs *Discrete Series*; there are no loose bolts or unattached beams "to be a frame for a portrait of mother or a deceased wife." *Discrete Series* does, however, include several "portraits" of a young and very much alive Mary Oppen, not as sentimental ornaments, but as essential components in the structural economy of the work. Their eroticism is not a diversion from the urban realities of crane operators, tug boats, or elevators. These love poems function according to the same rigorous principles of composition as any others; they are objects "empirically derived" which nevertheless "explain each other."

These poems are not, in any sense, a group, implying some thematic development or dependence of one on the other. But neither are they randomly distributed through the series, any more than a carpenter could randomly space 2 × 4 studs under a plasterboard wall. To be thorough, we would need to consider what similarities exist among these poems (their paradigmatic value), their pro- and antagonistic interaction with other contexts in the series, and their syntagmatic relations (the points of tangency or combinative effect of one poem and another). This examination would be fairly exhaustive, and so I have chosen, somewhat arbitrarily, the twenty-fourth poem of the series as a focus for discussion.

Oppen claims to be "a fairly passionate mechanic" (MP 205), and this passion seems to enhance the pleasure he finds in a photograph that juxtaposes a woman and a car:

> No interval of manner
> Your body in the sun.
> You? A solid, this that the dress
>                 insisted,
> Your face unaccented, your mouth a mouth?
>                 Practical knees:
> It is you who truly
> Excel the vegetable,
> The fitting of grasses—more bare than
>                 that.
> Pointedly bent, your elbow on a car-edge
> Incognito as summer
> Among mechanics.
>
>                                 (CP 12)

Flattery is not the intention of this poem; twice he questions whether the image is actually of his lover. The woman is an unaccented solid— the dress does nothing for her figure, the photographer has caught her, as happens, expressionless. She has, like any Econo-Car, "practical knees." And finally, it is as an elemental solid that the poet praises her: "you who truly / Excel the vegetable." She is, like the other subjects of Oppen's poetry, and the poems themselves, unornamented by the traditional metaphorical blandishments, "more bare than / that."

Oppen has said that he has a sense of "the greater reality of certain kinds of objects than of others. It's a sentiment," perhaps the only sentiment he allows himself. He continues, "I have a very early poem about a car closed in glass. I felt somehow it was unreal and I said so— the light inside that car." In the ninth poem of the series, that car, a limousine, elicits "a feeling of something false in overprotection and over-luxury" (CW 180–81). The "sentiment" to which Oppen refers is partly Marxist, a distaste for the accumulation of wealth; he assigns to such objects a lower level of veracity—the car appears in "a false light." So the unflattering portrait of a woman in bright sun, "among mechanics," not chauffeurs, is a positive counter in his argument, true praise.

The sixteenth poem in the series can be related to the twenty-fourth poem; their points of contact are very precise and easily evident.

> She lies, hip high,
> On a flat bed
> While the after-
> Sun passes.
>
> Plant, I breathe——
>                     O Clearly,
> Eyes legs arms hands fingers,
> Simple legs in silk.
>
>                                 (CP 9)

This is a more private scene, charged with a passive eroticism; only the master mechanic himself is present, pretending to be a houseplant. The bright sun continues to shine on his lover; we notice that the "noon" of "afternoon sun" has fallen away under the scissors of Oppen's cut-and-paste method of revision. The two most discrete lines of the poem, "Plant, I breathe—— / O Clearly," flower with a gentle sprinkle of Oppen's own explication: "My own presence is like a plant, just breathing, just being, just seeing this. Well, no, I was talking about eroticism, just internal sensations, like a plant. I don't exist otherwise. It's the closure of eroticism within oneself. It's two things, the tremendously sharp vision of erotic desire, together with a kind of closing of one's self, within oneself emotionally" (CW 203). "O Clearly," a syntactically detached exclamation, is then a marker for the empirical observation of the Objectivist campaign, brought to the intensity of an erotic passion. When we consider that the poet's lover "excels the vegetable," she may then be said to be more open to an emotional-physical exchange (certainly her posture indicates this), in contrast to the poet's solipsistic pleasure. The concluding metonymic list of body parts (might they not include a fender, exhaust manifold, or headlight?) stops, like "practical knees," on "simple legs." They are, however, adorned with silk, since Oppen claims that he hoped it would be "an erotic poem . . . a dirty poem" (MP 203).

Another circular disc that can be placed edge to edge with the first love poem we examined is the twenty-second poem of the series:

> Near your eyes——
> Love at the pelvis
> Reaches the generic, gratuitous
>            (Your eyes like snail-tracks)

> Parallel emotions,
> We slide in separate hard grooves
> Bowstrings to bent loins,
>                 Self moving
>     Moon, mid-air.
>
> (CP 11)

In " 'The Shape of the Lines': Oppen and the Metric of Difference,"
Marjorie Perloff takes a moment in the midst of her exacting prosodic
analysis of this poem to note that " 'Love at the pelvis' is hardly a very
pretty image, despite the near-rhyme of 'Love' and 'pelvis,' " and that
the poet, "perceiving his beloved's eyes quite unromantically as 'snail-
tracks,' " attempts a rather desperate simile (MP 224–25). Although
this poem is the most sexually explicit one in the series, concluding in
an active engagement, it is curiously similar to the twenty-fourth
poem in its unflattering images of the woman. This poem and the
sixteenth are joined, like Siamese twins, at "hip high" and "pelvis";
both focus our attention to the erogenous zones without much prior
ambient description. The initial conjunction of eyes and pelvis, the
parallel and yet separate grooves of the lovers, and their "self moving /
Moon" shape suggest the less conventional, less "generic," "69" position. But then the design of the poem, the positioning of the predominant noun phrases, is more significant than the finally undiscernible
bodies of the lovers. Oppen is, after all, an Objectivist poet, not the
casting director for a blue movie.

About this positioning, Oppen has said, "I do believe in a form in
which there is a sense of the whole line, not just its ending. Then
there's the sense of the relation of the speed, of the alterations and
momentum of the poem, the feeling when it's done that this has been
rounded" (CW 180). As Kenner has said, casually embracing Mallarmé
and Oppen, the words, not the bodies of the lovers, are the only
substantiality to be discovered in the poem. Or there is Williams's
desire, with one eye on Juan Gris, to write a poem that is "pure
design."[42] So Oppen is concerned that each poem, and the series entire, be a made thing, "rounded," with no sense of an undone.

Although "bent loins" provides an erotic charge missing from the
twenty-fourth poem's "Pointedly bent, your elbow on a car-edge," in
the most intimate of poems Oppen consistently gives priority to the
design of the poem, the form of his lines, and a cubist's attention to
geometrical shapes, ignoring the flattery or sentimentality attendant
upon mere subject. (We might even say that he mocks the traditional
"your eyes are like limpid pools" encomiums.) His hip high, bow-

strings, and bent elbows are all bolts in the frame of his series, points of tangency which demonstrate that these are not single lyrics but poems at once discrete and related.

Oppen claims that in "Drawing," the twenty-ninth poem of the book, he was "talking about form . . . primarily, since that's a major preoccupation of this whole volume."[43] "Drawing" and the last poem of the series are explicit comments on the form of *Discrete Series*; they are the construction foreman's blueprints.

DRAWING

Not by growth
    But the
Paper, turned, contains
This entire volume

(CP 14)

The organic form of romantic poetry, like the growth of a plant in which the form of the bud is preceded and determined by the form of the seed or stem, is rejected; instead, with epigrammatic brevity, Oppen describes the mechanistic program of the Objectivists—each page turned as one would, at the start of a new day, turn over the engine of one's car. "Each term is empirically justified rather than derived from the preceding term."[44] The car either starts or it doesn't. The effect of this formal description relies heavily on the 1934 edition of *Discrete Series*, in which each page, turned, revealed a separate but related poem.

But Oppen, who employs so few finite verbs, says that the turning of pages "contains" the entire volume; we assume that his careful choice of the verb has formal implications for the series. A discrete series is a finite series, a system of containment. Oppen has said that "discrete" means "empirically true" and "separate." This containment, then, indicates the Objectivist preference for the finite series, or "rounded object," over the unbound and ongoing process of the infinite series. Oppen constructs a system of containment with his pages; he does not, as we have mentioned, try to encompass *all* the world. Nor does he endeavor to take, as Creeley does in his infinite series *Pieces*, "a common audit of days." The Objectivist selects discretely from the incidents of the day, and it is only in the combination of these separate pages, turned, that he constructs a meaning, contains his empirical observations in a closed structure.

The last poem of the series also concerns itself with formal arguments:

> Written structure,
> Shape of art,
> More formal
> Than a field would be
> (existing in it)——
> Her pleasure's
> Looser;
> 'O—'
>
>      'Tomorrow?'—
>
> Successive
> Happenings
> (the telephone)
>
>                    (CP 14)

Oppen will not let us forget that the poem is a made thing, a construction; it is, like a machine, assembled, so that there are no redundant, nonfunctioning parts, no loose bolts. As in the twenty-ninth poem, he contrasts his structural approach to poetry with the organic: a field and a woman's pleasure are "looser" than the forms of art. Williams records in his *Autobiography* the first meetings of the Objectivists in George Oppen's apartment—or, at least, he records their arguments for an implicit formal necessity in the poem:

> The poem, like every other form of art, is an object, an object that in itself formally presents its case and its meaning by the very form it assumes. Therefore, being an object, it should be so treated and controlled—but not as in the past. For past objects have about them past necessities—like the sonnet—which have conditioned them and from which, as a form itself, they cannot be freed.
>
> The poem being an object (like a symphony or cubist painting) it must be the purpose of the poet to make of his words a new form: to invent, that is, an object consonant with his day.[45]

In *Discrete Series*, Oppen has invented an object, a new form consonant with his day; only the series, not the sonnet sequence, responds to the current necessities of "Successive / Happenings / (the telephone)." Each call is discrete, not derived from the information provided by a preceding call. Calls can be entirely unrelated (a wrong number), or fairly intimate: " 'O—' / 'Tomorrow?' " And until recently, "G Oppen" was assigned a number in the Pacific Bell System's San Francisco telephone book. The telephone, which did not exist when the sonnet was invented, becomes the contemporary analogue for a poetic form in which individual poems are at once separate and part of a system of communication.

The binding of my New Directions Paperbook 418, *The Collected Poems of George Oppen*, is already beginning to loosen around the few pages allotted to *Discrete Series*. When they finally fall out, I will cut and paste the poems, much as Oppen revised and edited his manuscripts, each on its own page. *Discrete Series*, an object consonant with its own day, continues to be the most economical formal example of the correlation of a metonymic mode of language and a serial structure. Empirically true in its particulars, yet the whole a finite, closed system. When Oppen says, with all Objectivist sincerity, that he "was attempting to construct a meaning by empirical statements," that meaning is nothing but the form of the series itself.

## Sounding and Resounding Anew: Louis Zukofsky and Lorine Niedecker

When that particle of light which is the poet's clear perception falls within the field of force which is the poet's desire for structure, the arc that the particle traces will close on itself to form a circle. For Louis Zukofsky and Lorine Niedecker the apparition and resonance of particulars is the first condition of poetry; but apparitions may fade in time. They seek the more permanent state of rest which such particulars describe within a circular orbit. In 1956 the orbital cloud that was the poetry establishment neither knew nor cared that Zukofsky and Niedecker were among them. And yet Niedecker's essay on Zukofsky's short poems announces the existence of the new form they both practiced: "Aside from the fact that Zukofsky's short poems are intensely individual and their energy sings in a new way, they move in a circular path 'so that we may think in our time.' Indeed they seem to move in all directions at once—each of the smallest and the most quiet a field of magnetic force. The subject matter of *55 Poems* (1941) is various—the young man excited by what he sees around him."[46] From her vantage point Niedecker marks an essential structural law of the series: these poems are "intensely individual" and yet they move together; as light is discovered to be both particle and wave, so these poems are both separate and in series.

Likewise Zukofsky, who instructed the young physicists at Brooklyn Polytechnic in the craft of writing, supplies as the note to poem 29 of *Anew* (1946) a quotation from Lorentz's *Theory of Electrons*: "It is not the motion of the single electron, nor the field produced by it, that can make itself felt in our experiments, in which we are always concerned with immense numbers of particles; only the resultant effects produced by them are perceptible to our senses."[47] The various subject matter of the single poems ensures against the linear progression of theme, character, or narration by which the Office of Poetics identifies the sequence. The field of magnetic force which the smallest of these poems produce—their energy singing with the resonant hum of a return to the tonic chord—is evidence of their permanence in a structure at rest. The "resultant effect" in a finite series such as Zukofsky's *Anew* or Niedecker's "Lake Superior" is the movement of numerous particles in a circular path.

### Zukofsky's Musical Inventions

In his review of Zukofsky's *Anew*, William Carlos Williams speaks of "the necessity for a new form *before* a *new* poetry of any sort can be written."[48] Zukofsky's renovation of the canzone and sestina, and his deployment of musical forms such as the fugue and the round through both *"A"* and *All*, meet Williams's prerequisite of formal invention. But the new form to be found most frequently among Zukofsky's shorter work is the finite series. Of the collected short poems from 1923 to 1964, "29 Poems" and "29 Songs," *Anew*, "Light," *Barely and Widely*, "The Old Poet Moves to a New Apartment 14 Times," and a number of other poems are serial structures. Most of the short poems in *All* are participants in a serial form. Zukofsky's commitment to formal invention, like his commitment to his twenty-four-book epic *"A"*, was lifelong.

There is an intimate connection between the poetics of the finite series and Zukofsky's program for the Objectivist movement. In an interview with L. S. Dembo, he offers his most concise and least convoluted definitions of the two significant terms of the movement: "Sincerity is the care for detail. Before the legs of the table are made, you can see a nice top or a nice grain in the wood, its potential, anyway, to be the complete table. Objectification is the structure. I like to think of it as rest, but you can call it movement."[49] Care for detail, or attention to "particulars," is an indication that the preferred mode of language in Objectivist poetry is metonymic.[50] "Strained metaphor," which often obscures the object with comparisons, "carries the mind to a diffuse everywhere and leaves it nowhere." If metaphor is used, he says, let it have the conciseness of "the single word which is in itself a relation" (P 278–79). In sincerity, "the mind is attracted to the veracity of the particular craft" (P 275). The metonymic mode, like Pound's "direct treatment of the thing" or Williams's "contact," is a care for significant details, the grain in the wood; it is, above all, the craft of particulars.

Zukofsky continues, "Writing occurs which is the detail, not mirage, of seeing, of thinking with the things as they exist, and of directing them along a line of melody" (P 273). The series, which is the structural correlative of the metonymic mode of language, is a syntagmatic chain of particulars—details directed along a line. He recognizes that a metonymic writing occurs along the combinative, or horizontal, axis of language; the metaphoric mode, or writing on the vertical axis of similarity, is the "mirage of seeing." This combination of single details into a serial structure is, however, an intermediate phase in Zukofsky's poetics—we have not yet arrived at the condition of rest, objectification. Thinking *with* the things and not *about* them, as he would say, applies to both the infinite serial form of Robert Creeley's *Pieces* and the finite form of George Oppen's *Discrete Series*.

Objectification is structure. The metonymic particulars so carefully tended "in sincerity" are but the precursors of a "completed sound or structure, melody or form" (P 273). Objectification is the construction or "arrangement, into one apprehended unit, of minor units of sincerity" (P 274).[51] For Zukofsky, objectification is also "rest," which indicates that his serial structure seeks a finite rather than infinite form. If objectification is a "rested totality . . . the apprehension satisfied completely as to the appearance of the art form as an object" (P 274), then Objectivist form stands opposed to the Coleridgean "form as proceeding" on two counts: (1) rested, and so not an ongoing process; and (2) a totality, leaving no sense of the incomplete or undone. The final product need not be static (the imagist dilemma), as the series denotes movement. But when we consider the analogues presented by the Objectivists (the machine with no redundant parts, the subway, or the neon tube) we realize that the poem-as-object must be a complete circuit. By contrast, the romantic analogue for organic form, the plant, is constantly growing and changing.

Zukofsky's finite series is not, like the sonnet, a predetermined form. *A new line is a new measure*, Williams exclaims in his review of *Anew*; likewise, each individual poem in the series is a new shape. The structure of the series is not imposed from the outside (as in the epic) but built-in, like the steel girders that disappear from public view as the skyscraper nears completion. In "Sincerity and Objectification," Zukofsky appropriately offers a prosodic analysis of those poems of Charles Reznikoff which achieve objectification (P 275–76); he rejects external contexts, such as the information that Gaudier-Brzeska is the unnamed subject of an epitaph, as irrelevant to the poem-as-object. Neither predetermined nor imposed, the finite form of the objectivist series calls for the middle voice: it *asserts itself.*

"Points define a periphery," said Pound, and three points are sufficient to graph a circle. I will select three of the consecutively numbered "29 Poems" in order to define the series. Admitting with Zukofsky that "at any time, objectification in writing is rare" (P 276), I nevertheless consider these single poems to have achieved a prosodic "rest," which is also the intended condition of the series as "completed structure."

Zukofsky lists "the materials of poetry" as "images—that's pretty solid—music, it's liquid; ultimately if something vaporizes, that's the intellect," or as he says elsewhere, *sight, sound,* and *intellection.*[52] Poem 2 is an exemplary Objectivist poem, possessing all of these materials:

> Not much more than being,
> Thoughts of isolate, beautiful
> Being at evening, to expect
> > at a river-front:
>
> A shaft dims
> With a turning wheel;
>
> Men work on a jetty
> By a broken wagon;
>
> Leopard, glowing-spotted,
> > The summer river—
> Under:    The Dragon:
>
> > > > (AL 24)

L. S. Dembo suggested to Zukofsky that "the poet here was seeing as an objectivist, in terms of particularities rather than wholes. He seems to be literally thinking with things as they exist and not making abstractions out of them" (MP 272). Certainly, the two central couplets are metonyms, minor units of sincerity; prosodically, the second lines of each couplet are in a nearly identical trochaic meter, ´x ´x ´(x); despite their harmony, the couplets are contextually autonomous, or as George Oppen would say, discrete—though the association of wagon and wheel is enticing.

Zukofsky, always the picador in this interview, drives the bull away from his horse: "But the abstract idea is particular, too. Every general word is particular, *as against another*—glass, table, shoe, arm, head . . .

'reality,' if you wish. Individually they're all, apart from their sound, abstract words" (MP 272). In his program essay, he claims, like Oppen, a "faith" in words as "absolute symbols for objects" (P 279). But he also recognizes that all words are abstractions, arbitrarily attached to their signifieds—and so he rejects, as does Oppen, any claim for the greater veracity of "the little words." Words are particular, he underscores, "as against another," related within an internally coherent system that is *la langue*, or the poem. Only the sound-shape of words is not abstract, in the sense that the poet measures and controls it as a quantity outside of the word-thing axis. The musical form of the assembled words is nearly synonymous with objectification; "prosodic rest" is then, for Zukofsky, of far greater veracity than the abstract, semantic meaning of the word.

In addition to the "rested totality" of musical form, poem 2 is exemplary for sight and intellection. He explains, "The first part is intellective, 'gaseous'; the second part would resemble the 'solid' state" (MP 273). In the first stanza, the poet begins with a general statement concerning the proximity of being and not-being; he then qualifies this condition in line 2. The Objectivist intellect finds "the beautiful" in that which is "isolate," as Oppen found the empirically true in discrete observation. At the river-front, itself a tangible edge, the poet's intellection makes contact with the "solid" state, the particular things seen: wheel, wagon, men on the jetty. In the final stanza, haiku and Greek astronomy, sight and intellection, join as the constellation of the Dragon is seen "reflected in the river—inverted" (MP 273). What is the existential state of such a dragon floating in a summer river? No firm answer, though Zukofsky reminds us of his objective: "There is a question of movement and enough rest; notice the space after 'Under.'" Or *An Objective: (Optics)— The lens bringing the rays from an object to a focus* (P 268).

The "completed structure" of Zukofsky's poems may seem to be predominantly shaped by the intellect (design) and the ear (prosody) of the poet. So Robert Creeley recognizes, in a review of *"A" 1–12* and *Barely and Widely*, that "the terms of a world depend on that intelligence which can relate them, making of senseless sound, a music, as Bach's."[53] In the fifth of "29 Poems," Zukofsky, relating a siren and signal, makes of senseless sounds on the East River a dialogue, a musical design:

Ferry

Gleams, a green lamp
In the fog:

Murmur, in almost
A dialogue

Siren and signal
Siren to signal.

Parts the shore from the fog,
Rise there, tower on tower,
Signs of stray light
And of power.

Siren to signal
Siren to signal.

Hour-gongs and the green
Of the lamp.

Plash. Night. Plash. Sky.

(AL 27)

There is only one image in the poem, the gleaming green lamp in the fog. The ferry itself is lost in the fog, as invisible as the elevator that does not finally make its appearance in the second poem of Oppen's *Discrete Series*. Images are, for Zukofsky, the "solid" state, but the presentation of images—if that were all the poem did—would relegate the poem to a secondary relationship with the real. The final line, "Plash. Night. Plash. Sky," is blind of image and symbol—it is all rhythm and blackness. Precisely because Zukofsky's poem itself "intends a solid object," it does not merely represent an image but becomes a design, a made thing in the world. The green lamp is an expression of Objectivist sincerity, care for details, but it is not design. "Each word," Zukofsky reminds us, "possesses objectification to a powerful degree; but . . . the facts carried by one word are, in view of the preponderance of facts carried by combinations of words, not sufficiently explicit to warrant a realization of rested totality such as might be designated an art form" (P 274). Details, images, must be brought to form, which for Zukofsky is completed design.

Bronk, Oppen, and Creeley would agree with Zukofsky that "the mind may construct its world" (PR 18). Siren and signal should be brought into a murmuring dialogue of statement and counterstatement, just as "the parts of a fugue, Bach said, should behave like reasonable men in an orderly discussion" (PR 19–20). The pilot of this ferry is not the romantic poet of the imagination but the offspring of a baroque musician and the Saussurean semiotician. The single sign is unintelligible; the audience is deaf to the tonality of a single note held indefinitely by the soprano. But an internally coherent system is an apt definition of both semiotics and the form of the fugue.

Poem 17 is an inversion of poem 2, moving from the "solid" state to the "gaseous," from sight to intellect:

> Cars once steel and green, now old,
> Find their grave at Cedar Manor.
> They rust in a wind
> The sky alone can hold.
>
> For the wind
> Flows heavily thru the mind like cold,
> Drums in the ears
> Till one knows its being which soon is not.
>
> (AL 34)

Though he preferred to walk to his work at Brooklyn Polytechnic, Zukofsky nevertheless admires the facilities of the "mechanic": in "A Statement for Poetry" he endorses Williams's contention that "a poem is a small (or large) machine made out of words" (PR 19). The opening of the poem invites comparison to the work of his Brooklyn neighbor George Oppen; both the junker, the most proletarian of objects, and the limousine, the most obvious denominator of the upper class, appear in *Discrete Series*. But the off-balance skid of three adjectives in the first line is righted by the verb securely placed in the initial position of the second line. Whereas Oppen expresses empirical observations of the "solid" state in verbless, fragmented syntax, Zukofsky maintains a quatrain form, rhymes lines 1, 4, and 6 in cantilever fashion, and completes syntactical constructions—all evidence of the "totality" he imparts to both the individual poems and the entire series.

In the second stanza, the wind signifies the "gaseous" state of intellection. The graveyard-junkyard simile of line 2 is reinforced as the wind, which rusts the cars, hastens the mind to a recognition of its own eventual decay. The final line, which turns on the brink of "being" and not-being, reminds us of the first line of poem 2: "Not much more than being." The intellection somehow tries to order the particularities of a rusted car or broken wagon. Zukofsky says in "An Objective" that "the order of all poetry is to approach a state of music wherein the ideas present themselves sensuously and intelligently and are of no predatory intention." The closed form of these poems is an expression of the way in which facts, particularities, "must receive the signet of the form" (PR 18).

In his review of *Anew*, Williams immediately recognizes the importance of music to Zukofsky's poetry: "Zukofsky has the intention of
singing *anew* when almost all poets otherwise have forgotten the
objective. *Singing*. Singing *anew*: in that order."[54] Praise goes to
Zukofsky for being a lyricist, or as he himself claims in poem 28 of "29
Songs," " 'Specifically, a writer of music.' The composite of notes
proceeded with assumed qualities in a definite proportion" (AL 69).
But he is also an inventor; Williams devotes much of his essay to the
importance of Zukofsky's metrical invention, the "devastating" discovery that "a new line is a new measure." But there is a second type of
invention in Zukofsky's poetry, beyond measure—the invention of
musical form in poetry. As if, the musicologists might say, he were to
write a book of simple but beautiful counterpoint pieces and call
them, as did Bach, Two-Part Inventions.

Zukofsky's pervasive concern with musical form, especially baroque form, can be found in his epic *"A"* and in several of the single
lyrics, but it is particularly appropriate to the structure of the finite
series. Although other serial poets have adopted analogues from the
world to describe the form of their poems—the mobile, the road, the
subway—Zukofsky translates, with modification, the structural characteristics of another art form. In *"A"*, he asks:

> Can
> The design
> Of the fugue
> Be transferred
> To poetry?[55]

Both Creeley and Duncan in their infinite serial poems have acknowledged the importance of Cage and Schönberg; but the elder Zukofsky
returns to the baroque era for the formal analogies of his finite series.
Michael Heller partly explains this influence by claiming that Zukofsky found sincerity and objectification "exemplified in musical form,
in particular in the musical forms of the baroque and classical periods
with their muted programmatic intention. In the works of Bach and
Handel, for instance, the 'meaning' is not in the creation or coloration
of some occurrence external to the music but is, in the most profound
sense, in the music itself, in the interrelations of notes, themes, tonal
effects, etc. The sense of totality or completeness of such music is in
its absence of a residue, in its simultaneity of means and ends."[56]
Musical form is not equated with poetic form, but it is traduced: the
tone row in Schönberg's serial music is as programmatic as the imitation of subjects in a Bach fugue; John Cage's pieces for prepared piano

and Bach's preludes and fugues for the "well-tempered klavier" are as programmatic as the serial poetics of Creeley's *Numbers* and Zukofsky's *Anew*. For Zukofsky, the baroque fugue is also a "rested totality."

"The parts of a fugue, Bach said, should behave like reasonable men in an orderly discussion." The statement-counterstatement form of the fugue provides a valid analogy for the relation of the individual poems of the finite series to one another. In the polyphonic fugue, no one of the four voice parts is predominant; each maintains its autonomy as it waits to enter the "discussion." In the monophonic lute song, the accompaniment assumes a subordinate role to the melody. No single poem in the series is subordinate to or dependent on another in theme, structure, or narrative.

The orderly discussion of the parts is directed one to another, not externally. That is, the voice parts of a fugue function as an internally coherent system; they do not "evoke" in any metaphorical or symbolic fashion an external world, either real or ideal, as the first movement of Beethoven's Pastoral Symphony (No. 6) evokes the "Awakening of Cheerful Feelings on Arrival in the Country." Insofar as they are parts, they are metonymic of the whole of the orderly discussion, which is undoubtedly *about one another* and not about the weather.

The multiple lines or voice parts of fugue structure are, like the individual poems of the finite series, both *related* by the recurrence of the "subject" and *separate* in that none are harmonically subordinate. An "orderly discussion" refers to the frequent discordance as the staggered lines vie with one another for the listener's ear; this "unrest" drives them on, from one entry to the next, one after another. But as the Irish novelist Flann O'Brien remarks, in an effort to describe the "multi-clause colloquy" of *At Swim-Two-Birds*, "Counterpoint is an odd number . . . and it is a great art that can evolve a fifth Excellence from four Futilities."[57] As the listener hears the entry of one voice part, he must also hear the reverberating presence of the whole fugue—a metonymic complexity that supplants the "harmonic depth" or "external evocation" of a metaphoric structure such as the symphony. For Zukofsky, this "fifth Excellence" is a "rested totality."

In polyphonic music, the term "imitation" describes the repetition of a phrase or subject in another voice part: in canonic form, the entire voice part repeats itself; in fugal form, the repeated subject is joined by new material.[58] Lorine Niedecker, avoiding the mimetic implications of "imitation" in a discussion of poetics, prefers the term "recurrence" to describe the fugal structure present throughout Zukofsky's work: in *"A"*, in his serial poems, and in several of the single lyrics collected in *All*. She claims that *"A"* "presents an order of succession but also of interweaving themes uniting with new and related matter, tightening often into such forms as canzones or ballades" (FC 292) which are also musically derived. Among the more tightly closed forms that Niedecker cites (FC 303–5) are those cyclic forms, appearing in *All* either singly or as part of a series, whose repetitions approach the canonic—the repetition of the entire voice part with little or no new material.[59]

"Technically," says Niedecker, "a recurring thing, for all but the apathetic student, is never the same—though the *idea* of *recurrence* is useful to establish relationships, to reveal kinship" (FC 292). At the very least, a "recurring thing" is altered by the new context in which it appears, joined by new materials. As Roland Barthes says, in "a fugal continuity . . . the new is ceaselessly accompanied by the old."[60] However, the proportion of "new" materials to "recurrent" things, as in any recipe, is structurally essential. In an epic of eight hundred pages, a recurrent subject such as the horses that cavort through *"A"* represents a small percentage of that discursive volume and so is subordinate to larger structural plans or devices.[61] In the tightly wound cyclic forms, the recurrent subject, like a snake swallowing its tail, consumes 95 percent of the poem's volume—these canons permit the entrance of so little new material that they are, as a result, almost invariably single lyrics. In the finite series, the proportion of old to new materials maintains an equilibrium—fugal recurrence becomes the constitutive structure of the series.

In *Anew*, whose forty-two consecutively numbered poems comprise the entire book, the most frequently recurrent subject is song or musical form itself. Nearly half of the poems in the series contain some reference to song or music—the parts of the fugue are indeed discussing one another. By comparison, the infinite serial poems of Duncan, Blackburn, and Creeley are considerably more diverse contextually. Niedecker is attentive to the finite serial form of *Anew*, claiming that it "contains the lovely, minutely in-wreathed flowering of Zukofsky's poetic genius. The poems are at once objective and intimate," and all are "more or less subject to the order of Mozart's 'poetry must be the obedient daughter of music' " (FC 305). The individual poems are in no way subordinate to one another, yet the chain of this series is more tightly linked than any other previously discussed. The "subject," in the strictly musical sense of "figure" and not in the literary sense of "theme," is not developed—*development*, as Barthes claims, is the hallmark of a rhetorical continuity that "will agree to repeat only if it can transform" or amplify; a fugal continuity does not develop but "distributes" the figures.[62] In the series, however, the subject need not be a verbatim repetition of a particular phrase, as is often the case in the canonic single lyrics.

Zukofsky thwarts development of his subject by offering a potpourri of musical forms: a ballade (17), a madrigal (27), a marriage song (30), and a birthday carol (40). He also offers bird song (25 and 34) and a translation, perhaps the best of our age, of Catullus's *Carmen* viii (22). Additionally, "song" appears as a figure in seven other poems, three of which,—9, 10, and 20—define Zukofsky's poetics. Poem 9 begins at one limit,

> For you I have emptied the meaning
> Leaving the song

while 10 strains toward the inverse,

> What are these songs
> straining at sense—
> you the consequence?

(AL 89)

Within the frame of an address, "for you," these two poems, linked in the series by the recurrent figure of song, pull against one another, enacting the diametrically opposed limits expressed in Zukofsky's now familiar statement of poetics found in *"A"* 12:

> I'll tell you.
> About my *poetics*—
>
> $$\int \begin{array}{l} \text{music} \\[12pt] \text{speech} \end{array}$$
>
> An integral
> Lower limit speech
> Upper limit music

(A 138)

The terminology is mathematical, but no musical form exploits the rational, programmatic, and mathematical aspects of music more than the baroque fugue. The prose version of his poetics occurs in "A Statement for Poetry": "Poetry may be defined as an order of words that as movement and tone (rhythm and pitch) approaches in varying degrees the wordless art of music as a kind of mathematical limit" (PR 19). A sampling of Zukofsky's work indicates that he often approaches this upper limit, that virtually all the poems of *All* are songs. Examples include: 16 of "29 Songs," "Crickets' / thickets"; 38 of *Anew* which

manages to rhyme "Oakie" in four successive lines; and the entire
eleven parts of the series "I's (Pronounced Eyes)," including "Azure / as
ever / adz aver" (AL 219)—all words found in *Webster's*, but pushed to
the limit of song and so emptied of meaning. In Zukofsky's brand of
*melopoeia*, phonetic similarity akin to punning *is* the poem, crowding
out not only denotative meaning but other forms of equivalence such
as metaphor; ornament in the New Critical formalist poem becomes
substance for the Objectivist.

   *Anew* 20, a third instance in which the recurrent figure of song is
employed reflexively as a statement of poetics, establishes the relationship of musical form and objectification:

> The lines of this new song are nothing
> But a tune making the nothing full
> Stonelike become more hard than silent
> The tune's image holding in the line.
>
> (AL 97)

"Singing anew," Zukofsky argues that as the musical shape of the line
approaches the substantive, integral "1," meaning approaches "0." The
tune's image, or musical form, becomes stonelike and so achieves
objectification. He recognizes that all words are abstract, apart from
their sound, and so it is by ear that the Objectivist constructs the
poem.

   Although poems 9, 10, and 20 are reflexive statements of Zukofsky's
poetics, there are several instances in which the recurrent figure of
song enters amidst new material. Poem 16 is a brief and beautiful
example of this recurrence:

> I walk in the old street
> to hear the beloved songs
> afresh
> this spring night.
>
> Like the leaves—my loves wake—
> not to be the same
> or look tireless to the stars
> and a ripped doorbell.
>
> (AL 95)

These songs are the old songs of love which the poet hears afresh,
anew. They, like the light-green and tender spring leaves, return; and
yet they are not the same. As Niedecker reminds us, a recurring thing

is never the same; at the very least it is altered by its new context.
Although the tireless stars may appear not to have shifted, the "ripped
doorbell" provides a strange new accompaniment to bird song, the
*Carmen* of Catullus or the troubadour ballade of Guillaume de Machault (poem 17).

One of the adapted musical forms in *Anew* of particular interest to
the fugal structure of the series is poem 27, "A madrigal for 3 voices":

> Hail the tree's meadow
> Where the watch
> Fees no property
>
>> Where bread crumbs strike
>> Red raked leaves
>> Pigeons redden shadow
>> Under red feet
>
>>> When pigeons greet
> Workers meeting—
> In the valley
>> of the city—
> Not a chimney's
>> made of putty
> And the lampposts
>>> are high
>>>> high
>>>>> and white—or
>>>> red, like
> no property of
>>> night.
>
> (AL 101)

Why a song in praise of communal property in a madrigal form? In a
city park where workers, tossing bread crumbs, gather among the
pigeons, the central tree, emblem of *Natura*, stands opposed to the
capitalist system of private property and its taxation. The multiple
voices of the madrigal form freely exchange certain recurrent items
which the single lyric voice might identify as either "mine" or "not-
mine." Structurally, the three stanzas each represent one of the voices;
their "entries" are both temporally and visually staggered. The
"where" in line 4, which marks the entry of the second voice, is a
repetition and syntactical extension of the "where" in line 2. The
pigeons and the red of leaves and shadow in the second voice recur at
the start and at the close, respectively, of the third voice—except that

the recurrent adjective "red" now modifies a new object, the lamp-posts. The penultimate line of the third stanza repeats the "no prop-erty" that closes the first stanza. The structure of this multivoiced madrigal is in many ways representative of the fugal structure of the entire finite series: subjects recur, either modifying or modified by new contexts.

Niedecker concludes her assessment of *Anew*: "Sounding out pretty much all of life, the first note of the fugue is present when the last note is struck" (FC 306). The cyclic structure of the fugue, the ceaseless return of the subject, is adapted by Zukofsky to the series. In a letter to Niedecker which has found its place in *"A"* 12, Zukofsky explains:

> —Each writer writes
> one long work whose beat he cannot
> entirely be aware of. Recurrences
> follow him, crib and drink from a
> well that's his cadence—after
> he's gone.
>
> (A 214)

Creeley also notes, in his review of *All*, that Zukofsky has written "a continuing *song*."[63] Fugal structure and a system of recurrence bind the entire Zukofsky canon together—an eight-hundred-page epic, a finite series of forty-three poems, and intricately wound single lyrics all share a structural device and what Zukofsky would simply call "the facts." But the statement and counterstatement of the multiple lines of the fugue, harmonically unsubordinated and yet intimately related, are most clearly the controlling structural device of his finite series.

### Niedecker's Geological Cycles

In July of 1966 Lorine Niedecker and her husband set out by car to tour the Lake Superior region—a tour that promised a welcome vaca-tion for them both, but that Niedecker was predisposed to think of as a field trip in preparation for the writing of a long poem. In letters to Cid Corman, then in Kyoto, Japan, she remarks that the region bordered by Minnesota, Michigan, and Wisconsin represents "not only for the geologist, a massive, grand corruption of nature," but for the poet also a grand corruption "of language," the blending of native Indian, French, and British tongues.[64] And although "some kind of poetry has been felt by several of the geologists" of the region, the Northwest Passage to the Orient has had its chief recognition in "weak verse like Longfellow's *Hiawatha*" (L 91). Longfellow entertained his Boston audiences with an embellished account of Indian lore appropriated from the ethnologist and Indian agent Henry Rowe Schoolcraft, much as Schoolcraft appropriated the title to lands and mineral resources from the Indians in questionable treaties.[65] But Niedecker's presentation of the region in her poem "Lake Superior" is considerably more elemental, or in an Objectivist sense of the word, "sincere." She writes to Corman, "I'll use a little time to walk beaches since this country is part of the agate, jaspar, carnelian, Thompsonite region. . . . The gift shops," she jokes, with their stock of commercially dyed agates and other curios most likely made in Japan, "are our modern day Passage to the Orient" (L 91). Upon her return to Milwaukee, she claims to have amassed "a millen[n]ium of notes for my *magma* opus" (L 94). Her research into the region's natural history and geology continued in the city's public library and included a request for "geological maps from the office in Washington, D.C." (L 94). Niedecker's poem mines the mineral resources of the Lake Superior region to uncover the glinting of time measured in millennia; it is not a historical record of human presence measured in the confrontation of natives and explorers.

"Lake Superior" is the first of three serial poems that comprise the volume *North Central* (1968), published when the poet was sixty-five years of age. Together with "Traces of Living Things" and "Wintergreen Ridge," this poem represents some of Niedecker's finest writing. But it is also an expression of "the new form" (L 155) toward which she felt compelled and yet was hesitant to articulate. She laments to Cid Corman, "I've been going through a bad time—in one moment (winter) I'd have thrown over all my (if one can) years of clean-cut, concise short poem manner for 'something else' (still don't know what to call it)" (L 153). She did have a name, though, for the source from which her earlier poems were drawn—"from this condensery."[66] Slowly she revealed to the world such lapidary poems as:

> Remember my little granite pail?
> The handle of it was blue.
> Think what's got away in my life—
> Was enough to carry me thru.

> (FC 22)

The fine edge on this poem bears the mark of an Objectivist poetics, an acute attention to particulars which Niedecker never lets get away from her. I have seen the "granite" of the pail glossed as "enamel,"[67] but certainly that stone and the blue of the Rock River and Lake Koshkonong, which flowed past and frequently flooded the Niedecker cabin on Blackhawk Island, are the most prominent topological features of her region. The form of the later "Lake Superior" series retains her characteristic concern for "the hard, clear image, the thing you could put your hand on," but it is also an expression of what she proposed to call a "reflective" poetics, "what the visual form gives off after it's felt in the mind." She concludes that "modern poetry . . . proceeds not from one point to the next linearly but in a circle."[68] Compelled by the immensity of the region in which she lived her life, Niedecker encounters the recurrent form of natural history directly. She writes the poem that the Lake Superior region had made in her.

In 1948 Louis Zukofsky included one of Niedecker's earliest poems (c. 1935) in his anthology-textbook *A Test of Poetry*, citing it in the company of Keats, Herbert, and Shakespeare as a worthy example of "Recurrence." It reads:

> There's a better shine
> on the pendulum
> than is on my hair
> and many's the time
>
> .. ..
>
> I've seen it there.
>
> (FC 6)

Zukofsky comments, "The less poetry is concerned with the everyday existence and the rhythmic talents of a people, the less *readable* that poetry is likely to be."[69] Recurrence in the sound-shape of poetry is intimately connected to the daily routine of a people and the cadence of their speech. The action described in the poem, the natural and unobtrusive rhymes, and the delicate pause between the fourth and fifth lines confirm Zukofsky's appraisal with great economy of means. In her early thirties and separated from her first husband, the poet sees in the brass pendulum the fading luster of her own blond hair. The pendulum, which is time and immutable, marks the changes in her own appearance. But this observation has little to do with vanity. Her comments (quoted earlier) on Zukofsky's poetry in an essay that appeared in 1956 also apply to her own work:"Technically, a recurring thing, for all but the apathetic student, is never the same—though the *idea* of *recurrence* is useful to establish relationships, to reveal kinship" (FC 292). The reflection on the pendulum is such a recurring thing, familiar but never quite the same. It also reveals the kinship between a poet at home on an isolated island in Wisconsin and a poet living in an apartment house in Brooklyn.

In October of 1966 Niedecker remarked in a letter to Cid Corman, "I've finished the Lake Superior poem—5 pages long—after much culling but I might just make a small book out of it with a short poem on each page" (L 101–2). The twelve poems that comprise the series were never to enjoy such a presentation, similar to the first edition of George Oppen's *Discrete Series*, a self-published volume whose generosity of white space no doubt depended on the finances of its author. In the Fulcrum Press setting of "Lake Superior," several poems appear together on a page, each separated by the tiny imprimatur of a leaf frond.[70] Such fuss over the presentation of the poem on the page is intended chiefly to indicate that Niedecker thought of "Lake Superior" as a series whose individual poems deserved a certain degree of autonomy; they were not to be stacked on top of one another as if they were stanzas of a single continuous poem, and the intervening characters only partially alleviate such an impression. Her understanding of modern poetry as proceeding in a cyclical rather than linear form is reinforced by a presentation that stresses the autonomy of the poems rather than their attachment. She sought to express not a single chain of cause and effect but an "awareness of everything influencing everything."[71]

I want to make reference to an essay by Donald Davie, "Lyric Minimum and Epic Scope," which, despite its having been twice reprinted, so thoroughly undervalues and misinterprets the intentions of the "Lake Superior" series that it seems to me to be of some use; at the very least it teaches us how not to read Niedecker.[72] Davie encounters the readily acknowledged "brevities" of "Lake Superior" and feels obliged to "annotate" the poem with reference to such prose histories of the region as Francis Parkman's *France and England in North America* and Janet Lewis's *The Invasion*, among others; it should not have to be said that he grinds the delicate pebbles of Niedecker's series to dust under the weight of such multivolume nonfiction mortars. His requirement that the full historical context be present in the poem displays either his ignorance of or aversion to an Objectivist poetics, which defines itself as "desire for what is objectively perfect, inextricably the direction of historic and contemporary particulars" (PR 12).

The Objectivist conviction that, in the words of Zukofsky, it is "*impossible* to communicate anything but particulars" (PR 16) is illustrated by the third poem of Niedecker's series:

> Radisson:
> 'a laborinth of pleasure'
> this world of the Lake
>
> Long hair, long gun
>
> Fingernails pulled out
> by Mohawks

(FC 161)

Davie claims that in Pierre Esprit Radisson, credited by Parkman with having discovered the confluence of the Mississippi and the Missouri in 1658, "we have a subject that seems to cry out for heroic treatment." He argues that Niedecker has "either missed the possibility or else firmly set her face against it."[73] Certainly the latter is the case. "Heroic treatment" is a call for a rhetorical contextualization that invariably lies about the particular historical facts. Depending on the disposition of the writer, Radisson is either a heroic explorer or a colonialist exploiter, and his deeds would be cast as such. "Heroic treatment" violates the Objectivist concern for sincerity, care for details. Niedecker consequently presents a paratactic list of particulars: a clipping from Radisson's journal, whose blend of French and English with the odd Indian word rather engagingly describes the ecstasy of an explorer lost in a pristine lake country; a juxtaposition of the metonyms "long hair" and "long gun," providing the essential image of the backwoodsman; and finally, his mutilated fingers presented as evidence of the endurance that must have been characteristic of the man. Niedecker prefers a direct treatment in which the contexts of particulars must be supplied; she rejects a heroic treatment in which the whole context is a rhetorical forgery.

In the fifth and sixth poems of the series, geologic formations and the presence of the French missionary Jacques Marquette among them are of equal concern to Niedecker:

> Through all this granite land
> the sign of the cross
>
> Beauty: impurities in the rock
>
>
> And at the blue ice superior spot
> priest-robed Marquette grazed
> azoic rock, hornblende granite
> basalt the common dark
> in all the Earth
>
> And his bones of such is coral
> raised up out of his grave
> were sunned and birch-bark-floated
> to the straits
>
> (FC 162)

Before further annotating these poems from Parkman's historiography, Davie unwittingly describes the Objectivist's "approach to the real world" under the guise of a reproach: "Marquette's heroic status is at it were official; a marble effigy of him, a gift of the people of Wisconsin, stands in the rotunda of the Capitol in Washington. But as with Radisson so more conspicuously with Marquette, Lorine Niedecker shows no interest in heroic exploits; Marquette in her verses is subdued to, and identified with, what he saw or what he moved among."[74] This treatment of materials which Davie disapproves is precisely that which the Objectivists extol. George Oppen selects as the epigraph to his aptly titled volume *The Materials* (1962) this passage from Jacques Maritain: "We awake in the same moment to ourselves and to things."[75] Or as Zukofsky claims, "Writing occurs which is the detail, not mirage, of seeing, of thinking with the things as they exist" (PR 12). Against the symbolic method that Eliot and the New Critics ply, Zukofsky and Oppen reject as mirage a consciousness that is coextensive with the world. The Objectivist poets think with things, not about them; they can know and communicate truthfully only the particulars of the world. Thus Niedecker's Marquette exists, literally, among the geologic materials of the Lake Superior region, identified with what he saw or moved among.

When, in the second stanza of the sixth poem, Marquette's bones are exhumed, they are found to have become like coral. This one allusion in the series, to Shakespeare, pleases Davie no end, since it is a departure from the "drabness" of language throughout; for the New Critic, only metaphor, allusion, or irony constitute figurative language—not metonymy. But Marquette's bones are not merely an ornamental figure; as part of the "azoic rock" of the region, as *stone*, they participate in the principal recurrent figure of the series.

The first poem of the series states:

> In every part of every living thing
> is stuff that once was rock
>
> In blood the minerals
> of the rock
>
> (FC 161)

That which now is living once was stone; and as evidenced by Marquette's bones, the living turns to stone again. On this cycle of the organic and inorganic, Niedecker has fashioned the cyclic structure of her series. Minerals and stone are the recurrent figure in the series, as they are in nature. In each age, they return in or among new organic materials, new contexts. The penultimate poem of the series, which itself returns to the proposition of the first poem, reaffirms the cyclic structure of recurrence:

> The smooth black stone
> I picked up in the true source park
>         the leaf beside it
> once was stone
>
> Why should we hurry
>         home

>                                        (FC 165)

When we consider that geologic time is measured in millennia, our haste becomes insignificant. With the stone and leaf we are already at home. In a cyclic structure, everything returns home eventually; closure is nothing more than a return to the place of origin. Niedecker's reference to the "true source park," the location designated as the source of the Mississippi River, carries a certain irony. We tend to think of time and space in linear terms, and it is our peculiar obsession to want to trace the river back to some initial point, to discover where it all comes from. But in the cycle of the organic and the inorganic, such a return is taken for granted. Niedecker's spare use of punctuation throughout the series reinforces this concept of an endless cycle: there are no full stops, no periods. Writing to Corman, she describes an agate purchased on her trip: "Thin circling lines in the agate with a rather wide orange band. Seems petrified wood and agate have a connection—almost all petrified wood is agate-ized wood, I've read. The circles in the agate are of growth" (L 94). Within the closed cycle of stone-leaf-stone, the "recurrent thing" does not extinguish itself or encounter a full stop, but returns in a new and separate environment.

Schoolcraft's return from Sault Sainte Marie is described in the tenth and eleventh poems of the series:

> Schoolcraft left the Soo—canoes
> US pennants, masts, sails
> chanting canoemen, barge
> soldiers—for Minnesota
>
> Their South Shore journey
>         as if Life's—
> The Chocolate River
>         The Laughing Fish
> and The River of the Dead
>
> Passed peaks of volcanic thrust
> Hornblende in massed granite
> Wave-cut Cambrian rock

painted by soluble mineral oxides
wave-washed and the rains
did their work and a green
running as from copper

Sea-roaring caverns—
Chippewas threw deermeat
to the savage maws
'*Voyageurs* crossed themselves
tossed a twist of tobacco in'


Inland then
beside the great granite
gneiss and the schists

to the redolent pondy lakes'
lilies, flag and Indian reed
'through which we successfully
passed'

(FC 164–65)

These two poems at first appear to be a straightforward if somewhat condensed account of the travels of an historical figure; they rely on Schoolcraft's own account for much of their information. But in fact the natural and mineral resources along the way are the true focus. Schoolcraft has "acquired" the rights to these resources, and with his pennants, masts, and flags, appears to lord it over both the land and the natives. When the travelers make their superstitious donations to the "sea-roaring caverns," it is the Chippewas who recognize a natural force for what it is and return to nature something of what it has given them; the *voyageurs* who sign themselves with the cross make an appeal to the supernatural for protection and then, ironically, vitiate their gesture of faith by tossing in a twist of tobacco. Niedecker's attention to such historical confrontations extends only to a critique of the participants' respect for the natural resources of the region.

Lisa Pater Faranda, in an essay that compares the journal publication of "Lake Superior" to its revised version in *North Central*, observes that in their original arrangement the poems were ordered by Roman numerals, giving them "a relentless linear movement."

This forces the reader to leave each section behind and creates the impression of a whole marked off in measured sections. Further, the demarcation of the past and present tenses layers time too boldly; the original arrangement of the sections clearly separates the speaker's exploration from those of the past so that while the past influences the present, it is nonetheless distinct. The arrangement of the individual sections, by so clearly distinguishing past from present, puts historical time in opposition to the evolutionary time evoked by the opening proclamation.[76]

The series originally appeared in the Fall 1967 issue of a University of Wisconsin publication, *Arts in Society*. In November, Niedecker writes to her friend Gail Roub, "I sort of hope you don't see it, a couple of small but important revisions (last week) make all the difference as *North Central* will show."[77] By eliminating the Roman numerals and rearranging the poems to displace the historical sequence of events as an ordering principle, Niedecker emphasizes the minerals as the recurrent figure in a circular rather than linear form.

The eighth and ninth poems of the series illustrate how this recurrent figure asserts itself in the presence of new contexts:

> Ruby of corundum
> lapis lazuli
> from changing limestone
> glow-apricot red-brown
> carnelian sard
>
> Greek named
> Exodus-antique
> kicked up in America's
> Northwest
> you have been in my mind
> between my toes
> agate

> **Wild pigeon**
>
> Did not man
>     maimed by no
>         stone-fall
>
> mash the cobalt
>     and carnelian
>         of that bird

(FC 163–64)

The carnelian color present in the minerals recurs in the plumage of the pigeon. Like the "wave-cut Cambrian rock" in the tenth poem, the bird has been "painted by soluble mineral oxides." In turn, the cobalt and carnelian of the bird are "mashed," as if with mortar and pestle, returned to the mineral powder with which they began. As Davie suggests, the exploitation by whites of North America's natural resources is not the primary "theme" of "Lake Superior"; such pathos, like the mutilation of Radisson's fingers or the burial of Marquette, is subordinate to the cycle of the inorganic and the organic. So the carnelian color of the mineral occurs among the geological formations of the North Central region, and then recurs, identical and yet changed by its new context, in a native species of the region.

Gneiss, agate, and hornblend—the minerals of Niedecker's Lake Superior region, like the native Mohawks and Chippewas, outnumber the French explorers. The historical figures in the series must be content to exist among the recurrent figure of the minerals. Davie concedes, at the conclusion of his essay, that Niedecker's treatment is "profoundly *un*historical." He then says, somewhat facetiously, that "the minerals of the Lake Superior region are in a real sense the only true 'heroes' of the poem first and last."[78] His own intention has been from the first to read the poem as a historical *sequence*; he abandons this approach only when he fails to discover such linear structures as heroic narrative or, in the exploitation of natural resources, thematic development. The profoundly historical, because its structure is one of temporal linearity, must be sequential. Niedecker's intention has been to construct a series of poems whose cyclic structure is bound together by a recurrent figure. She enacts her claim that modern poetry proceeds from one point to the next in a circular rather than linear fashion. Davie's frustration is fine evidence of her success.

In the poem "If I were a bird," Lorine Niedecker pays tribute to those poets who most influenced her work, among them Zukofsky:

> I'd plunge the depths with Zukofsky
> and all that means—stirred earth,
> cut sky, organ sounding, resounding
> anew, anew.
>
> (FC 105)

Both Zukofsky's *Anew* and Niedecker's "Lake Superior" are finite serial poems within whose cyclic structures a fugal subject sounds and resounds. As Bach's favorite instrument was the church organ, their favorite mode of language is one of particulars. Song and stone echo through their poems until the first note of the fugue joins the last.

# PROCEDURAL FORM

# A Predetermined Form

## Renovated Form:
## The Sestinas of John Ashbery and Louis Zukofsky

When in the late 1890s a Sicilian mason decided to begin a small winery producing rough reds for local and family consumption, a cave in the hills outside of town offered the cool and humid environment necessary for fermenting the grape pressings—a premium site on a parched and sunstruck Mediterranean island. It remained for the mason to enlarge the cave and to construct, with mortar and the readily available stone, the facilities for wine making. The family story goes—and all family stories are in part apocryphal—that his artisanship was such that the winery was concealed from the curious and the passersby, becoming (so it appeared) a part of the hill in which it had been constructed.

Recently, architects have chosen the brownstone, which once housed immigrants from the Old World, as the preferred property for renovation. These urban artisans have gutted the brownstones, retaining only their shells; the buildings are chunks of a salvageable but not sentimentally restored past. The irreproducible hue and texture of their brick, baked in kilns now demolished and according to ephemeral formulae now forgotten, remain; but within these structures one can find new hardwood, track lighting, framed lithographs, Boston ferns, and Italian furniture. The artisan of this postmodern urbanity does not hope to conceal his work within an ethnic tradition or period style but strives to display new and culturally diverse shapes within an old form. The impression of artisanship is enhanced by the presence, among the new, of the previously *made*.

A question that Ezra Pound might pose is "Chi é il miglior fabbro?" Who is the better craftsman? Is it the artisan who removes all trace of his trowel, conceals all evidence of his craft within the natural cave, even as he turns it to his purpose, or the artisan whose every device is laid bare and who marks every work as a made thing, an assemblage? John Ashbery, in his renovation of such Old World forms as the sestina, the pantoum, and the canzone, declares himself to be an artisan of the latter sort. By selecting continental forms that are relatively unfamiliar in Anglo-American verse (unlike the sonnet, which was adopted from the Italians at an early age and remained for centuries the only son and heir to the nation's wealth), Ashbery has been able to evict the immigrant content and retain only the structural shell of these forms. The sestina and the pantoum are predetermined forms that, in his hands, have been excavated of all obligation to traditional themes: the passage of time, the pastoral setting, the proposal to the beloved. They offer complex and programmatic restraints that, Ashbery claims in an interview, "uncover unexpected things" or "get directly into one's less-conscious mind." The sonnet, by comparison, is "much less demanding, less analytic."[1] He does not wish to restore the form to its antique beauty but to refurnish it; paradoxically, he expects to discover, at the instigation of these old and demanding forms, a new furniture not found in any downtown showroom. Such an assemblage, in which the radically new is joined to the salvaged structure of that which has previously been made, continually points to itself as the work of the finest artisan.

To solve the new riddle of a literary Sphinx, one must answer that there are three ages in the life of every poetic form. The sestina enjoyed an initial intimacy of form and content cradled in the arms of the twelfth-century troubadour Arnaut Daniel, whom Dante, a later practitioner, acknowledged in the *Purgatorio* as "il miglior fabbro." For its creator, the sestina was the appropriate form for what needed to be sung. As Marianne Shapiro points out, "The fit of complex forms with a subtlety of content underwrote the spontaneity of creation" for the troubadours. These were poets who viewed loving, composing, and singing as "an inseparable unity."[2] The second age of any poetic form is characterized by the decay of familiarity; insufferable at home and lately unable to find work, the now mature form is forced to seek its meager fortune abroad. Louis Zukofsky, in a verse "Interpretation" of his sestina "Mantis," describes the shabby condition of this form in the nineteenth century:

What is most significant
Perhaps is that C—and S—and X—of the 19th century
Used the "form"—not the form but a Victorian
Stuffing like upholstery
For parlor polish,
And our time takes count against them
For their blindness and their (unintended?) cruel smugness.

Again: as an experiment, the sestina would be wicker-work—
As a force, one would lie to one's feelings not to use it[3]

The complexity of the form is no longer a force that expresses a subtle content; the sestina has become an exercise or parlor game in which form and content sue for a real divorce. In its third age, the sestina does not search for its cane like an elderly man but instead undergoes a transubstantiation of an odd sort—its old body receives a new soul, a rebuilt engine is lowered into a classic chassis. Both Ashbery and Zukofsky, as renovators of the sestina in its third age, reinstate an intimacy of form and content. They express in the sestina what Dante called "la battaglia delli diversi pensieri," the battle of diverse thoughts, but they do so in a radically new manner.

### John Ashbery: The Pastoral and the Urbane

From the very start of his career, Ashbery—among other post-modern poets—has been concerned to renovate elaborate fixed forms. In his book *Some Trees* (1956), he presents a pantoum, a canzone, and three sestinas. The sestina is a thirty-nine-line poem composed of six strophes of six lines each and an envoi of three lines. The end-words, numbered 1 2 3 4 5 6 in the first strophe, are reordered according to a procedure called *retrogradatio cruciata*, based on repetition and inversion, to form the sequence 6 1 5 2 4 3 in each succeeding strophe. Formal closure is assured since the mathematical permutation of six elements is exhausted—nothing is left undone. In this pattern, the strophes are linked head-to-tail: the last end-word of one strophe becomes the first in the next. The envoi, a half-strophe, also brings this spiraling form to closure; it contains all of the end-words, generally in the order of first appearance.

In *Hieroglyph of Time: The Petrarchan Sestina*, Marianne Shapiro says that "contiguity relationships among words dominate the sestina." The vagabond *parole rime* are mainly responsible for the predominance of the contiguity relation and the relative absence of metaphor. Unlike the "abba" rhyme scheme of the sonnet quatrain, these end-words do not establish a similarity relation, an equivalence of sound, with other words. Instead, the end-words themselves recur, each time semantically altered by the new context. Shapiro, taking her cue from Roman Jakobson, calls this behavior of the end-words a metonymic progression. "Even on the level of selection," she claims, "each line of a sestina is determined by the context of the rhyme-words." Poets are quick to recognize that the sestina is "inhospitable to the conceits and feats of metaphor's daring." They are most likely, in the end-word's recurrence throughout the poem, "either to produce oscillations of meaning by maintaining lexical constancy and altering the context, or to introduce semantic nuances that transgress but do not obliterate boundaries." The language of the sestina is drawn "definitively toward the metonymic pole. Metonymy there rises to the status of a means of signification that shapes the poem."[4] The sestina form is particularly inviting for postmodern poets such as Ashbery and Zukofsky: the renovation of a predetermined form in which recurrence and not equivalence, contiguity and not similarity, the metonymic and not the metaphoric mode of language, is predominant dissolves the association of the closed form with a symbolic language attributed to it by the New Critics.

The end-words of the sestina are governed by the contiguity relation; semantic nuances are introduced by the shifting contexts in each succeeding strophe. But in this predetermined form it is appropriate to observe that the six occurrences of an end-word function as a class—that is, as a paradigmatic relation. Shapiro informs us that the sestina has always involved "a play of homonymic equivalences with a concomitant prevalence of semantic significance over narrow lexical meaning."[5] This peculiar kind of equivalence does not, as Jakobson observes of the sonnet, attempt to join two largely unlike terms in metaphor or rhyme; in an extreme example, Zukofsky and Niedecker consider the possibility of rhyming "lute" with "boot," in which the disjunctive contexts of the signifieds obstruct the otherwise comfortable phonic equivalence.[6] Rather, in the sestina, we have a single term, the end-word as lexical constant, repeated but with a slight semantic variation. A linguistic example of such a paradigmatic relation would be the declension of the noun in Latin: *homo, hominis, homini, hominem, homine.*

Roland Barthes defines the paradigm as "a group, a reservoir—as limited as possible—of objects," from which we select. "What characterizes the paradigmatic object is that it is, vis-à-vis other objects of its class, in a certain relation of affinity and of dissimilarity: two units of the same paradigm must resemble each other somewhat *in order* that the difference which separates them be indeed evident."⁷ In the case of the end-word, the affinity is obvious enough—lexical repetition; the dissimilarity is less marked—the oscillations of meaning. The repeated evaluation of the end-word's own affinity and dissimilarity generates in the sestina its centripetal force, a turning in on itself. Certainly, other structural aspects of sestina form, the head-tail linking of the strophes and the *tornada* or envoi, contribute to this cyclic effect, but the centripetal force of the paradigm will be felt in all procedural forms. The paradigmatic recurrence of the end-word in the sestina, Barthes tells us, is the very stuff of form: "The constraint of recurrence . . . has an almost demiurgic value: it is by the regular return of the units and of the associations of units that the work appears constructed, i.e. endowed with meaning; linguistics calls these rules of combination *forms*. . . . [F]orm, it has been said, is what keeps the contiguity of units from appearing as a pure effect of chance: the work of art is what man wrests from chance."⁸

Shapiro is not being entirely precise when she says that the contiguity relationships among words dominate the sestina, since chance cannot possibly govern a predetermined form. It would be more correct to say that contiguity relationships dominate *the mode of language* in the sestina. The form of the sestina, its shell or structure, based on a process of repetition and inversion, is dominated by paradigmatic relations. In traditional closed forms such as the sonnet, one would expect the paradigmatic structure to be joined by the metaphoric mode of language. What makes the sestina and other procedural forms exciting, to the postmodern poet in particular, is a rather unusual combination of paradigmatic structure and a metonymic mode of language.

In addition to the three sestinas in *Some Trees*, Ashbery has included in the early collection *Turandot and Other Poems* (1953) an example that, Richard Howard suggests, is surely the only sestina in English in which one of the teleutons is "radium";⁹ yet another sestina, "Faust," appears in *The Tennis Court Oath* (1962). None of these poems can be approached by the reader with less than a whip and a chair; they have not been tamed, nor have their teeth been pulled. But certainly the most ferocious example appears in a later volume, *The Double Dream of Spring* (1976):

Farm Implements and Rutabagas in a Landscape

The first of the undecoded messages read: "Popeye sits in thunder,
Unthought of. From that shoebox of an apartment,
From livid curtain's hue, a tangram emerges: a country."

Meanwhile the Sea Hag was relaxing on a green couch: "How pleasant
To spend one's vacation *en la casa de Popeye*," she scratched
Her cleft chin's solitary hair. She remembered spinach

And was going to ask Wimpy if he had bought any spinach.
"M'love," he intercepted, "the plains are decked out in thunder
Today, and it shall be as you wish." He scratched
The part of his head under his hat. The apartment
Seemed to grow smaller. "But what if no pleasant
Inspiration plunge us now to the stars? *For this is my country*."

Suddenly they remembered how it was cheaper in the country.
Wimpy was thoughtfully cutting open a number 2 can of spinach
When the door opened and Swee'pea crept in. "How pleasant!"
But Swee'pea looked morose. A note was pinned to his bib. "Thunder
And tears are unavailing," it read. "Henceforth shall Popeye's
          apartment
Be but remembered space, toxic or salubrious, whole or scratched."

Olive came hurtling through the window; its geraniums scratched
Her long thigh. "I have news!" she gasped. "Popeye, forced as you know
          to flee the country
One musty gusty evening, by the schemes of his wizened, duplicate
          father, jealous of the apartment
And all that it contains, myself and spinach
In particular, heaves bolts of loving thunder
At his own astonished becoming, rupturing the pleasant

Arpeggio of our years. No more shall pleasant
Rays of the sun refresh your sense of growing old, nor the scratched
Tree-trunks and mossy foliage, only immaculate darkness and
          thunder."
She grabbed Swee'pea. "I'm taking the brat to the country."
"But you can't do that—he hasn't even finished his spinach,"
Urged the Sea Hag, looking fearfully around at the apartment.

But Olive was already out of earshot. Now the apartment
Succumbed to a strange new hush. "Actually it's quite pleasant
Here," thought the Sea Hag. "If this is all we need fear from spinach
Then I don't mind so much. Perhaps we could invite Alice the Goon
          over"—she scratched
One dug pensively—"but Wimpy is such a country
Bumpkin, always burping like that." Minute at first, the thunder

Soon filled the apartment. It was domestic thunder,
The color of spinach. Popeye chuckled and scratched
His balls: it sure was pleasant to spend a day in the country.[10]

Ashbery's renovation of the sestina form is extensive and complete—
he knocks layers of old thematic plaster off the brick walls of structure. In a diachronic analysis of the sestina, one composes a history of
images or themes associated with the form; in a synchronic approach,
one undertakes a detailed analysis of the poem's structure at a particular moment in its evolution. The postmodern renovation of the sestina
forbids a diachronic analysis since it is precisely the history of images
associated with the form that has been gutted; we are comfortably
confined to a synchronic analysis of the poem in its third age of
renovation. Marianne Shapiro, who insists on both modes of analysis
in *Hieroglyph of Time*, readily admits in her brief discussion of Ashbery that his sestinas "seem a prominent exception to the preoccupation with time that characterizes the diachrony of the form. His ar-
chaeological layers of diction, from biblical to colloquial, seem to take
no measure of sequentiality."[11] Despite Shapiro's best efforts, Ashbery's sestinas cannot be treated as a modern appendix to a pastoral
tradition that includes Sir Philip Sidney and Edmund Spenser. These
are not modern examples of a traditional *kind* of poem. Shapiro fails to
recognize that the absence of a diachronic preoccupation ushers in a
new, third age of the sestina form; because postmodern renovation
excises traditional themes and symbolic content, it requires a separate, synchronic analysis.

The title, "Farm Implements and Rutabagas in a Landscape," is a
pastoral tease, a gossamer-clad nymph sipping from a bubbling spring
who vanishes at our approach; the fact is that this is a painterly title,
screwed to a wall somewhere in the Metropolitan Museum of Art.
Ashbery has said that he often begins with a title, before any conception of content or form: "A possible title occurs to me and it defines an
area . . . to move around in and uncover."[12] In this sense, the title, like
the form of the sestina itself, is predetermined—a sort of exploratory
device or probing tool. He also admits that his titles are often ironic or
satirical. Since this sestina has virtually nothing to do with agrarian
landscapes, we could say that the title functions ironically, as an
unkept promise, or as a practical joke—offering a chair and then
pulling it out from under the guest. But most interestingly, Ashbery's
title, our greeting to the poem, is a bold mark of artifice. It points to
something previously made, to art and not to nature; his joke is on the
artist who agrees, for the sake of an exhibition, to provide a descriptive
title for what is plainly visible—except that in Ashbery's sestina there
is not a rake or a rutabaga in sight. Such a contextual disjunction
between title and poem encourages the reader to uncover and explore,
joining the poet in his task.[13]

In his interview for the *New York Quarterly*, Ashbery describes the sestina form as "highly artificial," more so than such "conventional forms" as the sonnet (NYQ 124). The complexity of the *retrogradatio cruciata* pattern of the end-words and the form's only occasional appearance as an exotic foreign import to the English tradition reinforce this sense of artificiality. To select such a form is to reject the romantic notion of an organic form and the Coleridgean preference for "form as proceeding." Ashbery's membership in the New York School, with Frank O'Hara and Kenneth Koch, and his long-held position as an editor of *Art News* place him in a "museum culture" that does not hesitate to extol the artificial over the natural, or the imported over the homegrown; the sestina is an elaborately gilt frame which previously held the portrait of a French baron or his Italian mistress but now, with Ashbery as curator, holds the work of an abstract impressionist.[14] Charles Altieri claims that Ashbery exhibits "the ontology of the aesthete seeking to reverse the Romantic dream of erasing art so nature will stand clear. He dreams instead of erasing nature so that the book might stand free as a dynamic interchange of self-referring elements."[15] Certainly, the highly artificial form of the sestina erases nature and chalks itself up as a made thing.

The predetermined form of the sestina, the canzone, or the pantoum is opposed to Coleridge's "form as proceeding," but Ashbery's use of these forms does not constitute an endorsement of "form as superimposed." He does not have a preexisting subject matter to which poetic structure is applied; rather, he employs elaborate forms—or, occasionally, goofy titles—as exploratory or generative devices. In the *New York Quarterly* interview, he says that "these forms such as the sestina were really devices at getting into remoter areas of consciousness. The really bizarre requirements of a sestina I use as a probing tool rather than as a form in the traditional sense. I once told somebody that writing a sestina was rather like riding downhill on a bicycle and having the pedals push your feet. I wanted my feet to be pushed into places they wouldn't normally have taken" (NYQ 124). Form, in this description, is neither superimposed on, nor an extension of, an existing content. Ashbery fully exploits the predetermined aspect of these forms; the bizarre requirements of the form are not restraining but generating content. The objection of those with a classical sensibility might be that the poet ought to have something to say—a determinate subject which is then embedded in form. But Ashbery's use of a procedural form as a probing tool into remoter areas of consciousness enables him both to evade traditional subject matter and to discover new material. This exploratory use of the sestina is an important characteristic of renovated form: the old, preexisting structure finds a new content.

The first three lines of "Farm Implements and Rutabagas in a Landscape" confirm our suspicions that the complicated form of the sestina views itself as a game, puzzle, or assemblage; the form has an accomplice in this endeavor, namely the multiple contexts and voices which function as the shifting signs or counters of the game. In line 1, we receive "the first of the undecoded messages." This piece of rhetoric, stolen from a secret agent novel of Ian Fleming caliber, is a mighty contextual leap from the title, itself on loan from the art museum. The two counters, which function metonymically, only fit together from one angle. Both refer to something less than high art, tainted by the botulism of popularity—the secret agent novel as a genre for the semiliterate (though it has recently been described as a closed form by the semiotician Umberto Eco), and the barnyard school of scenic painting.[16]

The renovated sestina points to its own artificiality by referring not to the teeming city of Hong Kong or to the clucking of hens in the barnyard but to their prior depiction in another genre. This self-consciousness marks the sestina as artifice, and admittedly, as high art. Although a modernist such as Ezra Pound packs his bag with allusions to the high art of distant epochs—his "Sestina: Altaforte" is an example of *translatio*, an imitation in homage of the troubadour Arnaut Daniel—the postmodernist is comfortable with references to more popular modes.[17] Ashbery comments, "I want the reader to be able to experience the poem without having to refer to outside sources to get the complete experience as one has to in Eliot sometimes or Pound. This again is a reflection of my concern for communicating which as I say many people don't believe I have—but for me a poem has to be all there and available to the reader and it of course is very difficult to decide at certain moments what the ideal reader is going to know about and what he isn't going to know about" (NYQ 122–23). Although references to popular culture may be readily accessible to the reader, their import may not in fact be any less elusive. Ashbery's first message still requires decoding.

Roman Jakobson has said that "a CODE fully, or at least partially, common to the addresser and the addressee (or in other words, to the encoder and decoder of the message)" is necessary in any verbal communication.[18] Ashbery's ideal reader, as addressee, will have as common knowledge the rhetoric or codes of the art gallery or the 007 (itself a code meaning "licensed to kill") secret-agent novel. The author's request for an ideal reader is not new. Ashbery's communicative difficulty lies not with the role of the reader but with the role of the addresser. The first line issues a challenge to the reader and/or the critic to decipher these still "undecoded messages," to interpret the entire poem. We are offered a "tangram" (l. 3), or Chinese puzzle in which a variety of small geometrical shapes can be assembled into a larger square. But who is the encoder? From where is the first message delivered? The addresser in "Farm Implements" is not a traditional speaker, as, for example, in the Arnaldian sestina, the persona of the poet as lover is easily established and thought to preside over the poem. In Ashbery's renovation of the sestina, the reader encounters a collage or multiplicity of voices—the curator and the double agent are only the first of many—none of which is assigned priority.

The message, as we are given it, begins, "Popeye sits in thunder." What is the decoder to do with a comic, cartoon character who ascends to an Olympian throne? Is this Zeus of the massive forearms and an anchor tattoo? One implication is that popular culture has spawned its own versions of mythological heroes—just as Zeus sends the meddlesome Hephaistos crashing to earth with a single lightening bolt, so Popeye sends Bluto, for his aggressive pursuit of Olive Oyl, spinning into the ground with a single spinach-enriched punch. Ashbery claims that he has been influenced by both "Hollywood B-pictures" and "Gilbert Murray's Greek drama," and that he is interested in both "debased and demotic forms of expression" (APR 30). When the Sea Hag inquires if Wimpy has bought any spinach, he "intercepts" in the second strophe with his trademark address, "M'love," but continues, "the plains are decked out in thunder / Today, and it shall be as you wish." The debased, bombastic rhetoric of a Silver Age epic and the demotic, slurred lingo of the World War II vintage cartoon intersect in a single utterance. In this minestrone of diction, it is the addresser who remains undecoded by the reader. None of the voices is false—rather, all are programmatic. They are a foregrounded device, a recognized element in the poem as assemblage.

The sestina is not a Rube Goldberg machine in which language inexplicably drops through chutes or is catapulted into the air; in this predetermined form, language is controlled by the elaborate but precise movement of the end-words. The end-words arrange themselves into groups which to a great extent control the immediate context: "apartment," "scratched," and "spinach" evoke the comic and the low; "thunder" and "country" most often instigate epic bombast and lofty sentiment; "pleasant" plays it up the middle, in such banalities as "How pleasant!" We remember that Dante described the sestina as "la battaglia delli diversi pensieri," and that these diverse thoughts and contexts are controlled by the selection of the end-words. In Ashbery's renovated sestina, a "battaglia nova" takes place in which the language, even if it be a variety of recycled rhetoric, speaks for and contends with itself. The subtle and disputatious content of the Renaissance sestina gives way to the multiple, foregrounded voices of the postmodern sestina. Ashbery's contentious contexts are as intimately related to the elaborateness of the form as were the traditional subjects of Arnaut or Dante. The game continues; Ashbery has only replaced the players.

Marianne Shapiro has said that the sestina poet, in handling the end-words, is most likely "to produce oscillations of meaning by maintaining lexical constancy and altering the context, or to introduce semantic nuances."[19] The end-words in Ashbery's "Farm Implements" enjoy such oscillations and nuances; by examining these semantic and contextual shifts, we can very nearly arrive at the solution to this "tangram." In the first strophe, the end-word "country" is an appositive to the tangram itself (l. 3); the solution to the Chinese puzzle is related to our understanding of the role of "country" in the poem. In the second strophe, Wimpy's italicized statement, *"For this is my country,"* introduces a sort of breast-beating patriotism in which "country" is semantically equivalent to "nation." But in the third strophe we note a shift: "they remembered how it was cheaper in the country." The earlier elevated tone slips to one of mundane observation; "country" is semantically equivalent to "rural environs." Since we recall that Popeye in line 2 has abandoned "that shoebox of an apartment," we understand that, at one level, the poem describes the escape of the inveterate city-dweller on a hot, summer weekend to a home in Westchester or the Hamptons.

The fourth strophe marks the return of an elevated tone. Olive breathlessly reports that Popeye has been forced "to flee the country" by "the schemes of his wizened, duplicate father." Not only has "country" reassumed the semantic value of "nation," but there is also a significant expansion of the context of escape. Olive tells us, in language that might seem wildly inappropriate in any other poem, that Popeye's duplicate, jealous of her and the apartment, "heaves bolts of loving thunder / At his own astonished becoming, rupturing the pleasant / Arpeggio of our years." "Thunder," as an end-word, evokes an Olympian context and its attendant elevated tone in all appearances (except for the *tornada*, in which it is the "domestic thunder" of a burp). Here, Popeye's "duplicate father" indulges in the ultimate solipsistic fantasy, attempting to reproduce himself, or at least, as Athena is said to have sprung directly from the forehead of Zeus, to engender and give birth to one's offspring unassisted. According to the psychomythologists, this desire is most often manifested by the male jealous of the female's apparent control of childbirth. The shifting semantic value of "country" controls the oscillations in the context of escape: the apartment-dweller from the city, Popeye from his duplicate's solipsistic indulgence.

On an aesthetic level, the poet must consider his or her own escape from the form of the sestina. Charles Altieri claims that "the organicist ideal in art" emphasizes "the act of synthesis as the primary figure for the mind's powers." But Ashbery engages the "processes, not of synthesis, but of repetition and variation."[20] The end-words of the sestina are engaged in such a process of repetition and variation and, as a result, resist the semantic synthesis of a single determinate meaning. Certainly the sestina, which exhibits a formal closure, can be said to manifest a particular type of synthesis. But as Marianne Shapiro explains, "It is well to make the distinction between *semantic* (conceptual end-stoppage) and *formal* (the end of the poem) closure apparent from the outset. Sestina-writing poets will be seen as operating with the self-imposed constraints of this form to produce, ultimately, a way of achieving emancipation from *semantic* closure."[21]

The formal closure and semantic openness of the sestina are a function of its rather unique combination of a paradigmatic closed form and a metonymic mode of language. The most obvious place in which to observe this distinction in Ashbery's sestina is the *tornada*. All six of the end-words return in this half-strophe, providing a sense of formal closure. But Ashbery's language insists on a semantic openness: the ominous thunder that heralds the Olympian contexts throughout the poem is ironically undercut by the "domestic" context of a burp; Popeye, who had been referred to as if he were Zeus, "chuckled and scratched / His balls" as an act of dismissal or denial of any threat (of castration?) from a "duplicate father." As Shapiro says of an earlier sestina in *Some Trees*, "Attempts to read the 'Poem' under some hypotactic shelter fail, and two antinomic structures emerge: a poetic structure that is whole and a narrative structure that is fragmented, much like a matrix of fossils."[22] The poet escapes from "his own astonished becoming" because the sestina is semantically open—no end-word has a single determinate meaning; as addresser or encoder, he remains unknown, indeterminate.

Ashbery's interest in procedural forms extends beyond the sestina to other elaborate, continental forms such as the Italian canzone and the French pantoum. A diachronic study of the structure of the Renaissance canzone would trace its evolution from the sestina form practiced by twelfth-century troubadours, but it will suffice to discuss the form as Ashbery employs it in the volume *Some Trees*. The canzone is

composed of sixty-five lines: five strophes of twelve lines and a *volta* of
five lines. The remarkable "advance" of the canzone is its distribution
of only five end-words among the twelve lines of each strophe, in the
following pattern: 1 2 1 1 3 1 1 4 4 1 5 5. As a result of this invariable
pattern of repetition, the first end-word in each strophe controls six, or
one-half of the lines; its recurrence dominates the context of that
strophe. The final end-word of each strophe becomes the initial end-
word of the next, linking the strophes head-to-tail as we observed in
the sestina. The movement of the end-words is a retrograde loop,
somewhat simpler than the retrograde cross of the sestina. Eliminating the repetitions, we can observe the movement, beginning with the
second strophe, as: 5 1 2 3 4, 4 5 1 2 3, 3 4 5 1 2, and so forth, until the
permutation of the five elements is complete. The strophes of the
canzone lack the crossing "pincer" movement exhibited by the sestina, but they emphasize the cyclicism that these forms possess. The
final *volta* of five lines contains, as expected, the return of each of the
five end-words.

The relatively short, two- or three-beat line that Ashbery employs in
his "Canzone" exacerbates the effect of the repeated end-words in each
strophe, as if he were winding a skein of yarn into a tighter ball:

> Until the first chill
> No door sat on the clay.
> When Billy brought on the chill
> He began to chill.
> No hand can
> Point to the chill
> It brought. Where a chill
> Was, the grass grows.
> See how it grows.
> Acts punish the chill
> Showing summer in the grass.
> The acts are grass.
>
> Acts of our grass
> Transporting chill
> Over brazen grass
> That retorts as grass
> Leave the clay,
> The grass,
> And that which is grass.
> The far formal forest can,
> Used doubts can
> Sit on the grass.

Hark! The sadness grows
In pain. The shadow grows.

All that grows
In deep shadow or grass
Is lifted to what grows.
Walking, a space grows.
Beyond, weeds chill
Toward night which grows.
Looking about, nothing grows.
Now a whiff of clay
Respecting clay
Or that which grows
Brings on what can.
And no one can.

The sprinkling can
Slumbered on the dock. Clay
Leaked from a can.
Normal heads can
Touch barbed-wire grass
If they can
Sing the old song of can
Waiting for a chill
In the chill
That without a can
Is painting less clay
Therapeutic colors of clay.

We got out into the clay
As a boy can.
Yet there's another kind of clay
Not arguing clay,
As time grows
Not getting larger, but mad clay
Looked for for clay,
And grass
Begun seeming, grass
Struggling up out of clay
Into the first chill
To be quiet and raucous in the chill.

The chill
Flows over burning grass.
Not time grows.
So odd lights can
Fall on sinking clay.[23]

Repetition, even more pronounced in the canzone than in the sestina, is the constitutive formal device of the poem. The recurrence of a dominant end-word in one-half of the lines in each strophe gains a pervasive control of both context and structure. Repetitions in addition to those prescribed by the form are in evidence. In the first strophe, the fifth end-word, "grass," appears in line 8 in a position other than that of the teleuton—governed by its semantic affinity to the fourth end-word, "grows." Repetitions of non–end-words such as the verb "brought" in lines 3 and 7, and the noun "acts" in lines 10 and 12 and in the first line of the next strophe (a head-to-tail link), are carried by the shifting contexts and positions of the end-words themselves. Syntactical structures imitate the retrograde loop of end-word movement: "When Billy brought on the chill / He began to chill. / No hand can / Point to the chill / It brought" (ll. 3–7); clauses proceed but then seem to back over themselves. In general, sentence structure proceeds incrementally as if written for "A Child's Own First Reader." Ashbery is not reluctant to allow us to hear the voice of Billy reading, "the grass grows. / See how it grows" (ll. 8–9). We are not encouraged to hear the poem as the *address* of a single speaker, but to hear the poem as *writing*, a made thing. One context, governed by the dominant end-word, is particularly strong in each strophe; although minor shifts occur, and a more pronounced shift is apparent with each new strophe, the centripetal force of the repetition prevents any significant contextual—or certainly, narrative—development. This one context is so strong in each strophe that a semantic incongruity is occasionally induced, as in "Where a chill / was, the grass grows" (ll. 7–8)—knowing as we do that grass grows in sunlight. So repetition, as the predominant formal device of the poem, overcomes referentiality.

The dominant end-word in each strophe of the canzone repeatedly evaluates its own affinity and dissimilarity, both semantically and contextually; such reevaluations indicate the predominance of the paradigmatic relation in a form with a high degree of recurrence. Roland Barthes distinguishes between symbolic and paradigmatic attitudes toward form: "The symbolic consciousness implies an imagination of depth; it experiences the world as the relation of a superficial form and a many-sided, massive, powerful *Abgrund*. . . . The paradigmatic consciousness, on the contrary, is a formal imagination; it *sees* the signifier linked, as if in profile, to several virtual signifiers which it is at once close to and distinct from: it no longer sees the sign in its depth, it sees it in its perspective."[24] Paradigmatic form is an articulation of "introversive semiosis" in which one signifier is examined in its relation to another signifier; the symbolic is, by contrast, an "extroversive semiosis" in which the signifier is subordinate to a referential signified.[25] The elaborate structure of recurrence which is codified in the canzone form responds gratefully to an introversive semiotic analysis but is decidedly inhospitable to the exegesis of symbolic content, narrative development, or deposits of philosophic gems. As Barthes concludes, "The formal (or paradigmatic) imagination implies an acute attention to the *variation* of several recurrent elements," and accommodates those works "whose esthetic implies the interplay of certain commutations."[26] Repetition and variation displace metaphor and rhyme as the "figurative" language of paradigmatic forms. Ashbery's selection of the sestina and of the canzone, with its even greater proportion of repetition and more intensive centripetal force, allows him to displace both symbolic content and a metaphorical mode of language.

The formal parameters of the pantoum, which enjoyed its greatest popularity in nineteenth-century French poetry, are somewhat simpler to notate than those of the sestina but in many ways are no less difficult to practice. In the pantoum, the second and fourth lines of each quatrain become the first and third of the next quatrain. The repetition of two lines in each successive quatrain constitutes a much higher "percentage by volume" than that of the sestina, in which only the six end-words are recirculated. The leap-frog alternation of lines induces syntactical reevaluations and contextual shifts. The number of quatrains is not prescribed as it is in the sestina, but formal closure is made equally unavoidable by the repetition of the first and third lines of the first quatrain as the second and fourth of the last. In many cases, though not in Ashbery's "Pantoum," the first line of the poem recurs as the final line. This closing device emphasizes the cyclicism of the form and relates the pantoum to another French form, the rondeau. As a result of this pattern, every line of the poem is repeated once. Ashbery introduced his "Pantoum" at a reading by saying, in his self-deferential manner, that with this form, you get twice as much poem for your effort. But as Lorine Niedecker has said, "A recurring thing, for all but the apathetic student, is never the same."[27] We do not get half the semantic or contextual import but rather observe a complex interplay generated by the commutation of the lines.

Pantoum

Eyes shining without mystery,
Footprints eager for the past
Through the vague snow of many clay pipes,
And what is in store?

Footprints eager for the past,
The usual obtuse blanket.
And what is in store
For those dearest to the king?

The usual obtuse blanket?
Of legless regrets and amplifications
For those dearest to the king.
Yes, sirs, connoisseurs of oblivion,

Of legless regrets and amplifications,
That is why a watchdog is shy.
Yes, sirs, connoisseurs of oblivion,
These days are short, brittle; there is only one night.

That is why a watchdog is shy,
Why the court, trapped in a silver storm, is dying.
These days are short, brittle; there is only one night
And that soon gotten over.

Why, the court, trapped in a silver storm, is dying!
Some blunt pretense to safety we have
And that soon gotten over
For they must have motion.

Some blunt pretense to safety we have:
Eyes shining without mystery
For they must have motion
Through the vague snow of many clay pipes.[28]

The handbooks of poetic form claim that the pantoum sustains a binary system of argument; the semantic thrust, if one can follow it at all, proceeds in two complementary but opposed directions. We think of Dante's "battle of diverse thoughts" in the sestina, or Bach's description of the parts of a fugue as "reasonable men in an orderly discussion." In the pantoum, the contestants are reduced from six end-words or four voice parts to two pairs of lines which are engaged in repetition and alternation. In Ashbery's pantoum, the *ennui* of present "safety" (l. 25) casts nostalgic backward glances, "eager for the past" (l. 2)—but also muses over "legless regrets" (l. 10); coincidentally, the man of the hour questions the future, "And what is in store?" (l. 4) but seems to dread upcoming events, as would a shy "watchdog" (l. 14). This ambivalent attitude toward both past and future is a rich French pastry glazed with a "vague snow" (l. 3), or an "obtuse blanket" (l. 6), all for the delectation of the "connoisseurs of oblivion" (l. 12). If this is binarism, it is a very indeterminate brand, or as Ashbery says elsewhere, "a kind of fence-sitting / Raised to the level of an esthetic ideal" (DD 18).

The repetition of entire lines and the alternation of their position in the quatrain indicate that the pantoum is predominantly a paradigmatic form. But several refinements of this device of repetition and variation can be made to distinguish the pantoum from the sestina or canzone. Ashbery's pantoum contains a prominent example in the fifth and sixth quatrains of how repeated lines often undergo a syntactic reevaluation. Line 18, "Why the court, trapped in a silver storm, is dying," appears as the second term in a cause-and-effect relationship— because the days grow short, the court is dying. When the line recurs in the next quatrain, it is in the initial position: "Why, the court, trapped in a silver storm, is dying!" Although the words repeat, the punctuation has been altered so that there is both a semantic shift from explanation to exclamation and a syntactic shift from dependent to independent clause. The language calls attention to itself as paradigm, not as symbol; the structure of the poem demands that the reader evaluate these two lines as "dissimilar but sister signs" (introversive semiosis) and discourages any inquiry to the reference, or signified, of "silver storm."

A second significant effect of the repetition and alternation of lines is a contextual shift. In the fifth quatrain, the demonstrative pronoun in the line "And that soon gotten over" refers directly to "night" in the previous line, but indirectly to the context of dying and oblivion. In the sixth stanza, "that" refers to the "blunt pretense to safety we have," a context opposed, however inadequately, to that of dying. Such contextual shifts are pervasive and, as indicated by the disparity of dying and safety, often reinforce the binary argument in the pantoum. But contextual shifts also prevent any line from having a single determinate meaning; such ambiguity replaces the function of symbol and metaphor with their multiple connotations or exterior referents.

Finally, each line of the pantoum takes on a semiautonomous, molecular quality. Lines such as "Yes, sirs, connoisseurs of oblivion," are discontinuous and mobile, combining and recombining with new elements in the text. They refuse to be bound to a semantic progression or a particular syntactic construction. Quite frequently, the lines are not enjambed, so that the thought, the syntax, and the line are coextensive: "Eyes shining without mystery, / Footprints eager for the past" (ll. 1–2). Such insularity, required by the repetition and shifting of the lines, encourages us to examine the bonds between the word-atoms:

Can eyes shine *without* mystery? can footprints proceed eagerly toward what they have already *passed?* But whatever parallelism of
thought or syntax is established in these first two lines, like the crystal
lattice structure of a grain of salt, is dissolved when line 2 is reconstituted in the context of the second quatrain and line 1 is displaced to
the seventh and final quatrain. Each line relies largely on its own
mystery and cannot be dependent on any prior contextual or narrative
information. The commutation of lines in the pantoum demands a
molecular autonomy.

### Louis Zukofsky: The Renaissance and Brooklyn Heights

Louis Zukofsky's renovation of the sestina began when Ashbery was
still a grade-schooler. But in the diachronic record of an eight-hundred-
year-old form, Zukofsky's "Mantis" and Ashbery's "Farm Implements" are practically simultaneous events. Both poems pursue a new
content suitable to the twisting spiral of the sestina's end-words, a new
expression of "la battaglia delli diversi pensieri." Their "discovery" of a
postmodern, predetermined form whose shape was familiar to many
Renaissance poets in France and Italy has its scientific analogue: Crick
and Watson, unveiling the double-helix model of DNA, must have
seen the resemblance to that ancient timepiece, the hourglass; but
their model contained a map of genetic coding, not grains of sand. That
Zukofsky intended to write the sestina "anew" is clear from his discussion of the poem with L. S. Dembo:

> I suppose there are two types of natures. One is aware of the two-hundred-
> year-old oak, and it's still alive and it's going to have some use to him; the
> other one is going to say cut it down and build a supermarket. I'm not
> inclined to be the latter, nor do I want to imitate a traditional form, but if
> that thing has lasted for two hundred years and has some merit in it, it is
> possible I can use it and somehow in transferring it into words—as I said
> in *"Aleatorical indeterminate"*—make something new of it. And the
> same for the form of the sestina. Musicians have done that with fugues.[29]

Zukofsky encounters several hazards in the renovation of poetic form.
He does not wish to imitate lamely a traditional form; to do so would
be "absolutely useless . . . just a facility—like that of Sunday painters"
(MP 276). Such was the case in the nineteenth century—a reference to
the efforts of Swinburne perhaps—in which the sestina form became
mere "wicker-work," "not the form but a Victorian / Stuffing like
upholstery" (AL 76–77). Nor has he any intention of restoring the

form to its original condition with period furnishings from the age of Daniel, Petrarch, or Dante. Any sort of restoration attempt would validate the criticism of "the so-called 'modern' [who] will say you cannot write a sestina anymore, that Dante did it and it's dead and gone. . . . There's no use in writing the same sestina as Dante, because . . . you couldn't do it, except by copying it word for word and believing it's yours—an extreme case" (MP 275). But neither will Zukofsky relinquish the possibility of the form for the twentieth century—he will not cut down the oak to build "supermarkets." He disagrees with Williams's statement, quoted in " 'Mantis,' An Interpretation," that "Our world will not stand it, / the implications of a too regular form" (AL 77). Zukofsky will not join in the modernist rejection of predetermined forms; with the oak already felled by the high modernists, he does not feel compelled to haul out new lumber and build from scratch. His distinction as a postmodernist is that he neither restores nor abandons the old forms of the sestina or the canzone—he renovates the form by "making it new" from the inside out.

"Mantis"

Mantis! praying mantis! since your wings' leaves
And your terrified eyes, pins, bright, black and poor
Beg—"Look, take it up" (thoughts' torsion)! "save it!"
I who can't bear to look, cannot touch,—You—
You can—but no one sees you steadying lost
In the cars' drafts on the lit subway stone.

Praying mantis, what wind-up brought you, stone
On which you sometimes prop, prey among leaves
(Is it love's food your raised stomach prays?), lost
Here, stone holds only seats on which the poor
Ride, who rising from the news may trample you—
The shops' crowds a jam with no flies in it.

Even the newsboy who now sees knows it
No use, papers make money, makes stone, stone,
Banks, "it is harmless," he says moving on—You?
Where will he put *you*? There are no safe leaves
To put you back in here, here's news! too poor
Like all the separate poor to save the lost.

Don't light on my chest, mantis! do—you're lost,
Let the poor laugh at my fright, then see it:
My shame and theirs, you whom old Europe's poor
Call spectre, strawberry, by turns; a stone—

You point—they say—you lead lost children—leaves
Close in the paths men leave, saved, safe with you.

Killed by thorns (once men), who will now save you
Mantis? what male love bring a fly, be lost
Within your mouth, prophetess, harmless to leaves
And hands, faked flower,—the myth is: dead, bones, it
Was assembled, apes wing in wind: On stone,
Mantis, you will die, touch, beg, of the poor.

Android, loving beggar, dive to the poor
As your love would even without head to you,
Graze like machined wheels, green, from off this stone
And preying on each terrified chest, lost
Say, I am old as the globe, the moon, it
Is my old shoe, yours, be free as the leaves.

Fly, mantis, on the poor, arise like leaves
The armies of the poor, strength: stone on stone
And build the new world in your eyes, Save it!

(AL 73–74)

The six-page, verse "Interpretation" that accompanies Zukofsky's
sestina is a remarkable reassembling of the poem's scaffold; the
closed-form poet refuses to stow the construction materials and devices, the evidence of his artifice, after the poem has been made. Step
by step, the decisions by which Zukofsky arrives at the necessity of the
sestina form for his poem are enumerated. The genesis of this poem is
an "incident"—a mantis, lost in the subway, flying at the poet's chest,
startling him. Its "inception" is a first draft of twenty-seven words
which fail to do more than write up the "ungainliness" of the creature.
The incident itself is insufficient, not *"all* that was happening." There
has been a coincidence of "six thoughts' reflection (pulse's witness) of
what was happening / All immediate, not moved by any transition"
(AL 75). These six thoughts are the first indication that the poem will
assume the form of a sestina, with its six end-words and six stanzas.
Finally, the poet questions:

> Consider:
> "(thoughts' torsion)"
> la battaglia delli diversi pensieri . . .
> the battle of diverse thoughts—
> The actual twisting
> Of many and diverse thoughts
> What form should *that* take?
>
> (AL 75–76)

Zukofsky describes his arrival, after the "incident," after the "inception" of the poem, at the question of an appropriate form. Of course, by citing Dante's description of the sestina, the question contains its own answer. The lyric of a single, concentrated vision is inadequate to express the many and diverse thoughts that the poet, in that one moment, encounters. The "ungainliness" of the mantis is replicated in the twisting of the sestina form itself. But the mantis that is "lost," or contextually displaced, in the subway initiates contextually diverse thoughts on entomology, self-extinction myth, and especially the plight of the poor who find themselves begging in the subways.

> One feels in fact inevitably
> About the coincidence of the mantis lost in the subway,
> About the growing oppression of the poor—
> Which is the situation most pertinent to us—,
> With the fact of the sestina:
> Which together fatally now crop up again
> To twist themselves anew
> To record not a sestina, post Dante,
> Nor even a mantis.
>
> (AL 77)

Zukofsky does not want to imitate the traditional form, post-Dante. His renovation of the sestina occurs as the inevitable consequence of two facts: the twisting structure of the poetic form and a *new* battle of diverse thoughts expressing the most pertinent issue of the day.

Zukofsky's analysis of his poem's content—thoughts' torsion—precedes his identification of the sestina "as the only / Form that will include the most pertinent subject of our day" (AL 77). For Ashbery, as we noted earlier, the elaborate twisting of the sestina form serves as an exploratory probe of the remoter areas of consciousness. In Ashbery, the form generates an appropriate content; in Zukofsky, the content discovers an appropriate form. Despite this difference in craft, neither poet alters the form of the sestina, retaining the outer shell of the structure intact. Both adhere to Dante's description of the shape of the content—notice that Dante's "battaglia" does not specify an appropriate subject but the manner in which content behaves when intimately related to the sestina form. Each poet guts the sestina of traditional amorous or pastoral subjects, introducing a "battaglia nova": in Zukofsky, the coincidence of a mantis lost in the subway and the plight of the urban poor; in Ashbery, the multiple voices in a cosmopolitan blend of high and low culture. But postmodern renovation also involves a new attitude toward predetermined form: Ashbery employs its strictures as an exploratory device, to find "the new" itself; Zukofsky, convinced that a predetermined form can express the most pertinent situations of contemporary life, rejects the modernist view of closed form as a false sense of order and regularity imposed on the (as Pound says in "Hugh Selwyn Mauberley") "accelerated grimace" of our age.

Zukofsky's renovation of the sestina form is intended as a refutation of the modernist rejection of predetermined forms, but his assertion of two corollary characteristics of procedural form also identifies his efforts as distinctly postmodern. The first of these characteristics is the predominance of recurrence as both structural device and paradigmatic figure, displacing metaphor. Although most obviously present in predetermined forms, recurrence is significant in all of Zukofsky's work, including "A" and the finite series in *All*. In fact, Zukofsky ventures to say in an interview, "All art is made, I think, out of recurrence. The point is to have recurrence so that it isn't mere repetition, like Poe's 'Bells, bells, bells, bells.' The idea is to have these recurrences so that they will always turn up as new, 'just' different. Something has happened to the movement or you see the thing 'differently'" (MP 279). His distinction between static repetition and shifting recurrence is particularly attractive when one considers that the project at hand, the renovation of the sestina, is an attempt to have an old form turn up as new, seen differently. Additionally, Zukofsky is aware that the structure of the sestina exploits recurrence to a degree greater than most poetic forms. When he finally decides on a form for "Mantis," he concludes:

> That this thoughts' torsion
> Is really a sestina
> Carrying subconsciously
> Many intellectual and sensual properties of the
>        forgetting and remembering Head
> One human's intuitive Head

> (AL 76)

In the sestina, recurrence of the six *parole rime* enacts the intellectual and sensual properties of the "remembering Head." The shifts in context from one strophe to the next indicate that much is forgotten while much that is new takes the place of the old. The end-words of the sestina avoid static repetition by always turning up in the company of new materials, new contexts; in each strophe, their semantic import and contextual value must be seen differently. Zukofsky examines the role of the end-words:

> The sestina, then, the repeated end words
> Of the lines' winding around themselves,
> Since continuous in the Head, whatever has been read,
>     whatever is heard,
>         whatever is seen
> Perhaps goes back cropping up again with
> Inevitable recurrence again in the blood . . .
>
> (AL 76)

He recognizes that the *retrogradatio cruciata* motion of the end-words is the most appropriate form in which to express the coincidence of several thoughts' torsion, winding around themselves in the head. But Zukofsky also identifies the sestina and the action of its end-words as the most concentrated example in poetic form of an inevitable recurrence, both intuitive and physiological, structural and figural.

John Taggart, in his discussion of "Mantis," notes one effect of a structured recurrence in the sestina: "All of Zukofsky's rhyme words appear at more than their predetermined end positions throughout the poem. . . . The result is a heightened fugal complexity of very few words."[30] In fugue structure, a repeated subject is joined by new material. The proliferation of the end-words in "Mantis" indicates an even greater proportion of recurrent material and a greater centripetal force than usual in the sestina. If all art is made of recurrence, Zukofsky is determined to display this property to an undeniable degree in his practice of procedural forms.

An instance in which recurrence demonstrates the ability of the form to record the most pertinent situation of the day occurs in the third strophe. The newsboy who notices the poet's concern for the mantis declares that it is "no use." The boy's resignation—the mantis is "harmless" anyway, as the poor are impotent—and his employment cause the poet to remember something read: "papers make money, makes stone, stone, / Banks." This observation is a condensed version, glossed by Zukofsky in his "Interpretation," of a clever interlocking statement on the economics of the very poor: "Rags make paper, paper makes money, money makes banks, banks make loans, loans make poverty, poverty makes rags" (AL 79). The newsboy is "unable to think beyond" this cyclic repetition that conspires to retain the poorest at the subsistence level. In this manner, Zukofsky claims that the recurrence of the sestina form is quite pertinent to the cycle of poverty, and yet, by its avoidance of exact repetition, by its attempt to see things differently and encourage new modes of thinking about an old problem, the poem may offer some hope to those lost and begging in the subway.

The second distinctly postmodern characteristic of a procedural form which Zukofsky's "Mantis" illustrates is an antagonistic attitude toward symbolism. In his "Interpretation," Zukofsky argues:

> But the facts are not a symbol.
>
> There is the difference between that
> And a fact (the mantis in the subway)
> And all the other facts the mantis sets going about it.
>
> No human being wishes to become
> An insect for the sake of a symbol.
>
> (AL 78)

The mantis and the poor are coincidental facts that twist themselves together, relationally, within the fact of the sestina form; the mantis is not a symbol for the poor. Such symbolism is antithetical to the form of the sestina. It implies that there is a superficial structure or set of signifiers which momentarily conceals a more important, referential signified. Zukofsky's point throughout his "Interpretation" has been that there is a correlation of the "fact" of the sestina's twisting structure and the "thoughts' torsion" that comprises the poem's content. Recurrence in the sestina presents these coincidental facts in *profile*, examining their variations and commutations; the symbolic mode insists on an imagination of *depth*, a hierarchy of issues so large as to squash our poor insect. As Zukofsky says, the mantis sets other facts going about it; it does not "stand for" the poor as if it were a pin in a man's lapel.

The postmodern renovation of closed forms is most obvious in its effect on traditional content: although the structure of the building remains intact, the dumpster on the street is full of old plaster and floorboarding. For poets like Ashbery and Zukofsky, it is easier to displace traditional subjects in the sestina, canzone, and pantoum because they are foreign imports—their continental heritage is considerably devalued in United States currency. But in general, it is easier for the contractor to gut a building than to determine how and with what materials it may be made newly inhabitable. The contemporary function of closed form is the first consideration. Both poets reject the romantic concept of closed form as superimposed upon content: Ashbery is most avant-garde in his use of elaborate forms as exploratory devices to uncover remoter areas of consciousness; Zukofsky considers the twisting form of the sestina and the ungainliness of the mantis to be a coincidence of related facts that find one another. But there is also the furnishing to consider. The absence of rhyme and the predominance of recurrence in these procedural forms allow the poet to displace symbol and metaphor in favor of the commutation of several elements. Ashbery shuffles the several voices of kings and knaves like a Las Vegas blackjack dealer; Zukofsky offers the thoughts' torsion of a mild Marxist economics, entomology, and Melanesian myth. The postmodern renovated form is a paradigmatic structure of repetition and variation, invariably opposed to the symbolic consciousness in which form is a superficial film over the depths of a significant content.

## Canonic Form in Weldon Kees, Robert Creeley, and Louis Zukofsky

In music the device is called a ritornello, and it seems appropriate to begin this essay on canonic forms with a "little return" to passages by Louis Zukofsky and then Roland Barthes:

> All art is made, I think, out of recurrence. . . . The idea is to have these recurrences so that they will always turn up as new, "just" different. Something has happened to the movement or you see the thing "differently."[31]

> The constraint of recurrence . . . has an almost demiurgic value: it is by the regular return of the units and of the associations of units that the work appears constructed, i.e. endowed with meaning; linguistics calls these rules of combination *forms*. . . . [Form] is what keeps the contiguity of units from appearing as a pure effect of chance: the work of art is what man wrests from chance.[32]

Zukofsky and Barthes agree that recurrence is an essential structural ingredient in a work of art. The degree to which recurrence occurs and is deemed acceptable, however, varies with the literary genre. In the realistic novel, narrative development proceeds largely by the contiguity of units of plot, character, and setting; recurrence, although implicit as a function of the novel's theme, is explicit (observable on the level of discourse) only as leitmotif, a decorative figure.[33] Likewise, in the epic poem, which also exhibits a developmental superstructure, recurrent motifs are subordinate to larger structural plans.

But the fugal recurrence exhibited by Zukofsky's finite series tips the balance in the other direction: the new is ceaselessly accompanied by the old, and the old is constantly being reevaluated in its new context; fugal recurrence becomes the constitutive structure. All poetic recurrence is formal, though we can identify two types: the phonic recurrence of meter, rhyme, or alliteration in a sonnet; and in the sestina or pantoum, the lexical recurrence of end-words or entire lines approaching 50 percent of the poem's volume. Lexical recurrence is most prominent in such tightly wound cyclic forms as the round or canon, where repeated phrases consume up to 95 percent of the poem's volume. In canonic form, the repetition of the entire voice part permits the entrance of so little new material that these tightly wound forms are almost invariably brief. Weldon Kees's "Round," several of Robert Creeley's "feedback" poems, and a few pieces from what Louis Zukofsky might call "The Art of the Canon" will serve to illustrate this most recursive of procedural forms.

Those who were first to appreciate the work of Weldon Kees did not fail to recognize the importance of recurrence in his poetry. The editor of *The Collected Poems of Weldon Kees*, Donald Justice, observes that "with the devices of enumeration, repetition, and variation, which have attracted so many modern poets, Kees experiments endlessly, from the early 'Fugue' to the late 'Round.' "[34] As Robert E. Knoll points out, "His most prominent literary device is repetition."[35] In some ways a precursor of John Ashbery by a generation, Kees is also attracted to elaborate fixed forms such as the sestina and the villanelle in which recurrence is codified to the utmost; he anticipates Ashbery's stylistic range in "Farm Implements and Rutabagas in a Landscape" by writing what Justice has called the "first truly prosy sestina." But Kees's formalism is at its most innovative in the highly recursive forms he has derived from music: the fugue and the round. Kees may have been aided in this formal crossover by his experience as a musician and composer—though jazz improvisation and highly programmatic canons rarely take the stage together. But whether Kees renovates the fixed-form sestina or derives elaborate constraints from musical forms, recurrence provides the steady downbeat in his poetry.

Kees's poem "Fugue," from the first of his three books, *The Last Man* (1943), is not as tightly wound as his later poem "Round." In fugal imitation, as we noted earlier, the repeated "subject" is joined by new material, whereas in canonic imitation, the entire voice part repeats itself. But it will be of interest to compare the degree of recurrence in these two poems; in each case, Kees is true to the formal implications of his title.

Fugue

When the light
Begins to fail,
Many now alive
Will fall.
Falling night
Will darken drives,
Spread the darkness
Over all.

Though the sun
Is blinding now,
Spreading heat
On grass and skin,
Minutes tick
With steady beat,
Saying sun
Will soon be gone.

Light will fail,
Alive will fall;
Sun that blinded
Will be gone.
Heat will vanish
With the sun.
Falling night
Will cover all.

(CP 36)

This fugue, with three stanzas of eight lines each, is in three voice parts. Both phonic and lexical recurrence occur, within each stanza and between stanzas. Kees operates according to no fixed rules or constraints as he would in the sestina but rather adopts the polyphonic model of counterpoint in the poem. In the first stanza, several modes of recurrence are audible. The most familiar in poetic form is rhyme, and although Kees abandons the scheme in the second and third stanzas, here he ties an intricate knot: "light" and "night" (ll. 1 and 5) and "fall" and "all" (ll. 4 and 8) bind the two quatrains of the first stanza together by connecting beginnings and endings; "alive" (l. 3) and "drives" (l. 6) mark the center. Kees does not employ the alternating couplet of traditional quatrains but rather causes a recurrence or return of sounds from the first four lines of the stanza in the latter four.

We notice two other types of recurrent sounds. The assonance of "light" (l. 1) and "alive" (l. 3), and the alliteration of "fail" (l. 2) and "fall" (l. 4), are equivalences of sound which, as Jakobson claims, inevitably involve semantic equivalences. Brightness and darkness, living and dying are reinforced as related terms. The repetition and variation of words also support this semantic bond: "fall" in line 4 is a synecdoche (as a characteristic action) for the impending death of "many now alive." The verb is repeated in the present participle, "falling" (l. 5), as a dead metaphor for the coming on of night, darkness. Again, the repetition and variation of a word involves the semantic connection in the poem of death and darkness. Other examples in the stanza are "darken" (l. 6), which appears to refer to the moral decay of "drives," and "darkness" (l. 7), which is again the decay of light.

The second stanza functions in the fugal scheme as a related counterstatement, the entrance of a new voice part. New material such as sun, heat, and skin is introduced. Rhyme—again, between the two quatrains—is present in "heat" (l. 11) and "beat" (l. 14). The repetition of an end-word, "sun," is similarly dispersed between the first and seventh lines of the stanza.

Only in the third stanza can we fully appreciate how the above effects of poetic recurrence, familiar in traditional forms, are employed as fugal counterpoint. If we consider the first and second stanzas as the entrances of two voice parts, the third stanza enacts their simultaneous counterpoint, a splicing or knitting together of the two. The first two lines of the third stanza recombine the first four end-words of the first stanza; "light" and "alive," "fail" and "fall," the corresponding terms in the equation, are now stacked one over the other, although previously they had alternated like the red and black cards in a game of solitaire. A rhetorical and syntactical condensation has occurred—as often the baroque composer will shorten or abbreviate a motif—which nevertheless reintroduces the essential thematic material of the first stanza. The third through sixth lines of the final stanza reintroduce material from the second stanza. The seventh line repeats the fifth line of the poem; the final line is a variant of the last line of the first stanza. Thus, the entire third stanza is composed, not of static repetitions (Zukofsky's complaint), but of recurrences, variants on the materials of the first two stanzas—light and sun, life and heat, blindness and darkness. As Barthes claims, "The formal (or paradigmatic) imagination implies an acute attention to the *variation* of several recurrent elements" and the interplay of "commutations."[36]

The fugal recurrence of Kees's poem is a paradigmatic function; the repeated "subject," combining with new materials, continually reevaluates its own affinity and dissimilarity. Barthes distinguishes between rhetorical development and the formal commutation that one finds in a poem like "Fugue": "Rhetorical continuity develops, amplifies; it will agree to repeat only if it can transform. [Formal] continuity repeats, but combines differently what it repeats. Thus rhetorical continuity never returns to what it has set forth, while [formal] continuity returns, recurs, recalls: the new is ceaselessly accompanied by the old: it is, one might say, a fugal continuity, in the course of which identifiable fragments ceaselessly reappear."[37] The rhetorical continuity found in narrative works is a syntagmatic function—movement from units of plot, to units of character, to units of setting. If we are told that Emma Bovary's eyes are brown, we will later be disturbed to read—as it happens—that Emma Bovary's eyes are blue. We will only tolerate the amplification of what has been set forth in a narrative work, not its repetition or variation. But in the paradigmatic form of the fugue, the end-words of lines 1–4 are "combined differently" in the third stanza; they are joined by new material from the second stanza; development is rejected in favor of commutation.

If we could attach Kees's later poem "Round" (1954) to some kind of recurrence meter, our reading would indicate that it lies between the fugue, which permits the introduction of new material, and the canon, which repeats the entire voice part. The form of Kees's poem is most likely derived from the round in music, a perpetual canon in which, typically, three voices enter at staggered intervals, imitate one another strictly, and lead back to where they began. But there is also the model of the sixteenth-century French form, the *rondeau*, a fixed form of thirteen lines, three stanzas, and only two rhymes; the form includes a *rentrement*, or partial repetition of the first line at the end of the succeeding stanzas—aabba aabR aabbaR. Kees neither attempts the strict imitation of the perpetual canon nor does he adhere to the fixed form of the *rondeau* but rather plays a variation on aspects common to both the musical and poetic forms.

"Round" consists of three stanzas of eight lines each (as did the earlier "Fugue"), retaining in a sense the three voice parts of the musical round and, though the number of lines differ, the three stanzas of the *rondeau*. Another requirement of cyclical forms is the repetition of the first line as the final—rhetorical development is stymied by this return to the beginning. Further affinities or dissimilarities require a closer look at the poem; Kees's "Round" is as much a formal invention as it is a derivative of literary or musical models.

Round

"Wondrous life!" cried Marvell at Appleton House.
Renan admired Jesus Christ "wholeheartedly."

But here dried ferns keep falling to the floor,
And something inside my head
Flaps like a worn-out blind. Royal Cortissoz is dead,
A blow to the *Herald-Tribune*. A closet mouse
Rattles the wrapper on the breakfast food. Renan
Admired Jesus Christ "wholeheartedly."

Flaps like a worn-out blind. Cézanne
Would break out in the quiet streets of Aix
And shout, "Le monde, c'est terrible!" Royal
Cortissoz is dead. And something inside my head
Flaps like a worn-out blind. The soil
In which the ferns are dying needs more Vigoro.
There is no twilight on the moon, no mist or rain,
No hail or snow, no life. Here in this house

Dried ferns keep falling to the floor, a mouse
Rattles the wrapper on the breakfast food. Cézanne
Would break out in the quiet streets and scream. Renan
Admired Jesus Christ "wholeheartedly." And something inside my head
Flaps like a worn-out blind. Royal Cortissoz is dead.
There is no twilight on the moon, no hail or snow.
One notes fresh desecrations of the portico.
"Wondrous life!" cried Marvell at Appleton House.

(CP 100)

When a round in three voice parts is sung, the first voice, called the
*dux* or leader, enters alone for the duration of a measure; the second
and third voices, called the *comites* or companions, enter at equal
intervals—as Kees's stanzas are of equal length. When the round is
completed, the third voice will be heard alone for that same duration
of a measure. Now if Kees were to write a strict perpetual canon, his
three stanzas would be identical—and of course there is no way, short
of an actual performance, to read the stanzas in an overlapping manner. But I think that Kees, by his use of phrasal repetition, attempts to
convey the audible effect of a sung round in which the listener, unable
to comprehend simultaneously the text in all three voices, hears snippets and snatches of first one and then another. The only point at
which the voices do not interfere with one another is in the first and
last measure; so Kees repeats clearly the entire first line as the last,
solo. Between the head and the tail lies the body: here phrasal repetition imitates the vying of the overlapping voices for the attention of
the audience.

In the fixed-form pantoum, each line is repeated in the poem, intact,
and only once. Kees's phrasal repetition allows him to vary, commute,

and recombine motifs. Despite the programmatic constraints of the cyclic structure, the poet is still free to enjoy the many permutations of phrases, as Bach was said to have improvised fugues at the keyboard. The effect is distinctly contrapuntal. No line, other than the first, survives the round intact, either as a syntactical or a prosodic unit. Kees varies the wording of phrases, commutes phrases both within and between stanzas, and combines old "subjects" with new predicates. Although recurrence in the pantoum reaches 50 percent by the repetition of each line one time, certain phrases in the round are repeated several times; perhaps two-thirds of Kees's "Round" is comprised of phrasal recurrence. Kees also shifts a line or phrase, otherwise intact, across line breaks. Since the line break in verse alters emphasis, the effect is significant; in the more fluid musical form, the staggered entrances of the voice parts produce a similar, if less prominent, effect. This phrasal shift is the primary device of variation in the canons and reverberations of Zukofsky and Creeley.

As in the "Fugue," each stanza of "Round" has a slightly different contrapuntal function. The first stanza is the *dux* or leader since it first introduces material which then recurs: every phrase in this stanza, except "A blow to the *Herald-Tribune*" (l. 6) (which helps to identify a now obscure art critic, Royal Cortissoz, who died in 1948), is repeated at least once more in the poem. The reader encounters the citations from Marvell and Renan in lines 1–2, but an evaluation of the speaker's attitude toward his allusions must be suspended until the final line of the stanza or of the entire poem. The cyclic structure of the round forces a secondary reading in which each recurrence of a phrase must be interpreted differently. These two citations are unqualified exclamations of praise: "wondrous" and "wholeheartedly." In his poem "The Garden," Marvell praises life's munificence, its fruitfulness; Renan admires Christ from a humanist point of view. "But," in line 3, it becomes apparent that the speaker endorses neither of these appraisals. In his house, as opposed to the gardens at Appleton, "dried ferns keep falling to the floor." Psychologically disturbed, the speaker is no more able to accept Christ the man with enthusiasm than he can accept the mystical Christ. The speaker's attitude is reminiscent of the spiritual desiccation expressed by Eliot in *The Waste Land* some thirty years earlier.

The most startling image occurs as the central hinge of the stanza: "And something inside my head / Flaps like a worn-out blind" (ll. 4–5). The speaker describes a violently abrupt and humiliating self-exposure. As anyone can testify who has been caught at an inopportune moment by a blind's worn-out spring, the effect is one of frayed nerves and an insuppressibly paranoid suspicion of the mechanism; as the simile indicates, when the object of such suspicion is one's own mind, the effect becomes devastating. The semantic importance of the phrase is matched by its structural prominence. The phrase "Flaps like a worn-out blind" recurs in the first line of the second stanza, reinforcing the rebuttal of Marvell's exclamation, "Wondrous life!" The entire sentence recurs at the center of both the second and the third stanza. In addition to the frequency of recurrence, the line gains structural significance because it is the only phrase that commutes to an identical—and prominent—position in each stanza.

Of course, there are contextual shifts in each of the succeeding stanzas; the phrase, to recall Barthes's description of fugal continuity, combines differently when it repeats. The elegiac phrase (though it is difficult to ascertain how much remorse the speaker or the *Herald-Tribune* feels), "Royal Cortissoz is dead," precedes this central image in the second stanza, but follows it in the final stanza. The result in this latter instance is that the fifth line of the third stanza is, except for punctuation, an intact repetition of the fifth line of the first stanza. (In accord with the "round" structure, only the first line of the poem, a complete sentence, repeats exactly; no portion of it recurs before its repetition as the final line.) Such structural emphasis of a phrase is appropriate to the severity of the speaker's psychological disturbance, a suicidal despair. We learn from one biographical note that in July of 1955, within a year of the publication of this poem, Kees's car was "discovered on the north approach to the Golden Gate Bridge where it had been abandoned in the deep fog of mid-summer. He has not been seen or heard from since."[38]

The close of the first stanza insists that we return to, and reinterpret, the exclamations of Marvell and Renan; the succeeding contexts have made it apparent that, although initially presented with a benign neutrality, these exclamations are not only unendorsed by, but suffer the malignant irony of the speaker. The closet mouse that "rattles the wrapper" (an evocatively arid phrase, and a possible allusion to *The Waste Land*) on a package of dry cereal rebuts Marvell's assessment of life as a fruitful garden. For those of us who do not recall the first lines, the round form obligingly recalls them for us. "Renan admired Jesus Christ 'wholeheartedly'" is the only line that recurs within the bounds of the first stanza and its reassessment brings the stanza to a close. The phrase returns intact, but it is now shifted across the line break. "Renan" himself is isolated at the end of line 7; the increased emphasis that the line break's pause places on his name hints at a rebuttal by the speaker: *Renan*—but not I—admires a secular Christ.

This phrasal shift combined with a context of ironic reassessment indicates that the lines in "Round" do not merely repeat but recur; as Zukofsky claims, "Something has happened to the movement or you see the thing differently." Such recurrence illustrates the predominance of the paradigmatic function in canonic forms: nearly every phrase reevaluates its own affinity and dissimilarity.

The second stanza functions as the *comes* or companion of the first, although its composition indicates that this "Round" is not a strict perpetual canon in which the initial voice part is repeated exactly and in its entirety. This stanza is an illustration of a fugal recurrence in which repeated subjects are joined with new material. Between the flapping blind and the lament for Royal Cortissoz, Cézanne's exclamation "Le monde, c'est terrible!" is introduced as a refutation of Marvell which the speaker endorses. In the final two lines of the stanza, the observation that there is "no life" on the moon further expresses the speaker's suicidal bitterness. The stanza also contains an interesting example of recombination in which the "ferns" of line 3 return in a similar but amusingly different statement: "The soil / In which the ferns are dying needs more Vigoro" (ll. 13–14). Kees's black humor comes to the fore: surely this miracle compound, guaranteed to make gardening easier, will fail; it may be that both speaker and houseplant have overdosed on such modern improvements, unknown and unnecessary at Appleton House.

The commutation of phrases from one stanza to another and their recombination in a new arrangement or with new material require that each phrase possess a molecular independence. There is an abrupt contextual disjunction between the domestic images of ferns, blinds, and breakfast food, and the citations of a seventeenth-century poet, an impressionist painter, and a contemporary journalist. Such phrases as "Flaps like a worn-out blind" function more like the modular parts of a mobile than the pieces of a jigsaw puzzle in which the cat's eye has a single, fixed position. Fugal recurrence and the cyclic form of the round prevent any linear, narrative development. Each phrase functions as a free, not bound, motif.

The first two stanzas contain several desultory end rhymes: "House" (l. 1) and "mouse" (l. 6); the central couplet in the first stanza, "head" and "dead" (ll. 4–5); and in the second stanza, "Royal" (l. 11) and "soil" (l. 13). But these end rhymes are at the mercy of phrasal shifts, often reappearing as internal rhymes: in the second stanza, "dead" and "head" recur as an internal rhyme in line 12. Rhyme as a type of phonic recurrence is structurally subordinate in the round to phrasal recurrence. By contrast, one can distinguish between the Shakespearean and

Petrarchan sonnets largely because the stanzas are shaped by a predetermined rhyme scheme (some variation by the poet being admitted). In a fixed form, rhyme schemes assert both a structural and
semantic control; in the highly programmatic round form, rhyme is
desultory because it is subject to the incessant recombination of
phrases.

In the third stanza, however, the scattered rhymes of the earlier
stanzas devolve into a structurally significant pattern in support of the
formal closure that the return of the initial line asserts. The effect is
similar to one frequently observed in commercial advertising: film
footage is run backward and a beverage appears to spill into a glass, not
out of it. In this case, the product advertised is formal closure and not a
soft drink. The pattern of rhyme in the last stanza resembles the cyclic
form of the entire poem: abbccdda. "Mouse" and "House" form the
outer pair; "head" and "dead," as in the first stanza, occupy the central
couplet. The "b" and "d" rhymes, less prominent, have not appeared as
end rhymes earlier in the poem. The rhyming of the first and last lines
of the third stanza is coordinate with the recurrence of the first line of
the poem as the last. But Kees has not established such a rhyme
scheme in each stanza because any attempt to fix the pattern of rhyme
would have restricted the molecular independence of the shifting and
recurring phrases. In canonic forms, paradigmatic recurrence may be
accompanied by types of phonic recurrence such as rhyme or alliteration, but it remains the predominant structural device of the poem.

The first and the last stanza of "Round" are like the print and the
negative of a photograph: every phrase in the first stanza (except for
one) subsequently recurs in the poem; every line in the third stanza
(except for the penultimate) is composed of phrases that have previously appeared. Kees's "Round" cannot then be a strict canon since it
allows old material to "fall out" and new material to enter, but the
percentage of recurrence is nevertheless higher than that of a pantoum
or his earlier "Fugue." The frantic acceleration of recurrence in the
third stanza, and this sense of an inversion, culminates in the exact
recurrence of the initial line as the final line of the poem. Cyclic forms
create ambiguities in both formal and semantic closure. Formally,
beginning and end are identical: the poem cannot proceed any further,
and yet it must continue; it executes a return rather than a full stop.
Semantically, one cannot return to the initial line with the same
innocence: there is a pointed shift from the joyous "cry" of Marvell to
the despairing "shout" and "scream" of Cézanne (the only three verbs
of "saying" in the poem). When Marvell utters his cry a second time,
we are well aware of the speaker's malignant irony. In the penultimate

line (the only new line in the last stanza), the contrast between the speaker's graffiti-scored home and Appleton House cues us to his dissatisfaction: "One notes fresh desecrations of the portico" (l. 23). The difference we observe in the repeated line denies us the satisfaction of semantic closure. Not only does the cyclic form obstruct thematic or narrative development in favor of recombination and variation, it also denies the resolution that development promises. Although Weldon Kees may, or may not, have chosen to end his own life, the speaker of the poem considers and reconsiders his own arguments, perpetually reciting his soliloquy.

Robert Creeley's canonic-form poems have less in common with Pachelbel than with the structure of a Charlie Parker chorus. But if his model is jazz rather than classical, his description of the technique retains a distinctly musical phraseology: he is interested in poems that "make use of feedback, that is, a repetitive relocation of phrasing, where words are curiously returned to an almost objective state of presence so that *they* speak rather than someone speaking with them."[39] Ekbert Faas notes that Creeley widely employs this technique in his poetry through "the recurrence of certain phrases like the leitmotifs of a musical score, and above all by the use of key words which through repetition are slowly emptied of all meaning they had in the context of their first occurrence."[40] But "feedback" becomes the constitutive structure in a handful of canonic poems in which the entire voice part, the entire stanza, is repeated.

One example is the poem "3 in 1" from the volume *Pieces* (1969):

3 in 1

The bird
flies
out the
window. She
flies.

•

The bird flies
out the
window. She
flies.

•

The bird
flies. She
flies.[41]

Arthur Ford comments that this poem is less "abstract" than other poems in *Pieces* in that it portrays the "physical movement" of the flight of a bird. "The referents are there," he claims, though the poem "rides on its own physical insistence."[42] But to discover the referential bird nesting in the poem, the critic must insist that the physical movement of the poem itself be mimetic of an avian lift-off: the line break "She / flies" is a "sudden movement, suggesting, of course, the moment of the bird's flight." Of course, if the movement of the poem is considered strictly as a mimetic gesture, the poor bird launches itself thrice without any hint of its having landed. If we abandon attempts to parse the poem referentially, we discover that the only "Bird" in the poem is Charlie Parker, whose choral work induces a rhythmic *feedback*. To account for the physical movement of the entire poem, and not one gesture, we must examine its canonic form.

Except for the abbreviation in the third stanza, the entire voice part in this canon is repeated. But again, to recall Zukofsky's comments on recurrence, "Something has happened to the movement." Creeley's feedback technique relies on a "repetitive relocation of phrasing." The phrase "The bird flies" is repeated (relocated) in the second stanza, but as we noticed in Kees's "Round" and will discover in Zukofsky's canons, a shift of the phrase across the line break accounts for the delicate variation that recurrence requires. The five lines of the first stanza become four in the second stanza; an abbreviation reduces the third stanza to three lines. Creeley comments on the improvisational techniques of Parker: "Listening to him play, I found he lengthened the experience of time, or shortened it, gained a very subtle experience of 'weight,' all by some decision made within the context of what was called 'improvisation'—but what I should rather call the experience of possibility within the limits of his materials (sounds and durations) and their environment."[43] The gradual shortening of the three stanzas of "3 in 1" may be read as Creeley's attempt to bend meter away from the strictness of the metronome and toward a relative measure, as, he argues, Parker's "intensive variation on 'foursquare' patterns such as 'I've Got Rhythm' " bends that rhythm.

In a canonic-form poem such as "3 in 1," in which 95 percent of the poem's volume is consumed by repetition, attention is naturally focused on the remaining 5 percent, the material or effects that constitute variation: the phrasal shifts, an abbreviation. But this is typical of paradigmatic forms whose elements continually evaluate *their own* affinity and dissimilarity. Ford comments, I think correctly, that "3 in 1" is difficult poetry with no margin for error because "here is not the secure haze between two halves of a metaphor."[44] The paradigmatic relation in a canonic form invites us to compare the similarity or difference among the three stanzas; we are not encouraged by "3 in 1" to ask what the bird "stands for." We may not ask: how did the bird get inside the house? does the sudden release of the bird signify elation or dejection for the speaker? In fact, as Creeley's comments on feedback indicate, when repetition returns the words to an "objective state of presence," the persona of the speaker recedes entirely. The title, "3 in 1," should direct our questioning; it says remarkably little about avian behavior, but provides the most economical description of the poem's form. One thinks of a set of drinking cups or screwdrivers in which similar but progressively smaller units are contained within one another. The gradual reduction of the stanzas from five to four to three lines demands that we read the poem as a paradigmatic and not a metaphoric relation.

A second instance of the feedback technique occurs in the volume *In London* (1972):

> Mouths Nuzz
>
> Mouths nuzz-
> ling, "seeking
> in blind
> love," mouths nuzz-
>
> ling, "seek-
> ing in
> blind
> love . . ."

(CP 516)

The ellipsis promises a perpetual canon. In "Mouths Nuzz," the stanza length of four lines and the exactly repeated phrase are the constants. But there is a phrasal shift across the stanza break which, like an earthquake, sets off subsequent tremors in the line breaks of the second stanza. The initial phrase is not shortened in its delivery as it was in "3 in 1," but instead is drawn out with, I think, erotic effect. The variation focuses attention on the word particle "nuzz." The sound is deliberately onomatopoeic. The image is a metonymic representation of two lovers. But the mouths are blind because (1) there is a cliché, "love is blind," (2) lovers close their eyes in standard representations of a passionate embrace, and (3) the eyes of the lovers are not represented in the poem. Only the nuzz is. Creeley employs the canonic repetition to upset both the cliché and the mimetic effect of "nuzzling." The line break that hyphenates the word, the phrasal shift that suspends it between stanzas, and the repetition itself gradually cause the "nuzz" to lose its status as the root of the participle and become a thing in itself. The clichéd image takes on a monstrous quality, like a flea viewed under a powerful microscope. But this objectification of the "nuzz" underscores Creeley's claim that in the feedback technique, "words are curiously returned to an almost objective state of presence so that *they* speak rather than someone speaking with them." Do the mouths speak these words, is the poet a voyeur? No, the words mouth themselves. Repetition is the catalyst of the effect.

In a canonic-form poem, the repetition of the entire voice part functions as a constant in each stanza while phrasal shifts constitute the only permissible variant. As a result, the canon is the most recursive of paradigmatic forms; it is difficult to execute, and those pure examples that we do find are very often brief. But the presence of canonic form in a poet's work is often accompanied by other paradigmatic forms that, while less severe, operate according to similar rules. Certain poems of Creeley and Kees belong to a related class of paradigmatic form, the variation; this one is from Creeley's volume *The Charm* (1967):

A Variation

1

My son who is stranger
than he should be, outgrown
at five, the normal—

luck is against him!
Unfit for the upbringing he would otherwise
have got, I have no hopes for him.

I leave him alone.

I leave him to his own
devices, having pity not so much that he is
strange

but that I am him.

2

Myself, who am stranger
than I should be, outgrown
at two, the normal—

> luck is against me. Unfit
> for the upbringing I would otherwise
> have got, I have no hopes.
>
> I leave him alone.
>
> I leave him to his own
> devices, having pity not so much for
> myself, for why should that happen
>
> but that he is me, as much as I am him.
>
> (CP 38)

In "A Variation," Creeley maintains the form of the utterance as a constant. The first line, "My son who is stranger," becomes in the second stanza "Myself who am stranger." The stanzaic pattern is never transgressed; the syntactical construction and rhythm in this and in most of the lines remains unchanged, even if the literal content of the utterance is altered, instigating a semantic shift. The two lines have a formal affinity, a dissimilarity of meaning. The chief variant in the poem, then, is the shift in the "subject," from the son in section 1 to the father in section 2. Without wishing to trivialize the emotions presented (Creeley outgrows the normal at age two with the loss of his eye), we can say that all the poetic effects of the "variation" actualize what Michael Riffaterre calls the "hypogram,"[45] an inscribed phrase—in this case a cliché—not actualized in the poem but previously encountered by the reader: "like father, like son." Father and son are themselves a paradigm, existing in a relationship of affinity and dissimilarity. The form of the poem, as variation, is mimetic of the form of this relationship. Because the "subject" of the poem is itself a paradigm, the repetitive relocation of such phrases as "I leave him alone" (ll. 7 and 18) does not erase the speaker but in fact reinforces his presence in the poem. As is often the case in paradigmatic forms, however, the repeated (lexically constant) phrase undergoes a semantic shift. The "him" in the second section now refers to the father; the phrase entails a different sort of permissiveness, personal rather than parental. So every phrase in the poem, whether lexically constant or not, must evaluate its own similarity and difference between the two sections. Although the canon permits virtually no lexical or content variation and only minor variations in rhythmic or stanzaic form, the "variation" allows both lexical and formal shifts.

Weldon Kees provides an example of the variation which bears comparison not only to Creeley's offering but to his own cyclical-form poem "Round" as well:

Variations on a Theme by Joyce

The war is in words and the wood is the world
That turns beneath our rootless feet;
The vines that reach, alive and snarled,
Across the path where the sand is swirled,
Twist in the night. The light lies flat.
The war is in words and the wood is the world.

The rain is ruin and our ruin rides
The swiftest winds; the wood is whorled
And turned and smoothed by the turning tides.
—There is rain in the woods, slow rain that breeds
The war in the words. The wood is the world.
This rain is ruin and our ruin rides.

The war is in words and the wood is the world,
Sourceless and seized and forever filled
With green vines twisting on wood more gnarled
Than dead men's hands. The vines are curled
Around these branches, crushed and killed.
The war is in words and the wood is the world.

(CP 10)

The first line, recurring in four additional positions, establishes itself as the constant, or given, upon which the variation is played. The line itself is constructed as a variation in which *w*, *o*, *r*, and *d* are "unmarked," common to at least three of the four nouns, whereas the other vowel *a* and consonant *l* are "marked" as variants. Linguistic aptitude, the WORDplay recognizable as a central concern of *Finnegans Wake*, is at once the subject of the poem and the explanation of its Joycean theme. Words vie with one another—twisting within the cyclical form of the poem—as, in the third stanza, vines and trees compete to strangle or crush one another. The woods are at war, but the war is also in words. They too are alive and so in the world.

A second characteristic of the variation, as we observed in Creeley's example, is the patterning of the second stanza upon the first. In line 7, which retains the form of the utterance in line 1, the unmarked or common word is "ruin." Despite this shift, our initial "theme" makes a comeback: the variant "rain" reintroduces the woods and finally "breeds / The war in the words" (ll. 10–11). As Creeley predicts, the repetitive relocation of phrasing invokes the word as substantive, returned to an almost objective state of presence. Consequently, there is no identifiable speaker, no sense of an address being made; the words speak, rather than someone speaking with them.

Kees's "Variations" also exhibits structural characteristics of a cyclical form. As in "Round," the first and last lines are identical. But in this poem, Kees adopts the cyclical form in the stanzaic structure as well: all three of the six-line stanzas begin and end with the same line. In fact, the formal constraints in "Variations" are somewhat more rigid than those in "Round." Rhyme—an excellent indicator—is desultory in the first two stanzas of "Round," only collecting itself into a recognizable pattern in the third stanza. In "Variations," a rhyme scheme modeled on the French rondeau is observable in all three stanzas: ab(a)abaR, in which one of the rhymes of the central couplet is "off" (e.g., "gnarled"/"curled "in ll. 15–16) and the final rhyme is of course identical. The immediate consequence of this rigid rhyme scheme is the diminished proportion, when compared to "Round," of recurrent phrases in each stanza. A predetermined rhyme scheme obstructs the facility and autonomy (both syntactic and semantic) with which phrases recur. Despite the calcification of formal constraints in "Variations," a cyclical structure is very much in evidence; in fact, a variety of words present in the text lexically support the spiral structure of the poem itself: "swirled" (l. 4), "twist" (l. 5), "whorled" (l. 8), "twisting" and "gnarled" (l. 15), and "curled" (l. 16).

Although the variations of Creeley and Kees do not display the very high proportions of recurrence found in rounds and canons, the characteristics of paradigmatic form are still in operation. Structural differences evident among the fugue, canon, round, and variation are directly related to the changes in the proportion of recurrence. If an aspect of structure is altered, such as Kees's adoption of a rhyme scheme in "Variations," there will be consequent alterations in the mode of language displayed by the poem.

Lorine Niedecker, in her review "The Poetry of Louis Zukofsky," both succinctly and brilliantly charts the evolution of cyclic form in *All*. She begins, "Among the songs in 55 [*Poems*] is at least one so tightly evolved that we see it now as a precursor of a style that may point the future for Zukofsky and others highly sensitized."[46] The poem is number 7 in "29 Songs":

> Who endure days like this
> with me   the room's inference
> foghorns' tuned discs amiss
> dropped our wrists would be
> seconds   impatience' stem
> gestures' graft   arms difference
> eyes' blue iris splicing them[47]

One doesn't find an embryonic cyclical structure in this poem. But there are two qualities of the language here which do anticipate that of the canon. One is the centripetal force, which the reader experiences as "intension" and which leads Niedecker to describe the poem as "tightly" evolved. Closely related to, and perhaps the cause of the centripetal force, is the extreme condensation of language in the poem. Niedecker, whose own poetry is described as emanating "from this condensery," is responding, I think, to the syntactic abbreviation—the absence of a completed noun-verb clause. We notice in addition our own inability to paraphrase a narrative or identify a scenario, though we can identify someone (perhaps the poet's wife) "Who endure days like this / with me." Metaphor and symbolic depth—frequent components of the "intensive" poetry practiced by, for example, Hart Crane—are lacking in Zukofsky's poem. But curiously, in this instance, so is recurrence. This early poem of Zukofsky anticipates his cyclical forms entirely through the centripetal force and condensation of its language.

Niedecker next comments that "ten years later (1950) the tension finds a simpler equation." She quotes the poem "And Without":

> And without
> Spring it is spring why
> Is it death here grass somewhere
> As dead as lonely walks
> As living has less thought that is
> The spring.
>
> Spring it is spring why
> Is it death grass somewhere
> As dead as walks
> As living has less thought that is
> A spring. And without.
>
> (AL 138)

The "tension" manifested by the language of the earlier poem has found the "simpler equation" of the cyclic form and canonic repetition of this example. The centripetal mode of language makes a comfortable match with a paradigmatic form. As in all rondeau forms, the poem begins and ends with the same phrase. The second stanza illustrates Zukofsky's definition of canonic recurrence in which "something happens to the movement." In this stanza, he adds no new material but omits the deictic "here" and the adverb "lonely" and changes an article. The matrix sentence of the poem seems to be "without spring, there is death." The poet observes the change of season, in March perhaps, when evidence of the persistence of winter, bare ground, is co-present with the emergence of spring grass. As in the previous example, Zukofsky's syntax is considerably more paratactic (clauses juxtaposed, without connections) than hypotactic (dependent clauses or constructions).

The poem that immediately follows "And Without," though passed over by Niedecker, is a rather tightly controlled variation:

> Perch Less
>
> Perch less, bird
> Fly on the
> Leaves
> Be heard
> Spatter drops
> So nothing is
> But light
> So light so well
> Foolishness is joy.
>
> Butt age, boy
> Have it not tell
> You, *swift but*
> *Is nothing so*
> *Light it drops—*
> From such high
> Slurred notes
> Bow-hair dares bird:
> So light so well
> Foolishness is joy.

> (AL 138–39)

This variation is played on a matrix sentence, a simile extended to include all details of the poem: the high slurred notes on a sheet of music are like birds. These notations do not perch, but seem to hover above the music stave; they fly, however, "on the leaves" of the sheet music; their chirping is indeed "heard" as music; and, somewhat disconcertingly, they "spatter" the page with other notes, their "drops." In the second stanza of the variation, Zukofsky attempts to preserve the form of the utterance in the first line, from "Perch less, bird" to "Butt age, boy." Rhythm is the constant, sense is the variant. The reference may be to the poet's son, Paul, a child prodigy on the violin who would have had difficulty manipulating a full-size instrument. The italicized words in the stanza very nearly perform an "inversion," reversing the order of words in ll. 5–7; such a compositional strategy is common in contrapuntal pieces. But Zukofsky as virtuoso violinist may be bowing the same note, first in one direction and then back, listening not for the change in meaning but for the difference in tonal quality; the "inversion" then is a claim that, like his son, he too performs in the nonreferential mode of music. "Swift" (l. 12) may well be a pun, referring to the apodal sparrow which is rarely seen to perch, but flits from tree to tree; in this sense also, the bird does not "light." The repetition of the final two lines, "So light so well / Foolishness is joy," functions as a somewhat more abstract ground on which the two stanzas of the variation rest.

Niedecker culminates her essay on cyclic form in Zukofsky by citing the most extended example of a canon in his work, the first two "Songs of Degrees":

1

With
a Valentine
(the 12 February)

Hear, her
Clear
Mirror,
Care
His error.
In her
Care
Is clear.

2

With a Valentine
(the 14 February)

Hear her
(Clear mirror)
Care.
His error.
In her care—
Is clear.

Hear, her
Clear
Mirror,
Care

His error.
In her,
Care
Is clear.

Hear her
Clear mirror
Care his error
In her care
Is clear

Hear
Her
Clear
Mirror
Care
His
Error in
Her
Care
Is clear

Hear
Her
Clear,
Mirror,
Care
His
Error in
Her—
Care
Is
Clear.

(AL 151–53)

Lexical recurrence in all of the canon's six stanzas is perfect: the voice part is repeated exactly and in its entirety. The repetition of "clear" and "care" within the twelve-word stanza reinforces the lexical recurrence of the canon.[48] This virtuosic showpiece is further enhanced by the phonic recurrence in almost every word of a syllable composed of a vowel followed by an *r*. As a result, each stanza constitutes a grand rhyme on a single sound. Naturally, this poem is the quintessential illustration of Zukofsky's requirement that recurrences "always turn up as new." Like an organist performing an elaborate toccata, Zukofsky manipulates phrasal shifts and alters punctuation in each stanza to create delicate semantic shifts. Each stanza, though lexically constant, evokes a new aspect in the relationship of these valentine sweet-hearts; each stanza has a new emphasis, a different nuance.

The moves are almost as numerous as openings in a game of chess, but we can at least catalog a few. The first stanza begins with a general exhortation to "hear" and observe. The comma that follows "Mirror," in line 3, seems to separate and so contrast "her / Clear / Mirror," and "Care / His error." She as mirror or companion is without distortion, still, and calm; reading "Care" as a noun in line 4, his fault is presum-ably a nervous anxiety (Zukofsky was an elegant, dignified man, but he was also a chain-smoking, skittish insomniac and a hypochondriac as well). In Celia's care, Louis finds his cure (both care and cure are etymologically derived from the Latin *cura*): "In her / Care / Is clear."

The phrasal shifts and altered punctuation of the second stanza offer no startling revelation, but a somewhat different aspect of their rela-tionship does emerge. "Clear mirror," as a parenthetical appositive, refers directly to Celia; her supportive attitude is so unwavering that the poet feels an identity between them. The main clause of this first sentence now reads, "Hear her . . . Care." The poet praises the soothing comments of his wife. On the other hand, "His error" is now isolated as a sentence fragment at the center of the stanza. It would seem that the poet places a greater emphasis on his own guilt for some more specific act of misconduct. In this second stanza, the apportionment of praise and blame is much more deliberate.

It would of course be possible to notate the altered emphasis in all six stanzas, but the effect should already be "clear": although each stanza is lexically constant, the phrasal shifts and altered punctuation bring new meaning to the poem and demand different readings.

The canonic forms of Weldon Kees, Robert Creeley, and Louis Zukofsky are remarkable for their tightly wound construction. The perpetual canon, or round, of Weldon Kees, in which the first and the last lines are identical, illustrates the centripetal force, the structural and semantic "turning in upon themselves," which these poems pos-sess. The "repetitive relocation of phrasing" in Creeley's poems obstructs the more familiar metaphoric mode of language in the lyric; words no longer "stand for" the poet's hidden meaning but are re-turned to "an objective state of presence." As a result, the persona of a speaker recedes from the poem and the words themselves speak. All of these effects are finally aspects of paradigmatic form. The highly recursive structure of Zukofsky's canons demonstrates the constant evaluation of affinity and dissimilarity in paradigmatic relations. Only by its spiral twisting does the poem get round to a good look at itself.

# 5

# A Generative Device

## Constant and Variant: Semantic Recurrence in Harry Mathews, William Bronk, and Robert Creeley

In a letter to Robert Creeley, Ezra Pound observes: "Verse consists of a constant and a variant." Insofar as a poem manifests form and not chaos, the observation holds. In the "made" poem there will be materials both familiar and extraordinary. One can interpret Pound's remark along fairly traditional lines: in metrics, for example, the poet may select iambic pentameter as a constant, but if the line is to have any rhythmic interest, an occasional foot must vary from a methodical ta-tum, ta-tum. In fact, good verse can be said to demand a constant and a variant. But Pound applies and elaborates his observation in an innovative way. Creeley comments in a short essay, "His point was that any element might be made the stable, recurrent event, and that any other might be let to go 'hog wild,' as he put it."[1] Pound does not accept *de iure* the rules of a traditional verse which dictate what poets must leave as is, and with what they may take liberties. As Philip Dacey and David Jauss point out, "In the past, it was chiefly content and diction that distinguished one poet's envelope quatrain from another's."[2] William Carlos Williams offers a harsher indictment of traditional form: "All sonnets say the same thing of no importance."[3]

Pound proposes that the poet designate *de facto* the element that serves as a constant: *any* element can be made to recur; on another occasion it may well be the element allowed to run wild. The procedure is entirely at the poet's discretion. Poetry in traditional forms requires *certain* constants; poetry that is formally innovative will require at least *some* constant. Creeley concludes (citing Pound) that "such a form could prove 'a center around which, not a box within which, every item' " moves. The advantage of a form whose constant is at the poet's discretion is that the form does not stiffen into one that *contains* its various materials but remains one that *generates* the motion of its materials, enabling them to go "hog wild." In short, Pound begins with a convention (that all verse has constant and variant elements) and ends with a revolutionary concept of form: constant and variant elements can, like a reversible belt or jacket, change to suit the occasion. The resulting structures will be innovative rather than traditional; they will adhere to rules, but the rules are most likely to be *sui generis*.

In the preceding chapter, I have featured poems that display an increasing degree of lexical recurrence: in the sestina, the six end-words recur in a prescribed pattern; in the pantoum, each line recurs once again in a succeeding stanza; in Weldon Kees's "Round," phrases recur several times so that the third and last stanza is almost entirely composed of phrases from the first two stanzas; and in canonic forms (as I've called them), entire stanzas recur with only minor changes in line breaks or punctuation. These forms are either traditional (in the case of the sestina or pantoum) or derived from some musical model (as in the round or canon). The constant in these poems is *lexical*: words, phrases, lines, and stanzas are repeated. I have presented the poems in an order of increasing quantity of lexical recurrence, from a structure in which only a few words recur in a fixed pattern, to structures in which the entire text recurs. The variant in these poems consists of the significant shifts in the semantic or contextual value of the words. So to characterize these poems as a group, and perhaps to oversimplify for that reason: *the words stayed the same, but their significance changed*.

In this chapter I wish to turn the jacket of constant and variant inside out. I've selected poems of Harry Mathews, William Bronk, and Robert Creeley which I believe display a *semantic* rather than a lexical recurrence. In explaining what I mean by semantic recurrence, I want to call to my aid Michael Riffaterre. In an otherwise very complicated essay, "Paragram and Significance," Riffaterre arrives at the following lucid formulation: "The text's true significance lies in its consistent formal reference to and repetition of what it is about, despite continuous variations in the way it goes about saying it."[4] For Riffaterre, *meaning* in the text refers to "information conveyed . . . at the mimetic level"; *significance* refers to "the formal and semantic unity" of the poem.[5] In his analyses, he proposes to find a "semantic given" for which the text is a string of successive "lexical transformations."[6] In other parlance, the "significance" of the poem as Riffaterre defines it is its "system" or "paradigm" and the "lexical transformations" are "discourse" or "syntagm."[7] Or as Riffaterre says elsewhere, each poetic sign is "perceived as a variant in a paradigm, a variation on an invariant."[8] Now to relate this to our discussion of constant and variant: in these poems, the constant is a semantic value, the repetition of a concept initially *given*; the variant is lexical, "the way it goes about saying it." So, to oversimplify again: in these poems, *the significance remains the same, but the words used to express it change*. In these instances, we do not encounter a "content" contained in a box; rather, a *concept* exists which at once precedes and is enacted by the language of the poem. This concept is the invariant to which every turn in the language and structure in the poem refers.

Like turning over a page, verso, the relation between the lexical and semantic elements of the poems under discussion seems to be an inverse variation. As lexical recurrence assumes the role of a constant, the poet is forced and/or liberated, by the repetition of the utterance, to exploit all the various contexts in which it could occur and the available meanings or senses in which the utterance can be taken. As semantic recurrence assumes the role of a constant, the poet is encouraged, by his or her singular obsession, to explore the liveliest means of expression for an insistent concept; the poet is driven beyond the initial or complacent response. That this inverse relation holds true for poetic structures suggests a fundamental linguistic connection: we exploit a multiplicity of meaning in each word; we employ a variety of words to convey a single meaning; and we refuse to assign a one-to-one correspondence of word and thing. Given a system involving constant and variant, the poet can of course exploit a number of similar relations involving rhythm, sound, structure, and so on. But the poet must initiate the process by making certain formal choices and not others. In the poems I have chosen, the poets have made innovative choices. As Creeley says, "Any element that stays decisive in the context can be used as the variant, any element that stays decisive in the context can be used as the constant."[9] These poets have not allowed convention to decide for them.

Harry Mathews's career as both poet and novelist is exemplary for its exciting inventions in both form and language. He has, like another genius of language experiment, Gertrude Stein, spent much of his creative life in Paris. In 1972 he was elected to membership in the Ouvroir de Littérature Potentielle (the Workshop of Potential Litera-

ture) in Paris, whose list of members also boasts Georges Perec, Italo
Calvino, Marcel Duchamp, and Raymond Queneau. The workshop
encourages the cultivation of elaborate constraints as stimuli for creativity; several of their procedural forms appear in Mathews's set of
variations, *Trial Impressions*, which I will turn to later in this chapter.
But for the moment I would like to discuss an early poem included in
the selection of his poetry published in 1987, *Armenian Papers*. Written in 1954, "The Pines at Son Beltran" is a clear example of semantic
recurrence and lexical variation:

The Pines at Son Beltran

If marriage is separation
"To meet again," where is that country?
The high pines bend
Seaward in slow acknowledgment of mountain wind.
Clouds coast over blurred blue water,                                          5
Away, whiteness heavy with gold.

At such a table should marriage be broken—
The square stone set with blue figs,
The young bride hiding among red trunks,
Running (a little), with naked legs.                                          10
Sea-mirrored clouds are heavy with loss.
The pines incline, for another reason,
Toward water that is pulled blue silk
Ermine-edged, wrinkled by mountain wind.
She has run past the trees into a field of rushes                             15
Or some other sea-grass; but she is gone.
Who waits for her? The stone is bare.

The pines are fixed in a seaward posture.
Marriage is separation, and we
Who are ourselves most when we kiss                                           20
Practice for that lonely touching
In voyages on the sheeted sea
Toward unknown islands that must be found,
Mapped, and redeemed. The laden clouds
Glide to romance and rain; but the virgin bride                              25
Will bear a child whose name is love, and die.
(And the white thighs gone in the sand and eel-grass!
The beauty was there; we can ask no more.)

"But where shall we meet again?" On the far
Face of the moon at the earth's eclipse;                                      30

Or never; or some afternoon in Budapest;
Or, at a square stone table set
With blue imaginary figs
And a view of the water, under these bending trees.[10]

The first line of the poem presents a paradox; marriage is not separation but union. About the couple, it would be difficult to say for
certain whether they are characters of the present or the distant past. It
would be ridiculous to claim that the speaker of the poem bears any
more relation to the poet than that both may have stood on French
soil. At the risk of being fanciful, I would say that the speaker bears
some resemblance to the Provençal troubadour who often sings to an
inaccessible beloved. The "young bride" is gone, and it seems as if the
speaker scans the sea for a sail, or some such sign of her return. But
each stanza ends with *nothing*: the whiteness of the clouds, the bare
stone, a beauty that can no longer be sought, the empty water. If
anything, I'd say the groom, if that is what he is, holds out considerably less hope than the average troubadour that they will meet again.
Each stanza declares the absent spouse; each presents the same bare
stone for a table where a marriage feast ought to be laid. This loss, this
emptiness, is the semantic *given* in the poem. Virtually every element
in each stanza functions as a variant of this invariant setting. And
what is most disturbing is that all indices point not to a presence but
to an absence.

The stanza lengths in the poem attain a symmetry: the first and last
stanzas are six lines each; and the two interior stanzas are eleven lines
each. When lexical recurrence is the predominant device, as in the
sestina or pantoum, it seems to require that a pattern be imposed on it;
the "retrograde cross" motion of the sestina exhausts the permutations of the six end-words and comes to a halt. Otherwise, the repetition of words and phrases might continue indefinitely, or to exhaus-
tion. Lexical recurrence often demands that the poet codify a stanzaic
pattern, and that choice is frequently a traditional, "received" form
rather than one concocted from scratch. But a poem whose constant is
semantic recurrence does not require much stanzaic patterning; it
generates its own centripetal force, a circling back to its given concept
(in this case, absence or loss), often accompanied by a tone of insistence or resignation. It is, as Pound predicts, "a center around which,
not a box within which, every item" moves. The stanzas in "The Pines
at Son Beltran" exhibit no fixed patterning of rhyme or repetition, but
the symmetry in the lengths of the "exterior" and "interior" stanzas
indicates a centripetal movement. Like the "sea-mirrored clouds" (l.

11), these stanzas reflect one another; like the horizon line at which sea and sky converge, a correspondence occurs between them. Each pair is a blank slate (as the clouded sky has no sun, and the sea is empty of any sail), reflecting one another's barrenness. The last stanza courses back to the first, and the third flows back into the second; all four, however, are finally identical expressions.

I would like to propose two distinct readings of this poem. The first reading follows the progress of discourse, from the top of the page to the bottom, recording the lexical changes being rung on the semantic constant of the poem. In a second, systematic reading, I examine the correspondence of the two exterior stanzas, and then the two interior stanzas, in order to ascertain the poem's centripetal force. There is, as far as the poem's *significance* is concerned, no advance, transformation, or in general, any sense that we have arrived somewhere other than where we started. In this sense the poem is radically opposed to the tradition of the greater romantic lyric. Riffaterre describes this first strategy as a "heuristic reading," one that "follows the syntagmatic unfolding" of the text. The reader attempts to assemble a referential meaning for the text but is troubled by certain perceived "ungrammaticalities."[11] In the text at hand, the ungrammaticalities are the lexical variations, *contra naturam* in the normal flow of conversation.

The first stanza serves as the point of departure: no recurrence is found here, since every element is the initial statement of what will undergo a variation in the stanzas to come. Certain words appear to be part of the constant of the poem. For example, the nouns "marriage," "pines," and "clouds" occur in stanzas 1, 2, and 3, but not in 4; the adjective "blue" and the noun "water" appear in stanzas 1, 2, and 4, but not in 3. No words appear in all four stanzas. The repetition of words is not systematic nor as complete in their permutation as one finds in the sestina. Even though some lexical repetition occurs in the poem, these words are not the constant *per se*. What we do notice in a sequential reading is their variation. In the first stanza, the conditional statement "If marriage is separation" becomes in the second stanza "should marriage be broken." The paradoxical concept remains (in the subjunctive mood), though the verb employed varies. In stanza 1, "The high pines bend / Seaward" in the wind; in 2, "The pines incline" (substituting a synonym for the verb); in 3, "The pines are fixed in a seaward posture"; and in 4, there are "bending trees," substituting a synonym for the noun. Employing these four variants, the poet "represents" the seaward yearning of the groom for his departed bride. But such variation in the text foregrounds the rhetorical trope of pathetic fallacy rather than insisting that we share the speaker's emotional urgency. In stanza 1, the phrase "Clouds coast" employs a verb that, as a noun, identifies the setting. In 2, the "clouds are heavy" with loss (again, the pathetic fallacy in which rain represents tears); in 3, "The laden clouds / Glide to romance and rain." In this instance we have the substitution of a synonym for the verb ("glide" rather than "coast"), as well as for an adjective ("laden" in place of the predicate "heavy"). Each variant phrase expresses the pathos of the clouds whose drift is away from the groom and toward the absent bride.

The sea is closely associated with the sky throughout the poem: in stanza 1, the clouds coast over "blurred blue water." The reference to sight, "blurred," influences the subsequent description of the clouds as "sea-mirrored" in stanza 2. The "blurred blue water" changes to the rhythmically similar "pulled blue silk" in 2, a transformation that also depends on the repetition of *b*, *l*, and *u* sounds in "blue" as well as in "blurred," "pulled," and "silk." In 1, the "whiteness" of the clouds is "heavy with gold," a gilding or "lining" that the sun's light imparts; in 2, the silk is not lined but "ermine-edged." The constant here appears to be regal materials. The "silk" is "wrinkled" by the wind, an extension of the metaphor. So in 3, we find "the sheeted sea." A fairly elaborate set of transformations has been brought about in the three stanzas, motivated by similarity of sound and by metaphor. The phrases "pulled blue silk" and "sheeted sea" are lexical variants made possible by the fixed semantic "posture" of the poem. Other elements make less elaborate transformations: the bride's "naked legs" in 2 become "white thighs" in 3; the "sea-grass" in 2 becomes the "eel-grass" in 3. I could continue with an exhaustive catalog of all the elements that participate in the scheme of semantic constant and lexical variant, but these few examples should make the point. The reader encounters a number of transformations in the way things get said; such variations are troubling because we do not expect in normal discourse either an incessant substitution of terms or a repeated reference. These troubles demand for the poem a second reading.

Riffaterre describes a second, *retroactive* reading as a truly "hermeneutic" reading. After a reading that follows the "syntagmatic unfolding," we now perform a "structural decoding." At this point, "successive and differing statements, first noticed as mere ungrammaticalities, are in fact equivalent, for they now appear as variants of the same structural matrix."[12] In the poem at hand, lexical variants such as "naked legs" and "white thighs" amount to successive and differing statements of a semantic constant, an equivalence that one seeks in a second reading. By comparing the two exterior and the two interior stanzas, one arrives at the structural matrix of the poem. If in the first reading I emphasized the lexical variants, here I identify the semantic constant; this reading does not attend to the "syntagmatic unfolding" but to the system, or paradigmatic structure.

Only two phrases in the poem appear within quotation marks, and they form a kind of dialogue between the first and last stanzas. I believe that it is the bride who proposes "to meet again" (l. 2), to which the groom responds, "But where shall we meet again?" (l. 29). The speaker then proceeds to answer his rhetorical question, since by now the bride must indeed be gone. But the answer in the last stanza is also an answer to the question of line 2: "where is that country?" or, where are *you* going? Several extreme responses are provided: the first, on the far side of the moon, is classic hyperbole; the second, "never," seems to reinforce the pessimism that closes stanzas 3 and 4; the third gives a rather specific answer to the question, proposing the capital of Hungary—but here again the answer is exotic and, geographically, appears headed in the wrong direction.

The final alternative is most telling, especially regarding the proposal of a semantic given, or structural matrix. The "square stone table," at which the marriage "should" be broken in stanza 2, is now proposed as the place of reunion. In a variant of line 8, the table is now set with "imaginary" figs. From a narrative standpoint, the poet appears to propose a reunion at the very location of the departure: we "arrive" at the same pine grove in which we began. We could say, if this were a poem whose narrative we could comfortably endorse, that the event itself recurs. From a rhetorical standpoint, we noted that the poem opens with a somewhat paradoxical hypothesis, "If marriage is separation," followed by the question "where is that country?" But the stanza that purports to answer that question and resolve that paradox is colored, if you will, by the presence of the blue *imaginary* figs. The final stanza matches the troubling hypothesis with an insistence on the fictional nature of the setting and by extension the characters themselves. It is as if the poet were to declare, "This, ladies and gentlemen, is an exercise in literary portraiture," so that the only "country" in which these elaborate variations can occur is the fiction itself. The final stanza enforces a semantic recurrence (providing four different answers to the same question), returning to the concept with which the poem began and which has been present all along: the proposal of loss.

Notably, Mathews claims among his themes "discovery, loss, rediscovery. . . . (and no stopping at that point)," a sentiment that is certainly applicable to a structure that *demands* recurrence.[13] His themes have a resolutely fictive element about them. Although "boy meets girl, boy loses girl, boy gets girl back" is a common plot, exploited precisely because it is plausible, Mathews's *insistent* recurrence (no stopping at the tearful reunions) declares its literariness. So he reiterates, "Another way of saying this: language and what it cannot say, or: how poetic language says that it cannot say what it means and so succeeds in meaning what it doesn't say." The elaborate play of constant and variant in "The Pines at Son Beltran" is a literary device that declares itself, like the offering of "blue imaginary figs."

If the first and last stanzas of the poem demand recurrence, making the reply equivalent to the proposition, the second and third stanzas function as two nearly parallel channels moving toward a convergence. At the start of the second stanza, the speaker introduces the square stone table, claiming that this setting is most appropriate for the marriage/separation. He then describes the young bride, apparently fantasizing about her behavior, at once enticing and evasive. The first four lines of the third stanza are similarly set in the sea-cliff pine grove. In both cases, it is not entirely clear whether the speaker describes an *event* (a departure scene) or whether he is merely conjecturing about their presence together. The first use of the pronoun "we" occurs in line nineteen: "and we / Who are ourselves most when we kiss / Practice for that lonely touching." Each stanza begins with the speaker and bride either actually or conjecturally together in the grove. The indeterminacy created by the subjunctive mood in line 7 ("At such a table should . . .") impairs our ability to locate this scene temporally: has the departure occurred, or is it impending; or does he anticipate yet another? At the center of each stanza the action moves offshore as the weather (or whatever) carries off his bride. Both the pines inclined seaward "for another reason" (l. 12) and the clouds that "glide to romance and rain" (l. 25) indicate the direction of the groom's yearning. Stanza 3 specifies "unknown islands that must be found, / Mapped, and redeemed," a partial expression of the theme of discovery, loss, and rediscovery.

The last lines of each stanza plunge into despair. In 2, the bride flees "into a field of rushes / Or some other sea-grass; but she is gone. / Who waits for her? The stone is bare." The indirect response to the rhetorical question indicates that no one awaits or expects her; otherwise, there would be an offering of figs. A similar resignation closes stanza 3: "The virgin bride / Will bear a child whose name is love, and die." The marriage is unconsummated, a victim of the immediate separation. Does the "bride" herself die, or is it rather the love that is stillborn? The closing lines of 3 are virtually identical in import to the closing lines of 2. In each case the bride is "gone" and cannot be expected to return.

The exterior stanzas impart a centripetal force to the poem, turning it back on itself; they "redeem" the more pessimistic conclusions of the interior stanzas, seen here as moving in parallel. In "The Pines at Son Beltran," the predetermined element is not the stanzaic structure or a pattern of repetition but a concept that precedes all aspects of the poem and to which all poetic signs point. That concept is the bond, not of bride and groom, but of discovery and loss.

In a review of William Bronk's work, Gilbert Sorrentino remarks that Bronk "writes the same poem over and over again, explaining the quality and reality of despair. Each rings a variation on his dark theme." If Bronk is, as Sorrentino suggests, "a scandalously neglected poet," it is not because so many of his poems are locked in an aesthetic battle with the nature of reality, but because their outcome is unremittingly "tragic." Nevertheless, Sorrentino notes, "the darker and more intransigent the world they inscribe, the more salutary they become."[14] As evidence of the neglect that Bronk's reputation has suffered, an anonymous reviewer for the *Virginia Quarterly Review* comments that "his voice is . . . austere. I don't suppose he is for every palate, but those with a taste for the fine, tart, and clear."[15] For Bronk, the issue is far more serious and consuming than a dispute over "taste," as if his collected poems, *Life Supports*, were a basket of Hudson Valley apples. But I don't propose to engage in a retrospective survey of Bronk's accomplishments; one poem will suffice. "The Arts and Death: A Fugue for Sidney Cox" can be read as a variant of that dark theme present to some degree in all of Bronk's poems. *Life Supports* then is something of a constant, and each poem rings its changes. What is true for the poet's *oeuvre* remains true in this instance: Bronk's "Fugue" enacts the play of a semantic constant and elaborate lexical variants.

The Arts and Death: A Fugue for Sidney Cox

I think always how we always miss it. Not
anything is ever entirely true.

Death dominates my mind. I
do not stop thinking how time will stop,
how time has stopped, does stop. Those dead—       5
their done time. Time does us in.

Mark how we make music, images,
how we term words, name names,
how, having named, assume the named begins
here, stops there, add this attribute,                                    10
subtract this other: here the mold begins
to harden. This toy soldier has
edges, can be painted, picked up,
moved from place to place, used to mean
one or many. Within the game we play,                                     15
we understand. See his leaden gun
or saber, how deadly for aid or for
destruction as we aim him, and he is bold,
a game soldier. We play games
however serious we aim to be.                                             20
A true aim, a toy soldier. I think
always, how we always miss the aim.

Ponder the vast debris of the dead, the great
uncounted numbers, the long, the endless list
of only their names, if anyone knew their names.                         25
Joined to the dead already, to those known
who have died already, are we not also joined
to many we would have known in their time—
to one in Ilium, say, who thought of the dead?
In the world's long continuum, it is not                                 30
the names of the dead, but the dead themselves who are like
names, like terms, toy soldiers, words.

I think always how we always miss it; how the dead
have not been final, and life has always required
to be stated again, which is not ever stated.                            35
It is not art's statements only, not
what we try to say by music, not the way
this picture sculptures sight itself
to see this picture—not by art alone
the aim is missed, and even least of all                                 40
by art (which tries a whole world at once,
a composition). No, it is in our terms,
the terms themselves, which break apart, divide,
discriminate, set chasms in that wide,
unbroken experience of the senses which                                  45
goes on and on, that radiation, inward and out,
that consciousness which we divide, compare,
compose, make things and persons of, make forms,
make I and you. World, world, I am scared
and waver in awe before the wilderness                                   50

of raw consciousness, because it is all
dark and formlessness: and it is real
this passion that we feel for forms. But the forms
are never real. Are not really there. Are not.

I think always how we always miss the real.                    55
There still are wars though all the soldiers fall.

We live in a world we never understand.

Our lives end nothing. Oh there is never an end.[16]

For those who have read even a few poems by Bronk, the first two
lines of "A Fugue" articulate a familiar motif. "It" is the world, a
reality that "we" are never able to perceive in its entirety. Because we
"miss" the big picture, nothing we perceive is ever a "true" estimate.
Several critics have succinctly paraphrased this central theme (one
might as well say obsession) of Bronk's.[17] Norman Finkelstein comments: "The single great constant in the poetry of William Bronk is
desire; specifically desire for *the world*, which can never be known as a
totality. Despite the self-limiting fact that consciousness is aware of
its inability to experience this totality, it continually struggles for the
achievement of its goal. Cut off from any ground of belief, secure only
in its desire, consciousness therefore creates *a world*, which despite its
insufficiency in metaphysical terms nevertheless allows for the rendering of form—the poem."[18] Having analyzed the constant in Bronk's
work, Finkelstein then points out that, although the poems move
through "many essential human situations," they "echo each other so
hauntingly that they seem like endless variations on the same theme."
Indeed, Bronk's opening proposition in the poem at hand functions
much as the statement of a fugue, the motif around which all further
repetitions and elaborations are built. Though it recurs with slight
lexical variation, this statement is the constant *pre*occupation of the
poet. It is impossible for any language construct to express what *it* (the
real) is; but even though he knows this, the poet struggles to approach
the real in language. The result is much as Riffaterre predicts: continuous variations in the expression of the text's "true significance." For
this task, the fugue structure is a convenient analogue. Consequent to
Bronk's epistemology, his approach to the world, is his opinion of the
efficacy of language—it is obviously insufficient, as much as the real
is inexpressible. In this sense, Bronk's theme is also Harry Mathews's,
"language and what it cannot say."

The poet, unable to state *the* world directly, creates *a* world; as

Finkelstein says, he "allows for the rendering of form—the poem." So one of the things we are doing while we are "missing it" is known inclusively as "the Arts." And just as the *made* world of the poet must face the world as "universal field,"[19] so "the Arts" must confront a ubiquitous "Death." In the second stanza, Bronk accepts this idea in rather blunt terms. "Death," he says, "dominates my mind." This fixation, or isolation of a single concept, contributes substantially to the semantic recurrence that characterizes the poem's form. It is also apparent in the poet's opening statement: "I think *always* how we *always* miss it" (my emphasis). The presence of a semantic constant in this poem is brought about by the poet's intensive meditation, a turning over and over in his mind, of the arts and death: despite a wealth of "salutary" elaborations, there are no contexts other than those announced in the title.

We should say at this point that the lyric is no stranger to the theme of death, though death often appears as the dark stranger. So, shadowing the fugal structure of the poem is the additional consideration of genre; in this case, the appropriate term is "elegy." Riffaterre explains the difference between form and genre: "The genre sets limits to a text's potential verbal associations and allows the reader to harbor certain expectations once he has identified the text as belonging to the maxim, for instance, or to the Gothic novel. The difference between a fixed form (like the sonnet) and a genre is that the genre has a grammar and this grammar merely develops a very limited number of matrix sentences."[20] In the sonnet, a variety of (though certainly not all) contexts can be employed to fill the container; but the elegy brings with it a *decorum*, a code of appropriate gestures and topics. The limits imposed by such a generic choice are largely semantic.

Many elegies, of course, have a fairly general quality to them, as if written for "Everyman." Bronk's fugue is no exception since it can hardly be said to enumerate any specific characteristics of Sidney Cox. Reserve regarding personal affairs might well be one of the traditional limits imposed by the genre, though it appears to have crumbled in the era of confessional poetry. But Sidney Cox's role in Bronk's career as a poet has much to do with the link established here between the arts and death. Sidney Cox was Bronk's instructor in creative writing at Dartmouth in 1938. In an interview with Robert Bertholf, Bronk describes Cox as something of a *sine qua non* for his aspirations: "I'm fairly sure there wouldn't have been anything without Sidney."[21] When asked to describe Cox's influence, Bronk replies that he advocated "plain speaking, and what you might call honesty." Certainly these traits have become part of Bronk's "austerity." Hayden Carruth, in a review of *Life Supports*, points out that Bronk "soon discarded [metaphor] along with all poetic figures, retaining only rhythm and rhetoric. His poems became direct statements of ideas, even simpler, plainer."[22] Carruth then cites a portion of "A Fugue" as evidence. Only the direct statement, in Bronk's view, has any chance of approaching the real.

For a less kind appraisal, the anonymous reviewer for the *Virginia Quarterly Review* snorts that Bronk is "a frequently abrasive and vulgar poet of the vernacular."[23] As in all dedications, we must exonerate Sidney Cox from responsibility for his pupil's product; but according to Bronk, what Cox recommends against is an academic "practice in technique" and the use of "elaborate verse forms." Bronk has in fact avoided a fixed form in his tribute to Cox in favor of the constraints offered by the elegiac genre. He avoids the containment of a traditional form in favor of the (actually no less difficult) constant/variant structure of the fugue. Cox's presence in the poem unites the poet's preoccupations: how does one confront the reality of death with art? Bronk employs the "art of the fugue," appropriate not only to the funereal decorum of the occasion, but also to Cox's demand for a poetry of direct statement.

Before leaving the second stanza, I want to point out an effect of the constant/variant structure at the linguistic level. Line 3 begins with an alliterative phrase, "Death dominates," and in the remaining lines of the stanza there is a deliberate insistence on the *d* sound. The frequent alliteration reinforces the sense of a mind continually returning to the same thought: "I / do not stop thinking how." Words beginning or ending in *d* are prominently placed, especially in line 5, at the caesura or at the end of the line. Against this phonic constant, a temporal variant plays: the changes in tense involving the verb "to do." The rehearsal of past, present, and future tenses conveys the poet's preoccupation with time itself, and how *its* passing signals *our* mortality. Most interesting is the oddly "vernacular" usage in line 6: "their done time. Time does us in." Doing time. Done in. The semantic constant allows the poet to search his file of idiomatic expressions; but all these phrases are to the point, that life is a sentence, and it is invariably carried out.

The third stanza of the poem elaborates on the inability of the arts in general and language in particular to account for reality. We "make" music, as we make a poem (l. 7); form is rendered in order to confront the real. All writers "term words, name names" (l. 8). Bronk's position is essentially Saussurean in that he considers language to be a closed system of arbitrary signifiers; words are assigned to things as a matter of expediency, not because (as in the myth of Adam in the garden) names have an absolute connection to the thing named. In this appraisal Bronk joins Gertrude Stein, for whom all nouns are inadequate to their task of naming: "A noun is a name of anything, why after a thing is named write about it. A name is adequate or it is not. If it is adequate then why go on calling it, if it is not then calling it by its name does no good. . . . And therefore slowly if you feel what is inside that thing you do not call it by the name by which it is known."[24] Bronk illustrates his point with a spatial relation: "the named begins / here, stops there, add this attribute, / subtract this other" (ll. 9–10). He argues that language has not been and cannot be coincidental with the real. The word never possesses precisely those attributes that the thing itself possesses, no matter how we fiddle with it. If we try, "the mold begins / to harden." We shape some portion of the real to our own specification and seal it in the container we have made.

Bronk next employs an extended simile, or conceit, to illustrate this same point about language. Each word is like a "toy soldier" (l. 12) whose attributes are easily altered and which can be moved as a counter in the mock battle that is the whole of language. Bronk concisely evaluates the relation of language to *the world*: "Within the game we play, / we understand" (ll. 15–16). Language is only *a world*, one that we understand because it operates according to rules we have devised; without those rules, there is no guarantee of understanding anything. For both Bronk and Saussure, language is hermetic, a closed system that is capable of meaning, but only by prior agreement. It's a game, not the real thing.

As Bronk attempts to bring the compass of his conceit back to its origin, we observe an increasing amount of lexical repetition. This repetition is often the effect of his skillful manipulation of a cumulative syntax; clause builds on clause, not unlike the rhetoric of the metaphysical poets. As he describes the toy soldier's weapons, the *lead*en gun reintroduces the motif of the *dead* (ll. 16–17). Even a conceit that involves a toy is not allowed to stray too far from the central theme of the elegy. Language, Bronk seems to be saying, has its own potency, is not negligible or frivolous for not being "the real." It is capable of aid or destruction however we aim it. In line 19, he puns on "game" to mean "ready for action." Nevertheless, "We play games / however serious we aim to be." Words can destroy, but they are not nearly as formidable as the real itself, whose capacity for death is much greater. Bronk plays on the various meanings of both "game" (three times) and "aim" (four times) in these few lines, ringing changes that summon the four occurrences of "names" in lines 8–9. So the rhyme of important words constitutes a phonic constant. Lexical repetition in the sestina often leads to fresh contexts; Bronk's repetition of words also exploits their various imports, but he is careful always to return them to his central theme. Thus the stanza concludes with a variant of his opening statement, "I think / always, how we always miss the aim" (ll. 21–22). Here the diction of the military conceit is co-opted—that is, it is drafted to serve in a lexical variant of the original phrase. But we are certain that Bronk has returned to the poem's significance: death is more potent than the arts, and language can neither capture the real nor defend us from it.

I have expended a fair number of words in glossing the structure of this third stanza. But the play of constant and variant in a fugal structure is irregular and so cannot be succinctly charted. By comparison, David Lehman claims, "The more constrictive the form, the likelier it is that a poem cast in that form will gloss itself." Even the novice "will have no trouble discerning the pattern of insistence" in a villanelle, and the author "may thus be reasonably confident that his poem will divulge its form and illustrate its rules and regulations at least as well as a prose explanation could." This nearly immediate recognition is true, however, only in "a form built around regularly scheduled repetitions."[25] In the poems by Mathews and Bronk, repetition is irregular and not cast in a fixed stanzaic structure. We are taught to recognize regular patterns such as "2 4 6 8, fill in the blank," or a fixed form. Not surprisingly then, more regular forms have a higher degree of lexical repetition; the irregular forms rely on a semantic anchor in the midst of the lexical whirlpool.

In the fourth stanza, Bronk plays an elegant counterpoint on motifs that have appeared in three prior stanzas. "Ponder," he demands, "the vast debris of the dead" (l. 23). His insistence (cf. l. 7, "Mark how . . .") is rhetorical rather than a formal pattern of insistence. The entire text is a variation on the confrontation of an individual's "name" and the vast consortium of "the dead." A name and a language provide one with an identity; death and loss dissolve it. The stanza is a variant of a hidden sentence (in Riffaterre's term, a *hypogram*), the clue to which is located in line 29. It is spoken by "one in Ilium," Aeneas at the shores of Dis, and by Dante at the rim of the Inferno: "I had not thought death had undone so many."[26] The line is a shadow blooded by the earlier appearance of "Those dead— / their done time" (ll. 5–6). The final two lines of the fourth stanza function as a cadence, bringing all motifs to resolution: "it is not / the names of the dead, but the dead themselves who are like / names, like terms, toy soldiers, words" (ll. 30–32). The counterpoint devolves finally upon a single note. All the motifs or counters at play for four stanzas are actually equivalent to "the dead"; they are all variants of the same recurrent idea.

After this momentary resolution, Bronk reiterates the phrase with which he began; this key phrase is the only one that repeats exactly. The fifth stanza offers some hope of redemption: death is not "final," and "life has always required / to be stated again, which is not ever stated" (ll. 34–35). Apparently Bronk sees in life itself a fugal recurrence, stating over and over the well-tempered phrase, though it never utters that one perfect and lasting harmony. The poet next exonerates art, setting it above experience: "the aim is missed . . . least of all / by art (which tries a whole world at once, / a composition)" (ll. 40–42). Art is capable of making a world that is entire to itself, and like the "game," one that we can understand. Without the synthesis of art, the conscious mind divides the "unbroken experience of the senses," making of it parts that bear no resemblance to the whole. Bronk discusses much the same issue in stanza 3, but there he employs a conceit, whereas here he uses a more abstract, philosophical diction.

The poem reaches a rhetorical climax in the last six lines of this stanza. Conceding that it is we who "make forms, / make I and you" (ll. 48–49), the poet then turns to the world itself in an apostrophe. He is in awe "before the wilderness / of raw consciousness, because it is all / dark and formlessness." Bronk poses some mighty epistemological questions in this stanza: Is the "unbroken" (continuous) experience of the senses divided by the conscious mind (i.e., is perception discontinuous)? Is there no "divine or natural" order beyond that order, as Robert Duncan believes, which the human mind "contrives or imposes"?[27] Bronk argues, in terms most discomforting, that "the world" *is* the absence of form, and that all the "form" that we perceive is of our own making. This observation is in large part the tragic information that William Bronk conveys. But the mitigating circumstance is, with repeated insistence, that "it is real / this passion that we feel for forms." Unfortunately, "the forms / are never real. Are not really there. Are not" (ll. 52–54). Compare these lines from his poem "The Nature of Musical Form," which may serve as a gloss on the chosen analogue of the fugue:

> It is tempting to say of the incomprehensible,
> the formlessness, there is only order as we
> so order and ordering, make it so; or this,
> there is natural order which music apprehends
>
> which apprehension justifies the world;
> or even this, these forms are false, not true,
> and music irrelevant at least, the world
> is stated somewhere else, not there. But no.[28]

Bronk offers several alternatives, all of which he rejects: (1) human order, (2) natural order, and (3) transcendent order. He recognizes that the order we make cannot be thought to be part of the real—we cannot "make it so." What we "apprehend" as natural order is just that—our view of the cosmos, rather like a Rorschach test; and such impressions cannot be said to "justify" anything. Lastly, there is the transcendental view that the order is "somewhere else." This view, stated by Duncan's "divine order," or perhaps more systematically in something like Yeats's "gyres," must also be rejected. All three approaches to the real are false. What makes Bronk a post-humanist, postmodern thinker is his conviction that all forms are false, artificial. We make them, and we cannot pretend that they have a validity beyond us, in any way. So he says in "A Fugue" that "the forms are never real," they are always the product of artifice.

The final four lines of the poem restate or recapitulate prior claims of the poem. In line 55, Bronk substitutes "the real" for the "it" of lines 1 and 33. Only at the conclusion does he explicitly state the object of his meditation. The next line implies (with reference to the conceit in stanza 3) that the real (wars) persist even though language (the game) fails. The penultimate line refers us to lines 15–16; in this rephrasing, he contrasts the limited system of the language game which we *do* understand and the world itself which we can *never* understand. Finally, restating lines 33–34, Bronk returns to the theme of death; in keeping with the generic rules, he offers something other than despair at the close—not redemption, but not oblivion either. Our lives are part of the real, and as such persist; only our language closes, only forms have an end.

I began this chapter by discussing Robert Creeley's citation of Pound's advice, that there was such a thing as constant and variant operating in verse and that it was there to be used. I would like to finish by examining two short poems by Creeley, to see how he has employed this advice in new and constructive ways. Creeley's early poems, especially those in *For Love* (1962), display a high degree of what might be called closure. Certainly they are not exercises in imposed form, but they do hold themselves together. There is something of an irony of literary history here. Although Creeley was very much involved in Charles Olson's espousal of a "projective verse" during the fifties, the poems themselves might more readily answer to the phrase "retentive verse." They are not the Whitmanic or Ginsbergian or Duncanian outpourings of the vatic seer, nor are they writ large on the scale of the 6' 8" Olson, but are rather small, decidedly constricted works. This irony persists in part because of the inclusion of his early poems in anthologies that feature far more conservative, traditional versifiers such as Anthony Hecht, John Hollander, James Merrill, Alfred Corn, and John Frederick Nims. One such anthology, *Strong Measures: Contemporary American Poetry in Traditional Forms*, edited by Philip Dacey and David Jauss and published in 1986, does Creeley a particular disservice by implying that the included poems are in fact exercises in traditional forms with only the novelty of their having been composed recently. The editors even provide a "classification of poems" (Appendix C) whose rather too neat and reductive compartmentalization (i.e., "new" poems, in the same old molds) harms their contention that recent "formal" poetry is interesting on its own merit. The "structures" of the poems in this volume are "usually chosen," the editors claim, "not invented."[29] The implication is that there are no new forms of closure of any interest in contemporary poetry, only new examples of the old forms. Creeley's poems do in fact "choose" certain closural effects (such as rhyme), but they are almost always employed in a manner that radically undermines their familiar function. What's more, these "chosen" structures, so facilely classified by the editors, are only details in the blueprint of each poem's form. They are not the plan itself, which, following Pound, is invented. The editors complain that "in the Romantic times" the chosen form is rejected as "artificial." They do not recognize in Creeley a poet who is neither classical (as he detonates traditional forms with their own powder) nor romantic, since his "invented" forms are as unabashedly "artificial" as the sonnet or sestina. Being neither, he must therefore be a third: the postmodern destroyer of categories and classifications.

Dacey and Jauss offer Creeley's poem "If You" as an example of the "Short Couplet," defined as "a stanza or poem formed of two rhyming lines of iambic or trochaic tetrameter,"[30] a kind of dwarf couplet:

> If You
>
> If you were going to get a pet
> what kind of animal would you get.
>
> A soft bodied dog, a hen—
> feathers and fur to begin it again.
>
> When the sun goes down and it gets dark
> I saw an animal in a park.
>
> Bring it home, to give it to you.
> I have seen animals break in two.

You were hoping for something soft
and loyal and clean and wondrously careful—

a form of otherwise vicious habit
can have long ears and be called a rabbit.

Dead. Died. Will die. Want.
Morning, midnight. I asked you

if you were going to get a pet
what kind of animal would you get.[31]

There are at least two things wrong with our editors' categorization of this poem. First, the general assumption is that because these couplets *look* like those of the eighteenth century, they also *function* as their predecessors did; and second, the actual structure of the poem is considerably more complicated than the fact that the lines are arranged in pairs. The editors, not recognizing what might be the formal invention of the whole, classify the poem's structure according to what they think to be the inherited form of the part. Poets venture into anthologies at their peril.

One common concern of Duncan, Olson, and Creeley (who continue to be excluded from certain canonical anthologies) is that the anthology robs the poem of its context in the author's work, setting it among strange or even hostile neighbors. This is one of those instances. Creeley in no way employs the couplets in this poem as traditional, inherited form; in fact, he works hard to upset our expectations. It so happens that he singles out a couplet from this poem in a discussion apropos closure:

It seemed to me that the couplet, which I used a lot in my early writing, the disjunct couplet, that that was terrific because you could bring two things together as statement and have them seemingly hold together as a rhetorical situation, and also as a rhyming situation, or a rhythm, a parallel situation, but the information could be as disjunct as the man in the moon and a cat walking down the street. I mean, it could be some very different situations of so-called reality that could be compared. And a rhetorical poem could make them seem as reasonable as Pope, or at least hold them as instant in the mind as though they were reasonable, and then the attention would say, "Well, wait a minute now, these two things are not necessarily congruous." Again, in the mode of putting them together, you get different kinds of activity, like "when the sun goes down and it gets dark / I saw an animal go into the park," in which you can get disjunct syntax or tense, where you're following a line that's not really jarring the reader. It isn't surreal or collage, but it's getting awful close.[32]

Creeley understands that in the Popian couplet (an "otherwise vicious habit"), a phonic and/or rhythmic congruity encourages the reader to find a *semantic* congruity in the materials presented. Some context must be discovered which unifies or accounts for the inclusion of the most disparate materials.[33] Creeley's own intentions are the reverse: he provides a phonic *congruity*, but the contexts of the materials are *disjunct*; they are like two sets that do not intersect. We can correlate this effect rather more closely to Poundian than Popian practice. The phonic similarity or repetition functions as a constant (or "parallel"), thus allowing Creeley to introduce, as he says, "crazily diverse material." Sound is the "recurrent event" while context is allowed to go "hog wild." This poem does not faithfully represent the "short couplet," as our editors intend, but a "disjunct couplet." Creeley has set a charge under the traditional couplet and lit the fuse.

The couplet is not, however, the governing structure of this poem. Although Dacey and Jauss look for a "regular" form in this poem, I see one that is "irregular": an inward spiral, like that described by a gradually contracting compass or a sea shell. At the center of this spiral, there is a semantic constant that occurs as a contradiction. Here, what I wish to call structure has no more to do with content than it does with stanzaic pattern. It is the "formal and semantic unity" of the poem, which accounts for more than the brand of couplet employed. In keeping with Creeley's discussion of the disjunct couplet, the first couplet of the poem offers an apparently innocuous "rhetorical situation" which is almost immediately undermined. If the couplet were to conclude with the question mark appropriate to the interrogative phrase, "what kind," we could almost believe the speaker to be a child on a shopping trip to the mall and the question an innocent one. But the period forces us back on the couplet as a statement—rhetorically upsetting. The speaker is not asking but telling; he already knows the answer. This "ungrammaticality," as Riffaterre would call it, is our first indication that the poem is not "about" acquiring a pet. It is also our first indication that a *preconception* is involved, one that entertains a contradiction or reversal of sorts. This preconception is withheld for the moment from the reader.

The second couplet pretends to offer a suggestion or two, but that pretense is quickly exposed. A "soft bodied" dog suggests a stuffed animal, not a "real" one—no real pets to be had here. As for the hen, she too is a disjunction since few would keep her as a pet (after leaving college, Creeley made a meager living from raising chickens in New England). The closing line sounds distinctly like Stein: "feathers and fur" suggest a pillow, or a warm coat. These animal "products" offer physical comfort, but hardly the emotional companionship one seeks in a pet. As Creeley notes regarding the third couplet, the syntax of line 6 does not follow from line 5, and the tense shifts from the immediate present to the past. The expected conclusion might read: "a dog follows me home from the park." Instead, we get the more suspicious and indeterminate "animal." In each couplet, the poet reneges on his promise to provide "you" with a pet and the reader with a mimetic context.

The fourth couplet is a striking example of Creeley's ability to make something new with the old stuffing. The speaker proposes to present the stray animal to, presumably, his lover. The second line is virtually a non sequitur: "I have seen animals break in two." The "soft bodied" dogs have become, or have always been, brittle. The contradiction is an indication of the poem's central conflict. So too, these are brittle couplets. Although joined in an end rhyme, semantically they "break in two." But this couplet also conceals a reference to a text that provides a clue to the poem's preconception. Creeley's "Stomping with Catullus" (CP 68) indicates his familiarity with the Latin lyricist. The lines at hand recall the well-known "Lugete," Carmen 3, in which the poet's gift to Lesbia, a sparrow, has died, causing her to weep. The ambivalent nature of emotional commitment is summoned here, as well as the irony that Catullus exploits, that Lesbia both loves more deeply and weeps more profusely for the bird than for the poet. Carmen 3 is more a point of reference than a blueprint for "If You," though one can safely say that neither is primarily concerned with pets.

The next two couplets function rhetorically and syntactically as a pair. The poet's lover has been hoping for a gift that is soft, loyal, and clean, but the poet considers such a gift a "vicious habit." Again a reversal of expectation occurs: what is soft is actually malign; what appears reassuring is in fact "vicious." The contradiction is a restatement of the poem's central conflict. The next couplet offers some explanation. Like Lesbia's sparrow, the pet "will die." The short-lived rabbit betrays us with its death. What ought to offer companionship is actually guaranteed to provide the reverse, "Want." This longing is insatiable, as indicated by the use of present, past, and future tenses in line 13. Time becomes obscured; "Morning, midnight" are much the same, perhaps with a pun on "mourning." But surely the poem is not concerned with the mortality of pets; the stuffed dog and vicious rabbit are hardly realistic. The poem's given, its *initium*, is the conviction that our desires are destructive, that their satisfaction harms us more often than not. This apparent contradiction is the semantic constant of the poem, and we can see that it is acted out in every couplet.

The reversal also dictates the structure of the poem: while the classic rondeau ends with a reiteration of its initial premise (a confirmation that our direction is still the same), the final couplet in Creeley's poem assumes a tone that signals a reversal. Although identical, the first couplet can be construed as an innocent question, the last as an ominous warning. The structure of the poem resembles the cyclic closure of many traditional forms that employ the repetition of a first line as the last. But Creeley upsets this pattern, as his disjunct couplet upsets our expectations: the circle "comes around," but it misses its initial point and continues to spiral inwardly. All those elements that seemed uncomfortable in relation to the "realistic" scenario of the gift of a pet are swept into the actual significance of the poem: not the gratifications of companionship but its peril. This inversion is the one constant in the poem in relation to which all elements, as variants, make sense.

Another early poem by Creeley, "The Crow," bears comparison to "If You," not because of a common "pet" motif, but because it too undoes the mimetic plausibility of its situation in the pursuit of its actual significance.

The Crow

The crow in the cage in the dining-room
hates me, because I will not feed him.

And I have left nothing behind in leaving
because I killed him.

And because I hit him over the head with a stick
there is nothing I laugh at.

Sickness is the hatred of a repentance
knowing there is nothing he wants.

(CP 124)

Bird and man don't seem to provide much companionship for one another. The man is reluctant to indulge the bird's appetite; the bird, in what we would like to read as a comic overstatement of its emotions, "hates" him. Anyone who has refused a parrot one last grape can vouch for such hatred. But a crow, large, black, and hardly a domestic bird, should be found in the fields, not in a cage "in the dining-room." Not only is the bird an inappropriate pet, but its location seems calculated to antagonize its appetite. Given this breach of realism, the next two couplets then disrupt the logical sequence of cause and effect. The second couplet claims that "nothing" has been left behind, implying that the man flees the situation and does not plan a return. But line 4, "because I killed him," places an exaggerated importance on the bird—in that situation, the bird was *everything*, without compromise. The sudden shift in tense is also antirealistic; in line 2, the bird "hates" the man, but in line 4 the bird has already been "killed." In its failure of reasonable cause and effect, the third couplet also points to obsessive behavior by the man. He has not starved the bird but "hit him over the head with a stick." Although such abuse is certainly no laughing matter, the man now declares that "there is nothing I laugh at."

Short of venturing into the territory occupied by Edgar Allan Poe, how can we explain such an obsessive reaction? The final couplet at once provides an answer and undoes it. What is the "hatred of a repentance" if not *stubbornness*, unwillingness to admit or rectify a wrong. Stubbornness is the predisposition of the speaker in all four couplets; its description and not the crow's is the significance of the poem. The last line, "knowing there is nothing he wants," undoes more than it concludes. If "he" is the crow, he wants nothing because he is either dead or stubborn (a refusal of desire). In either case, there is a problem with the temporal sequence: the crow persists in his attitude beyond his own "murder" and the man's departure. The last couplet is a closural gesture that doesn't really explain much, except to say that the crow could be anyone and that the altercation is a serious one though its terms are unknown. What remains when the mimetic gesture collapses is the significance. What the poet contends with is not the crow but his own penchant for obsessive behavior.

Mathews, Bronk, and Creeley pursue a program of formal invention which manifests itself in diverse instances. But they appear in conjunction when they employ a structure of constant and variant as a means to limit, without "containing," the movement of a poem. The forms of the poems discussed are not inherited from the tradition of closed-form poetry but invented. The sonnet brings with it a stanzaic pattern into which some materials fit well and others do not. The breakthrough that these three poets have brought about is in their rejection of such a "box." They have designated as their recurrent event a concept, allowing the words that express that concept to respond to their own self-generated movements. By responding to the center around which they move, the words are held within a recognizable limit without falling into a rigid classification.

## Arbitrary Constraints and Aleatory Operations:
## Harry Mathews and John Cage

Ezra Pound proposes that all verse consists of a constant and a variant, but he allows that *any* element can function as constant, *any* element as variant. He rejects the authority of traditional forms, which tend to restrict that choice. Arnaut Daniel and Petrarch created forms appropriate to their age and condition; the poet today can do the same. By admitting variability into the terms of his equation, Pound allows that the selection of the constant and variant can be *arbitrary*, at the poet's discretion. I want to examine those invented forms that poets have brought about by the self-imposition of constraints. What, then, makes these invented forms different from those of a previous age, and more appropriate to ours? Again, Pound claims that such a form could prove "a center around which, not a box within which" each element moves. The reigning attitude toward form, perhaps since Aristotle's classifications, is that it works to *contain* the poetic "stuff." Robert Duncan addresses this point in an attack on the New Criticism of the 1940s: "We are just emerging from a period that was long dominated by the idea of a poem as a discipline and as a form into which the poet put ideas and feelings, confining them in a literary propriety.... The dominant school of that time thought of form not as a mystery but as a manner of containing ideas and feelings; of content not as the meaning of form but as a commodity packaged in form. It was the grand age of Container Design."[34] In the "container" theory, the idea or content of the poem is born of something called inspiration and is generally thought to *precede* the making of the poem. Ideas and feelings, as Duncan indicates, are then shaped, or packaged, by the poet's formal expertise, in accordance with "literary propriety." This school is of course heavily indebted to the capital fund of traditional verse forms, the leading indicator of such propriety.

The poet can buck this system in a variety of ways. Duncan's practice has led him to the invention of an infinite serial form. But a significant alternative (one that proceeds in the opposite direction) would be to employ arbitrary constraints. By deciding on a set of restrictions prior to composition, the poet attacks the notion of inspiration as a prior event, the persistence of which is due largely to the continued influence of romanticism. The poet begins not with the hallowed spark such as God imparts to Adam on the Sistine ceiling, but with a choice or decision; since formal choices *precede* content, the arbitrary constraints are thus relied on to *generate*, not contain, content. Or, as Edmund White says of the fiction of Harry Mathews, his "formal rigor is precisely what makes him modern. His structures are not imposed on preexistent contents; rather the exigencies of form generate incidents and even descriptions."[35] The use of arbitrary constraints in poetry is the most obvious instance of a procedural form.

But what constitutes a constraint, and how does a constraint generate content? If the Container School of Criticism gathered around Kenyon College in the 1940s, one enclave of those who espouse arbitrary constraints is the somewhat less formal Ouvroir de Littérature Potentielle (Workshop of Potential Literature), or Oulipo for short. Founded by Raymond Queneau and François Le Lionnais in Paris in 1960, the workshop's chief aim is the generation of literary forms employing elaborate constraints. Warren F. Motte, Jr., in *Oulipo: A Primer of Potential Literature*, provides us with considerable information on the subject of formal constraints, both in summary and by primary texts. In his introduction, Motte claims, "Erecting the aesthetic of formal constraint, then, the Oulipo simultaneously devalues inspiration." Citing Le Lionnais's "First Manifesto," he notes:

> There are many degrees of constraint, ranging from minimal to maximal. . . . Simplifying grossly, one might postulate three levels: first, a minimal level, constraints of the language in which the text is written; second, an intermediate level, including constraints of genre and certain literary norms; third, a maximal level, that of *consciously* preelaborated and *voluntarily* imposed systems of artifice. No text can skirt the minimal level and remain readable; perhaps no text can wholly avoid the intermediate level. But it is the maximal level that concerns the Oulipo: this is what they refer to in using the word "constraint."[36]

We have seen, for instance, the generic constraint of the elegy in William Bronk's "The Arts and Death: A Fugue for Sidney Cox," limiting his choice of materials and tone. The Oulipians are not at all disinterested in the more elaborate traditional forms, though the sonnet, as Motte says, brings with it a "rigid cultural codification" (OU 8–9) and is resistant to innovation. Certainly forms such as the rondeau or sestina occur within the third level of constraint; their study (and experiment with their parameters), as well as the resurrection of the old and obscure lipogram, acrostic, and palindrome, is dubbed *analytic* Oulipism. But it is in the creation of new forms of constraint, *synthetic* Oulipism, that the movement largely exercises its convictions. A constraint, then, should be "*consciously* preelaborated." The poet makes deliberate structural decisions, and elaborates a complete (hence procedural) form, before the actual composition takes place. Constraints are also "*voluntarily* imposed." The will of the poet is opposed to any operation left to chance or inspiration. Also, to the extent that "the tradition" works to compromise the individual will, an insistence on the voluntary leads to the synthesis of, or experiment with, forms. So, when the Oulipians do dabble in ancient forms, these forms tend to be noncanonic items rescued from disuse.

Marcel Bénabou, in his essay "Rule and Constraint," distinguishes between *rule* and *constraint*. He argues that such rules as the "laws of prosody" or the "three unities" of classical tragedy have been accepted as requirements for literary production; that is, they have become synonymous with "technique." These rules are motivated by the literary tradition and are often followed unconsciously by the writer. Bénabou argues, however, that

> it is actually in the passage from the *rule* to the *constraint* that the stumbling block appears: people accept the rule, they tolerate technique, but they refuse constraint. Precisely because it seems like an unnecessary rule, a superfluous redoubling of the exigencies of technique, and consequently no longer belongs—so the argument goes—to the admitted norm but rather to the process, and thus is exaggerative and excessive. It is as if there were a hermetic boundary between two domains: the one wherein the observance of rules is a natural fact, and the one wherein the excess of rules is perceived as shameful artifice. (OU 41)

We can distinguish the "accepted" rule from the "shameful" constraint by noting that the one is motivated by tradition, whereas the other seems unnecessary, or arbitrary.

Why then risk the opprobrium of readers by employing such reduplicative constraints? Bénabou argues that the boundary between rule and constraint "must be challenged in the name of a better knowledge of the functional modes of language and writing. One must first admit that language may be treated as an object in itself, considered in its materiality, and thus freed from its subservience to its significatory obligation" (OU 41). Constraints thus allow us to explore the "complex system" that is language. He concludes, "To the extent that constraint goes beyond rules which seem natural only to the people who have barely questioned language, it forces the system out of its routine functioning, thereby compelling it to reveal its hidden resources" (OU 41). Constraints function as a generative, or exploratory, device with regard to language itself. Such difficulties, as the Russian Formalists understood, force us away from the complacent or routine examination. Of course, if we have something to say, it is easy enough to say it and be done. But literary language "doesn't manipulate notions," as Jean Lescure points out in his essay "Brief History of Oulipo"; "it handles verbal objects. . . . Unusual designations point to the sign rather than to the signified" (OU 36). Constraints awaken our interest in, allow us to discover, language. Harry Mathews says, "There is no value inherent in the product of a constrictive form, except one: being unable to say what you normally would, you must say what you normally wouldn't."[37] The arbitrary constraint, because it impedes our attention, *generates* perception, reveals what may have been otherwise ignored. Motte summarizes the "seeming paradox" in Oulipian aesthetics as "the belief that systems of formal constraint—far from restricting the writer—actually afford a field of creative liberty" (OU 18). Or, in Bénabou's assessment: "Constraint is thus a commodious way of passing from language to writing" (OU 41).

It's no accident that a work whose structure relies on a constant and variant should employ arbitrary constraints. If Pound is correct that the poet can select any element for the constant, it is obvious that the voluntary preelaboration of a constraint becomes for the poem its constant. As an example, Georges Perec has produced a three-hundred-page lipogrammatic novel, *La Disparition*, written without the letter *e*. Although the constraint in principle is quite simple, its application is excessively difficult.[38] Because *e* is the most frequently used letter in both English and French, the constraint is constantly felt. It forces the writer to explore virtually every cranny of his lexical resources to provide for suitable substitutes—variants. Accordingly, no aspect of the generated text remains unaffected. The resultant text will run "hog wild" in order to accommodate the demands of the constraint.

I want to introduce two fairly sizable texts that employ arbitrary constraints. Harry Mathews, who became a member of the Oulipo in 1972, provides *Trial Impressions*, a work originally published in 1977 and subsequently included in *Armenian Papers: Poems 1954–1984*. *Trial Impressions* presents itself as a set of thirty variations on an "ayre" by John Dowland. The work, not surprisingly, employs several arbitrary constraints developed by the Oulipians. The second text is John Cage's *Themes & Variations* (1982), a series of mesostics (i.e., mid-line acrostic poems) using the names of fifteen writers, artists, and musicians who have influenced the author. Chiefly known as an experimental composer, Cage is also a prolific writer. His music, poetry, and lectures are a complicated play of arbitrary constraints and aleatory techniques. By introducing these works in tandem, I hope to show that the "macro" structure of each is a theme and variation.

## Mathews's *Trial Impressions*

The structure of Mathews's *Trial Impressions* has two dimensions. First, there is a macrostructure whose constraint motivates the entire set of thirty poems; and second, there are a number of microstructures, constraints that appear only on the occasion of a single poem but whose exercise is demanded by the exigencies of the whole. As I noted by comparison with Cage, the macrostructure is that of theme and variation. A selection from John Dowland's *Second Booke of Ayres* is offered as the first poem and identified in a subscript. This "original" lyric is the constant or theme from which the twenty-nine variants proceed. (The identification of the "original" from which the "copies" are made—a literary heresy when acknowledged, though often practiced—is not to be taken for granted. In his commentary on his poem "Condition of Desire" included in David Lehman's *Ecstatic Occasions, Expedient Forms*, Mathews notes that the "source" of his poem of personal loss is "a classic poem of loss and grief." Rather than provide the identity of that poem and its author, Mathews offers the matter "for puzzle-solvers," providing several clues.[39] Because the number of letters in the mystery author's name determines the number of letters in each line of Mathews's poem, the procedure functions as a constraint; the poem is generated by its predecessor.) The demands of *Trial Impressions* are indeed trying: how does one paint twenty-nine copies of *La Gioconda* and have them all appear fresh and new? The poet must provide a multiple record of his impressions of a single object, in this case twenty-nine poems that are not identical copies, as when the technically proficient painter produces a fake Rembrandt, but poems that are at least as exciting as the "original."

As in Mathews's earlier poem, "The Pines at Son Beltran," semantic recurrence is a factor; all thirty poems are saying essentially the same thing. That these poems are undeniably interesting on their own merits is an indication that what the poem says (its paraphrasable content) is not its chief recommendation. The constant presence of his material impels the poet to alter how he goes about saying it, a lexical variation. But let's not reduce this project to stylistic modifications; the poet is not merely drawing a mustache on the portrait of a bemused young woman. Mathews effects transformations that, to extend our metaphor, have more to do with his subject's personality than her appearance. Here is the source poem:

> Deare, if you change, Ile never chuse againe,
> Sweete, if you shrinke, Ile never think of love,
> Fayre, if you faile, Ile judge all beauty vaine,
> Wise, if too weake, my wits Ile never prove.
> > Dear, sweete, fayre, wise, change, shrinke nor be not weake,
> > And on my faith, my faith shall never breake.

Earth with her flowers shall sooner heavn adorn,
Heaven her bright stars through earths dim globe shall move,
Fire heate shall lose and frosts of flames be borne,
Ayre made to shine as blacke as hell shall prove:
  Earth, heaven, fire, ayre, the world transformed shall view,
  E're I prove false to faith, or strange to you.[40]

Critics have discussed whether *Trial Impressions* belongs to the genre the French call *exercises de style*. After assigning a "set text," usually well known, as Keith Cohen explains, "the imitator then composes a number of variations of the original according to slight modifications in style, tone, or register."[41] One notorious example of the technique is provided by a fellow Oulipian, Raymond Queneau; his *Exercises in Style* consists of ninety-nine versions of the same story. Certainly the charge of "stylistic exercise" eliminates any claim to the inspired, an admittedly Oulipian goal, but in the practice of both Queneau and Mathews there is a deliberate attempt to confuse the traditional valuation of "imitator" and "inventor." As Barrett Watten cautions, "Mathews's twenty-nine rewritings of Dowland's poem are not addressed only to 'style,' however. There is a deeper question of the relation of style to 'an original' that is identified with stated value of constancy [in Dowland's poem]. The work runs from farce . . . to more serious formulations."[42] We have become accustomed to accept some degree of "unconscious imitation" (which usually goes by the term "influence") under the current aesthetic. But the acknowledgment of deliberate imitation has been more difficult to redeem. To a large degree, the rebuttal lies in the properties of constraint itself. In an interview with the British poet John Ash, Mathews claims that an Oulipian constraint "distracts the ego and the superego sufficiently to keep them busy on this arbitrary problem so that the unconscious is made available to the writer."[43] The ego is directly involved with the constraint of an imitation, subdued finally by the need to say the same thing again and again, defeated in its desire for "self-expression." This preoccupation allows the unconscious to speak, saying more than or something other than the expected. The conscious mind concerns itself with the method and becomes the imitator, while the unconscious mind provides the essence and becomes the inventor.

Mathews employs a variety of microstructures that are chiefly motivated by the duress of having to produce twenty-nine variants of a given text. Without getting overly schematic, we can loosely collect the poems into three groups. The majority are what I would call transformations of the original text; a somewhat smaller group (which may overlap with some of these transformations) appropriates certain traditional forms, though not necessarily in the accepted manner; and a third group (keeping in mind that the whole project is essentially an Oulipian constraint) employs constraints patented by the Oulipo as their generating principle.

By using the term "transformation," I hope to dispel the impression that these poems are no more than "slight modifications in style, tone, or register." Certainly such modifications occur, but to halt our discussion at that revelation would be to consider them as exercises only. Mathews's transformations of the Dowland ayre are like soaking a fine white shirt in a permanent dye—every fiber takes on the intended color, and a reversal of the process seems impossible. These "new" poems are not "copies" any more than a shocking red button-down oxford can be taken for a white one. We could even say that the style of the shirt has remained the same; certain elements such as the placement of buttons or milling of the fabric stay the same. But a conceptual change that goes beyond style occurs. The occasion for which the brightly colored shirt seems appropriate will differ significantly from that on which the conservative white shirt is most apt.

Let's compare the "original" to its first transformation:

> If you break our breakfast date, I'll go begging in Bangkok;
> If you start stalling, I'll stop everything;
> If you phone that freak, I'll fall down Everest;
> If you take that trip, please tow away my truck.
>     A date, a freak, a trip—I implore you to be careful.
>     I don't claim to be reasonable, I just can't stop.
>
> We can't take this sharp awareness into yesterday,
> No pondered memory of tomorrow can exalt it.
> Can black holes yield light? Can sunlight weigh more than stone?
> Can the split atom be reassembled?
>     When today is tomorrow, and the electrons rejoin each other,
>     Only then will my unreasonableness fail to invest you.

*Up to Date*

Dowland certainly makes an impassioned plea for his lady's continued interest. It would not be unfair to say that the original is something of an exercise in that Elizabethan genre known as the lover's complaint; but we must also admit that it is a superb example of the genre. In the first stanza, the poet fears his beloved may be fickle. His response, if this is indeed the case, would be complete disillusionment, quitting the game altogether. The concluding couplet implores her to stability by citing his absolute constancy. The second stanza employs the familiar rhetorical device (familiar, that is, to the genre and the age) of hyperbole: sooner these incredible things will happen, than I'll do this to you. The figure is repeated several times for added emphasis. Mathews's first transformation retains the stanzaic structure of the original, including the medial caesura and as much of the alliteration and internal rhyme of the first stanza as possible. This poem, in a way the prototype, prepares us for the more "hog wild" variants to come. Constant in structure and statement, its modification is governed by the italic subscript, *Up to Date*. The subscript is thus the key to the transformation, the controlling element that governs all the changes. A translation from classic to modern, the poem suddenly becomes the property of a young urban professional, through whose persona or sensibility the poem is now told. Note the difference between style and sensibility: in Robert Lowell's *Imitations*, Baudelaire's style does not emerge into English, his thought assumes Lowell's style; Mathews not only alters the diction, he (re)considers the terms in which this new persona will express his plea. Mathews's poem is as much an insightful comment on modern mores as Dowland's poem is for his age. The easily detectable irony of Mathews's point of view is as suited to modern poetics as Dowland's classical rhetoric is appropriate to the Elizabethan lyric.

The constraint of bringing Dowland up to date results in a transformation from the fiery "heate" of Elizabethan passion to the more contemporary coolness. The diction is casual, even breezy ("If you break our breakfast date . . ."), and the plea sounds as if it had been made by someone refused a second date after a one-night stand. His shrill slang ("If you phone that freak . . .") is removed from Dowland, not only stylistically but culturally as well. Even so, his exotic and far-flung complaints ("I'll go begging in Bangkok," where in fact "today is tomorrow") are as hyperbolic (though perhaps more desperate) than those of Dowland's speaker. Which is to say, we are no more convinced by the complaints of our lover from SoHo than those of a man who claims he'll "never chuse againe." Mathews has, I think, very carefully selected a poem of unrequited love as his "set text," not the least because it illustrates that old cliché, "the more things change, the more they stay the same."

The sort of hyperbole on which Dowland builds the second stanza has been condemned in the current rhetorical market, but Mathews's pleasing transformation takes advantage of the contrary-to-all-terrestrial-logic theories of present-day physics: "Can black holes yield light? . . . / Can the split atom be reassembled?" Mathews makes the leap from sixteenth-century metaphysics to the quantum physics of the Einsteinian universe. Even so, his speaker appears to have gotten it all down without the equations in Physics for Poets.

Another poem in which a transformation occurs in the persona of the speaker is XIV, subscript *Male Chauvinist*: "You're a pain, and as long as you hang around, I'll keep playing the field. / You're a kvetch, and if you don't give me some room, there are friendlier beds," and so forth. In this example, the stanzaic structure and the rhetorical pattern remain intact, but the speaker suffers a reversal in attitude. Rather than swear to his constancy, he brags of his infidelity; instead of efforts to praise her, he insists on abusing her: "Pain, kvetch, potato nose, dope, keep acting this way / And as sure as there's sand in spinach I'll keep kicking your ass." The immaculate shirt we saw hanging on Dowland's line is now dipped in a vat of indelible black ink. Although Mathews retains the rhetorical structure of the original, he has allowed the persona of the speaker to "run wild." But don't these poems still say the same thing? The Elizabethan "complaint" becomes a more contemporary squabble; and the passive threats of Dowland's speaker become the active threats of physical abuse in the chauvinist mode.

By comparison, variation XI chiefly manipulates tone to achieve its effect:

> I could hardly expect you to love me if I couldn't make up my mind
>      about you.
> If I thought love was pointless, how could I fail to repulse you?
> I wouldn't expect your support if I derided beauty as skin-deep.
> If I was a jerk, why should your intelligence tolerate it?
>
> Who wants to fly his rocket ship through solid rock?
> Who cares for strolling on the unpaved void of night?
> Who takes icicles to bed in winter? Who likes his ice cream boiled?
> Nobody wants that kind of world. Please agree.

> *Of Course*

Each line could be preceded by the self-diminishing "Of course." Instead of the macho chauvinist, this speaker represents the very insecure "new" male; he is sensitive, but begs for assurances. This may be the first appearance of the celebrated "wimp factor" in poetry. His pathetic plea ("Please agree") is nearly as disagreeable as the chauvinist's bullying tactics. These two poems in particular summon a far different response from the reader than the original, whose speaker we are somewhat encouraged to cheer on. There is considerably more distance between "the poet" and the speaking "persona." But we observe this departure even as we recognize that the plea itself ("Stay with me") remains the same for each speaker.

One method that Mathews employs to great effect is a conceptual rather than stylistic transformation. As if issuing an order to be carried out, he begins with a concept that in some way modifies the structure of the poem. Poem III, subscript *Keep Talking*, represents an *expansion* of the original:

> Dear, if you, who are more polestar than polecat, change, I'll never,
>     when confronted with life's many-paged bill of fare, choose any dish,
>     no matter how succulent, again.
> Sweet and pretty as an advancing spinnaker, if you shrink like a boiled
>     sweater, I'll never so much as think of the high-rental havens of
>     love. . . .

Dowland's entire text is embedded in the rather amusing extended metaphors, most of which get horribly mixed by the line's end. The speaker has become almost unbearably prolix, as if afraid that his lady, bored by his attempts at verbal dexterity, will depart as soon as he's finished. He takes on something of the inept weaver of metrical delights who is more likely to provoke a giggle than to convince. But every gesture in the poem is motivated by the transformational command to keep talking, to expand.

Variation IV is an exercise in "haikuization," or *contraction* of the original, and so complements III:

> change love no next choice
> less love no love thought
> turn light all sight void
> weak wise no wise proof
> word faith gives faith faith
>
> first earth flower fills sky
> sky star lights earth dark
> fire bears cold ice flame
> grave dark light fills earth
> change earth heaven fire air
> than false being love being

*The Wang Way*

In Marcel Bénabou's comprehensive chart of Oulipian maneuvers, the "haikuization" of an existing text falls under the category of "word-deduction" (OU 45). Raymond Queneau, speaking of "redundancy" in the sonnets of Mallarmé, obtains the haikuization of two sonnets by "restricting" them to their rhyming sections. He defends the process by claiming (1) that he obtains a new poem which is also beautiful, (2) that "there is almost as much in the restriction as in the entire poem," and (3) that "without going to the limits of sacrilege, one can at least say that this restriction sheds light on the original poem; it is not wholly without exegetical value and may contribute to interpretation" (OU 59). Mathews's contraction of the original does not adhere strictly to its diction or word order, but the three results predicted by Queneau are in evidence. We may note that the haiku has always been "relevant to experimental interests" in Western poetry, and may be the forerunner of concrete poetry.[44]

Not holding himself to the traditional seventeen-syllable count of haiku, Mathews does restrict each line to five words, retaining the essence of the line if not its vocabulary. As John Cage points out in his introduction to *Themes & Variations*, "A haiku in Japanese has no fixed meaning. Its words are not defined syntactically."[45] Mathews's line exploits the semantic flexibility that the lack of a definite syntax makes possible; he offers Dowland's sense, but liberates other, I think more rarefied, interpolations. The second stanza, for example, displays more of the awe of nature and the humility, if not personal anonymity, familiar to oriental verse than the egotistical boasting of hyperbole in the Western tradition. The five-sign method in *The Wang Way* is much closer to Pound's interpretation of the ideogrammic method than the usual translations of haiku. The poem then is *new*: it is a fruitful adaptation of the haiku form, not merely a copy or parody; it offers very nearly as much of Dowland's sense as we need, and yet provides a scenario for interpretation well beyond that of courtship rituals. The first line in Mathews's version makes the struggle of personal choice and inexorable change more apparent, as the individual comes face to face with the cosmos. All of Mathews's variations have, I find, a salutary exegetical effect, almost as homages, on Dowland's poem.

Two of the variations are in fact successful not only as stylistic parody, but also as mock sonnets. The subscript of poem X, *L'Homme Mal Armé*, puns on both the symbolist poet Mallarmé and the title of Apollinaire's great "La Chanson du Mal-Aimé." In an interview with his friend and fellow poet John Ashbery, Mathews claims that, as a result of his long residence in Paris, he was forced to become more conscious of the resources of his own language. "I felt that I was surrounded by a language to which Mallarmé had a weird relationship.

Mallarmé wrote like nobody else; even his letters to his friends are very hermetic." Although inspired by Mallarmé's extreme retreat "towards formality, a kind of abstraction," Mathews concludes that he wouldn't "ever want to actually write like Mallarmé."[46] One solution is to parody that language:

> I and my pens disgorged by the finger in the fold
> Of thick literal leaves? or what if fabled art bunts
> From a racked best brim violation of brass that shunts
> The phoenix peering, defenestrated, through cold
>
> At (from the cream) the roe's stare like a buttonholed
> Rosette; coursing, from foxes' mutant pluck, old hunts
> To disaster; limp Coriolanus hacked by runts;
> Humpty Dumpty's cap crocked. All these your ears withhold:
>
> You only whose certain wits sheave parching winds and suck
> Assurance like a spring from this fagged stream's bed—tuck
> Me in its flux like an oar in the cleft of the thole
>
> Of your eyes! I am still theirs, hard-felt (if, as well, hung
> On cheeks, lips—thus of the wetted rose the strass soul
> Kisses the lobed rifts) and deeper than any tongue.

Keith Cohen aptly notes that Mathews targets "the tortured syntax, the nearly untranslatable word-plays, and the esoteric, seemingly private, system of symbols."[47] Just so, but it may be that it is this very "untranslatability" that Mathews parodies—the very impossibility of turning a Mallarméan sonnet into a perfectly rhymed sonnet in English. The only solution is to write your own without the bother of an original French text. As Mathews points out, "It's almost as though French and English don't mix in a fruitful way."[48] The result (about as far from the Dowland text as any, save that it is addressed to a woman) is that Mathews not only parodies the pitfalls of faithful translationese, but also mocks the sonnet form. The rhymes are particularly ridiculous: "bunts/shunts" and "hunts/runts" in the octet; and "suck/tuck" and "hung/tongue" in sestet. This sort of bawdy mockery is also found in poem VII, *A Disconsolate Chimaera*, whose target appears to be Shakespeare or Sidney.

Two of the variations seem to be largely motivated by analytic Oulipism, the revival of infrequently used forms whose resources have not been fully exploited. Poem XXIV is a miraculous example of the palindrome:

I

        (one who won)

                *"Deh!"*

sang

        —devil's aria:

                No-bed era

begat

        love's

                reverse

voltage.

        Bare, debonair

                as lived;

gnashed now.

        "Oh—we?"

                No: I.

                *To and Fro*

Without exaggeration I submit that, accommodating the constraint, this poem stays remarkably close to the "plot" of Dowland's original. The speaker, rejected, sings "love's reverse voltage." Once "debonair" he has now been "gnashed." She rejects the pronoun "we," leaving him with the solitary "I." I think the symmetry of the palindrome makes for some beautiful play of consonants and vowels, such as "Bare, debonair" and "devil's aria: No-bed era." Mathews's poem has as much musical verve as the internal rhymes and alliteration of Dowland's original.

The final poem in *Trial Impressions*, XXX, takes the form of a sestina. In an earlier chapter I discussed the renovation of elaborate fixed forms, and so I want to mention only those points that are peculiar to Mathews and the Oulipo. The analysis of fixed form among the Oulipians takes as its task the discovery of residual potential: what verbal resources have not been tapped, what innovations of its rules or structure will release additional literary energy? Raymond Queneau undertakes a mathematical analysis of the *permutational* character of the sestina's end-words. Is six the optimal number? He asks "whether it was always possible to construct $N$-inas when $N$ is a number other than six" (OU 78). Mathews's contribution to the renovation includes the poem "Ages and Indifferent Clouds." David Lehman comments, "The rhyming teleutons are the deliberately antipoetic *hippopotamus, geranium, aluminum, focus, stratum,* and *bronchitis.* It's two sestinas in one: the beginning of all the lines pun on the names of six out-of-the-way plants. The 'sea anemone' becomes 'An enemy, who has seen . . .' and 'sixty enemas'; the Jew's harp reappears in the guise of 'the deuce of hearts' and 'fused harps,' " and so forth.[49] Jacques Roubaud, in his "Mathematics in the Method of Raymond Queneau," points out that Mathews's sestina employs "a particularly efficient 'double helix' principle," in which "Daniel's permutation structures the ends of verses and Monge's permutation, the inverse, structures the beginnings" (OU 83–84).

In the example at hand, though, Mathews chooses his six end-words from the second stanza of Dowland's poem: *earth, heaven, fire, air, stars,* and *faith.* These teleutons are anything but antipoetic; they are in fact rather classical, reminding one of Sidney's pastoral double sestina "Ye Goatherd Gods." One can exacerbate the constraints of repetition in the sestina by selecting teleutons that are so idiosyncratic that finding them in the context of one stanza, let alone six, would be nearly impossible—or highly artificial, which is largely the point. In poem XXX, the constraint results from borrowing both the teleutons and the subject matter of the prior text. Mathews's appropriation of Dowland's metaphysical yet elemental diction nevertheless enables him to compose a poem of great passion and beauty. Any skeptic who charges only facile gamesmanship in this effort must face the intimacy with which Mathews ponders the infinite desire and fear of loss he finds in the original; he makes Dowland his contemporary. Here are the last stanzas:

> Without you, my thinking spins in thin air,
> Evening never warms its gradual stars,
> Choosing another is choosing a bed of earth,
> All love is decreed hallucinatory fire.
> But air and evening fill up with love from your faith,
> Which I could no more break than I could fly to heaven,
>
> Except that once I did: it was under a heaven
> Of night and eyes, our breaths made one air,
> Our eyes were struck open in pleasures of faith,
> There was nothing to be seen but stars,
> Only one night, and never to see dawn's fire
> Was all I wanted as we grappled on grass and earth.
>
> You make earth earth: who needs heaven?
> You give a heat to fire, you give a brightness to air
> Of that night's stars, of that broadcast faith.

Two forms that Mathews employs in *Trial Impressions* are the products of synthetic Oulipism, that branch devoted to the invention of forms, which "constitutes the essential vocation of Oulipo," as François Le Lionnais says in "Lipo: First Manifesto" (OU 27–28). Both forms are unprecedented in literary history; both employ arbitrary constraints to generate a new work. Poem XII is an example of the S + 7 method. In the official catalog, it is described as "a method of textual transformation elaborated by Jean Lescure in which each substantive in a given text is replaced by the seventh substantive following it in the dictionary" (OU 201). Essentially, it is a device of word-substitution (OU 45), but then so are the more familiar processes of simile or translation. Mathews's given text is of course the Dowland ayre, and the transformation that results is as follows:

> Deep, if you charge, I'll never chug again
> > (Deep, if you chant, I'll never chip again)
> Tall, if you shun, I'll never thrive on luck
> > (Swift, if you shrive, I'll never thirst for luck)
> Far, if you fan, I'll keep all bedclothes vast
> > (False, if you faint, I'll jug all beaver vast)
> Worse, if too weird, my wives I'll never puff
> > (Worse, if too webbed, my witch I'll never prowl):
> > Deep, tall, far, worse, charge, shun, and be not weird
> And by my fall, my fall will never bridge
> > (Deep, swift, false, worse, chant, shrive, and be not webbed,
> > And by my fake, my fake shall never breast.)

As you can see from the first stanza, Mathews carries out the transformation twice, substituting for nouns, verbs, and adjectives, but otherwise retaining the syntax of the original. The results vary with the dictionary one uses: the comprehensive *Oxford English Dictionary* produces more arcane results than the pocket *American Heritage Dictionary*. In the first transformation, Mathews has chosen to substitute for each noun, verb, and adjective of the pre-existing text the seventh entry that follows it in the dictionary of choice (I believe it's the pocket *American Heritage*). For the second transformation, indicated by the parentheses, the formula appears to be S + 1, substituting the very next entry. The S + 7 method must have been compelling to Mathews in the composition of *Trial Impressions* since the entire project involves the transformation of a preexistent text. Because both the original text and the method employed are decided upon in advance of the composition, the form is undeniably procedural. The determining number seven, as Mathews illustrates, is also wholly arbitrary, as in effect are the results. He claims, "The device is entertaining, apparently mechanical, apparently unpredictable."[50] Raymond Queneau concurs, "The results are not always very interesting; sometimes, on the other hand, they are striking. It seems that only *good* texts give good results" (OU 61). The S + 7 method is perhaps the most militant of those forms invented by the Oulipo which require the withdrawal of the poet's ego and the denial of inspiration, thus allowing the quality of the product to be entirely determined by the mechanism. The poet need only decide whether to save or abandon his file.

In an address delivered to a group of aspiring writers at Queens College, New York, Mathews defends the value of both the results achieved and the process itself. After providing a literal, published translation of a parable-length story by Kafka, he offers two translations of his own: the first retains the phrasing of the original but simplifies the syntax; and the second employs the S + 7 method. He then comments on the latter two translations:

> Putting it simply, one can describe what has been done in the two translations by saying that in the first the sense of the original is kept and its structure altered, in the second the sense is altered and the structure kept.... How, you may wonder, can the second [S + 7 method] translation even begin to be taken seriously?
>
> Let me reread the original and the two translations. . . . The first translation (unlike the original) is growing steadily more boring; the second translation is making more and more sense—or, at least, we seem more and more to be expecting it to make sense; and much of the sense we are persuading ourselves to discover sounds, while in no way replicating that of the original, like a kind of commentary on it. . . .
>
> Little by little, the "meaningless" second translation is accumulating an appearance of meaning. I suggest that this is no accident, and that the meaning of the second translation has its source in the original. I suggest that this meaning can certainly not be found in what the translation has changed—its vocabulary—but in what it has left intact: the structure and rhythm of Kafka's story. . . . This movement of discovery and resolution irresistibly survives the travesty of sense perpetrated by the second translation, just as it irresistibly succumbs to the "faithful" rendering of the [first] translation.[51]

The syntactical structure of Kafka's parable has been retained as a constant; its vocabulary varies wildly from the original. Mathews's point is that the structure of the story conveys more of its meaning than the words themselves, an observation that runs contrary to what we would probably surmise on first examination and thus validates Marcel Bénabou's argument in favor of literary and linguistic experiment. Turning back to Dowland, what *exactly* does he mean by "Sweete, if you shrinke, Ile never think of love"? Shrink how? Think what? As readers we are carried by the rhetorical momentum, the parallelisms of sound and rhythm, past and through such ambiguous diction to an understanding of the text. How different is the sense of the S + 7 transformation, "Tall, if you shun, I'll never thrive on luck"? If this tall, striking woman should "shun" (how apt!) the diminutive poet, he'd never boast good fortune. What critic's paraphrase could compete with such a variant? The transformation is interesting because it retains as a constant the cause-and-effect conditional, "If you . . . I'll . . . ." The transformation also functions as commentary on the original: don't we implore a distracted lover, when the relationship becomes untenable and he or she begins to look for any excuse to exit, "be not weird"?

The second of the Oulipian forms is poem XIII, subscript *Multiple Choice*. Eleven sections are numbered in sequence; each concludes by demanding that the reader make certain choices concerning the continuance or realization of plot. Multiple choice plot development is a type of *combinatorial* literature which presents not one proper sequence of events but several, all of which are equally valid and entirely at the reader's discretion. As in other Oulipian maneuvers, the author agrees to cede absolute authority over the text, allowing the reader to participate in its composition; the atmosphere is deliberately "ludic." The *potentiality* laden in the process is thus conveyed to the reader as co-creator. As with the S + 7 method, the multiple choice plot is intrinsically appropriate to the condition of Dowland's original. His ayre presents us with a limited either/or situation; *someone* must make a choice, and it appears to be the lady. The speaker's mind is made up: either she is constant, and they are inseparable; or she is fickle, and the world (at least for him) is in chaos. The power of the poem lies in the maniacal determination with which the speaker reduces all consequence to a single choice (presumably in an attempt to force her hand). The rhetoric of absolutes ("never . . . never") and hyperbole reinforces this desperate attitude. Mathews's combinatorial plot does not reduce options but multiplies them, dispassionately yielding the choice to the reader. In section 10, the intrusion of the reader as audience is even parodied, with the offending party scolded for "perplexing and irrelevant" remarks. Here is the first section:

> John comes to the city and meets
> Marian, a very affectionate girl.
> She loves him, and he her;
> But he finds that Marian has a changeable streak,
> So he leaves her. Do you think that he should never look

At another woman? Or do you think he should look
At some other woman? In the first case, proceed
To 7, if you're an optimist; to 8, if you're
A pessimist. In the second case, proceed to 2.

In the first five sections, variations on the name Marian (Marianne, Marie-Anne, etc.) make it somewhat unclear whether plain John is actually leaving the same woman or different women. Section 6 is a pivot, in which "the universe comes crashing down," much as Dowland's speaker predicts. Sections 7 through 11 offer five possible resolutions: (a) he lives alone and likes it, (b) he lives alone and dies of it, (c) she's miserable about it all, (d) she's indifferent, and (e) they live happily ever after. The reader is thus allowed to construct whichever poem is best suited to his or her taste. If Dowland intends to bind the reader to the authority of the poem, as his speaker attempts to bind his lady in love, Mathews's multiple choice plot frees both the players in the drama and its audience.

## Cage's *Themes & Variations*

When the name John Cage surfaces in a discussion of aesthetics, one immediately thinks of the composer who intends to abuse our every expectation of what music is. He tells us that *noise* is "the sound of a truck at fifty miles per hour"; that is, sound we cannot control. *Music* is "the organization of sound."[52] Nevertheless, a cassette tape of Cage's compositions, inserted into the car stereo, may well drive us to that exit known as Distraction. My interest at the moment is John Cage, poet; but one might well suspect that a book such as *Themes & Variations* (1982) instigates much the same reaction among some as his music. Cage is a prolific writer in defense of his aesthetics, filling more than half a dozen volumes. (In this matter, he is very much like his mentor Arnold Schönberg, a brilliant stylist as well as composer.) All of these writings are intellectually invigorating and humorously contentious; some of them are also poetry. There is no other name for them, though they often defeat our expectations of what poetry is. In his foreword to *Silence* (1961), Cage asserts, "As I see it, poetry is not prose simply because poetry is in one way or another formalized."[53] I want to examine the very deliberate methods by which Cage has "formalized" his text *Themes & Variations*.

In the final chapter of her widely acclaimed book *Poetic Closure* (1968), Barbara Herrnstein Smith addresses that "fugitive fraction of current poetic activity" which champions the practice of "anti-closure" (the negation of the favored term is an indication that the critic is willing to discuss the phenomenon only with regard to the assumptions it doesn't fulfill). One activity in which these naughty poets are engaged involves *chance*. Finding the germ of this disease lurking in musical compositions, Smith rather cogently turns her attention to Cage: "Although, for example, the techniques of serial music and John Cage's composition by 'random generation' are in many ways directly opposed to each other, both involve conceptions of the relation of art to determinacy and indeterminacy which, in turn, play some havoc with our assumptions regarding the place of expectation, determination, and predictability in the perception of structure and closure."[54] Smith usefully distinguishes between two modes of composition: one employs programmatic and predetermined rules of generation; the other employs a random generation by chance operations. Although the former would seem to value determinacy and offer the potential of closure and the latter indeterminacy and "anti-closure," Smith is well aware that the one is never entirely present without the other.

In his career, Cage has in fact practiced in both methods. Under the tutelage of Schönberg, Cage wrote several serial compositions; his pieces for prepared piano also utilize a procedural, programmatic method of composition and performance. But especially after his discovery of the Chinese *I Ching*, or Book of Changes, and the flowering of his study of Zen Buddhism, Cage began to employ chance operations in an effort to displace the individual ego from composition. Cage's career has not undergone any radical transformation of aesthetics; both modes accomplish his desired ends. *Themes & Variations* is a text generated by both programmatic rules and random operations. Its methods of composition include some constraints that are seemingly arbitrary and others that appear motivated by the poet's taste. At the same time, it admits material generated and arranged in an aleatory manner. The dust-jacket blurb from Station Hill Press describes it as "a poem, a score for oral performance, a typographic experiment, a musical composition in which the words are notes and the ideas phrases, a series of mesostics determined by chance operations and combined with the Japanese form of Renga." There is plenty of room here, as Smith suggests, to "play some havoc with our assumptions."

Cage's text is many things, but certainly these two: it is nearly "illegible" if by reading one seeks mainly to gather information; and it is nearly eighty pages long in this unpaginated edition from Station Hill. There is not enough space here for a systematic explication of the text, and not much to be gained by it. Instead, I propose to explain the system that generates the text, with excerpts as illustration. Harry Mathews claims that for the Oulipian, "the value of a structure is its ability to produce results, not the quality of those results."[55] The theorist need only discover whether the constraint does generate a text; however, the practitioner (and ultimately the critic) must worry about the quality. I want to evaluate Cage's use of constraints and aleatory methods, but also to evaluate the literary quality of the product. With literariness as final arbiter, the constraints are justified only by the quality of the product. A generative form is of dubious value if the poetry it produces is bad. One can then say, by examining the results, that these are good (useful) constraints, or they are not.

The most evident formal device in *Themes & Variations* is the mesostic, a version of the acrostic poem. The *Princeton Encyclopedia* defines the acrostic as "a poem in which the initial letters of each line have a meaning when read downward";[56] for the mesostic one uses the middle of the line.[57] In Oulipian parlance, the process is "letter-deduction" (OU 44). As our sources point out, the acrostic is hardly a new form, being familiar to the writers of the Old Testament, to Plautus, Jonson, Boccaccio, and Poe. At the very least, this project could be called an instance of analytic Oulipism as Le Lionnais defines it: "The analytic tendency investigates works from the past in order to find possibilities that often exceed those their authors had anticipated" (OU 27). Plautus, for instance, uses the acrostic as a billboard, the "argument" of his play spelling out its title. The chief resource that Cage uncovers is multiple repetitions of the acrostic. Whereas Plautus limits the summary of his comic plot to the extent of the letters in "Menaechmi," Cage "writes through" the given name five, ten, or fifty times. Although the acrostic has always functioned as a constraint, Cage investigates its generative properties for longer works. The acrostic acts as a locus for composition, not unlike the return of the six end-words in the sestina. At the same time, the multiple repetition of Cage's mesostics functions as a generator of subsequent text. The question to be asked is, what is the efficacy of such a constraint? Quite simply, it provides at once the place at which composition occurs, and the place to which composition will (perhaps indefinitely) proceed.[58]

John Ashbery asks Mathews, "What is your standard of a form being sufficiently constricting?" To which Mathews replies, "A form that makes you write something that you wouldn't normally say, or in a way that you would never have said it. The form is so demanding that you can't get around it."[59] The mesostic falls within this category, though not to the extreme degree of the palindrome or lipogram. Let's look at some of Cage's "introductory" mesostics:

we Don't know
whAt
we'll haVe
when we fInish
Doing
whaT we're doing
bUt
we know every Detail
Of
pRocess
we're involveD in
A way
to leaVe no traces
nothIng in between
herDed ox[60]

The mesostic method does in fact constrict both what the poet says and the way it is said, simply by demanding that certain letters fall into certain places and not others. Cage "knows every detail of the process" he is involved in, and so can't get around it. He further constrains himself by adopting what he calls "the Mink rule for a pure mesostic" (named for a Joyce scholar and professor of philosophy at Wesleyan), which is "not to permit the appearance of either letter between two of the spinal name or phrase."[61] Or as he says in his foreword to *M*, "A given letter capitalized does not occur between it and the preceding capitalized letter."[62] In the example given, the *D* of "herDed" precludes another *d* from appearing between the *I* of "nothIng" and itself; the *I* of "nothIng" precludes another *i* from appearing between the *V* of "leaVe" and itself, and so forth. This additional constraint more severely restricts the words that can be employed in any given line of the mesostic, thus forcing the poet to say something he wouldn't normally say. The poet hopes that the results will be revelatory, and not an exercise in obscurantism.

Cage claims in his introduction to *Themes & Variations*, "Ordinarily when I write mesostics, I write about the person whose name is a row going down the middle of the text, though some are a collection of mesostics 're and not re' that person. The mesostics in this text are exceptionally not about the men named at all, except coincidentally" [1]. Cage has attempted three types of mesostics, whose purposes are quite different. "James Joyce, Marcel Duchamp, Erik Satie: An Alphabet" is an example of the first type; it is a homage to the subjects *as* subject.[63] Cage is motivated by his admiration for the three artists (though he does use chance operations to execute the text). In "36 Mesostics Re and Not Re Duchamp," the poem occupies a middle ground between homage and materials accumulated by random methods.[64] Lastly, in the case at hand, the materials are arbitrarily related to the names that appear. In the first type we discover a traditional use for the acrostic form, as when Poe composes "A Valentine" to Frances Sargent Osgood employing her name. In the last type, we see the acrostic used in an entirely new way, purely as a generative device.

Cage says of *Themes & Variations*, "There are fifteen themes. They are mesostics on the names of fifteen men who have been important to me in my life and work: Norman O. Brown, Marshall McLuhan, Erik Satie, Robert Rauschenberg, Buckminster Fuller, Marcel Duchamp, Jasper Johns, Henry David Thoreau, James Joyce, Merce Cunningham, David Tudor, Morris Graves, Mark Tobey, Arnold Schoenberg, Suzuki Daisetz" [1]. I would call Cage's selection of names a motivated constraint since he has chosen these fifteen (that they are all men might also be considered motivated) because he admires and has been influenced by them.[65] Yet they (the fifteen men) are not themselves the themes (or subjects in the musical sense) of the work; the themes are the initial set of mesostics composed. "Many more could be added to this list," Cage claims, but he is limited by the duration that he has imposed on the text. So we can say that the essential structure of theme and variation in this book involves some constraints that are purely arbitrary and some that are motivated by taste. The text is written *through* the names of fifteen important artists and thinkers; it is not *about* them. He offers sound, not subject; musical figures, not literary themes.

As he says, the fifteen "themes" are not men but mesostics: "They are derived from three, four, or five mesostics of equal length written on any of the following one hundred and ten ideas which I listed in the course of a cursory examination of my books" [1]. In what must be an unprecedented gesture, Cage offers us a list of the materials from which the mesostics are drawn. This reservoir of content includes such Zen koan statements of Cagean aesthetics as "Purposeful purposelessness" [2], as well as more direct claims such as "Poetry is having nothing to say and saying it; we possess nothing" [4]. This chrestomathy of his thought takes up over four pages of the introduction. Not only does Cage adopt an extremely complicated generative structure (which we have not entirely discussed), but he also presents the content of the poem before the fact. Of course, these 110 ideas are not "the content" but its raw material; they are, in cursory fashion, what constitutes Cage's aesthetics. One might ask, why compose a poem that recycles ideas? Cage follows his list by addressing the generative structure of the poem: "This is one text in an ongoing series; to find a way of writing which though coming from ideas is not about them; or is not about ideas but produces them" [6]. Recombination, repetition with slight alterations, does not produce the same idea, the same text, but a new one. Recombination is the basis for theme and variation.

Once Cage has established the mesostic as form and his 110 ideas as material, he uses "I Ching chance operations to find which of these ideas would be the subject of mesostics on which name" [6]. Such chance operations, as an aleatory method, would appear at cross-purposes to the predetermined constraints set in place. Although I have been comparing some of Cage's methods to those of the Oulipo, their work is decidedly anti-chance. Raymond Queneau, taking aim at the automatic writing techniques of the surrealists, comments, "We are not concerned with . . . aleatory literature" (OU 51). Jacques Roubaud elaborates, "The intentional, voluntary character of constraints to which [Queneau] insistently alludes time and again is for him indissolubly linked to this lively refusal of chance, and even more so to the refusal of the frequent equation of chance and freedom" (OU 87). Queneau argues that "the inspiration that consists in blind obedience to every impulse is in reality a sort of slavery." The Oulipians do not wait on inspiration, but refuse to rely on chance as its successor. This dilemma of methods returns us to Barbara Herrnstein Smith's discussion of the issue. She cites as evidence for the opposition an article by Ernst Krenek, a serial-form composer whose comments on the issue parallel Queneau's:

> Generally and traditionally "inspiration" is held in great respect as the most distinguished source of the creative process in art. It should be remembered that inspiration by definition is closely related to chance, for it is the very thing that cannot be controlled, manufactured, or premeditated in any way. . . . Actually the composer has come to distrust his inspiration because it is not really as innocent as it was supposed to be, but rather conditioned by the tremendous body of recollection, tradition, training, and experience. In order to avoid the dictations of such ghosts, he prefers to set up an impersonal mechanism which will furnish, according to premeditated patterns, unpredictable situations. . . . The unexpected happens by necessity. The surprise is built in.[66]

For both Cage and Krenek, the highly complex, impersonal method of composition is "premeditated," but the results are "unpredictable."[67] Smith objects to this approach, falling back on a traditional definition of art: "In games we 'play' with chance . . . in art we *control* chance." As long as this traditional definition of art holds, "then works created by the artist's deliberate abdication of sovereignty are not works of art, but games (often, to be sure, requiring much intellectual skill of its players and yielding corresponding rewards). What is lacking is precisely what has been eliminated: not predetermined events (for as Krenek, Cage, and others would insist, the events are most scrupulously determined by certain operations) but *designed effects*."[68]

The conflict regarding the definition of art is insoluble: what Smith objects to, the likes of Cage and Queneau promulgate—though most likely it will be the work of artists that will decide. Jacques Bens, in his essay "Queneau Oulipian," appears to reiterate Smith's last point, but with all sincere approval: "Make no mistake about it: potentiality is uncertain, but not a matter of chance. We know perfectly well everything that can happen, but we don't know whether it will happen" (OU 67). From this patchwork of opinions one thing seems clear: arbitrary constraints and aleatory operations have a similar disposal toward the question "what is art?" Both methods signify an "abdication of sovereignty," a setting aside of the poet's will, of those elements of a work most motivated by taste. That is, what essentially binds Queneau to Cage, and Krenek to Bens, is not whether they are for or against chance, but that they are all against the intrusion of ego. The "designed effects" that Smith proposes are effects "on an audience" which reflect "the humanity of the artist: not necessarily his individual 'personality,' but his peculiarly human psychological organization, his sensations, perceptions, emotions, and experience."[69] Smith's dialectic sets emotions against "intellectual skill," the heart against the mind.[70] Cage employs both arbitrary constraints and chance operations in order to set aside both the ego and the humanist argument as definers of what art should be. So he claims, "CHANCE OPERATIONS ARE NOT MYSTERIOUS SOURCES OF 'RIGHT ANSWERS.' THEY ARE A MEANS OF LOCATING A SINGLE ONE AMONG A MULTIPLICITY OF ANSWERS, AND, AT THE SAME TIME, OF FREEING THE EGO FROM ITS TASTE AND MEMORY, ITS CONCERN FOR PROFIT AND POWER, OF SILENCING THE EGO SO THAT THE REST OF THE WORLD HAS A CHANCE TO ENTER INTO THE EGO'S OWN EXPERIENCE WHETHER THAT BE OUTSIDE OR INSIDE."[71]

Why is this opinion considered so heretical by the traditional-minded critic? The answer can be found in the *I Ching*, or at least in the foreword prepared for the Bollingen edition by Carl Jung, who claims that "in order to understand what such a book is all about, it is imperative to cast off certain principles of the Western mind." Our science, he points out, has until recently been based on the "principle of causality." However, Jung claims:

> The axioms of causality are being shaken to their foundations: we know now that what we term natural laws are merely statistical truths and thus must necessarily allow for exceptions. . . . If we leave things to nature, we see a very different picture: every process is partially or totally interfered with by chance. . . .
>
> The Chinese mind, as I see it at work in the *I Ching*, seems to be exclusively preoccupied with the chance aspect of events. What we call coincidence seems to be the chief concern of this peculiar mind, and what we worship as causality passes almost unnoticed. . . .
>
> While the Western mind carefully sifts, weighs, selects, classifies, isolates, the Chinese picture of the moment encompasses everything down to the minutest nonsensical detail, because all of the ingredients make up the observed moment. . . .
>
> Just as causality describes the sequence of events, so synchronicity to the Chinese mind deals with the coincidence of events.[72]

Smith demands to see *designed effects*, that is, effects whose causation is ultimately discernable and classifiable. Cage rejects the Western assumption of a temporal sequence in favor of an Eastern study of coincidence. As he says in his introduction, "In Buddhist thought . . . everything causes everything else; everything results from everything else. . . . Since everything is nothing but cause and effect, Buddhists see that it is unnecessary or impossible to speak in terms of cause and effect" [7]. For a serial composer like Krenek, or an Oulipian like Queneau, an "effect" is the result of an impersonal mechanism set in place by the composer or author; everything but the "effects" is predictable. For Cage, one may argue, the *I Ching* is another such impersonal mechanism; or, he allows the unpredictable to become part of the composition process, as well as part of its result.

Another manifestation of Cage's attraction to the Eastern sensibility is his adoption of the Japanese *renga* form. One wonders whether East can meet West in this work, whether the constraints of the mesostic (since its origin in Latin verse, dependent on the placement of *letters*) are compatible with the oriental renga (an *ideogrammic* composition). Cage claims that he initially "developed a library of mesostics," but "instead of using them as text in their own right, [he] used them as material for renga" [6]. Renga, like haiku, is a classical form of Japanese poetry (fourteenth–fifteenth centuries), a "linked" form "composed in alternation and according to extremely elaborate rules by a small group of poets." These rules are "of such formidable complexity that it is the least studied and understood of all Japanese genres."[73] For those of us familiar with haiku only in translation, Cage reveals that "a haiku in Japanese has no fixed meaning. Its words are not defined syntactically. Each is either noun, verb, adjective, or adverb. A group of Japanese of an evening can therefore entertain themselves by discovering new meanings for old haiku" [6]. Cage fastens on the asyntactic structure as a means to ensure multiple interpretation. Although haiku is short and composed by a single poet, "renga is long: five, seven, five; seven, seven expressed at least thirty-six times" (a stanzaic structure that Cage does not adhere to). "Successive lines are written by different poets. Each poet tries to make his line as distant in possible meanings from the preceding line as he can take it. This is no doubt an attempt to open the minds of the poets and listeners or readers to other relationships than those ordinarily perceived" [7]. This end, lifting the observer out of the mundane and familiar, has long excited the proponents of the avant-garde in Western art. For Cage, its source is that synchronicity which Jung ascribes to the *I Ching*, breaking the chain of cause-and-effect reasoning.

Cage concludes, "Thus an intentionally irrational poem can be written with liberating effect. This is called purposeful purposelessness. That renga is written by several poets conduces to its being free of the ego of any single one of them" [7]. If Cage were adopting the elaborate rules of classical renga, we might observe another instance of the paradoxically liberating effect of elaborate constraints. But his focus appears to be the asyntactic and semantically disjointed aspects of the form; its intentional irrationality sounds suspiciously like automatic writing. In either case, the intent appears to be the displacement of the individual ego as central focus for the poem, for which Cage claims these Eastern precedents. I do have one objection, however. If his goal is an "intentionally irrational" poem, deconstructing syntax will accomplish his end. But Cage has also employed the mesostic, an occidental form in which the placement of a letter in a certain position works to constrain conventional syntax (i.e., word placement), and so forces the poet to new expressions. If the poem is entirely asyntactic, much of the force of that constraint (and Cage's invocation of Mink's law) is dissipated. They seem at cross-purposes.

On the other hand, the entire compositional procedure must be liberating for Cage, or else, why bother? About "Joyce, Duchamp, Satie: An Alphabet," Cage admits, "I cheerfully set out to write the following text but for a week I could not put pen to paper. Then it occurred to me . . ." to base the text on permutations of the "presence" of the three "ghosts," the twenty-six letters of the alphabet, and chance operations.[74] The invention of a compositional method, or impersonal mechanism, was itself "inspiring," especially when inhabited by such ghosts. About "Writing through Finnegans Wake" (a series of mesostics involving Joyce's text), Cage admits, "It's the sort of work that I can take with me; and when I'm waiting in line or riding in the bus or subway or plane or what not, I can continue this work."[75] He unabashedly renounces any pretension to inspiration *during* composition (estimated at five hundred hours), only amusement; again, Herrnstein Smith would not approve of the ludic element in the art of Cage or the Oulipians, but it has in fact become a familiar element of postmodern art. We can only have the optimistic outlook that the results themselves will be unpredictably *inspiring*—that the text will not be about ideas but produce them. As with serial composition, the entire mechanism is premeditated, but the audible results are unpredictable. Krenek, answering charges as to the lack of "expression" or "communication" in his music, responds: "The interest it may evoke is similar to that elicited by the process of life, to which serial music is related in the paradox of the chaotic appearance of totally and systematically traceable causality. It may mean as much or as little as life itself."[76]

For the sake of illustration, here is a section from a variation written through the name of Cage's longtime friend and collaborator, Merce Cunningham, which (though not chosen entirely at random) I find as comprehensible as not:

> Many
> rulEs
> into poetRy
>
> no Climax
> no argumEnt
>
> that the Car
> shoUld
> Not
> possessioN
> where I parked it
> but i didN't
>
> Going

tHey send you
by stAying where we are
the inforMation

there isn't Much

somE
wheRe i was
Couldn't
bE found

beCome
anxioUs
aNd i could have
about how the liNe
or trIed
weNt on

you don't have to Go
as tHough
i hAd parked it

Moved to the other side of the bed

[62–63]

There is in these stanzas an integration of music and idea, of rule and observation, that is not at all sinister or distracting but playful and almost innocent. One sympathizes with Cage's dilemma of the car which is not where he parked it, his gentle excoriation of the Western obsession with possessions, how to acquire them, and how not to lose them. The renga "mix" encourages the involvement of this subject with a poetry that, though formal, has neither climax nor argument. Cage has no desire to assert ideas in an argument, but "by staying where we are," to allow "the information" to come to us.

The last parameter to be discussed is that of performance. Cage states that *Themes & Variations* "was written to be spoken outloud. It consists of five sections, each to take twelve minutes. The fourth is the fastest and the last one is the slowest" [1]. The overall running time for the text is thus sixty minutes; i.e., it can be experienced in the time one would view CBS's popular network news magazine. Perhaps it is likewise not meant to be pored over. He provides the elapsed time in the right-hand margin with the accuracy of an Olympic-quality stopwatch. So the "performance," limited in duration, presents one of the most rigid constraints. The pace, or should we say tempo, of each section varies with its length, against the fixed limit of twelve minutes. This constraint is clearly borrowed from serial techniques, rather than literary precedent. One must first hear the text as music, read it as score, before one can interpret it, if at all, as literature.

Both Cage and Mathews have given us texts for which the compositional methods are intricately worked out in advance; in fact, the Oulipian bibliography and Cage's own introduction set these strategies in print for our examination, before or after we encounter the text. A frequent question asked in interviews of literary figures concerns "craft." How does she do it, what is his formula, where do they get their material from? The question is disingenuous, and the questioner assumes the artist will respond with an modest shrug or an embarrassingly idiosyncratic admission. Of course, the interview is always conducted after the fact. But if the artist has the gall to assert that prior to composition a number of parameters were determined or that certain operations would be presumed, the accusations of intellectualizing art, of abandoning its essential human expressiveness, fall thick and hot as an August cloudburst. Mathews and Cage have given us amusing, engaging, and participatory art. We need not sit in a room with notepad and pencil, but can conduct our own arrangements. I for one cannot see how to resist such a performance.

# 6

## A Polemical Conclusion: The Language Poetries and the New Formalism

Under the guise of a friendly warning, one encounters the following complaint: that however impressive or fully articulated a new theory of poetic form may be, it is only as strong, as lasting, as the poets who practice it. Let us assume that the complaint stems from one who admires a contemporary poet, whom he or she holds to be of surpassing importance, and yet rightly observes that that poet is a practitioner of neither serial nor procedural form. Does this prove the validity of the complaint? No. It is only one case, and of course the significance of the poet under question is not unchallengeable. In fact, it is characteristic of the field of contemporary poetry that critics hotly contest the worth of any poet who they feel represents a rival or "invalid" poetics; there can be little or no agreement as to who the "important" poets are. But even though the importance of a poetic form may owe much to the reputation of a single masterful practitioner, the quality or useful life of the form is independent of—and thus indiscriminately available to—any one poet's practice. As for the dozen or so poets discussed in this work, I will just as adamantly take my stand by declaring each of them to be indispensable to any thorough discussion of postmodern poetry. They were not, however, selected as representatives of all that is interesting in contemporary poetry. This book is not a literary history of the period. In charting the development of a distinctly postmodern poetic form, some interesting poetry is necessarily set aside.

In pursuit of those postmodern poets who most clearly articulate a serial or procedural form, I have been equally concerned to choose works that I consider to be of exceptional quality. Surely the poetry of

George Oppen, Lorine Niedecker, and William Bronk deserves a place in those anthologies of modern poetry which claim an aesthetically unbiased editorship. Also, the poems chosen for discussion are significant instances in each poet's oeuvre, not at all sidelights or momentary diversions. An understanding of Ashbery would not be complete without an appraisal of his attitude toward elaborate, predetermined forms; a full sense of Creeley's thought in poetry would be impossible without an introduction to his notion of seriality. It is true that these poets may have attained their stature for reasons beyond their practice in the forms I have described. But I have not been concerned to account for the entire career of these poets (however much each of them deserves, and needs, such attention). Conversely, I do feel that an understanding of the novel and challenging forms of their practice should increase the appreciation and reception of these poets, where before their work may have met with only puzzlement or disdain.

A new theory of poetic form can be measured in its importance by the scope and diversity of its practice. The pursuit of the form has required the gathering here of a number of poets whose direct relationship to one another is not immediately apparent. The importance of the poetic form extends well beyond the reputation of any single poet, both synchronically (as a relation among peers) and diachronically. Thus it is possible to see, for example, the practice of seriality in the work of George Oppen in the 1930s, and currently in the work of several "Language" poets. The poetry of the 1990s and beyond will be indelibly marked by the practice of seriality and proceduralism, as a continuance of the practice of postmodernism.

No truly dominant poet has emerged in the past two decades, and this "lack" may account for the rather factional quality at the moment on the American poetry scene. But because the dominant presence of a single poet (perhaps Robert Lowell was the last) encourages an obedient rather than inventive entourage, that lack may not necessarily be bad for contemporary poetry. One finds instead a number of cliques—they are not full-fledged movements—associated with a place (Los Angeles), a technique (the new Rhymers Club), a political stance (leftist, feminist), or a magazine (*Sulfur, Conjunctions*). Such factionalism has its merits: the frequent clashes compel participants to define their poetics sharply; each faction must articulate and defend their poetics (because few assumptions will go unchallenged); and attention is swiftly focused on the hot spots, sparing the general audience a recitation of the obvious. The principal drawback of the situation reveals itself when poets, once associated with a particular faction, are unable to disassociate themselves in order to maintain what they perceive to be the integrity of their own work. The poetics of the faction becomes their poetics, even if they do not adhere to, or practice, all aspects of it.

Two factions that have courted both notoriety and serious critical attention recently are the New Formalism and "Language" poetries. Each group has been represented by the timely appearance of two anthologies, displaying its wares to what is, I think, a forewarned public. A "resurgence" in the practice of traditional forms has been touted by Philip Dacey and David Jauss in *Strong Measures: Contemporary American Poetry in Traditional Forms* (1986). A more exclusive membership policy is enforced by Robert Richman in his editing of *The Direction of Poetry: An Anthology of Rhymed and Metered Verse Written in the English Language since 1975* (1988). For Richman, it is not enough that the included sample meet strict formal criteria; the poet must consistently employ meter in his or her work—as though such consistency were a test of the poet's seriousness. Language poetry has been represented by Douglas Messerli's *"Language" Poetries: An Anthology* (1987), and rather copiously by Ron Silliman in *In the American Tree* (1986). Although these two factions are not explicitly reacting to one another, they establish opposing views on poetic form and the function of language, politics, and audience. In examining a few of the poets presented in these anthologies, I intend to provoke the differences between these two factions and sustain a fairly polemical opposition. I am less concerned with weighing individual poet against poet than with judging the vitality of these factions and the value of their poetics, based primarily on an evaluation of their attitudes toward poetic form.

Before turning to an example of New Formalist verse, I want to consider the veracity of several arguments made by Robert Richman in his introduction to *The Direction of Poetry*. We can begin with the anthology's title. Although Richman issues a disclaimer in his Editor's Note that the poems selected are not intended to be "entirely representative of the times," his book nevertheless "celebrates the work of . . . the most important group [of poets] to have emerged in the last fifteen years."[1] Thus we are introduced to a select company of poets who establish the "direction" of poetry. Although Richman is well within his rights to announce the arrival of a particular faction, he takes the rather presumptuous position that poetry as a genre will follow his chosen few.

It is virtually impossible to maintain a critically neutral, genial position in contemporary poetics. Richman, in his introduction to *The Direction of Poetry*, makes claims for the "quality" of formal poetry which are wholly inconsistent with the arguments of the Language school. One can admire the audaciousness of individuals in either school, but one must be prepared to challenge the claims and justifications of one school or the other. With this idea in mind, I would like to examine Richman's claims regarding "accessibility," the value of metrical language, and the "permissibility" of forms. He argues, "After two decades of obscure, linguistically flat poetry, there has been a decisive shift" to a poetics prizing "narration, characterization, and, perhaps most significantly, musicality."[2] Regarding "accessibility"—as opposed to the "obscurity" of Language poetries—it can be easily demonstrated that there is no cause-and-effect relationship between metered or nonmetered language and accessibility. The New Formalists may *also* seek a concrete setting and evocative characterization, but meter is not necessary for denotative coherence. In the canon of New Critical texts, complex metrical and rhyme schemes (while contributing to the "musicality" of the text) often function (due to the level of constraint) to make the text more "difficult."

Turning to the avant-garde, one might select a text such as David Antin's "Radical Coherency" (1987), in which the poet illustrates his thesis regarding extreme modes of associative coherence by leading his aging and somewhat senile mother (and hence the reader as well) through the lingerie section of a southern California Sears.[3] Truly this poem (which is nearly twenty pages long) passes the test of accessibility—as administered by forty or so night-school students of mine for whom poetry remains a "formal" genre appropriate only to eulogies. And yet the form of this "talk" poem (unpunctuated, with unjustified left and right margins, and absolutely unmetered) challenges Richman's association of the unmetered with the obscure and the metered with the accessible. The poem has narration, characterization (both the aging mother and the perplexed poet are adorable), and a musicality that only the *spoken* word can possess. Antin issues a radical challenge to our assumptions regarding "lyric" poetry; he is, in effect, an "oral" or performance poet.[4] Richman argues that the poetry he selects is "extremely appealing and accessible, and hardly the remote and unfamiliar territory contemporary verse has long been perceived to be."[5] But surely he must know that accessibility has never in itself been a reliable arbiter of poetry's quality; if so, Rod McKuen, or Jimmy Stewart, whose life's work of four poems emerged among the best-sellers of the 1989 holiday season, would be among our best poets.

Richman's second claim equates metrical language with "melodiousness." He argues that even "those with a poetically 'untrained' ear and eye" will appreciate the "return to musicality" among poets who practice metrical verse.[6] Again, as with the issue of accessibility,

Richman asks that metrical language take too deep a bow for this effect. Regular rhythms and rhymes can indeed be "sweet." But as modern music has proven, harmonious tunes are not all of "musicality." One wonders whether, like Orsino in *Twelfth Night*, we aren't moved to beseech our musicians, "Enough, no more. / 'Tis not so sweet now as it was before." Surely the implication that the poetry of the past two decades is "linguistically flat" because it is nonmetrical is also false. If one begins with Pound's injunction to follow the musical phrase rather than the tick-tock of the metronome, it must be acknowledged that the nonmetrical language of American poetry in this century is wondrously rich, from Williams's triadic line in *Journey to Love* (1955) to Robert Duncan's impeccable ear for the "tone leading of vowels" in *Ground Work* (1984).

By far the most objectionable of Richman's pronouncements involves the formal criteria according to which he selects the poems included in the book. One might say that since Richman has undertaken the anthology, one cannot object to his method of selection. But the attitude toward poetic form expressed in his introduction deserves a rebuttal. He argues that as a result of the prominence of nonmetrical poetry in the last twenty-five years, "the entire conception of form has been corrupted."[7] The result, he claims, is a "hybrid verse" in which the stanzaic form is retained but the metrical line abandoned. Here "the pretense of a traditional form is used without employing any of its technical attributes."[8] Richman demonstrates himself to be among the more retrogressive of the New Formalists; he promotes the traditional, "permissible" forms established by the canon, and he opposes all those "hybrid" (which is to say variant, or innovative) forms that the poets themselves have introduced.

Although he bases his criteria for inclusion in the anthology on the presence of strict meter, his prejudice implies a larger polemical complaint: poetic forms can only be "corrupted"; they can suffer decline or misuse, but viable forms cannot be newly created. Thus he must lamely and falsely argue that the use of metrical language "is clearly the best means for poets to come to terms with their experience now."[9] One may argue that it is possible to express contemporary experience in traditional forms—particularly if one is willing to modify either the form or the experience—but it is mistaken to assert that the Shakespearian sonnet is the "best" means by which poets give shape to the experience of the last two decades. Such a shape needed to be, and has been, invented. Those who see poetic form as a narrowly defined set of metrical rules and permissible variants gotten out of handbooks inevitably and misguidedly see formal innovation as mere decadence.

One must ask, is the New Formalism really "new"? Perhaps a more accurate title for the group would be the Old Formalism Revisited. An examination of the group's practice reveals how little these poets deviate from most basic assumptions of the New Criticism. James E. B. Breslin, in his essay on American poetry from 1945 to the present in the *Columbia Literary History of the United States*, refers to the current generation of traditionalist poets as the New New Formalists, since the appellation New Formalists had already been applied to the late-fifties work of such poets as James Merrill, W. S. Merwin, Adrienne Rich, and Richard Wilbur.[10] Of course, the most recent drive for a return to "traditional" poetic values seems to coincide with a general conservative swing in national politics, as was also the case in the fifties. The opposition between the retrogressive New Formalists and the avant-garde Language poetries comes at a crucial moment. Many of the poets in both groups were born after 1945 and constitute a fourth generation of twentieth-century American poets. As such, they have had no immediate debt to, or personal contact with, the great modernist poets, most of whom were born in the 1880s. The field of American poetry could be radically redefined before the turn of the century. Whether that redefinition of our poetics will be progressively or retrogressively inclined is still in question.

The editors of the second edition of *The Norton Anthology of Modern Poetry* (1988) delete the work of Louis Zukofsky, apparently convinced that neither he nor any other member of the Objectivist movement is of any further concern. (The Englishman Basil Bunting, however, is spared this dismissal.) On the other hand, Gjertrud Schnackenberg, a young (born 1953) and laureled member of the New Formalists, is newly included. Her poem "Supernatural Love" appears both here and in Richman's *The Direction of Poetry*. How is it that Zukofsky's brilliantly inventive—and difficult—formalism suffers exclusion, while Schnackenberg's competent—but familiar—exercises in traditional forms are so well received? I have come by both of these anthologies *gratis*, with the publisher's hope that I would employ them for classroom use. Schnackenberg's poem is indeed more "accessible" than most of Zukofsky, and "teachability" (since teachers determine the book's use) seems a primary consideration. And of course New Critical explication was fundamentally a teaching method, one that tended to exclude as "anti-poetry" whatever it couldn't neatly unfold in under an hour. "Supernatural Love" is as familiar to someone trained in New Critical precepts as an M-16 to a West Point cadet: it's standard issue; it's easily disassembled.

A snap inspection of Schnackenberg's poem reveals not only its New

Critical assumptions regarding poetic form but also its radical divergence from the Language poets on the question of poetic language. She selects a triplet stanza, rhyming aaa, for the form of the poem. As with most stanzaic forms, it is the rhyme pattern that determines structure; the number of stanzas is variable. She maintains a strict pentameter throughout. In order to sustain the triplet rhyme without ludicrous chiming effects, she permits several imperfect rhymes. There are two notable occurrences with respect to the rhyme scheme. In the eleventh stanza, the speaker describes her needlepoint: "Where following each X I awkward move / My needle through the word whose root is love."[11] The syntactic inversion in the first line to accommodate the rhyme is archaic; though John Crowe Ransom would have praised such a technique, Ezra Pound railed repeatedly at such musty use of language. It is the price of rhyme: a language no longer spoken. Later, Schnackenberg employs one identical rhyme: in the fifteenth stanza, the three lines each conclude with "nail," in reference to the crucifixion:

> He reads, "From French, for *clou*, meaning a nail."
> He gazes, motionless. "Meaning a nail."
> The incarnation blossoms, flesh and nail. . . .[12]

In a poem replete with religious symbolism, the rhymes acquire a symbolic value, there for the New Critic to uncover.

This poem should also appease those who demand from poetry a careful characterization and the development of a narrative frame. The precocious daughter, aged four, has a "habit" of identifying carnations as "Christ's flowers" (perhaps for the fleck of red on the white petals); the pedagogic father finds with his magnifying lens the etymological justification for the association in his unabridged dictionary. The poem increases in layers of significance as we move from a filial to a supernatural love, as the daughter, having pricked her finger on the needle, cries out, "Daddy daddy." A stable setting and characterization—not the indeterminacy of postmodernism—mark the poem. A clear sequence of events functions as a denotative surface level of meaning from beneath which the hidden meaning of symbolic significance arises.

But if the crux of the poem is the etymological search into the words "carnation" and "clove," why should we not also consider this a Language poem? For Language poets, words have an objective interest in and of themselves. For Schnackenberg, interest in the words themselves (through their buried meanings in Latin and French roots) yields to a symbolic value. "Carnation" (from the Latin *carnatio*, meaning flesh) and "clove" (from the French *clou*, meaning nail), reveal a religious or "supernatural" value. Once the revelation has occurred, the word becomes icon, and is no longer an object. Its linguistic value is trivial before such mystic significance. For the New Critic, this searching out of the hidden layer of meaning is a favorite pedagogical technique. One wonders, who is that man at the dictionary stand, if not John Crowe Ransom?

My primary criterion for judging the two factions of New Formalism and Language poetry has been their approach to poetic form. The New Formalist approach, heavily indebted to the New Criticism of the 1940s, is a retrogressive one, attempting to recapitulate the traditional forms and the theory of how poems "mean" from a movement now fifty years old. The Language poets, on the other hand, demonstrate a progressive and inventive approach to poetic form—in great variety— and manifest a theoretical apparatus that alternately supports or is the showpiece of their work. Although there is not room here to defend the full extent of Language theory—such work has been extensively undertaken in the prose of the poets themselves,[13] constituting a body of writing on poetics as impressive as that of Ransom, Tate, and Empson—I will nevertheless take the opportunity to argue the viability, and the quality, of their practice in both serial and procedural forms. The vitality that this movement signals is proof of the importance of these forms in contemporary poetry.

There is one absolutely radical divergence on the issue of language between the New Formalists and the Language poets. Charles Bernstein makes the case for the Language poets quite clearly in his essay "Thought's Measure": "Rather than making the language as transparent as possible . . . the movement is toward opacity/denseness— visibility of language through the making translucent of the medium. To actually map the fullness of thought and its movement."[14] Robert Richman, in contrast, pursues the transparency of an "accessible" verse in *The Direction of Poetry*; that is, he demands access *through* language to the narrated incident and the speaking character. For Bernstein, language *is* perception, the "grain" of the mind, the thought itself, already present. It is not the facilitator of character, story, or personal experience. Language is experience, is to be experienced. Beyond this point of departure are, of course, increasingly divergent conceptions of what poetic language is. Language poets such as Bernstein, Bruce Andrews, Susan Howe, Barrett Watten, and Lyn Hejinian evince a disdain for symbolic language and hidden layers of meaning, a technique that—as I've just shown—remains prevalent in New Formalist poetry.

Among Language poets, the emphasis on the "wordness" of words, the mechanics of syntax, and the vagaries of idioms represents an intensification of the language theory and practice of such predecessors as Gertrude Stein, Louis Zukofsky, and Ludwig Wittgenstein. In this pursuit, a welding of what Bernstein calls "the factness of the world in the factness of the poem" occurs.[15] There is no separation of fact from language, no layering of discourse, no transport from one plane of existence to another—only the intricate play of/at the surface of language itself.

The disagreement between New Formalists and Language poets on the relative merits of the transparency or the opacity of language also reflects a fundamental political polarization. As cultural neoconservatives, the New Formalists operate within a tradition of the "plain style," especially as it was practiced by such lobbyists for reason and "right thinking" in the arts as Yvor Winters and J. V. Cunningham. Thus the editors of *The New Criterion* (a venue for much New Formalist writing) deplore "the insidious assault on [the] mind that was one of the most repulsive features of the radical movement of the Sixties. The cultural consequences of this leftward turn in our political life have been far graver than is commonly supposed." Not surprisingly their criterion for aesthetic judgement is an explicit "truth" brought to serve in the "defense of high art in a democratic society."[16] In sharp contrast, Language poets such as Ron Silliman deplore such truth-speak as one further repressive effect of capitalism. He argues that "what happens when a language moves toward and passes into a capitalist stage of development is an anaesthetic transformation of the perceived tangibility of the word, with corresponding increases in its descriptive and narrative capacities." As a Marxist, Silliman argues that language under capitalism is reductively and oppressively "transformed (deformed) into referentiality."[17] The basic disagreement between these two movements on the nature of poetic language grows ever more intractable with the application of their respective neoconservative and leftist political theories.

Several poets associated with the Language group have recently produced intriguing examples of both serial and procedural forms. Such work indicates the continuing importance of both of these formal methods in postmodern poetry, and promises their further development. Leslie Scalapino has shown an ongoing interest in serial form in *that they were at the beach* (1985) and *Way* (1988). In both, references to physics contribute to the definition of the poetic form. The title poem of the former collection is subtitled "aeolotropic series." Aeolotropy refers to the condition of a body whose physical qualities—such as the refraction of light, elasticity, or conduction of electricity—are not the same in all directions. Aeolotropy is thus the opposite of isotropy, in which such qualities are equally exhibited in all directions. Many poetic forms, from the quatrain to the sestina, display a predilection for symmetry and balance. The diamond—of whatever shape—is always cut to a symmetrical form; any deviation of its refractivity is considered a flaw. But Scalapino, in her serial poems, ventures into a remarkable new modality, capturing the ever-changing and unequal refractivity of her subjects. Because human experience does not conform to the perfectly composed, balanced settings of the gem, the aeolotropic series more effectively confronts the limitless variegation of the real.

The title poem, "that they were at the beach," extends these shifting currents and reflections for some thirty-five pages. It is thus impossible to present its full range of effects in a short excerpt. But if one examines the beginning of the series, certain techniques become readily apparent:

> Playing ball—so it's like paradise, not because it's in the past, we're on a field; we are creamed by the girls who get together on the other team. They're nubile, but in age they're thirteen or so—so they're strong.
>
> (No one knows each other, aligning according to race as it happens, the color of the girls, and our being creamed in the foreground—as part of it's being that—the net is behind us).
>
> ———————————
>
> A microcosm, but it's of girls—who were far down on the field, in another situation of playing ball—so it was an instance of the main world though they're nubile but are in age thirteen or so.
>
> My being creamed in the foreground—so it's outside of that—by a girl who runs into me, I returned to the gym.[18]

Each phrase or clause—linked in the paratactic manner common to seriality—is like a free-floating particle. The recurrence of such phrases as "being creamed in the foreground" is not governed by some imposed, symmetrical scheme, but allowed to occur as the glint of light from the turning of an irregular, translucent stone. Time ("not because we're in the past") and space ("in the foreground") become indeterminate as the context gradually shifts. Individual words such as "creamed" and "nubile" (one of which appears in each of the four stanzas) also exhibit "unequal" qualities or shifting connotations, depending on the "turn" they take in each stanza. They assume both an erotic and a kitschy quality commonly found in the overused vocabulary of teenagers and B-movies. And at some point these words become detached from their function in the semantic packet, so that we do admire them solely for the sounds they make, or for the odd association. The speaker in this poem is something of an ingénue, not apparently dictating the revolving contexts, but subject to them. This insouciance (I refer here to the *tone* of the voice), or apparent artlessness, rhetorically supports the aeolotropic serial form, since the traditional "art object" has relied on the stable, isotropic form to bolster its authority.

Scalapino considers her more recent book *Way* to be one poem composed of "Later floating series" (in five sections) and "Way" (in two sections). The final section of "Later floating series" is titled "Delay series." Of particular interest here is the combination of a formal method based on concepts found in contemporary physics and a direct engagement with the distress of contemporary urban living. That is, the poem engages our experience both at the theoretical level and at the instinctual level of survival in an often hostile, urban environment. This poem is subtitled "the series as qualitative infinity." Prefatory to the book itself, Scalapino provides an extended excerpt from David Bohm's *Causality and Chance in Modern Physics*. Here we learn that every entity, no matter how fundamental, is far from being immutable. Rather it is "dependent for its existence on the maintenance of appropriate conditions in its infinite background of substructure." It experiences an interconnected, or reciprocal, relationship. Scalapino takes this "qualitative infinity" of nature as the formal principle of the poem. All sections of the series are interconnected; each part or entity in the series is thus subject to infinite qualification against its background. To return to Bohm (as cited by Scalapino), "we see that because every kind of thing is defined only through an inexhaustible set of qualities each having a certain degree of relative autonomy, such a thing can and indeed must be unique."[19] Although a short excerpt is again inadequate to a full description of the process Scalapino enacts in the form of the poem, let's consider the following:

it's irrelevant to
want to be like him—whether
it's the mugger—who'd
then run in
to the park—though not that aspect of it

                    a man—occurring now
                    dying from being sick—at a young age
                    —we're not

            able to do anything—so fear as an
                irrelevant
         point

the man's death—from
being sick at a young age—as not a
senseless point—not to—
by desire—reach such a thing in
that way

            which would be—for him—
            fear—whether
            it's the mugger—on
            our part—but in his
            doing that[20]

In the full extent of the series, every element undergoes a gradual but ceaseless qualification. Every element is in the process of becoming something else; or, as Bohm points out, "No such thing can even remain identical with itself as time passes." No element in this poetic form, or in this concept of the physical world, remains an immutable constant. This concept of aesthetic form is a radical departure from all those traditional forms that rely on some basic "measure" or fixed structure. One can, however, compare the formal method of Scalapino's "series as qualitative infinity" with Robert Duncan's espousal of an infinite serial form whose aperiodic structure is indebted to biophysics. Scalapino's paratactic style, which liberally employs the Dickinsonian dash as its only means of punctuation, supports the formal theory of an ongoing process of change.

Scalapino's poem also engages the issue of causality and chance in a sociological context: one must ask by what virtue is the speaker the victim of a mugging, and by what virtue is the young man a victim of a fatal disease. What is the interconnection that unites these figures in a constantly shifting background? And what is the role of chance, the intervention of the uncontrollable, in the victimization of all parties? The poet/speaker explores the irrelevancy of her desire to identify with the mugger—if only to understand the motivation for his act. At the same time, "occurring now," she encounters her powerlessness before the young man's death and her inability to empathize completely. "Fear," though deemed "irrelevant," is the common aspect: of crime, of death. In both cases a feeling of helplessness emerges, subsiding then into isolation. The "qualitative infinity" of the series underscores both our interconnectedness and our unique qualities in the world.

Michael Palmer's recent work in serial form permits a flexible and sensitive response to the exigencies of occurrence, both in the world and in the poet's act of composition. He pursues an "interstitial" method whereby an ongoing, open series of poems is interspersed with other poems not counted as part of the series itself. In *The Circular Gates* (1974) and *Notes for Echo Lake* (1981), Palmer sustains several such serial poems: "Notes for Echo Lake" itself, "Symmetrical Poems," and the generically titled "Series" and "Second Series." His practice in this form is related quite clearly to Robert Duncan's "Passages" series. Palmer comments that for him a book fails "when it's simply a gathering," having lost the additional "resonance" that occurs when the book assumes a "particular shape." So he states, "I think a lot of my earlier work in series, for example, proceeded from that same idea of defining things beyond their particular events as poems. But I think you can also lose the particular shape of a particular poem if it simply functions as a unit among other units in this larger program."[21] Palmer's method bears some comparison to Scalapino's, even if it is not expressed with reference to contemporary physics. In both cases, the poet feels compelled to account for the interconnectedness of "bodies," events, or ideas: each section of a serial poem is defined in its relation to all others (not simply to its proximate neighbors) and is not presented as a separate event. At the same time, Palmer employs an interstitial method in arranging poems to point out that each section is not locked into a series (as a sequential presentation would imply), thus losing some degree of its particularity. Both Palmer and Scalapino demonstrate that the series is the ideal form to assert both the interconnectedness and the uniqueness of things. The expression of this apparent paradox is supported by the claims of modern physics for the function of the physical world.

Palmer argues the same case for poetry: "When you have a poem which is an open series, like [Duncan's] 'Passages' or my 'Symmetrical Poems,' that is for me making possible that a voice has its place. . . . I found in the interstices of the section of 'Echo Lake' a breathing space . . . that created a balance that felt right to the book as I was making it."[22] In the opening lines of the third section of "Series," Palmer discusses the pitfalls of ignoring a serial order in the world:

> The machine keeps demonstrating a new way of counting
>         to three. We both lose our place
> looking for the prediscovered end
>         of the series, in this case
> a shadow instead of the light. In other words, the
>         colors come first, then numbers, without any

> special kind of memory for facts. More inquiries
> by the papers into the latest series
> of bombings. How much more
> for example than on Dresden and Tokyo.[23]

One should not excerpt reality, hold aside some portion of it, compel it to bear some added burden of significance. Nor can one, through the process of comparison, summary, or analysis, obscure the fundamental particularity of the body without obscuring the significance it does possess. The serial form is for poetry the most adept method of portraying both the interconnectedness and the particularity of objects in the world and our relationship to them and to one another.

Language poets have explored the capacity of seriality to accommodate the many ways beyond the logical and the sequential in which things come together. These poets also account for a significant number of the procedural forms in which constraint and invention join to reveal meaning and not merely to confirm a thing already understood. To choose but one poet and one such form, Rosmarie Waldrop contributes to David Lehman's collection *Ecstatic Occasions, Expedient Forms* an abecedarium that instructs us in the virtues of procedural form. Waldrop's poem, "Shorter American Memory of the American Character According to Santayana," limits itself to the words used in Santayana's essay "The American Character." The form of the abecedarium requires that the initial letters of the words strictly adhere to alphabetical order. Waldrop permits herself only the freedom of the "arrangement and articulation of the words beginning with the same letter." Though there are of course ancient examples of the abecedarium, each poet may affix or delete rules to attain desired effects. Here Waldrop offers further innovation to the prose poem by retrieving her text from Santayana's essay. All of the five stanzas are printed left- and right-justified. Here is the second stanza:

> An American does, distinguishes, dreams. Degrees, experience, economy, emergencies, enthusiasm and education are expected. For future forecasts, forces far from form fall and find fulfillment. Good God. Gets growing, goes handling himself and his help (hardly happy).[24]

Waldrop's title, "Shorter American Memory," appears to comment sarcastically on the growing impatience of Americans with anything resembling the philosophical essay, favoring the conciseness of the sound-bite. A crippled American memory, aided mainly by computer-generated bytes of information, has forgotten—among other things—why Richard Nixon is no longer in office. The abecedarium—with clear satirical effect—here condenses Santayana's essay. Both Santayana (1863–1952), born in Spain, and Waldrop, born in Germany in 1935, maintain their critical distance from the American character that "expects" degrees, a solid job, and a positive disposition. The future, with God's providence, will be a fulfilling one—though everyone seems "hardly happy." But this prose poem is not merely an abridged version of Santayana's essay. Waldrop's articulation and arrangement of Santayana's words permits, compels "immediate invention. Intense imagination," so that "ultimately understanding" becomes the goal.

Waldrop comments on the semantic value that accrues when procedural forms are employed:

> It was an important moment for me when I realized consciously that the encounter of a poem-nucleus with an arbitrary pattern (like a rhyme scheme) would tend to pull the nucleus out of its semantic field in unforeseen directions. The tension always generates great energy, not just for bridging the "gap" between original intention and the pattern, but for pushing the whole poem farther. When it works, the poem grows richer for being "stretched."
>
> I'm spelling out what Ashbery and others have called the liberating effect of constraints. But what matters is that *any* constraint, *any* pattern can be generative in this way. It does not need to be one of the traditional forms with their heavy closure effect of regularity and recurrence.[25]

For Waldrop, "Shorter American Memory" is "an extreme case of constraints." Yet the poem demonstrates the generative capacity of the procedural form to enunciate new and unexpected meaning. Waldrop, like Scalapino, recognizes that poetic form need not be limited to regular, isotropic shapes. Thus procedural forms, though displaying far greater constraints than the rhyme schemes of traditional forms, are paradoxically far more capable of liberating the poem's semantic field.

The rationale for setting the work of the Language poets against the work of the New Formalists has not been primarily to test the strength of the two movements; that would be to focus too narrowly on the contentions of the present moment, or to put it another way, on the politics of poetics. But there is a final point of some importance to be recognized in the clash of these two factions. The value of what we now call postmodern poetry can be measured in some significant degree by the attitude toward form that the poets display. Those poets who insist on a retrogressive revival of not only the traditional forms but also the poetics of half a century ago will inevitably create a

stagnant and derivative poetry. Some—though not the conformist
creative writing programs, the sanitized university press poetry series,
or the prestigious but predictable magazines of verse—already recognize the worthlessness of retreading old paths. Those poets who by
their practice have contributed to a formal approach that is exclusively
postmodern will sustain the creative energy of the period itself and
endeavor to further distinguish its aims and products from those of
modernism. Seriality and proceduralism are two such exclusively
postmodern formal approaches that now participate in poetry's unending design.

# Notes

## 1. Introduction

1. Williams argues, "Everything new must be wrong at first since there is always a moment when the living new supplants that which has been and still is right and is thus sure to be wrong in transit, or until it is seen that that which was right is dead." See "George Antheil and the Cantilene Critics" (1928) in *Selected Essays* (New York: New Directions, 1969), p. 60. Also, Arnold Schönberg laments a similar lag-time in understanding throughout his essay "How One Becomes Lonely" (1937) in *Style and Idea* (Berkeley and Los Angeles: University of California Press, 1984), pp. 30–53.

2. Ezra Pound, *Gaudier-Brzeska* (New York: New Directions, 1970), p. 126.

3. Williams, *The Collected Later Poems* (New York: New Directions, 1967), p. 5.

4. Williams, "A New Line Is a New Measure," *The New Quarterly of Poetry* 2 (Winter 1947–48): 11.

### Defining a Postmodern Poetics

5. Several critics have argued persuasively against a rupture between modernism and postmodernism. Ihab Hassan summarizes: "The degree to which modernism and postmodernism seem continuous or discontinuous, and indeed both at the same time, will always depend on historical presuppositions; probably, that degree will remain perpetually moot. There is a clearer consensus on the modernist break with *its* tradition. . . . The point is most recently and tersely made by Ricardo J. Quinones: 'Post-Modernists do not define themselves by a counter-Modernity in the way the Modernists defined themselves by a counter-Romanticism' [*Mapping Literary Modernism: Time and Development* (Princeton: Princeton University Press, 1985), p. 254]. This, of course, assumes a linear scheme of time that post-structuralists deplore." *The Postmodern Turn: Essays in Postmodern Theory and Culture* (Columbus: Ohio State University Press, 1987), pp. 214–15.

6. Charles Olson, "The Present Is Prologue," in *Additional Prose*, ed. George F. Butterick (Bolinas, Calif.: Four Seasons Foundation, 1974), p. 40.

7. As an example of the debate between the "contemporary" and the "avant-garde," compare the comments of the following two critics. Lynn Keller argues on behalf of continuity and against rupture: "Too often 'postmodern' is employed as a narrow evaluative label applied with either scorn or approbation to experimental works whose aggressive emphasis on textuality and on the web of society's semiotic codes may be linked to poststructuralist criticism. It is my belief that 'postmodern' may more usefully serve as a general period term encompassing a broad spectrum of work that both follows after and depends upon modernism. Contemporary literature's genuine distinction from modernist literature need not depend upon extreme or dramatic disruption of modernist aesthetics" (*Re-making It New: Contemporary American Poetry and the Modernist Tradition* [New York: Cambridge University Press, 1987], pp. 8–9). Marjorie Perloff seems to apply the very "narrow evaluative label" that Keller disdains: "The notion of the poem as language construction in which the free play of possible significations replaces iconic representation—this is perhaps at the heart of what we call *postmodernism*." Her approach is in alliance with an ahistorical avant-garde: "Everything that is *contemporary* is by no means *postmodern* and, conversely, some of the greatest postmodern works are . . . about thirty years old. And even these works have their roots in the earlier years of the century." "Contemporary/Postmodern: The 'New' Poetry?" in *Romanticism, Modernism, Postmodernism*, ed. Harry R. Garvin (Lewisburg, Pa.: Bucknell University Press, 1980), pp. 171–72.

8. For a further discussion of Toynbee's early negative assessment of postmodernism, see Matei Calinescu, *Five Faces of Modernity: Modernism, Avant-Garde, Decadence, Kitsch, Postmodernism* (Durham, N.C.: Duke University Press, 1987), pp. 133–36, 267–68.

9. Hal Foster, "Postmodernism: A Preface," in *The Anti-Aesthetic: Essays on Postmodern Culture*, ed. Hal Foster (Port Townsend, Wash.: Bay Press, 1983), pp. xi–xii. This collection of essays serves as a functional introduction to the conflict as Foster summarizes it.

10. Paul Blackburn, *The Collected Poems of Paul Blackburn* (New York: Persea Books, 1985), p. 216.

11. Elizabeth Bishop, *The Complete Poems 1927–1979* (New York: Farrar, Straus, Giroux, 1983), pp. 133–35.

12. William Carlos Williams, *Imaginations* (New York: New Directions, 1970), p. 166. Jerome Mazzaro, in *Postmodern American Poetry* (Urbana: University of Illinois Press, 1980), also considers the condition of language in modernist and postmodernist poetics as a fall from the "sacred" to the "secular": "In conceiving of language as a fall from unity, modernism seeks to restore the original state often by proposing silence or the destruction of language; postmodernism accepts the division and uses language and self-definition—much as Descartes interpreted thinking—as the basis of identity. Modernism tends, as a consequence, to be more mystical in the traditional sense of that word whereas postmodernism, for all its seeming mysticism, is irrevocably worldly and social" (p. viii). William V. Spanos, in *Repetitions: The Postmodern Occasion in Literature and Culture* (Baton Rouge: Louisiana State University Press, 1987), examines the same issue in Platonic terms. The *Logos* that modernism sustains, "Identity, the One, the Word, the realm of Forms, Presence," is "shattered and dispersed into difference (the many, words, the realm of existence, temporality)," a "fall" into what Spanos identifies as the postmodern "occasion" (p. 195).

13. For an engaging survey of the radical avant-garde in poetry, including con-

crete, sound, and performance poetry, see Richard Kostelanetz's collection of reviews and essays, *The Old Poetries and the New* (Ann Arbor: University of Michigan Press, 1981). That the laureled John Ashbery is classified among the "old" poetries in this volume provides an interesting measure of how the avant-garde outstrips in its lust for the "new" even what we would consider to be definitively "postmodern." Although the critic may equate the "postmodern" with the avant-garde, the true avant-gardist must consider himself already beyond, or post-postmodern.

14. Spanos, *Repetitions*, pp. 192–93.

15. Calinescu, *Five Faces of Modernity*, pp. 275–76.

16. For a thorough examination of the poem-as-lecture, see Marjorie Perloff's " 'No More Margins': John Cage, David Antin, and the Poetry of Performance," in *The Poetics of Indeterminacy: Rimbaud to Cage* (Princeton: Princeton University Press, 1981), pp. 288–339. One might also mention in this category the monumental performance of Laurie Anderson, *United States, Parts I–IV*. Performance art may well represent the epitome of postmodern fusion and mutation of genres and forms.

17. In Jean Baudrillard's formulation of a postmodern milieu, "The Ecstasy of Communication," he argues, "Something has changed, and the Faustian, Promethean (perhaps Oedipal) period of production and consumption gives way to the 'proteinic' era of networks, to the narcissistic and protean era of connections, contact, contiguity, feedback and generalized interface that goes with the universe of communication." In Foster, ed., *The Anti-Aesthetic*, p. 127.

18. Christopher Butler, *After the Wake: An Essay on the Contemporary Avant-Garde* (Oxford: Oxford University Press, 1980), p. ix.

19. Robert Creeley, *Contexts of Poetry: Interviews 1961–1971* (Bolinas, Calif.: Four Seasons Foundation, 1973), p. 186.

20. Malcolm Bradbury, "Modernisms/Postmodernisms," in *Innovation/Renovation: New Perspectives on the Humanities*, ed. Ihab Hassan and Sally Hassan (Madison: University of Wisconsin Press, 1983), p. 326.

21. Creeley, *Contexts of Poetry*, pp. 185, 186.

## Seriality and Proceduralism: A Typology of Postmodern Poetry

22. Creeley's assessment appears in his introduction to *The Collected Essays of Robert Creeley* (Berkeley and Los Angeles: University of California Press, 1989), p. xiii. He gives the title "Heroes/Elders" to the first section of the book, and the title "The Company" to the second. The allegiances forged by the indefatigable resistance he perceives are permanent.

23. Christopher Beach, "Interview with Joel Oppenheimer," *Sagetrieb* 7 (Fall 1988): 110.

24. Joel Oppenheimer considers the period 1958–64 to be the high point in recent American poetry. Most significant is the sheer number of people, many of them young, who sought out poetry as the most apt means of expression for social protest. In his interview with Christopher Beach, Oppenheimer remarks, "They came for the energy and some of them fell in love with the *poetry*, so that there were really live audiences, audiences of young people who would listen, who wanted to talk about poetry or wanted to hear poetry, to try and write it." *Sagetrieb* 7 (Fall 1988): 122. For other more extended analyses of the historical context for American poetry in the fifties and sixties, see Cary Nelson, *Our Last First Poets:*

*Vision and History in Contemporary American Poetry* (Urbana: University of Illinois Press, 1981); James E. B. Breslin, *From Modern to Contemporary: American Poetry, 1945–1965* (Chicago: University of Chicago Press, 1984); and Paul Carroll, *The Poem in Its Skin* (Chicago: Big Table, 1968).

25. See the proem to Charles Olson's essay "Projective Verse" for his distinction between an "open" poetics based on breath or speech and a "closed" poetics based on the printed page and the syllable counting it facilitates. Olson, *Human Universe*, ed. Donald Allen (New York: Grove Press, 1967), p. 51.

26. Robert Richman, ed. *The Direction of Poetry: An Anthology of Rhymed and Metered Verse Written in the English Language since 1975* (Boston: Houghton Mifflin, 1988), p. xiii.

27. This definition of the "open" characteristics of the poetic series is indebted to Umberto Eco's discussion of "open works" in postmodern music in *The Open Work*, trans. Anna Cancogni (1962; Cambridge: Harvard University Press, 1989), p. 4.

28. For more enthusiastic introductions to the world of visual and sound poetries, see Paul de Vree, "Visual Poetry," and Bob Cobbing, "Concrete Sound Poetry," in *The Avant-Garde Tradition in Literature*, ed. Richard Kostelanetz (Buffalo, N.Y.: Prometheus Books, 1982).

29. Victor Shklovsky, "Art as Technique" (1917) reprinted in *Russian Formalist Criticism: Four Essays*, ed. Lee T. Lemon and Marion J. Reis (Lincoln: University of Nebraska Press, 1965), p. 12. Although the "difficulty" that Shklovsky endorses may be equated with the elitist impulses of modernism, it should be recalled that in the theory of "defamiliarization" such difficulty is required to enhance the "process of perception." It still seems necessary that an artistic form break the hold of the habitual in our lives and actively engage us with our environment.

30. Eco, *The Open Work*, p. 13.

31. Eco, *The Open Work*, p. 14.

32. Charles Olson, *Human Universe*, p. 52.

33. Eco, *The Open Work*, p. 15.

34. Ihab Hassan, *The Postmodern Turn* (Columbus: Ohio State University Press, 1987), p. 14.

35. William Carlos Williams, *Spring and All*, in *Imaginations* (New York: New Directions, 1970), p. 133.

36. See James E. B. Breslin, *William Carlos Williams: An American Artist* (1970; Chicago: University of Chicago Press, 1985), p. 50. Breslin identifies *Spring and All* as a serial poem at the start of his chapter on the volume, but he is not at pains to discuss what he means by the term. Nevertheless, he, unlike some other critics of Williams, discusses the volume as a single structure.

37. For an interesting close reading of *Spring and All* which does much to reveal its structural nuances, see Marjorie Perloff, " 'Lines Converging and Crossing': The 'French' Decade of William Carlos Williams," in *The Poetics of Indeterminacy* (Princeton: Princeton University Press, 1981), especially pages 122–42. Perloff argues that *Spring and All* "provides the paradigm for the serial poems Williams wrote throughout the following decade: for example, *The Descent of Winter* (1928) and *A Novelette* (1932)" (p. 142).

38. Michael Palmer, *The Circular Gates* (Los Angeles: Black Sparrow Press, 1974). The poem "Series" in six numbered, untitled sections is included within a larger subdivision of the book, titled SERIES. Leslie Scalapino, *that they were at the beach* (San Francisco: North Point Press, 1985). Scalapino's designation of the

series as aeolotropic, as when "the refractive property of a transparent body is not the same in all directions" (as opposed to isotropic) (*Oxford English Dictionary*), is illustrative of the disjunctive rather than linear properties of the serial structure. More recently, Scalapino has published the poem "Delay Series: The Series as Qualitative Infinity" in *Temblor* 4 (1986): 23–32, and reprinted in *Way* (San Francisco: North Point Press, 1988).

39. Roland Barthes, *Critical Essays*, trans. Richard Howard (1964; Evanston, Ill.: Northwestern University Press, 1972), p. 210.

40. *Princeton Encyclopedia of Poetry and Poetics*, ed. Alex Preminger et al. (Princeton: Princeton Unversity Press, 1974), p. 759. Entry on "Semantics and Poetry" by Philip Wheelwright.

41. Barthes, *Critical Essays*, p. 210.

42. Barthes, *Critical Essays*, p. 211.

43. Barbara Herrnstein Smith, *Poetic Closure* (Chicago: University of Chicago Press, 1968), pp. 110–11.

44. Recent examinations of paratactic structure in modernist and postmodernist texts include Laszlo K. Géfin, *Ideogram: History of a Poetic Mode* (Austin: University of Texas Press, 1982), passim; and Stephen Fredman, *Poet's Prose* (New York: Cambridge University Press, 1983), especially in his discussion of Williams's *Kora in Hell*.

45. Smith, *Poetic Closure*, p. 99.

46. M. L. Rosenthal and Sally M. Gall, *The Modern Poetic Sequence* (New York: Oxford University Press, 1983), p. 9. It is interesting to note that these authors do not address the work of any of the poets discussed in the body of this book.

47. Coleridge's proclamation is quoted by Rosenthal and Gall in defense of their thesis of an organic sequence, p. 7. They cite *Coleridge's Writings on Shakespeare*, ed. Terence Hawkes (New York: G. P. Putnam's Sons, 1959), p. 68.

48. Eco, *The Open Work*, p. 217.

49. Eco cites Pierre Boulez, *Relevés d'apprenti* (Paris: Seuil, 1966), p. 297.

50. Eco, *The Open Work*, p. 218.

51. William Butler Yeats, *The Poems of W. B. Yeats*, ed. Richard J. Finneran (New York: Macmillan, 1983), p. 187.

52. Eco, *The Open Work*, p. 220.

53. Harry Mathews, *The Sinking of the Odradek Stadium* (Manchester, England: Carcanet Press, 1985), pp. 28–29. First published in 1971–72 by *The Paris Review* 51–54.

54. Rosenthal and Gall, *The Modern Poetic Sequence*, pp. 314–49.

55. Roland Barthes, *Critical Essays*, p. 207.

56. *Coleridge's Writings on Shakespeare*, ed. Terence Hawkes, p. 68.

57. Dylan Thomas, *The Collected Poems* (New York: New Directions, 1957), p. 10.

58. Barthes, *Critical Essays*, pp. 209–10.

59. M. H. Abrams, *The Mirror and the Lamp* (New York: Oxford University Press, 1953), p. 172.

60. Barthes, *Critical Essays*, p. 207, my italics.

61. S. T. Coleridge, "On Poesy and Art," in *Coleridge's Biographia Literaria*, Vol. II, ed. J. Shawcross (Oxford: Oxford University Press, 1907), p. 262.

62. Donald Wesling, *The New Poetries: Poetic Form since Coleridge and Wordsworth* (Lewisburg, Pa.: Bucknell University Press, 1985), p. 53.

63. Denise Levertov, "Some Notes on Organic Form" (1965), in *The Poet in the World* (New York: New Directions, 1973), p. 11.

64. Both Wesling (p. 52) and Levertov (p. 7) employ the term "exploratory" in their discussions of organic form.

65. Charles Olson, "Projective Verse" (1950), in *Human Universe*, p. 52.

66. Olson, *Human Universe*, p. 52.

67. Levertov, "An Admonition" (1964), in *The Poet in the World*, pp. 59, 60.

68. Robert Duncan, "Towards an Open Universe" (1966), in *Fictive Certainties* (New York: New Directions, 1985), p. 81.

69. Boris Eichenbaum, "The Theory of the Formal Method," in *Russian Formalist Criticism*, ed. Lemon and Reis, p. 127.

70. For a somewhat different anatomy of the meditative sequence in Stevens and Auden, based on the duress of psychological pressure, see Rosenthal and Gall, *The Modern Poetic Sequence*, pp. 353–91.

71. Duncan, "From a Notebook" (1954), in *Fictive Certainties*, p. 65.

72. Frank Kermode, in *Wallace Stevens* (New York: Grove Press, 1960), p. 118, claims that the "power" of the Canon Aspirin section of Stevens's "Notes" is "great in isolation; in its context, as sequel to the previous poem, it is overwhelming." The section "raises the temperature of the whole work." Of course, such a climactic movement is characteristic of the romantic sequence as a form. Marjorie Perloff recounts Kermode's testimony in her essay "Pound/Stevens: Whose Era?" in *The Dance of the Intellect* (New York: Cambridge University Press, 1985), p. 4.

73. Wallace Stevens, *The Collected Poems* (New York: Knopf, 1954), pp. 403–4.

74. Duncan, "Towards an Open Universe," in *Fictive Certainties*, pp. 81–82.

75. Stevens, *Collected Poems*, p. 165.

76. Stevens, *Collected Poems*, p. 130. Stevens's explication of "The Idea of Order at Key West" in a letter to Ronald Lane Latimer makes the tentative distinction between personal and general orders: "In 'The Idea of Order at Key West' life has ceased to be a matter of chance. It may be that every man introduces his own order into the life about him and that the idea of order in general is simply what Bishop Berkeley might have called a fortuitous concourse of personal orders. But still there is order. This is the sort of development you are looking for. But then, I never thought that it was a fixed philosophic proposition that life was a mass of irrelevancies any more than I now think that it is a fixed philosophic proposition that every man introduces his own order as part of a general order. These are tentative ideas for the purposes of poetry." *Letters of Wallace Stevens*, ed. Holly Stevens (New York: Knopf, 1966), p. 293. This argument is resumed in "Connoisseur of Chaos," *Collected Poems*, pp. 215–16.

77. Stevens, *Collected Poems*, p. 239.

78. Stevens, *Collected Poems*, p. 240.

79. *Coleridge's Biographia Literaria* II, p. 254.

80. Stevens, *Collected Poems*, p. 392.

81. Stevens, *Collected Poems*, pp. 411–12.

82. Stevens, *Collected Poems*, p. 466.

83. *Coleridge's Biographia Literaria* I, p. 202.

84. A. R. Ammons, *Sphere: The Form of a Motion* (New York: Norton, 1974), p. 79.

85. Ammons, *Sphere*, p. 11.

86. Ammons, *Sphere*, p. 12.

87. Ammons, *Sphere*, p. 11.

88. Ammons, *Sphere*, p. 14.

89. John Ashbery, *A Wave* (New York: Viking, 1984), p. 69.

90. Ashbery, *Self-Portrait in a Convex Mirror* (New York: Viking, 1975), p. 73.

91. Ashbery, *A Wave*, p. 70.

92. The most useful recent study of the modern epic is Michael André Bernstein's *The Tale of the Tribe: Ezra Pound and the Modern Verse Epic* (Princeton: Princeton University Press, 1980). I am indebted to the summary of the characteristics of epic verse presented in his introduction.

93. Charles Olson, "Mayan Letters," in *Selected Writings*, ed. Robert Creeley (New York: New Directions, 1971), pp. 82–83.

94. Robert von Hallberg, *Charles Olson: The Scholar's Art* (Cambridge: Harvard University Press, 1978), p. 59.

95. Von Hallberg, *Charles Olson*, p. 59. Joseph N. Riddel comments in a similar context, "Olson reads *Paterson* as a kind of serial poem, overwhelmed by the process of detail and the rush of history." *The Inverted Bell: Modernism and the Counterpoetics of William Carlos Williams* (Baton Rouge: Louisiana State University Press, 1974), p. 183. Riddel attempts to rebut the charge of "seriality" on behalf of *Paterson*, claiming that Williams lifts the process "to structure."

96. Olson, *Letters for Origin: 1950–1956*, ed. Albert Glover (New York: Paragon House, 1988), pp. 102, 103–4.

97. Robert Duncan, *Fictive Certainties*, p. 179.

98. A notorious example of this discriminatory exclusion involves the parties under discussion. Duncan's long poem "An African Elegy" had been enthusiastically accepted by John Crowe Ransom for the *Kenyon Review*. But following the appearance of Duncan's essay "The Homosexual in Society" in the August 1944 issue of *Politics*, Ransom revised his estimate of the "African Elegy" on the grounds of "homosexual advertisement" and rejected it. For a further discussion of this incident, see Thom Gunn, "Homosexuality in Robert Duncan's Poetry," in *Robert Duncan: Scales of the Marvelous*, ed. Robert J. Bertholf and Ian W. Reid (New York: New Directions, 1979), pp. 143–60.

99. Duncan, *Fictive Certainties*, p. 180.

100. See John Ashbery's comments on his pantoum "Variation on a Noel," in *Ecstatic Occasions, Expedient Forms*, ed. David Lehman (New York: Macmillan, 1987), p. 5.

101. Barthes, *Critical Essays*, p. 210.

102. Barthes, *Critical Essays*, p. 217.

103. Barthes, *Critical Essays*, p. 210.

104. One might also add Josef Albers's series of paintings, for which he is perhaps most famous, *Homage to the Square*. The relationship of form and colors in the quasi-concentric squares, from painting to painting, is certainly paradigmatic. Albers was an important faculty member of Black Mountain College from 1933 to 1949.

105. Barthes, *Critical Essays*, p. 210.

## 2. The Infinite Serial Form

### The Unbound and the Uneven: Robert Duncan's *Passages*

1. Robert Duncan, "Preface to a Reading of Passages 1–22," in *Maps* 6 (1974), a special issue on Robert Duncan edited by John Taggart, p. 53. The following abbreviations for works by and interviews with Duncan are used throughout:

BB    *Bending the Bow* (New York: New Directions, 1968)

BH    *Robert Duncan: An Interview* by George Bowering and Robert Hogg (Toronto: Coach House Press, 1971)
EF    Interview by Ekbert Faas, in *Towards a New American Poetics: Essays and Interviews* (Santa Barbara: Black Sparrow Press, 1978)
FC    *Fictive Certainties* (New York: New Directions, 1985)
GW    *Ground Work: Before the War* (New York: New Directions, 1984)
ID    *Ground Work II: In the Dark* (New York: New Directions, 1987)
M    *Maps 6 (1974)*
MS    *Medieval Scenes* (1950; Kent, Ohio: Kent State University Libraries, 1978)
OF    *The Opening of the Field* (1960; New York: New Directions, 1973)

2. Charles Olson, "Projective Verse," in *Human Universe and Other Essays*, ed. Donald Allen (New York: Grove Press, 1967), p. 53. Duncan and Olson shared an abiding interest in the philosophy of Heraclitus, as indicated by Duncan's comment that "when I read Heraclitus, which is all the time, and Charles has had it all the time, and Hesiod we share—how in the world do we do it? I mean . . . we were reading right close to the letter the same thing" (BH 15). Heraclitus is also the source of inspiration for Olson's important poem "The Kingfishers" in *Selected Writings* (New York: New Directions, 1966) which begins with the Heraclitean aphorism, "What does not change / is the will to change" (167), and includes Heraclitus's account of the struggle among the four primal elements (pp. 170–71). In his own notes to *Bending the Bow*, Duncan cites as the source of the book's title Fragment 51 in G. S. Kirk's edition of *Heraclitus, The Cosmic Fragments* (Cambridge: Cambridge University Press, 1954), which reads: "They do not apprehend how being at variance it agrees with itself: there is a connexion working in both directions, as in the bow and the lyre" (p. 203). Although Kirk's skill as a translator is suspect, Duncan clearly takes the Heraclitean struggle of opposites as the inspiration for the book in which the *Passages* series first appears.

3. Duncan complains that Olson, as a Roman Catholic, is a "dogmatist," whereas he is a "heretic" due to his romantic and theosophical interests. But Olson seems to be little interested in either theological position and objects to Duncan's theosophy in the essay "Against Wisdom as Such." In that essay the essential charge, with which I find myself sympathetic, follows: "I fall back on a difference I am certain the poet as least has to be fierce about: that he is not free to be a part of, or to be any, sect; that there are no symbols to him, there are only his own composed forms, and each one solely the issue of the time of the moment of its creation, not any ultimate except what he in his heat and that instant in its solidity yield. That the poet cannot afford to traffick in any other "sign" than his one, his self, the man or woman he is. Otherwise God does rush in. And art is washed away, turned into that second force, religion" (*Human Universe*, pp. 68–69).

4. As Duncan claims, "I'm not going to take Charles's alternatives, I'm not going to take the closed form versus the open form because I want both, and I'll make open forms that have closed forms in them and closed forms that are open" (BH 5). See also EF 61, 82–83.

5. Duncan claims that "in Olson, the universe has a beginning and it has declined" (EF 80); he associates this particular belief with Neoplatonism and opposes it to the Heraclitean "process of creation." Although Olson may indeed be a lapsed Catholic, Duncan insinuates that on this point he is also a lapsed Heraclitean.

6. See *The Waste Land*, line 430; for a thorough study of the fragment poem as genre, see A. F. Janowitz's unpublished dissertation, *Parts and Wholes: Romantic and Modernist Fragment Poems* (Stanford University, 1983). Janowitz argues, in

brief, that "the Modernist poem made up out of a collage, or compilation, of fragments is a radically different species of poem from the romantic poem fragment, which posits an ideal unity, but which remains open-ended and unfinished" (p. 2).

7. Umberto Eco, *The Role of the Reader* (1979; Bloomington: Indiana University Press, 1984), p. 56.

8. Eco, *Role of the Reader*, p. 48.

9. Eco, *Role of the Reader*, pp. 57, 50.

10. Duncan, *Of the War* (Berkeley: Oyez, 1966); *Tribunals* (Los Angeles: Black Sparrow Press, 1970).

11. See Duncan's extended attack on the publishing industry in "A Preface for MAPS #6: THE ISSUE" (M 1–16).

12. Ian W. Reid, "The Plural Text: 'Passages,'" in *Robert Duncan: Scales of the Marvelous*, ed. Robert J. Bertholf and Ian W. Reid (New York: New Directions, 1979), p. 161.

13. Duncan claims that "back of the field as it appears i[n] Olson's proposition of composition by field is the concept of the cosmos as a field of fields" (FC 168).

14. In "From Symbolist Thought to Immanence: The Ground of Postmodern American Poetics," *Boundary 2* 1 (Spring 1973): 609–10, Charles Altieri argues that Duncan's statement reveals a predilection for Wordsworthian immanence, rather than Coleridgean symbolism. To the extent that it does prefer a "natural order," it is Wordsworthian. But clearly the opposition of an "imposed" or mechanic order and a "natural" or organic order is derived as much from Coleridge.

15. M. H. Abrams, *The Mirror and the Lamp* (New York: Oxford University Press, 1953), p. 220.

16. See also "Crosses of Harmony and Disharmony" (OF 44).

17. In *Ideogram: History of a Poetic Method* (Austin: University of Texas Press, 1982), Laszlo K. Géfin provides this analysis: "Duncan calls the forms of control 'conventional,' 'regular,' or 'periodic,' in that they repeat the same structure again and again, as do the molecules of a crystal. The opposite is aperiodic structure, which does not seek to control but follows the processes of nature like the structures of organic matter in which atoms and molecules are part of a larger entity and yet play individual roles" (p. 101).

18. In Heraclitus's phrase *panta xorei*, "all things change," the verb *xorei* (which also means "to flow") is translated in Latin texts as *procedere*, "to proceed." So there is a linguistic bond between the Heraclitean concept of constant change and the romantic concept of ongoing process.

19. For a comprehensive examination of Heraclitean thought, see G. S. Kirk and J. E. Raven, *The Presocratic Philosophers* (Cambridge: Cambridge University Press, 1957), pp. 182–215; on the concept of "measure" within change, see especially pp. 186–92.

20. Eco, commenting on Henri Pousseur's definition of his composition as a "field of possibilities," states that "the notion of 'field' is provided by physics and implies a revised vision of the classic relationship posited between cause and effect as a rigid, one-directional system: now a complex interplay of motive forces is envisaged, a configuration of possible events, a complete dynamism of structure" (*The Role of the Reader*, p. 58).

21. Olson, *Selected Writings*, p. 238.

22. Heraclitus's account of the struggle of the elements is alluded to in Olson's "The Kingfishers," *Selected Writings*, pp. 170–71.

23. Ezra Pound, *Literary Essays* (New York: New Directions, 1954), p. 3.

24. William Carlos Williams, *The Collected Later Poems* (New York: New Directions, 1967), p. 4.

25. Roland Barthes, *Critical Essays*, trans. Richard Howard (1964; Evanston, Ill.: Northwestern University Press, 1972), pp. 211, 210.

26. Eco, *Role of the Reader*, p. 56.

27. This conjunction is suggested by Ian W. Reid in his essay "The Plural Text: 'Passages,'" in *Scales of the Marvelous*, pp. 178–79; but Reid turns to the attunement between *Passages* and the plural text only at the conclusion of his essay and without sufficient formal analysis of their similarity.

28. Barthes, *S/Z*, trans. Richard Miller (1970; New York: Hill and Wang, 1974), p. 4.

29. Barthes, *S/Z*, pp. 4, 5.

30. Eco, *Role of the Reader*, p. 62.

31. Eco, *Role of the Reader*, pp. 62, 63.

32. Barthes, *S/Z*, pp. 5–6.

33. Robert J. Bertholf, Introduction to *Scales of the Marvelous*, p. vi.

34. Despite Duncan's claim that there is no main entrance to his series, he seems unwilling to abandon the traditional rhetoric at the start of a long poetic enterprise, the poet's invocation to his muse. But if this rhetorical practice seems incongruent with his theory of form, he might excuse the indulgence by pointing out that Memory, the mother of the Muses, is referred to as "Her-Without-Bounds." Or as he claims, "My Heraclitean feeling is that the old feelings must be kept alive in the structure of what you do, and noticeably . . . [I] bring back into my poetry without too much shame the old rhetoric I had of earlier forms" (BH 8).

35. See Kirk and Raven, "Orphic Cosmogonies," pp. 37–48. Reid provides a thorough reading of this aspect of Passages 1 in *Scales of the Marvelous*, pp. 162–63.

36. After an extended visit with Pound at Rapallo, Yeats wrote to Lady Gregory of, among other things, Pound's "passion for cats" and how "large numbers wait him every night at a certain street corner knowing that his pocket is full of meat bones or chicken bones." Yeats's letter is cited by Noel Stock, *The Life of Ezra Pound* (1970; San Francisco: North Point Press, 1982), p. 274.

37. Jack Spicer in his "Vancouver Lectures" also employs the haunted house as an analogy for the structure of a serial poem. See "Excerpts from the Vancouver Lectures," in *The Poetics of the New American Poetry*, ed. Donald Allen and Warren Tallman (New York: Grove Press, 1973), pp. 227–34.

38. In "Ideas of the Meaning of Form," Duncan attacks "the imposing of rules and establishing of regularities" as "a tribal magic against a real threat of upset and things not keeping their place." For an example of periodic form, he turns to Mozart: "The tonal scale of Mozart, where, even among the given notes on the piano, scales are established, so that certain notes are heard as discordant in relation to other notes, threatening to harmony, is a scale imagined to hold its own against threat. A change in mode, in what was permitted, once threatened demonic disorder. Now, unconventional usages threatened loss of reason or insurrection. It is an architecture built up of symmetries, for the mind feels even visual departures from the norm will bring vertigo and collapse. There must be regular sequences and a repetition of stanzas, because thought must not wander, possibility must contain the reassurance of an end to possibilities" (FC 102).

39. The preface to *Medieval Scenes* is from the 1978 edition, no pagination.

40. The letter is reprinted in *Ironwood* 22 (Fall 1983): 104, a Special Issue on Robert Duncan.

41. Quoted from the tape of a class lecture, 11 November 1977, by Mark Johnson, "Robert Duncan's 'Momentous Inconclusions,'" in *Sagetrieb* 2 (Summer–Fall 1983): 75. See also BH 5.

42. Duncan's spacing of the text of "Passages 10" suggests Chinese writing and the Pound-Fenollosa ideogrammic method; Laszlo Géfin identifies the ideogrammic method with the paratactic composition, a "placing beside one another," and so opposed to hypotaxis, "to arrange under," "which signifies a dependent construction or relation of parts with connectives" (*Ideogram*, p. xii). The paratactic mode, then, is more appropriate to an ahierarchical poetic structure such as *Passages*.

43. Ian Reid also notes the interweaving of Eros and the Moon in "Passages 14," "Chords." The poem "alludes to a variant version of the Orphic creation story, found in Aristophanes' *The Birds*, where Love comes forth from a Moon-Egg begotten by the Wind upon Night." *Scales of the Marvelous*, p. 164.

44. Michael Riffaterre, *Semiotics of Poetry* (Bloomington: Indiana University Press, 1978), p. 82.

45. Jack Spicer, who did graduate work in linguistics, also employs the lecture course in linguistics as the structure of his book-length series *Language*. Spicer and Duncan frequently corresponded on the subject of linguistics and poetics (see *Ironwood* 22 [Fall 1983]: 97–100 for a sample of Duncan's letters), but the relationship deteriorated, as Duncan indicates in an interview: "Sapir I had read, and Jesperson I had read, and Spicer had been at Whorf, and often I would not read with Spicer—Spicer was sophisticated at the linguistic level so he could be very perverse, and he could beat me at that tic tac toe, but in later years he couldn't beat me because Spicer was obsessed. He was incapable of moving, I mean. He would just simply dissolve and go into pieces and at one time cry and usually feel I was cheating because my obsession was to fuse and his obsession was going in a trap towards fate" (BH 21).

46. Michael André Bernstein supports Duncan's criticism when he notes that "the thrust of the ideogram is indeed, as Pound said, 'totalitarian,' in the sense that it seeks a single, coherent synthesis of all its parts, but [Duncan's] *grand collage* is centrifugal not centripetal, and it often proceeds by undoing the certainties of its inaugural premises." The failure of Pound's *Cantos* to cohere produces a "liberating fragmentation, a dispersion in which separate motifs can now co-exist without being marshalled into a hierarchical totality." Bernstein, "Robert Duncan: Talent and the Individual Tradition," *Sagetrieb* 4 (Fall–Winter 1985): 189.

47. Bernstein, p. 189.


Against the Calendar: Paul Blackburn's *Journals*

48. Paul Blackburn, *Early Selected Y Mas* (Los Angeles: Black Sparrow Press, 1972), p. 130.

49. *The Collected Poems of Paul Blackburn*, ed. Edith Jarolim (New York: Persea Books, 1985), p. 258. All citations of Blackburn's poetry are from this edition, abbreviated CP.

50. Blackburn, *The Cities* (New York: Grove Press, 1967), p. 12.

51. Roland Barthes, *Critical Essays*, trans. Richard Howard (1964; Evanston, Ill.: Northwestern University Press, 1972), p. 181.

52. Compare Elizabeth Bishop's description of the cigarettes in the ashtray on her writing desk in "12 O'Clock News": "They are in hideously contorted positions, all

dead. We can make out at least eight bodies." *The Complete Poems: 1927–1979* (New York: Farrar, Straus, and Giroux, 1983), p. 175.

53. *Lorca/Blackburn: Poems of Federico García Lorca Chosen and Translated by Paul Blackburn* (San Francisco: Momo's Press, 1979), no pagination.

54. Annalisa Goldoni, "La Poesia di Paul Blackburn," in *Studi Americani* 15 (Rome: Edizioni di Storia e Letteratura, 1969), p. 384.

55. Robert Duncan, *Ground Work: Before the War* (New York: New Directions, 1984), p. 135.

56. See Robert Duncan, *Bending the Bow* (New York: New Directions, 1968), p. 68, and *Ground Work: Before the War*, p. 80.

57. Charles Olson, "Projective Verse," in *Human Universe and Other Essays*, ed. Donald Allen (New York: Grove Press, 1967), p. 52.

58. William Carlos Williams, *Imaginations* (1918; New York: New Directions, 1971), p. 18.

One Thing Finding Its Place with Another: Robert Creeley's *Pieces*

59. Robert Creeley, *Contexts of Poetry: Interviews 1961–1971*, ed. Donald Allen (Bolinas, Calif.: Four Seasons Foundation, 1973), p. 187. The following abbreviations for works by and interviews with Robert Creeley are used throughout:

CE    *The Collected Essays of Robert Creeley* (Berkeley: University of California
       Press, 1989)
CP    *The Collected Poems of Robert Creeley 1945–1975* (Berkeley: University of
       California Press, 1982)
CTP   *Contexts of Poetry*
EF    Interview by Ekbert Faas, in *Towards a New American Poetics* (Santa Bar-
       bara: Black Sparrow Press, 1978)
MS    *Mabel: A Story* (London: Marion Boyars, 1976)
QG    *A Quick Graph*, ed. Donald Allen (San Francisco: Four Seasons Foundation,
       1970)

60. John Cage, *A Year from Monday* (Middletown, Conn.: Wesleyan University Press, 1967), p. 26.

61. See Cage's "review" of *Arnold Schoenberg Letters*, ed. Erwin Stein (New York: St. Martin's Press, 1965), "Mosaic," in *A Year from Monday*, pp. 43–49.

62. Roland Barthes, *Critical Essays*, trans. Richard Howard (1964; Evanston, Ill.: Northwestern University Press, 1972), p. 210.

63. The *Princeton Encyclopedia of Poetry and Poetics*, ed. Alex Preminger (Princeton: Princeton University Press, 1974), pp. 32–33, notes that a sub-type of anacoluthon—when the apodosis of a conditional sentence is lacking—is anantapodoton; this is precisely the case in Creeley's "Do You Think. . . ."

64. Gerard Manley Hopkins, cited in Roman Jakobson, "Linguistics and Poetics," in *Conference on Style in Language*, ed. Thomas A. Sebeok (New York: John Wiley and MIT, 1960), p. 368.

65. Roman Jakobson, "Poetry of Grammar and Grammar of Poetry," *Lingua* 21 (1968): 605; reprinted in his *Verbal Art, Verbal Sign, Verbal Time* (Minneapolis: University of Minnesota Press, 1985), p. 43.

66. Kenneth Burke, *The Philosophy of Literary Form* (1941; Berkeley: University of California Press, 1973), p. 119.

67. Barthes, *Critical Essays*, p. 210.

68. Charles Altieri, *Self and Sensibility in Contemporary American Poetry* (New York: Cambridge University Press, 1984), p. 121.

69. Philip L. Gerber, "From the Forest of Language: A Conversation with Robert Creeley," *Athanor* 4 (Spring 1973): 13.

70. Cage, *A Year from Monday*, pp. 26, 29.

71. Altieri, *Self and Sensibility*, p. 112.

72. Charles Olson, "Projective Verse," in *Human Universe and Other Essays*, ed. Donald Allen (New York: Grove Press, 1967), pp. 52, 53.

73. Olson, *Human Universe*, p. 56.

74. Cage, *A Year from Monday*, p. 28.

75. Olson, *Human Universe*, p. 56.

76. William Carlos Williams, *The Collected Later Poems* (New York: New Directions, 1967), p. 5.

77. Williams, *Imaginations* (1918; New York: New Directions, 1970), p. 18.

78. Williams, *Pictures from Brueghel* (New York: New Directions, 1962), pp. 117–18.

79. Williams, *Pictures from Brueghel*, p. 109.

80. Williams, *Collected Later Poems*, p. 5.

81. Williams, *Imaginations*, p. 166.

82. Terry R. Bacon, "How He Knows When to Stop: Creeley on Closure," in *American Poetry Review* 5 (November–December 1975): 5.

83. See Altieri, *Self and Sensibility*, chapter 5: "Robert Creeley's Poetics of Conjecture," passim.

84. Cf. Creeley, in his interview with Ekbert Faas: "Or Kenneth Koch, well, he simply uses a very steady heroic couplet, and into that he can literally pour anything, throw in all this lovely garbage. He uses a contained, reasonably stated line of bullshit and you can read on and on and on despite the fact that it's obviously going nowhere" (*Towards a New American Poetics*, p. 195).

85. Gertrude Stein, "Poetry and Grammar," in *Lectures in America* (1935; Boston: Beacon Press, 1985), p. 227.

86. Robert von Hallberg, *American Poetry and Culture 1945–1980* (Cambridge: Harvard University Press, 1985), p. 47.

87. *Harvard Concise Dictionary of Music*, compiled by Don Michael Randel (Cambridge: Harvard University Press, 1978), p. 458.

88. William Sylvester, "Robert Creeley's Poetics: I Know That I Hear You," in *Boundary* 2 (Spring/Fall, 1978): 205.

89. Creeley, interview with Bacon, "How He Knows When to Stop," p. 6.

90. Cage, *A Year from Monday*, p. 28.

91. Creeley, interview with Bacon, "How He Knows When to Stop," p. 6.

92. Cage, *A Year from Monday*, p. 28.

## 3. The Finite Serial Form

### The Dark House: Jack Spicer's Book of *Language*

1. *Language* 28 (1952): 348–59. The cover of Jack Spicer's *Language*, for those of us who do not own a first edition, is reprinted in *Boundary* 2 6 (Fall 1977): 229.

2. This letter is included in *The Collected Books of Jack Spicer*, ed. Robin Blaser (Los Angeles: Black Sparrow Press, 1975), pp. 60–61. It forms part of the book *Admonitions* (1958). Further citations are abbreviated CB.

3. Excerpts from Spicer's "Vancouver Lectures" appear in *Caterpillar* 12 (July 1970): 175–212, and in *The Poetics of the New American Poetry*, ed. Donald Allen and Warren Tallman (New York: Grove Press, 1973), pp. 227–34. Further citations of the "Vancouver Lectures" are taken from Allen and Tallman and abbreviated NAP.

4. Robert Duncan, *Bending the Bow* (New York: New Directions, 1968), p. v.

5. See Wallace Fowlie, *Mallarmé* (Chicago: University of Chicago Press, 1953), pp. 54, 61.

6. *Mallarmé: Selected Prose Poems, Essays, and Letters*, trans. Bradford Cook (Baltimore: Johns Hopkins University Press, 1956), p. 24.

7. Ron Silliman, in his essay "Spicer's Language," pauses briefly to discuss the structure of Spicer's serial form in, I think, cogent terms: "The serial poem is the basic unit of Spicer's mature writing. Although booklength, this unit is considerably different from the openended modernist epic which extends from the model of Pound's *Cantos*. It is not merely a question of the serial poem's shorter size, but of closure and discreteness. The serial poem develops the internal unities of the book, while in the same moment emphasizing the distinctness of its individual parts. Each work within a serial poem bears its own scar of closure, but also displaces at least a part of its range of reference outside of the individual text. Spicer builds the superstructure in such a fashion as to avoid any instant in which (as often happens both in naive narrative and expository forms), the subject 'snaps' into clarity." *The New Sentence* (New York: Roof Books, 1987), p. 162.

8. Edgar Allan Poe, "The Philosophy of Composition," in *Edgar Allan Poe: Essays and Reviews*, ed. G. R. Thompson (New York: Library of America, 1984), p. 15.

9. William Carlos Williams, *In the American Grain* (1933; New York: New Directions, 1956), p. 227.

10. Poe, *Essays and Reviews*, pp. 14, 15, 14.

11. Roland Barthes, *Critical Essays*, trans. Richard Howard (1964; Evanston, Ill.: Northwestern University Press, 1972), p. 244.

12. Barthes, *Critical Essays*, p. 245.

13. Roman Jakobson, "Linguistics and Poetics," in *Style and Language*, ed. Thomas A. Sebeok (New York: John Wiley and MIT, 1960), p. 353.

14. Jakobson, "Linguistics and Poetics," p. 356.

15. Jonathan Culler, *Structuralist Poetics* (Ithaca: Cornell University Press, 1975), p. 56.

16. W. R. Johnson, *The Idea of Lyric: Lyric Modes in Ancient and Modern Poetry* (Berkeley: University of California Press, 1981), p. 3.

17. Johnson, *Idea of Lyric*, pp. 9, 10.

18. Louis Zukofsky, *Prepositions*, expanded ed. (Berkeley: University of California Press, 1981), p. 15.

19. Colin Christopher Stuart and John Scoggan air out the dirty laundry in "The Orientation of the Parasols: Saussure, Derrida, Spicer," *Boundary* 2 6 (Fall 1977): 228.

20. *The Collected Poems of Wallace Stevens* (New York: Knopf, 1954), p. 202.

21. Gerald L. Bruns makes the distinction between orphic and hermetic literature in *Modern Poetry and the Idea of Language* (New Haven: Yale University Press, 1974), pp. 1, 232–62. For instance: "The sign appears to derive its power of signification from the formal principles that determine its relative position within a semiotic system; at the same time, however, it claims for itself its ancient power

to transcend the system and to announce a meaning on the basis of its unity with the world of things" (233). Spicer, like Mallarmé, can be said to endorse only the first, or formalist, stance; Wallace Stevens could be said to endorse the second, or romantic, stance.

22. Culler, *Structuralist Poetics*, p. 18.

23. Barthes, *Elements of Semiology*, trans. Annette Lavers and Colin Smith (1964; New York: Hill and Wang, 1967), p. 80.

24. Barthes, *Elements of Semiology*, p. 86.

## The Subway's Iron Circuit: George Oppen's *Discrete Series*

25. Burton Hatlen and Tom Mandel, "Poetry and Politics: A Conversation with George and Mary Oppen," in *George Oppen: Man and Poet*, ed. Burton Hatlen (Orono, Maine: National Poetry Foundation, 1981), p. 41. The title of Williams's review of *Discrete Series*, to which I allude, is "The New Poetical Economy," reprinted in Hatlen on pp. 267–70 from *Poetry* 44 (July 1934). Further references to this volume are abbreviated MP.

26. *The Collected Poems of George Oppen* (New York: New Directions, 1975), p. 21. All poetry by Oppen is cited from this volume, abbreviated CP.

27. "George Oppen," in *The Contemporary Writer*, ed. L. S. Dembo and Cyrena N. Pondrom (Madison: University of Wisconsin Press, 1972), p. 174. First published in *Contemporary Literature* 10 (Spring 1969). Further references to this interview are abbreviated CW.

28. Rachel Blau DuPlessis, "George Oppen: 'What do we believe to live with?'" *Ironwood* 5 (1975): 65. Thomas Sharp also suggests the subway as a "prototype" for *Discrete Series*, but the Oppens, in conversation, were lukewarm to the idea (MP 277). Sharp nevertheless quotes a passage from Mary Oppen's autobiography *Meaning a Life* (Santa Barbara: Black Sparrow Press, 1978) which concisely illustrates both the "serial" and the "discrete" aspects of subway transportation: "We didn't yet know the subway system [in New York, 1929], and we got off at stations at random just to see what was above ground. Once we stuck our heads out into a cemetery, another time we were on clay fields with standing pools of water, and once we were among giant apartment buildings in the Bronx, block after block" (p. 89).

29. *The Complete Poems and Selected Letters and Prose of Hart Crane*, ed. Brom Weber (Garden City, N.Y.: Anchor, 1966), pp. 110–11.

30. Charles Tomlinson, "An Introductory Note on the Poetry of George Oppen," *Ironwood* 5 (1975): 13. Harold Schimmel rebuts in favor of a "Bonnard bathroom nude" (MP 299–300), but his arguments for "Under arm" and "red globe" as the erotic glimpses of a keyhole peeper seem unnecessarily Freudian. Thomas Sharp attempts to confirm Tomlinson's suggestion of the elevator in conversation with the Oppens (MP 281). However, his claim that "with this knowledge, the poem gains for the present reader total clarity" reduces the poem to a riddle that one declares satisfactorily "solved" when one has "discovered" the referent. Such a poem—filled in and thrown out like the puzzle page of a daily newspaper—would be dispensable when the reader arrives at the "total clarity" of the referential "solution." Gilbert Sorrentino has suggested in a letter to me that the object may be "a signal stanchion on the New York subway system platform (no longer, I think, in use). The signals were meant to alert passengers as to the identity of the next

arriving train (red and white were the 'colors' of the dead and departed Sea Beach Express). Each line had its own color code—two greens, the 4th Ave. local, etc. etc."

31. Louis Zukofsky, "Sincerity and Objectification," in *Poetry* 37 (February 1931): 273. In this special number edited by Zukofsky, the current first and third poems of *Discrete Series* appear in earlier versions, numbered 1 and 2, under the title "1930's." It is possible that "1930's" was a proto-title for the entire series. The decade, overburdening the single poem, becomes a more convincing referent for the thirty-one poems in a serial form. As Williams says, the Objectivist intends to make "an object consonant with his day."

32. Oppen, "The Mind's Own Place," *Montemora* 1 (Fall 1975): 133. First appeared in *KULCHUR* 10 in 1963.

33. In "Poetry and Politics: A Conversation with George and Mary Oppen," Mary claims, "We had no particular leanings toward the Communist Party—we were looking for someone who was active and who was doing something right now, and was something we could join. But we looked at the poets, we looked at the writers and we did not think that was any kind of art. Neither the paintings, the things that I was doing or—George can speak for himself—but we couldn't enter into that sort of artistic world. It was propaganda art" (MP 33). And George has said, in "The Mind's Own Place," "There are situations which cannot honorably be met by art" (p. 136), explaining in part his twenty-five-year hiatus from poetry—to confront the Fascists in Germany, and to evade the McCarthy hearings by self-imposed exile to Mexico.

34. Oppen, "An Adequate Vision: A George Oppen Daybook," in the special Oppen issue of *Ironwood* 26 (1985): 24–25. Oppen has testified to his admiration of Bronk's work in several interviews; he refers to Bronk in the series "A Narrative" (CP 138).

35. William Bronk, *Life Supports* (San Francisco: North Point Press, 1981), pp. 43–44.

36. Charles Altieri, "The Objectivist Tradition," *Chicago Review* 30 (Winter 1979): 6.

37. William Carlos Williams, *Selected Essays* (1921; New York: New Directions, 1969), pp. 33–34.

38. In "George Oppen's Serial Poems," *Contemporary Literature* 29 (Summer 1988): 221–40, Alan Golding argues that Oppen must not be considered as a kind of "miniaturist" but as a poet whose work is characteristically in serial form. Golding is of course quite right in his assessment. He does very little, however, to distinguish between the several types of long forms: "Oppen did distinguished work in the genre of—call it what you will—the long poem, the serial poem, the poetic sequence. My point, then, is this: that to overlook Oppen's sequences *as sequences*—to ignore *why* Oppen works in this genre—is to misunderstand, by limiting, the nature of his achievement" (p. 222). As with other critics, Golding makes the mistake of blurring rather than distinguishing these types of the long form in contemporary poetry. Oppen's serial poems are clearly *not* sequences, and they should not be described as such. Similarly, he compares Oppen's technique to Creeley's, but refers to the latter's volume *Pieces* as a "sequence of fragments" (p. 235). Such a description hardly clarifies Creeley's distinct practice of seriality, though the comparison with Oppen stands.

39. Williams, *Selected Essays*, p. 129.

40. Hugh Kenner, *A Homemade World* (New York: Knopf, 1975), p. 169.

41. Kenner, *Homemade World*, p. 170.

42. Williams, *Imaginations* (1932; New York: New Directions, 1970), p. 288.

43. Kevin Power, "An Interview with George and Mary Oppen," *Montemora* 4 (1978): 187.

44. Oppen here slightly rephrases his definition of the discrete series, in a letter to Rachel Blau DuPlessis, quoted in her essay in *Ironwood* 5: 64.

45. Williams, *The Autobiography of William Carlos Williams* (New York: New Directions, 1967), pp. 264–65.

## Sounding and Resounding Anew: Louis Zukofsky and Lorine Niedecker

46. Lorine Niedecker, *From This Condensery: The Complete Writing of Lorine Niedecker*, ed. Robert J. Bertholf (Winston-Salem, N.C.: The Jargon Society, 1985), p. 301. Subsequently cited as FC.

47. Louis Zukofsky, *All: The Collected Short Poems 1923–1964* (New York: Norton, 1971), p. 114. Subsequently cited as AL.

### Zukofsky's Musical Inventions

48. William Carlos Williams, "A New Line Is a New Measure," *The New Quarterly of Poetry* 2 (Winter 1947–48): 11.

49. This interview, "Sincerity and Objectification," one of the few ever given by the increasingly reclusive Zukofsky, has been reprinted in *Louis Zukofsky: Man and Poet*, ed. Carroll F. Terrell (Orono, Maine: National Poetry Foundation, 1979), p. 271. Further references to the interview and the other work contained in this volume are cited as MP. Dembo's interview was conducted 15 May 1968 and first appeared in *Contemporary Literature* 10 (Spring 1969); it was included in *The Contemporary Writer*, ed. L. S. Dembo and Cyrena N. Pondrom (Madison: University of Wisconsin Press, 1972).

50. Zukofsky prefers the word "particulars" (probably borrowed from Williams) in his essay "Program: 'Objectivists' 1931" for the now famous "Objectivists" number of *Poetry* 37 (February 1931): 268, subsequently cited as P.

51. We might compare Zukofsky's definition of objectivism with Robert Creeley's definition of the poem in *A Quick Graph* (San Francisco: Four Seasons Foundation, 1970): "A poem will be a *thing* of parts, in such relation, that the tension between them will effect an actual coherence in form" (p. 25). Both involve the construction of a relational whole from "minor units," or parts. The analogy is mechanical, not organic.

52. Zukofsky's triad is clearly dependent on Pound's phanopoeia, melopoeia, and logopoeia. "About the Gas Age," in *Prepositions: The Collected Critical Essays of Louis Zukofsky*, expanded ed. (Berkeley: University of California Press, 1981), pp. 169, 171. Subsequently cited as PR.

53. Robert Creeley, *A Quick Graph*, p. 122.

54. Williams, "New Line," p. 8.

55. Louis Zukofsky, *"A"* (Berkeley: University of California Press, 1978), p. 38. Subsequently cited as A.

56. Michael Heller, *Conviction's Net of Branches: Essays on the Objectivist Poets and Poetry* (Carbondale: Southern Illinois University Press, 1985), p. 27.

57. Flann O'Brien, *At Swim-Two-Birds* (1951; New York: New American Library, 1976), p. 156.

58. Poem 17 of "29 Songs" (AL 55–56) bears the title "Imitation," and Zukofsky's note supplies the musical definition: "*Mus.* The repetition of a phrase or subject in another voice part or in a different key." The poem itself presents the "imitation"

Gothic architecture, Swiss chalets, and assorted chinoiserie found among the "new" apartment buildings and taxis of New York. Structurally, however, 17 does not function clearly as a fugue itself, and Zukofsky may be playing the musical definition with its baroque vigor against a twentieth-century American culture that is content to "imitate," cheaply and without substance, European and Eastern forms.

59. I discuss these canonic forms and other "rounds" and "reverberations" of Robert Creeley and Weldon Kees in my next chapter, on procedural forms.

60. Roland Barthes, *Critical Essays*, trans. Richard Howard (1964; Evanston, Ill.: Northwestern University Press, 1972), p. 181.

61. As Niedecker notes, *"A"* tightens on several occasions into various closed forms: *"A"* 9, for example, is a canzone. Ron Silliman makes a very perceptive comment about the larger structures in *"A"* and the relation of the individual "books" to the whole epic: the "open-ended interconnectedness in [*"A"*] 1–6 marks the debt to *The Cantos*, but from 7 [a crown of sonnets] [w/wch he chose to represent himself in the Objectivist issue of *Poetry*, 2/31] forward, a new conceptualization as to the function of part-to-whole relations in the formation of a long poem starts to emerge: each moment is a totalization, complete to itself, capable of entering into larger structures as a relational fact. This integrity of units is radically unlike *Maximus* or *Passages*" (*Paideuma* 7 [Winter 1978]: 405–6). In the epic, especially one that assumes the classic formulation of twenty-four books, fugal recurrence functions much as does motif in the novel—subordinate to the superstructure of the whole as well as, in the case of *"A"* 9, to the canzone structure of the individual book.

62. Barthes, *Critical Essays*, pp. 175, 181.

63. Creeley, "paradise / our / speech," in *The Collected Essays of Robert Creeley* (Berkeley: University of California Press, 1989), p. 50.

### Niedecker's Geological Cycles

64. Lorine Niedecker, *"Between Your House and Mine": The Letters of Lorine Niedecker to Cid Corman, 1960–1970*, ed. Lisa Pater Faranda (Durham, N.C.: Duke University Press, 1986), pp. 90–91. Subsequently cited as L.

65. Faranda comments on the "equivocal" treatment of the Ojibwas and their legends by Schoolcraft and Longfellow in *Letters*, pp. 92–93, n. 3.

66. The phrase occurs in Niedecker's poem "Poet's work":

> Grandfather
> 　advised me:
> 　　Learn a trade
>
> I learned
> 　to sit at desk
> 　　and condense
>
> No layoff
> 　from this
> 　　condensery

*From This Condensery*, p. 141. All poems by Niedecker are cited as they appear in this edition. For helpful emendations and a much-needed index to this volume, see

*A Preliminary Index to Lorine Niedecker's "From This Condensery,"* ed. Harry Gilonis with Peter Quartermain (Vancouver: Slug Press, 1989).

67. See Kenneth Cox, "The Poems of Lorine Niedecker," in *The Cambridge Quarterly* 4 (Spring 1969): 170.

68. One of very few comments on her poetics, this occurs in a letter from the poet to her neighbor Gail Roub, first published by Cid Corman in "Letters to Gail," *Origin* 4 (July 1981): 42.

69. Louis Zukofsky, *A Test of Poetry* (New York: The Objectivist Press, 1948). Niedecker's poem appears on p. 41; Zukofsky's comment in a subsequent section, p. 99.

70. *North Central* (London: Fulcrum Press, 1968). The Jargon Society's *From This Condensery*, otherwise an exquisitely printed book, also refuses to spare the blank space, separating the several poems on each page with a boldface **o**. Cid Corman's edition, *The Granite Pail: The Selected Poems of Lorine Niedecker*, presents the poems several to a page, but without intervening characters. In addition to Oppen's *Discrete Series*, one can also cite the first edition of Louis Zukofsky's *Anew* (Prairie City, Ill.: Decker, 1946) whose forty-three short poems are printed each to a page. This seems to be the favored printed form for the serial poem, lacking more blatant types of division or organization.

71. Niedecker, "Letters to Gail," p. 42.

72. Donald Davie, "Lyric Minimum and Epic Scope: Lorine Niedecker," originally appeared in *PN Review* (Manchester, Eng.) 25 (Winter 1981). It has been reprinted in *The Full Note: Lorine Niedecker*, ed. Peter Dent (Devon, Eng.: Interim Press, 1983) and in *Sagetrieb* 1 (Fall 1982): 268–76.

73. Davie, "Lyric Minimum," p. 272.

74. Davie, "Lyric Minimum," p. 272.

75. *The Collected Poems of George Oppen* (New York: New Directions, 1975), p. 16.

76. Lisa Pater Faranda, "Composing a Place: Two Versions of Lorine Niedecker's 'Lake Superior,'" in *North Dakota Quarterly* 55 (Fall 1987): 354.

77. Niedecker, "Letters to Gail," p. 44.

78. Davie, "Lyric Minimum," p. 276.

## 4. A Predetermined Form

### Renovated Form: The Sestinas of John Ashbery and Louis Zukofsky

1. "John Ashbery: An Interview by Ross Labrie," *American Poetry Review* (May–June 1984): 32. Subsequently cited as APR.

2. Marianne Shapiro, *Hieroglyph of Time: The Petrarchan Sestina* (Minneapolis: University of Minnesota Press, 1980), pp. 30–31.

3. Louis Zukofsky, *All: The Collected Short Poems* (New York: Norton, 1971), pp. 76–77. Subsequently cited as AL.

### John Ashbery: The Pastoral and the Urbane

4. Shapiro, *Hieroglyph of Time*, pp. 13, 22, 23, 23, 23–24.

5. Shapiro, *Hieroglyph of Time*, p. 7.

6. Niedecker's correspondence with Zukofsky is recorded in *All*, p. 210: "'There are words that rhyme but / are never used together / You would never use *lute* with *boot*'— / So she has used them."

7. Roland Barthes, *Critical Essays*, trans. Richard Howard (1964; Evanston, Ill.: Northwestern University Press, 1972), pp. 216–17.

8. Barthes, *Critical Essays*, p. 217.

9. Richard Howard, "John Ashbery," in *Modern Critical Views: John Ashbery*, ed. Harold Bloom (New York: Chelsea House, 1985), p. 19.

10. John Ashbery, *The Double Dream of Spring* (New York: Ecco Press, 1976), pp. 47–48. Subsequently cited as DD.

11. Shapiro, *Hieroglyph of Time*, p. 205.

12. Ashbery, "Craft Interview with John Ashbery," in *The Craft of Poetry: Interviews from The New York Quarterly*, ed. William Packard (Garden City, N.Y.: Doubleday, 1974), p. 111. Subsequently cited as NYQ.

13. On the open engagement of the reader in text production, cf. Barthes's "plural text" in *S/Z* (New York: Hill and Wang, 1974); Umberto Eco on semantically open forms in *The Role of the Reader* (Bloomington: Indiana University Press, 1979); and Marjorie Perloff on "indeterminacy," especially her chapter on Ashbery in *The Poetics of Indeterminacy* (Evanston, Ill.: Northwestern University Press, 1983).

14. Harold Bloom has made several eloquent arguments for Ashbery as the heir to romanticism, via Wallace Stevens and Walt Whitman. Certainly, such poems as "A Wave" indicate Ashbery's interest, particularly in the later volumes, in "form as proceeding," or in roughly Stevensian terms, "the poem of the form of the mind." Ashbery demonstrates his capabilities in both closed and open form, but undertaking a sestina, he must reject for that instance organic form. It is interesting, however, that Bloom, in making his argument for the romantic Ashbery, must dismiss as misleading the substantial evidence of the artificial Ashbery: "Ashbery has been misunderstood because of his association with the 'New York School' of Kenneth Koch, Frank O'Hara and other comedians of the spirit." (*Modern Critical Views*, p. 6). Ashbery's involvement in the art world of Paris and New York, in the company of his comic cousins Koch and O'Hara, is at least as significant an influence as the paternal Stevens; his practice of continental forms has its source, I think, in the museum culture of the New York School association.

15. Charles Altieri, *Enlarging the Temple* (Lewisburg, Pa.: Bucknell University Press, 1979), p. 164.

16. See Eco, *The Role of the Reader*, chapter 6, "Narrative Structures in Fleming," in which Eco comments that "the success of the '007 saga' . . . has been due both to the mass consensus and to the appreciation of the more sophisticated readers" (p. 146). But he concedes, "Since the decoding of a message cannot be established by its author, but depends on the concrete circumstances of reception, it is difficult to guess what Fleming is or will be for his readers" (p. 172).

17. See Shapiro's discussion of Pound's sestina in *Hieroglyph of Time*, pp. 48–52.

18. Roman Jakobson, "Linguistics and Poetics," in *Style in Language*, ed. Thomas Sebeok (Cambridge: MIT Press, 1960), p. 353.

19. Shapiro, *Hieroglyph of Time*, p. 23.

20. Charles Altieri, *Self and Sensibility in Contemporary American Poetry* (New York: Cambridge University Press, 1984), p. 147.

21. Shapiro, *Hieroglyph of Time*, p. 16.

22. Shapiro, *Hieroglyph of Time*, p. 206.

23. John Ashbery, *Some Trees* (1956; New York: Ecco Press, 1978), pp. 44–46.

24. Barthes, *Critical Essays*, pp. 209–10.

25. Shapiro applies Jakobson's analysis to the sestina: "In the sestina, compared with other poems, recurrence is codified to the utmost. The proportion of introversive to extroversive semiosis increases accordingly, and *signans* and *signatum*

more closely approach fusion. Sestinas are not *about* ideas; they *are* ideas. Their form, more conducive to suggestive juxtaposition than to connected statement, thereby is more able to embody recurrence as process" (*Hieroglyph of Time*, pp. 6–7).

26. Barthes, *Critical Essays*, p. 210.

27. Lorine Niedecker, *From This Condensery* (Winston-Salem, N.C.: The Jargon Society, 1985), p. 292.

28. Ashbery's pantoum appears with the dedication "Homage to Saint-Simon, Ravel and Joseph Cornell" in Dore Ashton, *A Joseph Cornell Album* (New York: Viking, 1974), pp. 119–20. The "clay pipe" appears frequently in Cornell's box constructions. Ashbery has reviewed Cornell's work both as an editor for *Artnews* and as a contributor to *New York* magazine; it is certainly no accident that Ashbery's participation in the art world surfaces in the context of the elaborate and artificial pantoum form. The poem first appeared in *Some Trees*, pp. 30–31, without the dedication.

### Louis Zukofsky: The Renaissance and Brooklyn Heights

29. Dembo's interview is reprinted in *Louis Zukofsky: Man and Poet*, ed. C. F. Terrell (Orono, Maine: National Poetry Foundation, 1979), p. 275. Further references to this interview are abbreviated MP.

30. John Taggart, "Zukofsky's 'Mantis,'" in Terrell, ed., *Louis Zukofsky: Man and Poet*, pp. 255–56.

### Canonic Form in Weldon Kees, Robert Creeley, and Louis Zukofsky

31. Louis Zukofsky's statement in an interview with L. S. Dembo is reprinted in *Louis Zukofsky: Man and Poet*, ed. C. F. Terrell (Orono, Maine: National Poetry Foundation, 1979), p. 279.

32. Roland Barthes's comments are found in *Critical Essays*, trans. Richard Howard (1964; Evanston, Ill.: Northwestern University Press, 1972), p. 217.

33. See Roman Jakobson, "Two Aspects of Language and Two Types of Aphasic Disturbances," in *Selected Writings*, vol. II (The Hague and Paris: Mouton, 1971), especially: "The primacy of the metaphoric process in the literary schools of romanticism and symbolism has been repeatedly acknowledged, but it is still insufficiently realized that it is the predominance of metonymy which underlies and actually predetermines the so-called 'realistic' trend. . . . Following the path of contiguous relationships, the realist author metonymically digresses from the plot to the atmosphere and from characters to the setting in space and time. He is fond of synecdochic details" (p. 255).

34. *The Collected Poems of Weldon Kees*, rev. ed., ed. Donald Justice (Lincoln: University of Nebraska Press, 1975), p. x. Subsequently cited as CP.

35. Robert E. Knoll, "Weldon Kees: Solipsist as Poet," *Prairie Schooner* 35 (1961): 39.

36. Barthes, *Critical Essays*, p. 210.

37. Barthes, *Critical Essays*, p. 181.

38. See "The New York Intellectuals 1941–1950: Some Letters by Weldon Kees," ed. Robert E. Knoll, *Hudson Review* 38 (Spring 1985): 55.

39. Robert Creeley, *Contexts of Poetry: Interviews 1961–1970*, ed. Donald Allen (Bolinas, Calif.: Four Seasons Foundation, 1973), p. 88.

40. Ekbert Faas, *Towards a New American Poetics* (Santa Barbara: Black Sparrow Press, 1978), p. 155.

41. *The Collected Poems of Robert Creeley 1945–1975* (Berkeley: University of California Press, 1982), p. 416. Subsequently cited as CP.

42. Arthur Ford, *Robert Creeley* (Boston: G. K. Hall, 1978), p. 42.

43. Robert Creeley, "Notes Apropos 'Free Verse,'" in *The Collected Essays of Robert Creeley* (Berkeley: University of California Press, 1989), p. 494.

44. Ford, *Robert Creeley*, p. 42.

45. For Riffaterre's discussion of the hypogram, see "Sign Production," chapter 2 of *Semiotics of Poetry* (Bloomington: Indiana University Press, 1978), pp. 23–46.

46. Lorine Niedecker, *From This Condensery: The Complete Writing of Lorine Niedecker* (Winston-Salem, N.C.: The Jargon Society, 1985), p. 303.

47. Louis Zukofsky, *All: The Collected Short Poems 1923–1964* (New York: Norton, 1971), p. 50. Subsequently cited as AL.

48. Michael Palmer has suggested to me that Zukofsky was trying to compose lyrics to accompany a twelve-tone series composed by his son Paul. This would account for the maintenance of twelve words in each stanza. Strictly speaking, however, a twelve-tone row would demand that the tones be shifted into a new order in each statement of the row; Zukofsky here keeps the order of the words fixed, and so his lyric resembles the structure of a canon much more closely. In any event, Zukofsky certainly has a programmatic musical analogue in mind as the structure of this poem.

## 5. A Generative Device

### Constant and Variant: Semantic Recurrence in Harry Mathews, William Bronk, and Robert Creeley

1. Creeley's short essay in which he cites Pound's letter accompanies and explains the form of his poem "The Whip" in David Lehman, ed., *Ecstatic Occasions, Expedient Forms* (New York: Macmillan, 1987), p. 42. It is also reprinted under the title "Form" in *The Collected Essays of Robert Creeley* (Berkeley: University of California Press, 1989), pp. 590–92.

2. Philip Dacey and David Jauss, eds. *Strong Measures: Contemporary American Poetry in Traditional Forms* (New York: Harper and Row, 1986), p. 9.

3. William Carlos Williams, *The Collected Later Poems* (New York: New Directions, 1967), p. 5.

4. Michael Riffaterre, *Text Production*, trans. Terese Lyons (1979; New York: Columbia University Press, 1983), p. 76.

5. Riffaterre, *Semiotics of Poetry* (1978; Bloomington: Indiana University Press, 1984), pp. 2–3.

6. Riffaterre, *Text Production*, p. 76.

7. See also Kaja Silverman, *The Subject of Semiotics* (New York: Oxford University Press, 1983), p. 104, and Roland Barthes, *Elements of Semiology* (1964; Hill and Wang, 1984), p. 59.

8. Riffaterre, *Semiotics of Poetry*, p. 3.

9. Creeley, interview by Ekbert Faas, in *Towards a New American Poetics* (Santa Barbara: Black Sparrow Press, 1978), p. 194.

10. Harry Mathews, *Armenian Papers: Poems 1954–1984* (Princeton: Princeton University Press, 1987), p. 3.

11. Riffaterre, *Semiotics of Poetry*, p. 5.

12. Riffaterre, *Semiotics of Poetry*, p. 6.

13. Mathews's comments can be found on the back cover of *Armenian Papers*.

14. Gilbert Sorrentino, *Something Said* (San Francisco: North Point Press, 1984), p. 78.

15. Anonymous reviewer in *Virginia Quarterly Review* 58 (Spring 1982): 59.

16. William Bronk, *Life Supports: New and Collected Poems* (San Francisco: North Point Press, 1981), pp. 34–35.

17. Bronk shares this concern with George Oppen, whose work frequently addresses the relation of the "singular" and the "numerous," the individual and the world. See especially *Of Being Numerous*, in *The Collected Poems of George Oppen* (New York: New Directions, 1975), pp. 145–202.

18. Norman M. Finkelstein, "William Bronk: The World as Desire," in *Contemporary Literature* 23 (1982): 481.

19. W. S. Di Piero, untitled review of Bronk, *Life Supports*, in *TriQuarterly* 55 (Fall 1982): 219.

20. Riffaterre, *Semiotics of Poetry*, p. 154.

21. William Bronk, interview by Robert J. Bertholf, *Credences* 1 (May 1976): 13.

22. Hayden Carruth, "Jabs of Meaning," review of Bronk, *Life Supports*, in *New York Times Book Review*, 13 December 1981, p. 13.

23. Anonymous reviewer in *Virginia Quarterly Review*, p. 59.

24. Gertrude Stein, "Poetry and Grammar," in *Lectures in America* (1935; Boston: Beacon Press, 1985), pp. 209–10.

25. David Lehman, in his note to his own villanelle "Amnesia," in *Ecstatic Occasions*, p. 123.

26. The line is perhaps most familiar to the contemporary reader as line 63 of Eliot's *The Waste Land*. It is a translation of Dante's "si lunga tratta / di gente, ch'io non avrei mai creduto / che morte tanta n'avesse disfatta," *Inferno* III, 55–57. Of course, the echo reaches back to Vergil, and ultimately to Homer's *Odyssey*.

27. Robert Duncan, *Fictive Certainties* (New York: New Directions, 1985), pp. 81–82.

28. Bronk, *Life Supports*, p. 69.

29. Dacey and Jauss, *Strong Measures*, p. 4.

30. Dacey and Jauss, *Strong Measures*, p. 434.

31. Robert Creeley, *The Collected Poems* (Berkeley: University of California Press, 1982), p. 176. Subsequently cited as CP.

32. Creeley, interview with Terry R. Bacon, "How He Knows When to Stop: Creeley on Closure," *American Poetry Review* 5 (November–December 1976): 5.

33. Cf. Roman Jakobson on G. M. Hopkins: "Equivalence in sound, projected into the sequence as its constitutive principle, inevitably involves semantic equivalence." "Linguistics and Poetics," in *Style in Language*, ed. Thomas A. Sebeok (Cambridge: MIT Press, 1960), p. 368. The entry on the heroic couplet in *Princeton Encyclopedia of Poetry and Poetics* (Princeton: Princeton University Press, 1974), p. 347, offers this familiar example from Pope: "Here thou great Anna! Whom three realms obey, / Dost sometimes counsel take—and sometimes tea" (*Rape of the Lock* 3.7–8). Parallelism of sound, rhythm, and syntax make the rather outrageous anticlimax seem an acceptable observation.

Arbitrary Constraints and Aleatory Operations: Harry Mathews and John Cage

34. Robert Duncan, *Fictive Certainties* (New York: New Directions, 1985), p. 179.

35. Edmund White, "Their Masks, Their Lives—Harry Mathews's *Cigarettes*," in the "Harry Mathews Number" of *Review of Contemporary Fiction* 7 (Fall 1987): 78.

36. Warren F. Motte, Jr., trans. and ed., *Oulipo: A Primer of Potential Literature* (Lincoln: University of Nebraska Press, 1986), pp. 10–11. Further references to the essays in this volume are abbreviated in the text OU.

37. Harry Mathews, "Vanishing Point," in *The Avant-Garde Tradition in Literature*, ed. Richard Kostelanetz (Buffalo, N.Y.: Prometheus Books, 1982), p. 312.

38. For a complete history of the lipogram, see Georges Perec, "History of the Lipogram," in Motte, ed., *Oulipo*, pp. 97–108.

### Mathews's *Trial Impressions*

39. Harry Mathews, note to his poem "Conditions of Desire," in *Ecstatic Occasions, Expedient Forms*, ed. David Lehman (New York: Macmillan, 1987), p. 137. As evidence of the "procedural" form of his contribution, Mathews cites his "starting points," "procedures," and "results" for the composition of the poem.

40. Dowland's text, as it appears in *Armenian Papers* (Princeton: Princeton University Press, 1987), p. 35. I refer to other poems from this volume by their Roman numeral designations.

41. See Keith Cohen, "The Labors of the Signifier," *Review of Contemporary Fiction* 7 (Fall 1987): 180.

42. Barrett Watten, "Harry Mathews: An Experiment in Presence," *Review of Contemporary Fiction* 7 (Fall 1987): 132–33.

43. Mathews, "A Conversation with Harry Mathews," interview by John Ash, *Review of Contemporary Fiction* 7 (Fall 1987): 28.

44. For a brief account of the role of the haiku in Western poetry see *Princeton Encyclopedia of Poetry and Poetics*, ed. Alex Preminger et al. (Princeton: Princeton University Press, 1965), p. 334.

45. John Cage, *Themes & Variations* (Barrytown, N.Y.: Station Hill Press, 1982), unpaginated. For ease of reference, I take the first page of text as [1]; Cage's comments thus appear on [6]. Further references to this volume are indicated in similar fashion in the text.

46. Mathews, "John Ashbery Interviewing Harry Mathews," *Review of Contemporary Fiction* 7 (Fall 1987): 45.

47. Keith Cohen, "The Labors of the Signifier," p. 181.

48. Mathews, "John Ashbery Interviewing Harry Mathews," p. 44.

49. David Lehman, Glossary entry under "sestina," in *Ecstatic Occasions*, p. 235.

50. Mathews, "Vanishing Point," p. 311.

51. Mathews, "For Prizewinners," *Review of Contemporary Fiction* 7 (Fall 1987): 17–18.

### Cage's *Themes & Variations*

52. John Cage, *Silence* (Middletown, Conn.: Wesleyan University Press, 1961), p. 3.

53. Cage, *Silence*, p. x.

54. Barbara Herrnstein Smith, *Poetic Closure* (Chicago: University of Chicago Press, 1968), p. 261.

55. Mathews, "Vanishing Point," p. 312.

56. *Princeton Encyclopedia*, p. 4.

57. Cf. Cage's discussion of the mesostic method which accompanies his contribution to Lehman, ed., *Ecstatic Occasions*, p. 27, as well as Lehman's definition of the acrostic in his Glossary, p. 225.

58. Cf. Herrnstein Smith's discussion of paratactic structure in *Poetic Closure*, pp. 98–100. She concludes that "a generating principle that produces a paratactic structure cannot in itself determine a concluding point." Although Smith's examples include nursery rhymes and lists, Cage's mesostics can be seen to function similarly.

59. Mathews, "John Ashbery Interviewing Harry Mathews," p. 43.

60. Cage, *Themes & Variations*, [8]. Further citations appear in the text.

61. Cage, in Lehman, ed., *Ecstatic Occasions*, pp. 26–27.

62. Cage, *M: Writings '67–'72* (Middletown, Conn.: Wesleyan University Press, 1973), unpaginated foreword.

63. Cage, *X: Writings '79–'82* (Middletown, Conn.: Wesleyan University Press, 1983), p. 53–101.

64. Cage, *M*, pp. 26–34.

65. Cf. Harriet Zinnes, "John Cage: Writer," in *The Hollins Critic* 17 (February 1981): 10–11. She also observes the apparent discrepancy between Cage's profession of random procedures with his rather discriminate selection of texts or names of artists.

66. Ernst Krenek, "Extents and Limits of Serial Techniques," in *Problems of Modern Music*, ed. Paul H. Lang (New York: Norton, 1960), pp. 90–91. The excerpt cited by Smith appears on pp. 261–62 of *Poetic Closure*.

67. Krenek, "Extents and Limits," p. 81.

68. Herrnstein Smith, *Poetic Closure*, p. 262.

69. Herrnstein Smith, *Poetic Closure*, pp. 262–63.

70. Cf. Arnold Schoenberg, "Heart and Brain in Music," in *Style and Idea* (Berkeley: University of California Press, 1975), pp. 53–76.

71. Cage, as cited by M. C. Richards, "John Cage and the Way of the Ear," *TriQuarterly* 54 (Spring 1982), "A John Cage Reader," pp. 113–14. Richards's source is Cage's preface for *Lecture on the Weather* (New York: Henmar Press, 1975).

72. C. G. Jung, foreword to the third edition of *The I Ching, or Book of Changes*, trans. Cary F. Baynes (1951; London: Routledge and Kegan Paul, 1967), pp. xxii–xxiv.

73. *Princeton Encyclopedia*, p. 427.

74. Cage, *X*, p. 54.

75. Cage, interview by Richard Kostelanetz, "Talking about *Writing through Finnegans Wake*," in *TriQuarterly* 54 (Spring 1982): 216.

76. Krenek, "Extents and Limits," p. 94.

## 6. A Polemical Conclusion: The Language Poetries and the New Formalism

1. Robert Richman, *The Direction of Poetry* (Boston: Houghton Mifflin, 1988), p. v.

2. Richman, *Direction of Poetry*, p. xiii.

3. David Antin's "Radical Coherency" is reprinted in *American Poetry since*

*1970: Up Late*, ed. Andrei Codrescu (New York: Four Walls Eight Windows, 1987), pp. 182–99.

4. For a further discussion of Antin's challenge to the lyric, see Marjorie Perloff's essay "Postmodernism and the Impasse of Lyric" in *The Dance of the Intellect* (New York: Cambridge University Press, 1985), especially pp. 192–97.

5. Richman, *Direction of Poetry*, p. xv.

6. Richman, *Direction of Poetry*, p. xiii.

7. Richman, *Direction of Poetry*, p. xv.

8. Richman, *Direction of Poetry*, p. xvi.

9. Richman, *Direction of Poetry*, p. xxi.

10. James E. B. Breslin, "American Poetry: 1945 to the Present," in *The Columbia Literary History of the United States*, ed. Emory Elliott et al. (New York: Columbia University Press, 1988), pp. 1081–82, 1100.

11. Gjertrud Schnackenberg, *The Lamplit Answer* (New York: Farrar, Straus, and Giroux, 1985), p. 82.

12. Schnackenberg, *Lamplit Answer*, p. 83.

13. See for example Charles Bernstein, *Content's Dream* (Los Angeles: Sun and Moon Press, 1986); *The L=A=N=G=U=A=G=E Book*, ed. Bernstein and Bruce Andrews (Carbondale and Edwardsville: Southern Illinois University Press, 1984); Michael Palmer, ed., *Code of Signals: Recent Writings in Poetics* (Berkeley: North Atlantic Books, 1983); and Ron Silliman, *The New Sentence* (New York: Roof Books, 1987).

14. Bernstein, *Content's Dream*, p. 70.

15. Bernstein, *Content's Dream*, p. 70.

16. "A Note on *The New Criterion*," in the inaugural issue of that journal (September 1982): 2, 4. See also Hilton Kramer's critique of the triumph of post-modern philistinism, "Postmodern: Art and Culture in the 1980's," in that same issue, pp. 36–42.

17. Ron Silliman, "Disappearance of the Word, Appearance of the World," in Andrews and Bernstein, eds., *The L=A=N=G=U=A=G=E Book*, p. 125.

18. Leslie Scalapino, *that they were at the beach* (San Francisco: North Point Press, 1985), p. 17.

19. See David Bohm, *Causality and Chance in Modern Physics* (London: Routledge and Kegan Paul, 1957).

20. Scalapino, *Way* (San Francisco: North Point Press, 1988), pp. 104–5.

21. Interview with Michael Palmer by Lee Bartlett in *Talking Poetry: Conversations in the Workshop with Contemporary Poets*, ed. Lee Bartlett (Albuquerque: University of New Mexico Press, 1987), p. 139.

22. Palmer, in Bartlett, ed., *Talking Poetry*, pp. 139–40.

23. Palmer, *The Circular Gates* (Los Angeles: Black Sparrow Press, 1974), p. 56.

24. Rosmarie Waldrop, "Shorter American Memory of the American Character According to Santayana," in *Ecstatic Occasions, Expedient Forms*, ed. David Lehman (New York: Macmillan, 1987), p. 196. The poem has since appeared in the chapbook *Shorter American Memory* (Providence, R.I.: Paradigm Press, 1988). Waldrop reveals in a headnote to the book that "the texts are derived from sources collected in Henry Beston's *American Memory* (New York: Farrar & Rinehart, 1937)."

25. Waldrop, in Lehman, ed., *Ecstatic Occasions*, p. 197.

# Index

Abrams, M. H., 28, 51, 54
Albers, Josef, 289n104
Allen, Donald, 106
Altieri, Charles, 91–92, 174, 178, 291n14
Ammons, A. R.: *Sphere*, 33–34
Andrews, Bruce, 274, 308n13
Antin, David, 11; "Radical Coherency," 270
Apollinaire, Guillaume, 248
Ash, John, 243
Ashbery, John, 11, 35–36, 40, 168–85, 188, 191–93, 248, 257, 268, 281; and the sestina, 169–78; *Works*: "Canzone," 179–82; "Daffy Duck in Hollywood," 11; *The Double Dream of Spring*, 171; "Farm Implements and Rutabagas in a Landscape," 171–78, 185, 193; "Faust," 171; "Pantoum," 182–85; "Self-Portrait in a Convex Mirror," 35; *Some Trees*, 9, 169, 171, 178; *The Tennis Court Oath*, 171; *Turandot and Other Poems*, 171; "A Wave," 35–36
Auden, W. H., 9

Bach, J. S., 146, 148–49, 183, 198
Bacon, Terry R., 97
Barthes, Roland, 20–21, 23, 28, 30, 41, 56–58, 69, 73, 88, 91, 110, 120–21, 150, 170–71, 181–82, 192, 195–96, 199
Bataille, Georges, 110
Baudelaire, Charles, 245

Baudrillard, Jean, 285n17
Beethoven, Ludwig van, 90, 149
Bénabou, Marcel, 240–41, 247
Bens, Jacques, 261
Bernstein, Charles, 274–75, 308n13
Bernstein, Michael André, 69, 289n92, 293n46
Berryman, John, 2; "Homage to Mistress Bradstreet," 22
Bertholf, Robert, 58, 226
Bishop, Elizabeth, 8; "12 O'Clock News," 293n52; "Visits to St. Elizabeths," 8
Blackburn, Paul, 4, 7–8, 69–87, 150; and autobiography, 69–70, 79, 81, 86–87; and elegy, 70, 73–77; *Works*: "August 1969: Softness," 85–86; *The Cities*, 70–71, 81; *The Collected Poems*, 77–78; *Early Selected Y Mas*, 70; "From the November Journal: Fire," 84; "Journal: December 6, 1968," 76–77; "Journal: July 1971," 86; "Journal: June/August 1968 Saignon-par-Apt (Vaucluse)," 74–75; *The Journals*, 23, 69, 74–76, 79, 81–84, 86–87; "Paris-Toulouse Train," 81–82; "Phone Call to Rutherford," 7–8; "Plaza Real with Palm Trees: Second Take," 86; "Rituals I–XVII," 78–79; "Rituals XVII. It Takes an Hour," 82; "Roads," 83; "The Selection of Heaven," 69–73, 77–78; "Signals I: Tanger, August 1956," 79–80; "Signals II," 81; "Signals III," 80, 88; "Sixteen Sloppy Haiku," 74

Black Mountain College, 4, 29, 48, 88, 90. *See also* Creeley, Robert; Duncan, Robert; Olson, Charles
Blaser, Robin, 63, 105–7
Bloom, Harold, 302n14
Bly, Robert, 2
Bohm, David, 277–78
Boulez, Pierre, 24, 38
Bradbury, Malcolm, 12
Breslin, James E. B., 272, 286n24, 286n36
Bronk, William, 4, 215, 223–31, 237, 268; and Oppen, 127–29, 134; and Zukofsky, 146; *Works:* "The Arts and Death: A Fugue for Sidney Cox," 223–31, 239; *Life Supports,* 223, 227; "Metonymy as an Approach to a Real World," 127–29; "The Nature of Musical Form," 230
Bruns, Gerald, 121, 296n21
Bukowski, Charles, 11
Bunting, Basil, 272
Burke, Kenneth, 90–91
Burroughs, William, 50
Butler, Christopher, 12

Cage, John, 11, 50, 62, 92, 148, 241–42, 248, 255–66; and Creeley, 87–89, 91, 100, 103–4; *Works: Silence,* 255; *Themes & Variations,* 43, 241, 248, 255–65
Calinescu, Matei, 10
Calvino, Italo, 217
Canonic form, 149–50, 192–213, 215
Canzone, 142, 168–69, 178–82, 184, 191
Carroll, Paul, 286n24
Carruth, Hayden, 226–27
Catullus, 88, 112, 118, 151, 153, 235
Chomsky, Noam, 105, 114
Cohen, Keith, 243, 249
Coleridge, S. T., 15–16, 112, 130, 143; and organic form, 22, 27–35, 51, 53–54, 174
Corman, Cid, 154–56, 160
Corn, Alfred, 232
Cox, Sidney, 226–27
Crane, Hart, 118, 209; *The Bridge,* 27, 123; "Voyages," 22, 27
Creeley, Robert, 12–14, 87–104, 125, 148, 150, 193, 198, 202–8, 213–16, 231–37, 268; and serial order, 87, 89, 91; and Zukofsky, 145–46, 154; *Works: The Charm,* 205; *Collected Essays,* 12–14, 93, 95; *Contexts of Poetry,* 12, 88–89, 91, 100; "The Crow," 236–37; "Do You Think . . .," 89;

"The Flower," 104; *For Love,* 9, 87, 231; "Having to—," 93, 96; "If You," 232–36; *In London,* 87–88, 100, 104, 204; *Mabel: A Story,* 87, 92, 101, 103–4; "Mouths Nuzz," 204–5; "Numbers," 95, 98–102, 104, 131, 149; "Oh, Love . . .," 96; "One Day," 87; "One thing," 94–95; *Pieces,* 22, 87–88, 91–102, 104, 130, 139, 143, 202–3; "Pieces of cake," 97; "Post Cards," 102–3; *A Quick Graph,* 92–93, 100, 299n51; "The Riddle," 87; "Some nights," 99; "Stomping with Catullus," 235; *Thirty Things,* 87, 102–4, 122; "3 in 1," 202–4; "A Variation," 205–6
Culler, Jonathan, 111–12, 120
Cunningham, J. V., 275
Cunningham, Merce, 264

Dacey, Philip, 214, 232, 234, 269
Daniel, Arnaut, 168, 175, 177, 186, 238, 251
Dante, 168–69, 176–77, 183, 186, 188, 229; *Divine Comedy,* 38; *Inferno,* 305n26
Davie, Donald, 157–59, 163
Dembo, L. S., 122, 129, 134, 142, 144, 185
Dowland, John, 241–55; *Second Booke of Ayres,* 242
Duchamp, Marcel, 217, 259
Duncan, Robert, 47–69, 148, 150, 231, 233, 271, 278; and Barthes, 55–58, 69; and Levertov, 29; and New Critical formalism, 38–39, 238; and Pound, 58–59, 68; and Spicer, 62; and Whitman, 48, 57, 66; *Works:* "An African Elegy," 289n98; *Bending the Bow,* 49, 52, 54, 56, 61, 64, 66; "Crosses of Harmony and Disharmony," 63; *Fictive Certainties,* 30–31, 39–40, 51, 53, 55, 57, 230–31, 292n38; *Ground Work: Before the War,* 49–50, 79; *Ground Work II: In the Dark,* 49; *Medieval Scenes,* 62, 106; *Of the War,* 50; *Passages,* 23, 29, 47–69, 77, 79, 100, 106–7, 122, 279; "Passages 1" ("Tribal Memories"), 47, 58; "Passages 2" ("At the Loom"), 58–59; "Passages 5" ("The Moon"), 64; "Passages 6" ("The Collage"), 65; "Passages 9" ("The Architecture"), 60–62, 65; "Passages 10" ("These Past Years"), 63–65; "Passages 15" ("Spelling"), 67–68; "Passages 17" ("Moving the Moving Image"), 62;

Duncan, Robert (*cont.*)
  "Passages 18" ("The Torso"), 66; "Passages 20" ("An Illustration"), 82; "Passages 21" ("The Multiversity"), 68; "Passages 36," 82; "A Seventeenth Century Suite," 82; "Structure of Rime XXVI," 82; *Tribunals*, 50
DuPlessis, Rachel Blau, 123

Eco, Umberto, 15, 18–19, 23–25, 49, 56–57, 175
Eichenbaum, Boris, 30–31
Eliot, T. S., 8, 128, 130, 159, 175; *Four Quartets*, 132; *The Waste Land*, 11, 49, 132, 198–99, 305n26
Epic, 36–38, 49, 109, 115, 132, 142, 150, 154, 192

Faas, Ekbert, 87, 91, 99, 202
Faranda, Lisa Pater, 161–62
Finkelstein, Norman, 225
Ford, Arthur, 203
Foster, Hal, 7
Fredman, Stephen, 287n44
Fugue, 142, 146, 148–50, 153–54, 190, 192–96, 198–201, 208, 223–27, 229–30

Gall, Sally, 22, 27
García Lorca, Federico: "Song of the Small Dead Girl," 74
Gaudier-Brzeska, Henri, 144
Géfin, Laszlo K., 287n44, 291n17, 293n42
Ginsberg, Allen, 14, 231; *Howl*, 50
Golding, Alan, 298n38
Goldoni, Annalisa, 75
Gris, Juan, 138
Gunn, Thom, 289n98

Hallberg, Robert von, 38, 98
Hassan, Ihab, 283n5
Hecht, Anthony, 232
Hejinian, Lyn, 274
Heller, Michael, 148
Heraclitus, 48, 50, 52–55, 61, 69, 290n2
Herndon, James, 114–15
Herrnstein Smith, Barbara. *See* Smith, Barbara Herrnstein
Hollander, John, 232
Hopkins, Gerard Manley, 89
Howard, Richard, 171
Howe, Susan, 274

Jakobson, Roman, 89–90, 93, 105, 111–12, 170, 175, 195, 303n33, 305n33
James, Henry, 123
Janowitz, A. F., 290n6
Jarolim, Edith, 77–78
Jauss, David, 214, 232, 234, 269
Johnson, W. R., 112, 121
Joyce, James, 207, 259, 264
Jung, Carl, 262–63
Justice, Donald, 193

Kafka, Franz, 253
Keats, John: "The Eve of St. Agnes," 20–21
Kees, Weldon, 4, 193–202, 205–8, 213; *The Collected Poems*, 193; "Fugue," 193–96, 198; *The Last Man*, 193; "Round," 193, 196–203, 206, 208, 215; "Variations on a Theme by Joyce," 207–8
Keller, Lynn, 284n7
Kenner, Hugh, 134, 138
Kermode, Frank, 288n72
Knoll, Robert E., 193
Koch, Kenneth, 174, 295n84
Kostelanetz, Richard, 285n13
Kramer, Hilton, 308n16
Krenek, Ernst, 260–62, 264
Kunitz, Stanley, 13

Language poetry, 268–70, 273–75, 280–81; and Marxism, 275
Lehman, David, 229, 242, 250, 280
Le Lionnais, François, 239, 252, 257
Lescure, Jean, 240, 252
Levertov, Denise, 2, 29–30
Lévi-Strauss, Claude, 14
Lewis, Janet, 157
Lewis, Wyndham, 18
Longfellow, Henry Wadsworth, 154–55
Lorca, Federico García. *See* García Lorca, Federico
Lorentz, H. A., 142
Lowell, Robert, 2, 268; *Imitations*, 245
Lucretius: *De Rerum Natura*, 37, 52

Machault, Guillaume de, 153
Mallarmé, Stéphane, 106–7, 110, 112, 121, 134–35, 138, 248–49; *Un Coup de dés*, 121; *Livre*, 49
Maritain, Jacques, 159
Marquette, Jacques, 158–59, 163
Marvell, Andrew, 198–201

Mathews, Harry, 11, 215–23, 225, 229, 237–38, 241–55, 257, 266; *Armenian Papers*, 217, 241; "Condition of Desire," 242; "The Pines at Son Beltran," 217–23, 242; *The Sinking of the Odradek Stadium*, 25–26; *Trial Impressions*, 43, 217, 241–55
Mazzaro, Jerome, 284n12
McClure, Michael, 63
Merrill, James, 232, 272; *The Changing Light at Sandover*, 37
Merwin, W. S., 272
Messerli, Douglas, 269
Metaphor, 23, 42, 55, 85, 91, 110, 126, 130–31, 142–43, 149, 159, 170–71, 189, 204, 209, 213, 220
Metonymy, 55, 71, 78, 85, 91, 93, 110, 125–28, 130–33, 142–43, 149, 158–59, 170–71, 178, 204
Michelangelo, 77, 238
Moore, Marianne, 131
Motte, Warren F., Jr., 239, 241

Nelson, Cary, 285n24
New Criticism, 2–3, 30, 43, 159, 170, 270, 272–74; and formalism, 2, 39–40, 48, 90–91, 152, 238–39
New Formalism, 269–74, 281; and neoconservatism, 275
New York School, 4, 174. *See also* Ashbery, John
Niedecker, Lorine, 4, 154–63, 170, 182, 268; and Zukofsky, 141–42, 149–50, 152–54, 163, 208–9, 211; *Works*: "If I were a bird," 163; "Lake Superior," 142, 155–63; *North Central*, 155, 161–62; "Poet's work," 300n66; "Remember my little granite pail," 155; "There's a better shine," 156; "Traces of Living Things," 155; "Wintergreen Ridge," 155
Nims, John Frederick, 232

Objectivism, 4, 124–27, 129, 136, 138–40, 142–46, 152, 155, 157–59, 272. *See also* Niedecker, Lorine; Oppen, George; Reznikoff, Charles; Zukofsky, Louis
O'Brien, Flann: *At Swim-Two-Birds*, 149
O'Hara, Frank, 174
Olson, Charles, 1, 13, 231, 233; and Duncan, 48, 54; and postmodernism,

6; *Works: Additional Prose*, 6; "Against Wisdom as Such," 290n3; *The Maximus Poems*, 27, 37–38, 48, 54; "Projective Verse," 1, 14–15, 18, 29–30, 48, 83, 92
Oppen, George, 4, 121–41, 144–45, 268; and Bronk, 127–29, 134, 305n17; and eroticism, 136–39; and Mallarmé, 134–35, 138; and Marxism, 127, 136; and The Objectivist Press, 121, 125; and Williams, 122, 124, 127, 133, 135; *Works: The Collected Poems*, 122, 141; *Discrete Series*, 23, 121–41, 143, 146–47, 157; "Image of the Engine 5," 122; *The Materials*, 159; "A Narrative," 133–34; "Of Being Numerous," 129–30; *Of Being Numerous*, 130; "Party on Shipboard," 128–29, 135; "Psalm," 135; *This in Which*, 133
Oppen, Mary, 122, 135
Oppenheimer, Joel, 14, 285n24
Oulipo (Ouvroir de Littérature Potentielle), 43, 216–17, 239–41, 243–44, 247, 249–54, 257, 260–62, 264, 266
Ovid, 74; *Metamorphoses*, 37

Palmer, Michael, 278–80; and Zukofsky, 304n48; *Works: The Circular Gates*, 20, 279; *Code of Signals*, 308n13; *Notes for Echo Lake*, 279; "Second Series," 279; "Series," 20, 279–80; "Symmetrical Poems," 279
Pantoum, 168–69, 178, 182–85, 191, 197, 201
Paradigm, 41–43, 56, 60, 71, 90, 135, 170–71, 178, 181–82, 184, 189, 192, 195, 200–201, 203–6, 208, 213, 221
Parker, Charlie, 202–3
Parkman, Francis, 157–58
Perec, Georges, 217; *La Disparition*, 241
Perloff, Marjorie, 138, 284n7, 285n16, 286n37
Petrarch, 16, 186, 201, 238
Plautus, 257
Poe, Edgar Allan, 108–9, 237, 257, 259
Postmodernism, 3, 5–13; and the avantgarde, 6, 9–11; and contemporary literature, 5–9; poetics of, 5–13
Pound, Ezra, 4, 58–59, 77, 143–44, 168, 214–15, 218, 231–32, 238, 241, 248, 271, 273; and Bishop, 8; *Works: Canto 41*, 37; *The Cantos*, 9, 37–38, 68, 132; *Gaudier-Brzeska*, 4; "Hugh

Pound, Ezra (*cont.*)
Selwyn Mauberley," 11, 22, 132, 189; "In a Station of the Metro," 131; *Literary Essays*, 55; "Sestina: Altaforte," 175
Procedural form, definitions of, 3, 5, 11–12, 15–20, 40–44
Propertius, 74
Pythagoras, 50, 52–53

Queneau, Raymond, 217, 239, 243, 248, 250–51, 253, 260–62; *Exercises in Style*, 243

Radisson, Pierre Esprit, 157–58
Randel, D. M., 100–101
Ransom, John Crowe, 15, 273–74
Reid, Ian, 50, 293n43
Renan, Ernest, 198–99
Reznikoff, Charles, 125, 143
Rich, Adrienne, 2, 272
Richman, Robert, 15, 269–72, 274
Riddel, Joseph N., 289n95
Riffaterre, Michael, 66, 206, 215–16, 219–20, 225–26, 229, 234
Rosenthal, M. L., 22, 27
Roub, Gail, 162
Roubaud, Jacques, 251, 260
Round, 142, 193, 196–202, 208–9, 213, 215, 236, 239
Russian Formalism, 43, 240. *See also* Eichenbaum, Boris; Shklovsky, Victor

San Francisco Renaissance, 4. *See also* Duncan, Robert; Spicer, Jack
Santayana, George, 280–81
Sappho, 112
Saussure, Ferdinand de, 59–60, 105, 113, 120–21, 133, 146, 227–28
Scalapino, Leslie, 275–78; "Delay series," 277; "Later floating series," 277; *that they were at the beach*, 20, 275–77; *Way*, 275, 277–78
Schimmel, Harold, 297n30
Schnackenberg, Gjertrud, 272–74
Schönberg, Arnold, 3, 62, 69, 88, 100, 148, 255–56, 259
Schoolcraft, Henry Rowe, 155, 160–61
Schrödinger, Erwin, 52–54, 69
Sequence, poetic, 21–23, 27–36, 87
Serial form, definitions of, 3, 5, 11–12, 15–26

Sestina, 42, 142, 168–78, 184–94, 215, 239, 250–51
Sexton, Anne, 2
Shapiro, Marianne, 168–71, 173, 177–78
Sharp, Thomas, 297n28
Shklovsky, Victor, 16, 286n29. *See also* Russian Formalism
Sidney, Sir Philip, 173, 249, 251
Silliman, Ron, 269, 275, 296n7, 300n61, 308n13
Smith, Barbara Herrnstein, 21–22, 255–56, 260–62, 264, 307n58
Sorrentino, Gilbert, 223, 297n30
Spanos, William V., 10
Spicer, Jack, 4, 11, 62–63, 105–21, 123; and Duncan, 106, 113, 293n45; and Mallarmé, 106–7, 110, 112, 117; and Poe, 108–9; *Works: Admonitions*, 105, 107; *After Lorca*, 114, 116, 119; *The Collected Books*, 106; "Graphemics," 119–21; *Language*, 105, 109–21; "Morphemics," 116–17; *One Night Stand and Other Poems*, 106; "Phonemics," 117–19; "Thing Language," 109–12, 115; "Transformations," 113–15; "Vancouver Lectures," 62, 106, 108, 111, 113
Stanley, George, 113
Stein, Gertrude, 98, 100, 216, 228, 234, 275
Stevens, Wallace, 31; "The Auroras of Autumn," 20, 22, 33; *Collected Poems*, 9; "Connoisseur of Chaos," 288n76; "The Idea of Order at Key West," 32, 288n76; *Letters*, 288n76; "The Man on the Dump," 116; "The Man with the Blue Guitar," 32; "Notes toward a Supreme Fiction," 31–33; "Of Modern Poetry," 32; "An Ordinary Evening in New Haven," 33
Swinburne, Algernon Charles, 185
Sylvester, William, 101
Symphonic form, 90, 149
Syntagm, 20–21, 55–56, 59, 78, 88, 90–93, 96, 98, 136, 143, 219–21

Taggart, John, 190
Tennyson, Alfred: *In Memoriam*, 20, 22, 70
Thomas, Dylan, 28
Tomlinson, Charles, 124
Tone poem, 90
Toynbee, Arnold J., 6–7
Turner, Frederick: *The New World*, 37

Variation, 205–8, 210, 217, 229
Vergil: *Aeneid*, 37, 229, 305n26
Villanelle, 193, 229

Waldrop, Rosmarie, 280–81
Watten, Barrett, 243, 274
Wesling, Donald, 28
White, Edmund, 238
Whitehead, Alfred North, 48, 52
Whitman, Walt, 14, 48, 57, 121, 231
Wilbur, Richard, 13, 272
Williams, William Carlos, 3–4, 11, 20,
    143, 271; and Blackburn, 7–8, 85; and
    Oppen, 122, 124, 127, 133, 135; and
    Zukofsky, 142–43; *Works: The Auto-
    biography*, 140; "The Desert Music,"
    93–94; *Imaginations*, 9, 81, 138; *In
    the American Grain*, 109; *Kora in
    Hell: Improvisations*, 85, 93; *Pater-
    son*, 38; *Pictures from Brueghel*, 9; *Se-
    lected Essays*, 129, 131; *Spring and
    All*, 20; *The Wedge*, 4, 55, 92, 94, 214
Winters, Yvor, 275
Wittgenstein, Ludwig, 26, 275
Wordsworth, William, 112

Yeats, W. B., 24, 231, 292n36; "The Sec-
    ond Coming," 24

Zukofsky, Louis, 4, 125, 134, 141–54,
    168–69, 192–93, 195, 198, 200, 203,
    208–13, 272, 275; and Niedecker, 156;
    and sestina, 185–92; *Works*: "A," 9,
    142, 145, 148–49, 151, 154, 189; *All*,
    142, 149–50, 154, 189, 208; "And
    Without," 209–10; *Anew*, 142–53,
    163; *Barely and Widely*, 142, 145;
    "Ferry," 145–46; *55 Poems*, 208; "I's
    (Pronounced Eyes)," 152; "Light," 142;
    "Mantis," 185–92; " 'Mantis,' An In-
    terpretation," 168–69, 185–91; *An
    "Objectivists" Anthology*, 125; "The
    Old Poet Moves to a New Apartment
    14 Times," 142; "Perch Less," 210–
    11; *Prepositions*, 112, 144, 146–47,
    151, 157, 159; "Songs of Degrees,"
    211–13; *A Test of Poetry*, 156; "29
    Poems," 142, 144–45, 147; "29
    Songs," 142, 148, 151, 208–9

Library of Congress Cataloging-in-Publication Data

Conte, Joseph Mark, 1960–
    Unending design : the forms of postmodern poetry / Joseph Mark Conte.
        p.   cm.
    Includes bibliographical references and index.
    ISBN 0-8014-2469-0 (cloth : alk. paper).—ISBN 0-8014-9914-3 (paper : alk. paper)
    1. American  poetry—20th  century—History  and  criticism.   2. Postmodernism
(Literature)—United States.   I. Title.
PS325.C65   1991
811'.509—dc20
                                                                    90-55732